CANADIAN PENTECOSTALISM

MCGILL-QUEEN'S STUDIES IN THE HISTORY OF RELIGION
Volumes in this series have been supported by the Jackman Foundation of Toronto.

SERIES TWO In memory of George Rawlyk
Donald Harman Akenson, Editor

SERIES ONE: G.A. Rawlyk, Editor

Canadian Pentecostalism

Transition and Transformation

Edited by

MICHAEL WILKINSON

McGill-Queen's University Press
Montreal & Kingston • London • Ithaca

© McGill-Queen's University Press 2009

ISBN 978-0-7735-3457-5 (cloth)
ISBN 978-0-7735-3733-0 (paper)

Legal deposit first quarter 2009
Bibliothèque nationale du Québec

First paperback edition 2010

Printed in Canada on acid-free paper that is 100% ancient forest free
(100% post-consumer recycled), processed chlorine free

McGill-Queen's University Press acknowledges the support of the Canada
Council for the Arts for our publishing program. We also acknowledge
the financial support of the Government of Canada through the Book
Publishing Industry Development Program (BPIDP) for our publishing
activities.

Library and Archives Canada Cataloguing in Publication

Canadian Pentecostalism : transition and transformation / edited by
Michael Wilkinson.

(McGill-Queen's studies in the history of religion. Series two ; 49)
Includes bibliographical references and index.
ISBN 978-0-7735-3457-5 (bnd)
ISBN 978-0-7735-3733-0 (pbk)

1. Pentecostalism – Canada – History. 2. Pentecostalism – Social aspects –
Canada. 3. Social change – Canada – Religious aspects – Christianity.
I. Wilkinson, Michael, 1965– II. Series.

BR1644.5.C2C36 2009   270.8'20971   C2008-905654-X

Typeset by Jay Tee Graphics Ltd. in 10.5/13 Sabon

Contents

Contributors

PETER ALTHOUSE, PhD (Toronto), assistant professor of Theology, Southeastern University, and author of *Spirit of the Last Days: Pentecostal Eschatology in Conversation with Jürgen Moltmann.*

PETER BEYER, PhD (Toronto), professor of Religious Studies, University of Ottawa, and author of numerous articles and chapters on religion in Canada and the books *Religion and Globalization* and *Religions in a Global Society.*

ROBERT K. BURKINSHAW, PhD (British Columbia), professor of History and dean, Faculty of Humanities and Social Sciences, Trinity Western University, and author of *Pilgrims in Lotusland: Conservative Protestantism in British Columbia, 1917–1981.*

MICHAEL DI GIACOMO, PhD (Laval), associate professor of History at Valley Forge Christian College, and author and researcher on Pentecostalism in Quebec.

BRUCE L. GUENTHER, PhD (McGill), associate professor of Church History and Mennonite Studies, Mennonite Brethren Biblical Seminary / Trinity Western University.

RANDALL HOLM, PhD (Laval), associate professor of Biblical Studies, Providence College, and author of numerous articles on Canadian Pentecostalism.

PAMELA M.S. HOLMES, ThD candidate in Systematic Theology at Wycliffe College, Toronto School of Theology.

STEPHEN HUNT, PhD (Reading), reader in Sociology, University of the West of England, and author of numerous articles and chapters on Pentecostalism and the books *The Alpha Enterprise: Evangelism in a Post-Christian Era* and *Religion and Everyday Life*.

MARTIN MITTELSTADT, PhD (Marquette), associate professor of Biblical Studies at Evangel University, and author of *Scripture in the Pentecostal Tradition: A Contemporary Reading of Luke-Acts*.

DAVID REED, PhD (Boston), professor emeritus, Wycliffe College, University of Toronto, and author of numerous articles and chapters on Pentecostalism.

THOMAS A. ROBINSON, PhD (McMaster), associate professor of Religious Studies, University of Lethbridge, and author of numerous articles on Pentecostalism.

DONALD S. SWENSON, PhD (Notre Dame), professor of Sociology, Mount Royal College, and author of *Society, Spirituality and the Sacred: A Social Scientific Introduction*.

MICHAEL WILKINSON, PhD (Ottawa), associate professor of Sociology at Trinity Western University, and author of *The Spirit Said Go: Pentecostal Immigrants in Canada*.

Acknowledgments

In early spring 2004 I was sitting in a coffee shop in Vancouver with William Raccah talking about the need for a book on Canadian Pentecostals. William encouraged me to develop the idea and now it has become a reality. It was not difficult to find contributors who shared our enthusiasm. Everyone gladly gave of their time to write and rewrite. In October 2006 Trinity Western University hosted a symposium at which the authors presented their chapters to each other. There was a great turnout of scholars and people from across Canada and the United States interested in Pentecostalism. Blaine Charette, Jack Wisemore, and David Wells responded to papers. Roger Stronstad presented new material on his exceptional scholarly work on Luke-Acts. The day was filled with wonderful exchange.

The symposium was supported through the Aid to Small Universities program of the Social Sciences and Humanities Research Council of Canada. The Pentecostal Assemblies of Canada also made a generous grant that was very much appreciated. The grants were used not only to bring everyone together; they also supported a strong network of scholars who continue to engage in research on Pentecostalism. A website was also developed and is hosted by Trinity Western University where resources on Pentecostalism can be accessed by all (www.twu.ca/sites/cprn/). Jim Lucas of the Canadian Pentecostal Seminary helped facilitate the event. Above all, Laurel Archer must receive much credit. She is an exceptional administrator and the symposium's success was due to her attention to details. Permission to reprint the tables in the Introduction and some of the findings in chapter 12 from my book *The Spirit Said Go: Pentecostal Immigrants in Canada* was granted from Peter Lang Publishing.

Finally, I want to thank my wife, Valerie, for her love and support. I am grateful for such a generous partner. I also want to thank my children, Victoria, Ethan, Alexander, and Grace, who all share a great sense of humour about my work which keeps me grounded.

CANADIAN PENTECOSTALISM

Pentecostalism in Canada: An Introduction

MICHAEL WILKINSON

In 2006 Pentecostals from around the world paused to remember the one hundredth anniversary of the Azusa Street revival meetings led by William Seymour in Los Angeles, California. This is an important event in the history of the modern Pentecostal movement,[1] bringing together several ideas and movements from the nineteenth century that emphasized such things as sanctification, Holy Spirit baptism with the evidence of speaking in tongues, and eschatological themes around the imminent return of Jesus Christ. In spite of the various debates about the origins of the twentieth-century Pentecostal movement, Azusa is regarded as playing a significant role in establishing Pentecostalism as an important shift in the transformation of Christianity. While there are a variety of "Pentecostalisms" worldwide there is also something of an Azusa-*ization* process whereby all Pentecostal currents are influenced, directly or indirectly, by this one event and have had to reflect on their identity and Azusa's role as a modern revival.

Pentecostalism is a renewal movement representing an important transformation in Christianity alongside the Roman Catholic, Eastern Orthodox, and Protestant Churches.[2] It is characterized by "exuberant worship; an emphasis on subjective religious experience and spiritual gifts; claims of supernatural miracles, signs, and wonders – including a language of experiential spirituality, rather than a theology; and a mystical 'life in the Spirit' by which [its members] daily live out the will of God."[3] Pentecostalism, according to Harvey Cox, is effective precisely because of its emphasis on a primal spirituality that addresses the deepest need of all human beings, transcending all cultures throughout the world.[4]

Table 1: Pentecostals in Canada, 1911–2001

Year	Total
1911	515
1921	7,012
1931	26,349
1941	57,742
1951	95,131
1961	143,877
1971	222,390
1981	338,785
1991	436,435
2001	369,475

SOURCES: Derived from Dominion Bureau of Statistics, 1953, 1963, Statistics Canada, 1973, 1983, 1993, 2003 (www.statcan.ca).

In just over a hundred years, Pentecostalism has gone from a marginalized, obscure movement to the most significant reconfiguration within Christianity. At the beginning of the twentieth century there were a few rumours of revival and renewal but nothing to approximate a movement. However, by 1990 there were an estimated 14,000 different Pentecostal groups in about 200 countries worldwide claiming 372 million Pentecostal Christians. Approximately 21 per cent of all Christians were Pentecostal, mostly from non-Western regions of the world. The five largest Pentecostal *congregations* in the world in the early 1990s were in Korea (800,000 members), Chile (350,000 members), Argentina (145,000 members), Brazil (85,000 members), and Nigeria (65,000 members).[5] In 1995 it was estimated that approximately 450 million Christians worldwide were Pentecostal, growing to 500 million by the turn of the century. Scholars estimate that growth should reach over 800 million by 2025, mostly in Africa, Asia, and Latin America.[6]

In Canada, Pentecostals first appeared in the Canadian Census in 1911 when just over five hundred people indicated they were Pentecostal (see Table 1). The numbers continued to grow, and upon reflection, turn out to be quite substantial in light of other changes in Canadian religious identification. In just fifty years the figure grew to nearly 144,000 in 1961, reaching its peak in 1991 with just over 436,000 Canadians identifying with Pentecostalism.[7] The Pentecostal Assemblies of Canada (PAOC), the largest Pentecostal denomination in Canada, experienced phenomenal growth between 1951 and 2001 – from 45,000 members and adherents to 232,000, with over 1,000 congregations and approximately 3,000 credential holders (see Table 2).

Table 2: Pentecostal Assemblies of Canada,
membership and adherents, 1951–2001

Year	Total
1951	45,000
1961	60,000
1971	150,000
1981	125,000
1991	222,000
2001	232,000

SOURCES: Bibby, 1987: 14; 1993: 6; PAOC Vital
Statistics (www.paoc.org).

Table 3: Renewal movements in Canada, 2001

	Total (as percentage)
Pentecostals	504,551 (11)
Charismatics	2,596,361 (59)
Neocharismatics	1,324,088 (30)
Total	4,425,000 (100)

SOURCES: Burgess and van der Maas, 2002: 48

In Canada there are thirteen older or "classical" Pentecostal denominations including The Apostolic Church in Canada, The Apostolic
Church of Pentecost, The Church of God, The Church of God of Prophecy in Canada, The Elim Fellowship of Evangelical Churches and Ministers, The Foursquare Gospel Church of Canada, The Independent
Assemblies of God – Canada, The Italian Pentecostal Church of Canada,
The Open Bible Standard Church of Canada, The Pentecostal Assemblies
of Canada, The Pentecostal Assemblies of Newfoundland and Labrador,
The Pentecostal Holiness Church of Canada, and the United Pentecostal
Church. There are also numerous independent Pentecostal congregations
that have no affiliation with these denominations. Difficult to measure
are those who have had a Pentecostal or charismatic experience but
stayed within their established, historic, mainline denominations like the
Anglican Church of Canada and The United Church of Canada. Roman
Catholics have also been influenced by a theology of the Spirit. New
evangelical groups like the Vineyard Fellowship are clearly shaped by an
emphasis on experiential Christianity and the work of the Holy Spirit,
but they do not self-identify as Pentecostal. Some estimate the figures for
Pentecostals and Charismatics to be in the range of 4.4 million Canadians or approximately 15 per cent of the population (see Table 3).[8] To
date, no national study has attempted to assess the extent to which Canadians have been impacted by this spirituality of the Spirit.

These different estimates illustrate the problems with conceptualizing Pentecostalism, not to mention the different ways in which one counts. Census figures for Pentecostals most likely represent only the oldest of the Pentecostal denominations. However, the 2001 Census category for Pentecostals does not account for all the older denominations. The fastest growing category, "Christian," is said to include those who identified themselves as Apostolic, another older Pentecostal denomination.

The worldwide growth of Pentecostalism raises a number of questions. Where did they come from, why were they underestimated, how did they spread throughout the world, and what impact do they have on other forms of Christianity? How did Pentecostalism emerge and develop in Canada? What are its main characteristics? Is there anything unique about Pentecostalism in Canada? How does it compare with the movement worldwide? What needs to be understood is how Pentecostalism is related to the American story and the global story and, further, how it is rooted and established in Canadian culture.

A second question has to do with understanding the particularities of Pentecostalism in Canada. It is often thought that Pentecostalism is a global culture. Yet, that means different things to different people. It is usually claimed that Pentecostals share a common culture characterized by Spirit baptism and speaking in tongues, healing, dreams and visions, and prophecy. It is often thought that Pentecostalism is experiential, biblical, egalitarian, and motivated by mission. While this may be true, it cannot be assumed that these characteristics look the same in all cultures. Specifically, these cultural qualities of Pentecostalism also intermingle with the local cultures in which they take root. More specifically, Canadian Pentecostalism illustrates in important ways how these aspects play out in education, theology, mission, and women in ministry.

A third question of concern for scholars revolves around our understanding of how charismatic movements of the Spirit become institutionalized and globalized. Pentecostalism illustrates clearly the tension between "Spirit led" and "organization driven." These tensions swing back and forth in particular ways as illustrated in this volume among charismatic Anglicans and Roman Catholics. They also show in a unique way how Pentecostalism itself is thought to be in need of renewal as indicated by the "Toronto Blessing" renewal meetings in the 1990s. Still, while Canadian Pentecostalism develops in a particular cultural context, it is also shaped by experiences and expressions beyond its borders. Globalization is a long historical process which restructures religion and religions.[9] Pentecostalism, like all religions, is confronted with globalizing trends whereby the structures of modernity are spread throughout the world. But an account of globalization also has to take into consideration the ways in which so-called modern structures are reconfigured as they are planted in particular cultures.[10] An understanding of Canadian Pentecostalism must take into account how it is shaped by globalizing trends but also a contributor to them. While there is something to recognize about Pentecostalism as a global culture, Pentecostals are also rooted in particular cultures. In the same sense, one can speak of a variety of Pentecostalisms. The purpose of this volume is to situate Canadian Pentecostalism among the many "Pentecostalisms" around the world. While there is something that Pentecostals share across cultures, Pentecostalism is rooted in specific local cultures. In order to understand Canadian Pentecostalism, one has to locate it in a Canadian context but with an eye on the global. Pentecostals do share certain beliefs about the Holy Spirit, dreams and visions, healing, and the Kingdom of God. An analysis of Pentecostalism in Canada points to the ways in which it is a part of this global movement and a local phenomenon.

Despite some of the vast differences among Pentecostal and charismatic Christians, there is an underlying narrative, a shared spirituality, a set of beliefs about a "normative moral order."[11] This conception of "how life ought to be" has given rise to a set of practices and social institutions that constitutes and directs social life for these Pentecostal and charismatic Christians. The various chapters in this volume explore specifically the social consequences of Pentecostal and charismatic spirituality and how it continues to change. Transition and transformation offer two important concepts with which to think about its emergence, development, and contemporary situation.

Transformation works in two critical ways. Important for Pentecostals is the transformative experience with the Holy Spirit. Pentecostals call for an encounter that changes individuals and social structures through an emphasis on such things as Spirit Baptism and an encounter with the Kingdom of God.[12] But Pentecostalism itself is also going through a transformation. Contemporary social change is impacting all social life. Globalization scholars argue that all religions, including Pentecostalism, must come to terms with a restructuring of religion along the same lines as other social institutions like politics, economics, and culture.[13] Transition, on the other hand, illustrates the process of moving through a cycle. Historians and sociologists have examined many transitions, including the institutionalization of religious movements and the shift organizations make internally but often in relation to other processes in society. Transition captures the many issues revolving around process. Social process refers to recurring attitudinal and behavioural patterns that seem to reflect change in the short term but in the long term reflect cycles or recurring patterns. Transformation, on the other hand, is reflected in a broader context of change. In other words, a social change perspective examines how culture and social institutions like religion are altered over space and time. While previous paradigms have focused on the shift from sect to church[14] or the secularization of society and the loss of religion,[15] globalization is another optic that asks what we see when we look at religion in the context of global society. More specifically, we start to account for the development of Pentecostalism in Canada with different assumptions and conclusions (see the chapter in this volume by Beyer). The institutionalization of Pentecostal denominations like the PAOC reflects a cycle of emergence, bureaucratization, stabilization, institutional dilemma, and renewal. Transformation, however, is reflected in the larger social and cultural context of change and the implications for denominations regardless of where they are in the cycle. Globalization is one such example of change. Theories of globalization suggest that the entire world is adjusting to a transformation.[16] In this volume the various authors capture these two themes.

Specifically, the book is organized around three areas – the origins and development of Canadian Pentecostalism, aspects of the Canadian Pentecostal experience, and the institutionalization and globalization of Pentecostalism. The first section deals with several issues surrounding the origins and development of Pentecostalism. Pentecostal historiography is replete with issues and questions about origins.[17] Increasingly, the debates about Pentecostal origins have led to a number of new interpretations. Allan Anderson argues that Pentecostal historiography has focused too much on origins in the US, especially the influence of the Azusa Street revival, at the expense of understanding non-North American contributions. The four chapters in this section discuss a number of these issues. Michael Di Giacomo argues that in spite of early British influences on Canadian Pentecostalism, one cannot ignore the influence of Pentecostal currents in the US. Yet, Pentecostalism develops in a unique way in Canada as it takes root in the local culture. Furthermore, his account highlights the role of Spirit Baptism in shaping twentieth-century Pentecostalism. In chapter 2, Thomas Robinson, provides a more specific examination of one aspect of Canadian Pentecostalism,

Oneness Pentecostalism. Oneness Pentecostalism represents one of the earliest controversies among Pentecostals about water baptism and the Trinity. Robinson's point is that water baptism and not Spirit Baptism defines and shapes early Pentecostalism. In chapter 3 Peter Althouse explores the social meaning of the eschatological dimensions of Pentecostalism. He argues that their emphasis on the Kingdom of God and the imminent return of Jesus Christ has social implications about which Pentecostals, while close to evangelical views, have their own perspective. In chapter 4 Randall Holm provides an overview of Canadian Pentecostalism from the perspective of the spiritual ethos of Pentecostalism. Using the metaphor of "walking," Holm weaves the story of Canadian Pentecostalism as a journey. Experience is a hallmark for Pentecostalism but it is based on a particular reading of the Bible. While each chapter points to distinctive features in the development of early Pentecostalism in Canada, it is probably best to see these accounts as all contributing to an understanding of its emergence and its transition from a renewal movement to institutionalized form. Further, there are important transnational links between Canadians and Americans in the formation of early Pentecostalism.

The second section deals with aspects of the Canadian Pentecostal experience. Specifically, these chapters examine how Pentecostalism is worked out in education, theology, mission, and gender relations. It is often assumed that Pentecostals are driven by pragmatism and no doubt they have historically acted pragmatically.[18] Yet, Pentecostalism is far more motivated by normative concerns rooted in their commitments, beliefs, concerns, and practices. These "visions" of how life ought to be shape ministries and congregations. As Kydd says, "First and foremost, it was their religious experiences, their understanding of scripture, and their life experience that defined the nature of the emerging movement."[19] In chapter 5 Bruce Guenther illustrates how education was shaped by Pentecostalism's distinctive beliefs. Yet, while his focus is on one institution, he makes it clear that Pentecostal theological education must be understood in the context of the early twentieth-century Canadian evangelical Protestant world. In chapter 6 Martin Mittelstadt shows how Pentecostals interpret the Bible with a special emphasis on Luke-Acts. More specifically, Mittelstadt argues that understanding a Pentecostal reading of the Bible is crucial for comprehending the ways in which they see the world and their place in it. Robert Burkinshaw focuses on Pentecostalism among First Nations groups of Canada in chapter 7. He describes the early developments of mission work by Pentecostals on the West Coast, arguing that native initiative and leadership was far more important in the early years than is often recognized.[20] It was not until the 1960s that the PAOC was established in many native communities. Yet, the growth of Pentecostalism in native communities is due to the nature of Pentecostal spirituality and its emphasis on a spirit world which resonated with native peoples, not solely to the organizational efforts of the PAOC. Pamela Holmes writes in chapter 8 about the way in which gender, institutions, and Pentecostal spirituality interact. Holmes argues that Pentecostal belief in the Spirit empowered men and women in the early stages of the movement and, more importantly, opened a vital space for women in ministry in Canadian society. She then explains the decline of women's roles employing a feminist critique of institutionalized Pentecostal organizations and the way authority was used to devalue the contribution of women.

The last section examines issues of institutionalization and globalization. In chapter 9 David Reed examines the role of charisma in the Anglican Church. Reed explores the beliefs, practices, and views among Canadian Anglicans about renewal and the implications for the church. He concludes that in spite of what may seem like a decline in numbers of charismatic Anglicans, they have actually influenced the church in significant ways. In chapter 10 Donald Swenson gives an account of the charismatic movement among Roman Catholics in Canada. In both the Anglican and Roman Catholic cases, the traditional "sect to church" theory is not adequate to explain the charismatic movement within the historical churches. His analysis covers the vibrant emergence of Pentecostalism among Roman Catholics in the 1960s to its current state of near absence within the church. Swenson argues that the apparent rise and decline must be understood in the context of longer historical patterns of renewal in the Roman Catholic Church. The modern Catholic charismatic movement, argues Swenson, is actually a continuation of previous cycles. In chapter 11 Stephen Hunt asks questions about globalization in relation to the Toronto Blessing. Hunt's main concern is to question whether the Toronto Blessing illustrates global processes or is simply a matter of good marketing. Hunt believes it is incorrect to view the Toronto Blessing and its worldwide impact as simply the exporting of Pentecostalism from Toronto. Hunt highlights the importance of understanding Pentecostalism in the context of global society and its apparent success in light of the different ways in which it has been interpreted in a variety of local contexts. In chapter 12 Michael Wilkinson examines the reverse flow of globalization and explores how

Pentecostalism in Canada is transformed organizationally, theologically, and culturally with the migration of Pentecostals from Africa, Asia, and Latin America. Increasingly, global society is characterized by transnational networks which serve as religious social ties between Pentecostals in different locations. Clearly, Pentecostals share a common narrative about the Holy Spirit, but that story and its spiritual significance varies from place to place.

In conclusion, Peter Beyer evaluates the origins and growth of Pentecostal and charismatic Christianity in global society. Beyer parallels the story of twentieth-century Pentecostalism with other developments to show how Pentecostalism shares continuity with the larger social context. The global and the local are important factors, argues Beyer, for situating Canadian Pentecostalism. They are also important for understanding how renewal movements are institutionalized and how markets reflect growth and decline. These external factors are as important to understand as the internal organizational and theological motivations of Pentecostal groups as they transition from movement to institution, transform the world they live in, and are transformed by it. Beyer picks up one other thread in his chapter, examining why Pentecostalism went largely unnoticed by outside observers in Canada and why Pentecostalism, along with other religious movements, is currently important for thinking about the role of religion in society. It is is our hope that this introduction to Canadian Pentecostalism will contribute to our understanding of religion in Canada and beyond. This collection is not the final say and much still needs to be explored as religion generally, and Pentecostalism particularly, undergoes a transition and a transformation.

NOTES

1 Various terms are used to describe this modern movement including Pentecostal, charismatic, renewal, neo-Pentecostal, etc. In this volume Pentecostal and Pentecostalism are used inclusively to refer to the movement generally.

2 See Land, *Pentecostal Spirituality*. Land makes the point that Pentecostalism represents a major shift in Christianity as significant historically as the Protestant Reformation.

3 Burgess and McGee, *Dictionary of Pentecostal and Charismatic Movements*, 5.

4 Cox, *Fire from Heaven*.

5 Synan, *The Spirit Said Grow*.

6 See Anderson, *An Introduction to Pentecostalism*, 10–14.

7 See www.statcan.ca for statistics on religion in Canada.

8 See Burgess and van der Mass, "Canada," 48.

9 Beyer, *Religions in Global Society*; Wilkinson, "Religion and Global Flows."

10 Jan Aart Scholte makes a compelling case for understanding globalization as the spread of all things modern but also the pluralization and hybridization of modern structures like economics and politics so that what appears is characterized by continuity and discontinuity. See *Globalization: A Critical Introduction*.

11 Smith, *Moral, Believing Animals*.

12 Macchia, *Baptized in the Spirit*.

13 Beyer, "Social Forms of Religion and Religions in Contemporary Global Society."

14 See Niebuhr, *The Social Sources of Denominationalism*.

15 See Berger, *The Sacred Canopy*.

16 See Held and McGrew, *The Global Transformations Reader*; Waters, *Globalization*.

17 Anderson, *An Introduction to Pentecostalism*, 166–86.

18 Kydd "Pentecostal Assemblies of Canada," 1988; Wacker, *Heaven Below*. Blumhofer is critical of Wacker's view of pragmatism among early Pentecostals. See her "All Shook Up."

19 Kydd, "Pentecostal Assemblies of Canada," 1988, 695–6.

20 The terms used in reference to Aboriginal peoples of Canada vary and are in flux. While "Aboriginal" is currently in use, the term "native" was employed by the people Burkinshaw interviewed.

PART ONE

Origins and Development

Pentecostal and Charismatic Christianity in Canada: Its Origins, Development, and Distinct Culture

MICHAEL DI GIACOMO

INTRODUCTION

This chapter presents an introductory overview of Pentecostalism, broadly defined, including its origins and the socio-religious and ideological movements that contributed to its emergence and ethos, with an emphasis on Pentecostalism's beginning, development, and distinct culture in Canada. It seeks to answer the following questions: In an attempt to understand and define Pentecostalism, what are its fundamental components and characteristics, including its origins? In keeping with the special emphasis on Canadian Pentecostal and charismatic movements, when did these movements begin and how did they develop in Canada? What impact did Pentecostal/charismatic Christianity have in Canada? And finally, what is unique about Canadian Pentecostalism?

The most common feature of Pentecostalism is the emphasis placed on the Holy Spirit and spiritual gifts as listed in 1 Corinthians, chapter 12, and particularly on speaking in tongues. It is doubtful that there would even be a Pentecostal movement without the experience and practice of glossolalia. Robert Mapes Anderson follows Martin Marty in his insistence that an accurate definition of Pentecostalism should emphasize the actual *experience* or *practice* of speaking in tongues.[1] David du Plessis defined a Pentecostal as "someone who can testify to having enjoyed the very same experience as that which the Apostles of our Lord had on the Day of Pentecost according to Acts 2."[2] This association with the New Testament, and especially with the Book of Acts, is crucial to Pentecostal self-identity, as it validates the experience. The very word "glossolalia" is derived from the pages of the Bible, making the New Testament a fundamental element to any definition of Pentecostalism. Early Pentecostals like Parham and Seymour believed that the gift of tongues was actually *xenolalia*, or foreign languages, given for the specific purpose of accelerating the spread of the gospel in the mission fields of the world. However, in time, as disappointment and disillusionment set in because those to whom the gospel was preached in unknown tongues did not understand what was being said, Pentecostals resigned themselves to an understanding of glossolalia as a spiritual language whose main purpose is spiritual edification.[3] Although instances of xenolalia have been known to occur, when the language spoken but not understood by the speaker is understood by the hearer, such manifestations have been rather rare.[4]

As fundamental as glossolalia was and to some extent still is for defining Pentecostalism, the connection is no longer so straightforward. After five generations the reality is that not all people who attend Pentecostal churches actually speak in tongues.[5] The institutionalization of Pentecostalism and its move away from its sectarian origins, in Troeltsch's typology, precludes an exclusively experience-based definition. Allowance must be made for an expansion of the definition to include institutional affiliation, i.e., one who belongs to or identifies with a Pentecostal denomination but has not necessarily experienced the baptism of the Holy Spirit. The definition must take into account generations of Pentecostals who identify themselves as Pentecostal but who have never personally received the distinguishing Pentecostal experience of the baptism of the Holy Spirit with the accompanying glossolalia.

THREE WAVES OF CONTEMPORARY PENTECOSTALISM

The defininition of Pentecostalism must also take into consideration the many who practice speaking in tongues but have no affiliation with traditional Pentecostal denominations.[6] The widest possible definition of twentieth-century Pentecostalism encompasses three "waves" or surges that are linked by a common spirituality and yet carry distinct characteristics. The first wave comprises the "classical Pentecostals,"[7] of whom the most prominent representative in Canada is the Pentecostal Assemblies of Canada (PAOC). Their origins can be traced to events occurring in the ten years spanning the turn of the twentieth century. The second refers to Pentecostalism in the historic churches (Catholic, Anglican, Lutheran, etc.), commonly called the Charismatic Renewal, that traces its origins to the 1950s and 1960s. The third wave refers to the Pentecostal movement in the evangelical churches which began in the 1980s, of which John Wimber and the Vineyard Church and the Toronto Airport Christian Fellowship are two of the better known examples. A closer look at these three sub-groups of Pentecostalism will help us better understand Pentecostalism in Canada.

First Wave: Classical Pentecostalism

Most groups, but not all, included in the first wave of *classical* Pentecostalism trace their origins to one or more of three distinct events around the turn of the twentieth century characterized by Pentecostal/charismatic manifestations such as prophecy and healing, especially glossolalia: the first was a camp meeting in 1896 in Cherokee County, North Carolina organized by a small denomination that would later identify itself with the Pentecostal movement and become the Church of God, now headquartered in Cleveland, Tennessee; the second event was an outbreak of glossolalia in a Bible school in Topeka, Kansas in 1901, under the leadership of independent Holiness preacher Charles Parham; and finally, the Pentecostal revival meetings held on Azusa Street in Los Angeles under the leadership of William Seymour, also a Holiness preacher, which continued almost non-stop for three years from 1906 to 1909. While this chapter leaves to others the issue of the point of origin of the Classical Pentecostal Movement[8] and makes no attempt to resolve the matter, it does propose that all three be considered as part of the beginning of modern Pentecostalism but each with its own particular significance.

Cherokee County is the first documented case of a distinctively Pentecostal experience in a group setting in North America, which gives the Church of God (Cleveland, TN) the distinction of being the oldest Pentecostal denomination in North America. The second event in Topeka is significant for the distinct theology of Charles Parham that became the cornerstone of classical Pentecostalism, that glossolalia is the normative certifying initial sign of having received the baptism of the Holy Spirit, a second experience distinct from and subsequent to conversion. Even though the "initial evidence" doctrine may be defined as fundamental in the theology of most classical Pentecostal churches,[9] unanimity among Pentecostals on this point is elusive as the oldest Pentecostal denominations in Europe and South America do not include it in their creeds.[10] It was even challenged in the very early years of classical

Pentecostalism by its most influential leaders such as Azusa Street mission leader William Seymour[11] and Assemblies of God evangelist and general presbyter F.F. Bosworth.[12] Some non-North American classical Pentecostals such as Minnie Abrams of Pandita Ramabai's Mukti Mission in India, and Willis Hoover, founder of Chilean Pentecostalism, also challenged or did not include initial evidence in their statements of faith. In later years, parts of the second surge of Pentecostalism, Charismatic Renewal, as well as the Third Wave, have not included the doctrines of initial evidence and subsequence in their theologies.[13]

As for the third event in Los Angeles, its significance lies in the fact that it became the catalyst that transformed Pentecostalism into a global phenomenon. However, the assumption that all classical Pentecostal denominations trace their origins to the Pentecostal mission on Azusa Street in Los Angeles would be inaccurate. Pentecostalism in India, for example, pre-dated the events of Azusa Street and developed independently of the American movement. Chilean Pentecostalism, the first in Latin America, also began independently of the American Pentecostal movement. Founded by Methodist missionary Willis Collins Hoover (1858–1936), the Pentecostal movement in Chile began as part of a revival movement within Methodism and following its ouster from Methodism, became the Methodist Pentecostal Church that to this day still maintains a Methodist flavour with respect to doctrines, practices – including infant baptism – and an Episcopal polity.[14] Pentecostalism in Canada also began and, for a while, developed independently of Azusa Street, at the Hebden Mission in Toronto. While its pastors, Jim and Ellen Hebden, gave strong leadership to the fledgling Pentecostal movement for a decade, the Mission played no role in the long-term development of Pentecostalism in Canada.[15] While it can be strongly argued that the Hebden Mission influenced the development of Pentecostalism in Canada, the point should not be exaggerated. All early influential Canadian Pentecostal leaders probably came into contact with the Hebden Mission, and therefore its influence in the development of early Canadian Pentecostalism should certainly be recognized as significant. However, the US contribution, especially the Azusa Street Mission, is undeniable and must also be given due credit in the beginning and development of Pentecostalism in Canada. Aimee Semple McPherson[16] and A.H. Argue of Winnipeg received the baptism of the Holy Spirit in William Durham's North Avenue Mission in Chicago, Durham himself having received it at Azusa Street.[17] R.E. McAlister, who founded the Pentecostal movement in Ontario, was baptized in the Holy Spirit in

Los Angeles.[18] Charles E. Baker, who went on to spread the Pentecostal message in Quebec, received the Pentecostal experience through the ministries of R.E. McAlister and A.H. Argue. Baker's wife was healed in evangelistic meetings organized by McAlister in Ottawa. The guest speaker who prayed for Mrs Baker was A.H. Argue. Azusa Street directly or indirectly influenced the start of Pentecostal ministries by may Canadian leaders. The stamp of Azusa Street on Canadian Pentecostalism is indelible.

The Second Wave: The Charismatic Renewal

Pentecostalism's second wave was first identified as *neo-Pentecostal* and later as *charismatic*. Those who received the baptism of the Holy Spirit and its accompanying charism of glossolalia and who remained in the mainline historic churches or non-denominational churches admitted to having embraced Pentecostal spirituality in that they initially identified with the Pentecostals. This fact is underscored by the publishing of the first book on the Catholic charismatic renewal, aptly titled *Catholic Pentecostals*.[19] Later, a desire to distinguish themselves from classical Pentecostalism led to the neo-Pentecostals assuming the designation of "charismatic."[20] This designation was subsequently extended to encompass non-denominational churches, and still later, as it became more fashionable, classical Pentecostals began calling themselves "charismatic."

The announcement in 1960 by Anglican priest Dennis Bennett that he had received the baptism in the Holy Spirit is often considered the beginning of the charismatic movement. It is probably more accurate to think of this event as a time in which Pentecostalism entered popular culture and became part of the public consciousness due to the exposure from major media outlets.[21] In actuality, Bennett was not the first member of a mainline denomination to receive the Pentecostal experience and remain within his denominational structure. Classical Pentecostalism in Europe, Korea, and Chile began as charismatic movements in the mainline churches and not all of the first Spirit-baptized, glossolalia-speaking leaders in those countries left their denominations.[22] Examples include Anglican priest Alexander A. Boddy[23] in England, reformed minister Louis Dallière in France,[24] and Lutheran Pastor Jonathan Paul in Germany.[25] The Pentecostal movement began in the Presbyterian and Methodist churches of Korea, among the Methodists in Chile, within the Anglican Church in England, the French Reformed church in France, and the German Lutheran and Reformed churches.[26] The integrative character of the neo-Pentecostals desiring to remain attached to and work within their own familiar church traditions and structures contrasted sharply with the separatism and "come-outism" of many of the first-wave classical Pentecostals who could not believe that God could work with existing denominational structures. Other prominent charismatics include Lutheran pastor Harald Bredesen (1946), Methodist minister Tommy Tyson (1952), Disciples of Christ minister Don Basham (1953), Mennonite pastor Gerald Derstine (1954), Episcopalian Agnes Sanford (1953–4), Episcopalian rector Richard Winkler, and Presbyterian James Brown (1956).[27]

In North America, healing evangelists Oral Roberts, Gordon Lindsay, T.L. Osborn, and William Branham as well as the Full Gospel Business Men's Fellowship International (FGBMFI), under the leadership of Demos Shakarian, were instrumental in bringing the Pentecostal experience to mainline Christians in the 1940s and 1950s. The policy of FGBMFI discouraged mainline Christians who received the baptism of the Holy Spirit from joining denominational Pentecostalism.[28] The key figure in bringing the Pentecostal experience to the mainline churches was a minister from South Africa, David du Plessis. In 1949 he felt God telling him to visit the New York offices of the World Council of Churches. That initial visit and the warm reception he received was the beginning of an international ministry that brought him into contact with many mainline leaders, including top Catholic leaders, to whom he was given the opportunity to speak of the Pentecostal experience. [29]

The charismatic movement grew but did not reach its apex until it was embraced by the Catholic Church.[30] In 1967, at Duquesne University in Pittsburgh, the Pentecostal movement began within the Catholic Church as Catholic professors and students began seeking fulfillment in their spiritual lives in the wake of Vatican II. After having received the baptism of the Holy Spirit with accompanying glossolalia, not only did they perceive the Pentecostal blessing as an answer to their personal spiritual quest but also as an answer to the prayer of Pope John XXIII for a new Pentecost.[31]

The Third Wave: Pentecostalism and Conservative Protestants

In the 1980s Pentecostalism experienced new growth and expansion, with different emphases and characteristics, especially through the network of churches called the Vineyard Fellowship, founded by John

Wimber. This new surge was called, simply, *The Third Wave*, a term coined by Peter Wagner of Fuller Theological Seminary.[32] Although Wagner acknowledged continuity with Pentecostal/charismatic spirituality, he recognized this new surge of Pentecostalism as distinct from the former in that, although "Third Wavers" do recognize the validity and practice of spiritual gifts, they do not put the same emphasis on glossolalia and baptism of the Holy Spirit as do the previous two Pentecostal waves. The Third Wave was also distinguished by the openness of evangelical churches that were previously reticent to embrace the charismatic movement. And, finally, Wagner simply acknowledged quite openly that he and those churches influenced by him chose not to identify either with the classical Pentecostals or the charismatic renewal.[33]

Wagner and Wimber taught a course on "Signs and Wonders" that proved to be controversial at Fuller Theological Seminary. Thereafter, the Third Wave was associated with the notion that "signs and wonders" were a normal part of evangelism and church growth. Since Wimber's Association of Vineyard Fellowship Churches was a major part of this movement, one of its churches, the Toronto Airport Vineyard, now the Toronto Airport Christian Fellowship, had a significant impact on Christian churches in the 1990s. Certainly the most conspicuous church of the Third Wave, it brought personal renewal to many, albeit not without controversy, ultimately leading to a falling out with and formal disassociation from the Association of Vineyard Churches.

PENTECOSTAL/CHARISMATIC MOVEMENTS IN CANADA

All three sub-groups of Pentecostalism penetrated the Canadian scene. The very first Pentecostal centre in Canada was the East End Mission, in Toronto, commonly called the Hebden Mission after its pastors, British émigrés James and Ellen Hebden. Ellen is considered the first in Canada to be baptized in the Holy Spirit with accompanying glossolalia on 17 November 1906.[34] Thomas Miller called the Hebden Mission "the Canadian Azusa."[35] Besides Toronto, both the North Avenue Mission in Chicago and the Azusa Street Mission in Los Angeles contributed to the beginnings of Canadian Pentecostalism. In 1906, businessman and lay preacher A.H. Argue of Winnipeg received the Baptism of the Holy Spirit in the North Avenue Mission in Chicago whose pastor, William Durham, received the baptism of the Holy Spirit in Los Angeles. Argue went on to found what would become one of the largest Pentecostal churches in Canada. Around the same time Robert

E. McAlister, after having received the baptism of the Holy Spirit, returned to the Ottawa region to preach the message of Pentecost, going on to found the Pentecostal movement in Eastern Canada. A few years later, in 1910, a school teacher from Connecticut, Alice Garrigus, began her ministry in Newfoundland that eventually led to the formation of the Pentecostal Assemblies of Newfoundland and Labrador.[36] Pentecostalism in Canada took root, grew, and developed, therefore, as a result of the work of these leaders as well as others, but it should be noted, mainly on the basis of developments in the us.

The Canadian movement also looked to Britain for leadership and inspiration, especially in the early attempts to organize the movement. When it was perceived that the movement was taking a wrong turn, evidenced by bitter theological disputes, the increasing number of fraudulent preachers taking advantage of trusting congregations, and the misuse of spiritual gifts, some sought more accountability among their leaders. Practical considerations such as dealing with foreign governments, the building of hospitals and schools, and railway fare discounts for clergy, also motivated leaders to seek to form some legally recognized structure beyond the local church.[37] In Eastern Canada, following Great Britain's lead, with British Anglican Vicar A.A. Boddy's encouragement, as well as that of some us Pentecostals,[38] a first attempt at organizing the Canadians resulted in the formation of the Pentecostal Missionary Union in 1909.[39] It did not last long, though, as there was much opposition to any structuring of the Pentecostal movement.[40] The Hebdens went on record to show their opposition to any move to organize Pentecostals beyond the confines of the local congregation: "We desire to state most emphatically that in the Lord's work at 651 Queen St and at 191 George St., Toronto, we have no connection whatever with any general organization of the Pentecostal people in Canada. As a missionary church we stand alone in God's divine order, and extend the right hand of fellowship to every member of the body of Christ ... and we decline absolutely all responsibility for any so-called representatives of the Pentecostal work in Canada."[41] In spite of their opposition and decline in influence,[42] Pentecostalism in Canada continued to flourish.

The ever-increasing number of problems and challenges facing the Pentecostals led a few leaders to make another attempt at structuring the Pentecostal movement. A number of Pentecostal churches in Ontario and Quebec applied for and received a legal charter from the Canadian Parliament on 17 May 1919 incorporating them as The Pentecostal Assemblies of Canada (PAOC) giving them all the rights and privileges due any religious organization. The original intent of the new PAOC was to join the Pentecostal Assemblies of the World,[43] a Oneness Pentecostal denomination,[44] for the PAOC at this time officially adhered to the doctrine of Oneness or Jesus Only theology.[45] In fact, the leader and founder of Pentecostalism in Eastern Canada was R.E. McAlister, also one of the early proponents of Jesus Only doctrine (see chapter 2 in this volume).[46]

In that same year Pentecostals in Western Canada chose to affiliate, not with the PAOC, but with the Assemblies of God (AG) of the US, to become the Western Canada District Council of the Assemblies of God, USA.[47] The following year the PAOC voted to join the AG as the Eastern Canada District Council of the Assemblies of God, USA[48] and by so doing positioned itself squarely within mainstream Christianity by rejecting the Jesus Only stance. Consequently a split occurred among Canadian Pentecostals when Frank Small, one of the PAOC charter members, would not change his Oneness stance to join the AG with his fellow Canadian Pentecostals. He subsequently founded the Apostolic Church of Pentecost in 1921.

When the PAOC joined the AG the result was more unity among Pentecostals across Canada because the Canadian Pentecostals in the West joined with those in Eastern Canada under the PAOC banner. Eventually, because of differences over missionary policy, it was decided that the PAOC would withdraw from the AG to become a distinct national and administrative entity, albeit a fraternal organization to the US body.[49]

CANADIAN PENTECOSTALISM'S RELATIONSHIP WITH EVANGELICALISM

Also consistent with trends south of the border, Canadian Pentecostalism sought acceptance within the theologically conservative family of Christianity – first with fundamentalism and then evangelicalism. Kydd specifically addresses Pentecostalism's uneasy relationship with evangelicalism.[50] Tension was experienced in its co-operation and participation with evangelical groups such as the National Association of Evangelicals and Youth for Christ.

Pentecostal involvement with these conservative groups came mainly through the efforts of Pentecostal pastor J. Harry Faught who provided strong leadership in the founding of the Evangelical Fellowship of Canada (EFC). Faught, who became the first executive chair of the new organization, insisted that membership be limited to individuals to allow evangelicals within non-evangelical denominations to join. As a result, three of the first six presidents were Presbyterian and thereby prevented the EFC from being characterized as fundamentalist.[51]

Not all laud this close relationship as a totally positive development. Classical Pentecostalism's acceptance into the wider evangelical fold was done, so it seems, at too high a price, at the expense of forsaking the distinctiveness of Pentecostalism and betraying its own nature. In other words, Pentecostalism, by identifying itself with fundamentalism and accepting itself as a sub-group of evangelicalism, defined its *self-understanding* within the framework of a brand of Christianity it had originally critiqued by its very emergence and existence. It is not beyond the realm of possibility that the inherent tension between the ethos of the charismatic and the theological assumptions of evangelicalism has resulted in a smaller percentage of classical Pentecostals experiencing glossolalia, a situation causing much concern among Pentecostal leaders. If the theology and ethos of evangelicalism did apply a "cooling effect" on classical Pentecostalism, the latter, as a spiritual movement, refused to be contained and subsequently found expression in a different ecclesiastical framework as the charismatic movement.

CANADIAN CHARISMATIC RENEWAL MOVEMENTS

Anglican priest and television personality Al Reimers made the earliest attempt to document the full scope of the charismatic renewal in Canada by writing *God's Country: Charismatic Renewal*. Not intended to be a scholarly work or a history of the movement, as he himself acknowledges, it is more an attempt, based on testimonies, anecdotes, and loose statistics, to present and help the reader understand the spiritual experience of the movement. His numbers are not based on formal surveys or definitions, and there was no attempt to produce a scientific profile of the charismatic movement such as his colleague, fellow Anglican David Reed of Wycliffe College, produced more than a decade later (see chapter 10 in this volume).[52] However, even though Reimers' numbers need to be viewed with some skepticism, his work is valuable in that it gives us an idea of the scope of the movement in the late 1970s.

Reimers states that the Charismatic Renewal (CR) in Canada began first among Anglicans and a few members of the United and Presbyterian churches. At the time of writing, the CR was strongest among Roman Catholics with the greatest contingent in Quebec. He estimated that the movement among Catholics had about 2,000 prayer groups that involved over 100,000 people, whereas among Anglicans he estimated between seventy-five and one hundred and a couple of dozen based in churches of other denominations like the United, Lutheran, Christian Reformed, Presbyterian, and Orthodox.[53] Reimers was not able to obtain precise figures concerning the number of people involved in the CR, contenting himself with "a list of about a hundred United Church ministers known to be sympathetic" that was given to him. He writes, "I guess there are at least a hundred Anglican clergy involved and several hundred Roman Catholic priests, plus a few bishops in each of those churches."[54]

As to when the charismatic movement first came to Canada, relying on the testimonies of those involved in the movement, Reimers was able to determine that it originated with visits to Canada by Dennis Bennett in the early 1960s. Among the first to receive the Pentecostal experience were an Anglican priest and his wife, Ron and Judy Armstrong, in Etobicoke in 1962. In the following year, also in Etobicoke, charismatic renewal began among United Church ministers with the first prayer group meeting at the Alderwood United Church.[55] From then on the charismatic movement spread across Canada.

As for the first Catholic Charismatic Renewal (CCR) meetings in Canada, the record is somewhat confusing (see chapter 10 in this volume). Reimers states that Fr Duffy brought the charismatic experience from Madonna House (a Catholic retreat centre and charitable organization in Combermere, Ontario, approximately 160 kilometres west of Ottawa) to Regina in 1968. A paper was written that claims that the Canadian CCR began in Regina.[56] This is not certain, for the founder of Madonna House, an exiled Russian baroness by the name of Catherine de Hueck Doherty, invited American charismatic leaders to come and explain the initial charismatic events that occurred at Duquesne and Notre Dame Universities. Reimers does not explicitly say when the visit to Madonna House occurred, but he seems to suggest that it took place soon after the initial Catholic Charismatic rallies in the US in 1967. A charismatic prayer group began at Madonna House as a result of the visit from the US leaders. However, if Fr Duffy went to Regina from Madonna House, that suggests that Madonna House was already a hub of charismatic activity in Canada before 1968. In addition, Fr Robert Pelton of Madonna House claims to have been the first Catholic in Canada to speak in tongues.[57] However, the issue of the time and place of the beginning of Catholic charismatic activity in Canada is overshadowed by the fact that the CCR would have its greatest effect in Quebec through leaders, all of whom received their experience in the US.

In 1969 in Montreal, Sister Flore Crête, a nun of the Sisters of Providence and doctoral student at Notre Dame University, who had received the Pentecostal experience two years before in the US, began the first charismatic meeting in Quebec. Not being allowed by her superiors to hold such meetings on the premises of the convent, she held them in her family's home.[58] As for the introduction of the charismatic movement to English Catholics, Fr Joe Kane, OMI, a missionary from Peru, received his charismatic experience in Seattle on the way to Canada. After arriving in Montreal in 1970, he introduced English-speaking diocesan priests to the charismatic experience.

Although French Canadians were introduced to the renewal by Sr Crête, the movement did not expand in French Canada until Father Jean-Paul Régimbal arrived on the scene in 1969; he quickly became the best-known leader among Canadian Catholic charismatics. He also had received his Pentecostal experience in the US when working as an assistant pastor at St Theresa Catholic church in Phoenix, Arizona. An Episcopalian woman, having gone to him for marriage counselling, shared her experience of Spirit baptism, and as a trained psychiatrist, he immediately classified her as schizophrenic. However, her testimony intrigued him and motivated him to read the books of Acts and I Corinthians wherein he read about the *charismata*. Having finally concluded that the woman had been telling him the truth, he asked her forgiveness, then knelt as she laid hands on him and prayed for him. He received the Pentecostal experience immediately, and two weeks later he spoke in tongues and prophesied. This story, based on an interview with Régimbal, may be somewhat confusing to classical Pentecostals, who consider the normative pattern to be the immediate manifestation of glossolalia upon the reception of the baptism of the Holy Spirit.[59] In an interview with Prosser, now professor at Regent University in Virginia, he elaborated by saying that Fr Régimbal was convinced that he had received the baptism of the Holy Spirit when the woman laid hands on him and prayed for him; however, he was also convicted of the need for correcting a wrong against another person. Once reconciliation took place two weeks later, he immediately received the gift of glossolalia.[60]

Fr Régimbal was later appointed the head of a retreat centre in Granby, Quebec, where he was allowed to carry on his charismatic ministry, not without controversy and opposition, however. In March of 1971 he organized large charismatic rallies of up to 34,000 at the Montreal Forum, long-time home of the Montreal Canadiens professional hockey team, as well as in the famous St Joseph's Oratory. In the meantime, Régimbal's ministry and influence increased as evidenced by the growing attendance at his retreat centre. Whereas in the beginning in 1970 only a handful of people attended, more than 200 people per weekend would attend in 1972 and as many as 1,000 would attend the Monday prayer meetings by 1973. Not only did local people attend; busloads would come from other regions of Quebec, Ontario, and the US. English charismatic groups were growing as well as the French groups. By 1972 there were six English groups and eight French groups.[61]

The leadership information conference at the Grand Séminaire de Montréal on Labour Day weekend in September of 1972 was a watershed in the CCR. The main speakers at this conference, Kenneth Ranaghan and Sr Amata Fabbro, spoke to an audience of four bishops, forty priests, and 360 nuns. Thereafter, the number of religious leaders increased and the number of adherents joining the CCR doubled in size every six months.

In spite of the phenomenal growth, cultural tensions surfaced very early between the English and French contingents of the movement. In one conference attended by 4,000 people, half of whom were French Canadians, it was not appreciated that the leaders and coordinators, mainly English speaking, had failed to provide adequate language services for French-speaking Canadians. Cultural and linguistic tensions consequently led the French-Canadian charismatics to organize their own leadership structure and their own unilingual French conference in 1974. The main speakers at that Conference were Fr Régimbal, French Canadian lay leader Jean Vanier, and Belgian church leader Leo Joseph Suenens as the keynote speaker.[62] Ten thousand French Canadians attended. By July of 1974, Fr Régimbal compiled figures affirming 440 charismatic prayer groups in the province of Quebec, comprising some 20,000 people.[63]

There was no equivalent structure for English Catholic charismatics across Canada until 1973. Prior to some organizational efforts they operated closely with counterparts in the US. Not surprisingly, most CCR activity was in Ontario and Quebec, the provinces in Canada with the greatest number of Catholics. In mainly Protestant Western

Canada, the CCR was smaller and less pervasive.[64] Western Canada, especially British Columbia and Alberta, was mainly the domain of Protestant charismatics and the Jesus People movement.[65]

At the time Prosser wrote his thesis, the CCR leadership in Quebec, the biggest contingent of the charismatic movement in Canada, comprised Fr Jacques Cousteau; Jacques Dupuis, a Catholic layman from Montreal; Fr Cornelius Boekema from Ottawa-Hull (now Gatineau); Fr Jean-Paul Régimbal from Granby; Professor Vincent Therrien of Trois-Rivières; and Sr Jeanne Rousseau of Quebec City. In 1974, according to the *American Charismatic Year Book* published by Notre-Dame University, 1,500 prayer groups were listed in Canada, two-thirds of which were in Eastern Canada.[66] By the early 1980s, the best days of the CCR had come and gone.[67]

In addition to revitalizing people and churches, renewal or revival also had a habit of threatening ecclesiastical relationships and structures, sometimes to the point of rupture. This occurred within classical Pentecostalism during the Latter Rain controversy of the 1940s as well as in the 1990s as a result of the controversial Toronto Blessing. The Latter Rain Movement, put succinctly, began as a renewal movement within classical Pentecostalism in the late 1940s, originating in North Battleford, Saskatchewan. However, it quickly fell out of favour with many Pentecostals because of certain controversial teachings and practices. Denominational leaders frowned on such teachings as receiving spiritual gifts through the laying on of hands, or undue and exaggerated importance given to the spiritual gifts, seemingly elevating them to the status of scripture.[68] The controversy was particularly felt in the Saskatchewan District of the PAOC where there was serious disagreement between denominational officials and the leaders of the Latter Rain Movement who also happened to be the leaders in the PAOC Bible College, Bethel Bible Institute. Eventually the leaders of the Bible College left the PAOC along with the bulk of the student body.[69] In the 1990s, classical Pentecostals in search of renewal discovered the Third Wave Toronto Blessing. Although it did result in renewal in a great number of individuals, it also led to strained relationships between individuals and churches. To an observer living in Quebec in the 1990s, it seems that the strained relations within the PAOC over the Toronto Blessing were especially acute in Quebec. To my knowledge, there has been no scholarly study of the impact of the phenomenon in Quebec.

PENTECOSTAL MOVEMENTS AND SECULARIZATION
IN QUEBEC

Interestingly, the locus of Pentecostal and charismatic activity in the 1970s was Quebec. Not only was the greatest contingent of the CCR in Quebec, but classical Pentecostals themselves focused on expanding their presence in that province. The irony here is underscored when one realizes that Pentecostal Christianity surged in that part of Canada where the institutional and public secularization process of Quebec's Quiet Revolution had been the most dramatic.[70]

The Quiet Revolution of the 1960s was characterized by the questioning of everything traditional and all things once accepted as normal. One of the most revolutionary aspects of the Quiet Revolution was the secularization of institutions and national symbols that ultimately led to, or at least contributed to, a decline in the practice of Catholicism, and this in a relatively short period of time. The Quebec provincial government of Jean Lesage took over responsibility for Quebec's social services, especially those of education, health, and social welfare, which had been traditionally the domain of the Catholic Church. In addition, the responsibility to protect and promote the French language and culture, also traditionally the responsibility of the Catholic Church in Quebec – "*la foi, gardienne de la langue*" – has since been assumed by the Quebec government. In effect, internal and external social forces, including Vatican II reforms, led to the removal of the Quebec Catholic Church from its traditional and long-held position of social power. Whereas the Catholic Church had been so ubiquitous, so socially and culturally dominant in the past, the 1960s saw its withdrawal from many social services and its relegation to a strictly religious sphere. Journalist Ron Graham captures the essence of the fundamental transformation of Quebec society in a nutshell when he describes this period of Quebec history as that time when "the State replaced the [Church] hierarchy, language replaced faith, and nationalism replaced religion."[71] The transformation of Quebec from a highly religious society to a secular one permitted a greater openness on the part of the Québécois to other ideologies, philosophies, and religions, creating conditions favourable to Pentecostal growth and expansion.

Yet, in spite of a willingness to experiment with the new, in spite of the Quebecers' desire to break with their past, the abandonment of tradition, and the dramatic decline in church attendance, the classical Pentecostals never convinced more than 0.6 per cent of the Quebec population to embrace Pentecostalism.[72] As for the Catholic charismatics in Quebec, if we estimate a core group of participants of 15,000–20,000 at its peak in the late 1970s and add to that number friends, sympathizers, and the curious, we might find about 1 per cent of the Quebec population that would have embraced charismatic Catholicism.[73] The point here is that, at their finest hour, during a time of unprecedented growth, classical Pentecostals and charismatic Catholics could convince only approximately 1.5 per cent of Quebecers to embrace Pentecostalism, and this in spite of widespread interest, media attention, and unprecedented charismatic activity in Quebec. The impact on the population as a whole cannot be characterized as phenomenal, although many found meaning and fulfillment through their participation in charismatic and Pentecostal Christianity. By contrast, the separatist ideology, a marginal movement attracting relatively few people in the 1950s, was embraced by a sufficient percentage of the population that they almost voted Quebec out of Canada in October of 1995.

The reluctance of Canadians to change religious culture notwithstanding, Canadians have indeed changed their culture, and fundamentally so. The most obvious example is Quebec. The Quebec situation illustrates with high drama how a society can change the very core of its identity and self-perception in a short period of time. The most forceful example of radical change was the rapid and dramatic decline of the very significant power the Catholic Church had held in Quebec up until the 1960s. When it is underscored that Catholicism was a fundamental component of French-Canadian identity and had defined French-Canadian culture for so long, the relegating of such a powerful institution to the margins of society in such a short period of time is nothing short of staggering. Given its long and powerful reign in terms of social and cultural hegemony, could the secularization process of the 1960s not be likened to the overthrow of a government, albeit a "quiet" overthrow of an unofficial government? Such a radical change can only be qualified as revolutionary. And out of the ruins a new French Canadian emerged, with a new self-awareness and a new identity – the Québécois.[74]

The Quiet Revolution dramatically underscores that a society and a people can fundamentally change. In Quebec's case, a group of elites advocating the secularization of society were the most successful in convincing people to change. The question that needs to be asked by Pentecostals and charismatics is why they were unable to lead Canadians into a fundamental transformation of their religious (and cultural) identity? It is interesting that in other parts of the world, including Catholic societies, Pentecostalism is experiencing greater success. Whatever it was that prevented the Québécois from embracing Pentecostalism, it does not seem to exist in some traditionally Catholic countries in Latin America where Pentecostalism's growth can truly be characterized as phenomenal.[75] For example, evangelical Protestants, most of whom are Pentecostal or charismatic, now comprise 25 per cent of the population in Guatemala and 15 per cent in Chile[76] – a far cry from the 1 per cent in Quebec.[77] Canadian Pentecostalism does not encompass proportions of its population base similar to its counterpart in Latin America. Inevitably, these statistical distinctions lead us to examine the cultural specificities that allow for or impede the growth of the movement. Consequently, we are led to take a closer look at the cultural distinctiveness of Canadian Pentecostalism.

CANADIAN PENTECOSTALISM'S DISTINCT CULTURE

When considering the cultural distinctiveness of Canadian Pentecostalism, reference is naturally made to the historical, political, and cultural connections to both Britain and the US. Can we speak of a unique Canadian Pentecostalism? How distinct is Canadian Pentecostalism? Canadian Pentecostalism did indeed benefit and inherit much from Britain. In the first decade of the twentieth century, when the Dominion of Canada was, for all practical purposes, still a colony of Britain, a jewel of the British Empire, the relationship between British and Canadian Pentecostal movements was, in all likelihood, very close because the British connection, especially with English Canada, was strong. English Canadians were proud of their heritage in the British Empire as their participation in the Boer War and two World Wars attested. Even pre-World-War-II French Canada was not ashamed of or shy about its loyalty to the British Crown as demonstrated at the first nationalist mass meeting at Drummondville, in June 1902, when fidelity was proclaimed to "French-Canadian nationality and to its constituent elements of faith, language, laws, and traditions, and *to the British Crown*" (emphasis mine)[78] – a far cry from current sentiments. A British "flavour" in the Hebden's ministry is all but certain. After all, the Hebdens *were* British. Early attempts at organizing Pentecostals were inspired by the British model of the Pentecostal Missionary Union, helped along by British Anglican vicar Alexander Boddy, an early

Pentecostal leader in Sunderland, England, arguably Britain's Azusa.[79] J.E. Purdie, the founding principal of the first Canadian Pentecostal Bible College (see chapter 5 in this volume) who remained at its head for the next twenty-five years, was a priest of the Church of England in Canada and most certainly looked to Britain for leadership and inspiration.[80] And lest we forget, both Pentecostal antecedents in the Holiness movement, Wesleyan and Keswickian, had their origins in Britain. Even the dispensationalist-millenarianist-fundamentalist current that North American Pentecostals adopted was of British origin via John Nelson Darby and his Bible-and-prophecy conferences. British contributions to Canadian Pentecostalism are undeniable. But whatever British influence there might have been on Canadian Pentecostalism, it simply waned, especially after the end of the Second World War.

As the British influence on Canadian Pentecostalism on the one hand should not be exaggerated, the strength of US influence, on the other hand, should not be underestimated. The Azusa Street Mission undeniably was the main source to which most Pentecostals looked for leadership. Although Pentecostal outbursts occurred around the world independently of Azusa Street, including in Canada, key leaders who spread the Pentecostal message worldwide were baptized at Azusa Street or with the help of someone who had been to Azusa Street. Canadian A.H. Argue received the Pentecostal experience at the North Avenue meetings in Chicago whose pastor, William Durham, began Pentecostal ministry following his visit to Los Angeles. Argue subsequently spread the Pentecostal message in Western Canada. R.E. McAlister was baptized, probably at Azusa Street or at least en route there,[81] and then spread the message in Eastern Canada. Alice Garrigus also came to Canada from the US to help build Canadian Pentecostalism.

The dominance of Pentecostalism in the US over Canadian Pentecostalism was assured as the latter was formally a part of the AG from 1919 to 1925. Canadian Pentecostals looked for leadership and resources to this organization, headquartered in Springfield, Missouri. Since the friendly separation in 1925, Canadian Pentecostals – the PAOC particularly – have enjoyed a fraternal relationship with their US counterparts. Ministers on both sides of the border transfer their credentials with ease, and invitations cross the border on a regular basis. Some of the Canadian Pentecostals who have risen to prominent leadership in the US are long-time General Secretary of the AG, Joseph Roswell Flower; founder of the International Church of the Foursquare Gospel, Aimee

Semple McPherson; long-time AG preacher on the Revivaltime radio broadcast, C.M. Ward; college president and former head of the National Association of Evangelicals, Don Argue; and former AG Assistant General Superintendent and now President of Zion Bible College, Charles Crabtree.

Stark differences between Canadian and US Pentecostal cultures notwithstanding, the influence of American Pentecostalism on its Canadian counterpart is powerful and pervasive. Canadian Pentecostals, as well as other Christians, are aware of a steady stream of US religious production through television, film, music, and literature at all levels, whether scholarly, inspirational, devotional, or educational. The sheer size of US religious production can even be qualified as overwhelming, beginning with organizations such as Focus on the Family, the Billy Graham Evangelistic Association, Pat Robertson and the 700 Club, and the National Association of Evangelicals. In terms of size and cross-border influence there is no comparison – US ministries dwarf the biggest Canadian ones – understandably so, given the greater population and economic base of the US. Whereas most, if not all, Canadian evangelicals have heard of or been impacted in some way by these ministries, the reverse cannot be said of Canadian ministries that for the most part do not even appear on US evangelical "radar screens." No Pentecostal pastor, educator, or scholar living in Canada is able to deny the colossal US dominance of the Canadian conservative churches in general and Pentecostal churches in particular, for as long as one is able to remember. The fact is that Canadian evangelicals, Pentecostals, and charismatics usually look to ministries in the US for leadership and inspiration.

CONCLUSION

Although non-American inspiration should not be discounted in the early years of Pentecostalism, and non-Americans have given significant leadership and inspiration to Pentecostalism in general – Donald Gee and Smith Wigglesworth from Britain, and David du Plessis from South Africa – caution is in order to avoid any exaggeration of its influence. British leadership or influence on Canadian Pentecostalism, even before World War II when Canada, especially English Canada, still had a British "flavour," was minimal.

Although Canadian Pentecostals cannot help but be impacted in large measure by their US counterparts, Canadian Pentecostalism is not simply "American" for the very simple reason that, although there are

certainly similarities between Canadian and American cultures, they
are nonetheless quite different. The late George Rawlyk found out personally that Canadian Evangelicalism is distinctly not American after
he spent a year writing in South Carolina.[82] Sam Reimer's study con-
firms empirically that there are indeed differences between US and
Canadian Evangelicals. History, attitudes, expectations, practices,
issues, culture, and even political positions distinguish the two cultures.[83] It is, furthermore, too simplistic to speak of "Canadian" and
"American" cultures as if they were monolithic. The comparisons of
sub-cultures can reveal further similarities, common characteristics,
and stark contrasts. There are many in the Northeast corridor of the US
who would be comfortable in Ontario. Quebec's insistence on its
distinct status and culture within the Canadian federation would find
resonance in the American South.

So, is Canadian Pentecostalism unique? The best answer, it seems to
me, is yes and no. The uniqueness of Canadian Pentecostalism as distinct from British and American Pentecostalism stems from its
Canadianness, that is, the distinct Canadian history and culture that
provide a unique framework through which Canadian Pentecostals can
express their particular Pentecostal spirituality and ethos, that is, their
Pentecostalness. Canada's Pentecostal and charismatic story is unique
because its actors played out their roles on the unique stage of Canadian history and culture and geography. Canadian Pentecostals can put
just as much emphasis on the theology of the baptism of the Holy Spirit
as their American counterparts. Canadian, American, and British Pentecostals can all sing that "the Comforter Has Come" with equal zest
and enthusiasm. It is unlikely, though, that Canadians would sing
about Canada with the same religious zeal that American Pentecostals
sing "God Bless America" or "America the Beautiful." Canadians
would not necessarily identify with their American counterparts on a
range of cultural and political issues from gun control to the role of religion in the public place to the sanctification of national symbols and
myths. In other words, Canadian Pentecostals are unique simply
because they are Canadian. The mixing of Canadian patriotism and
Christianity, it seems to me, is much more likely to be found in English
Canada and in varying degrees, contingent on time and place. It might
range anywhere from a framed picture of the Queen in a church in Loy-
alist country or David Mainse of 100 Huntley Street broadcasting
month-long "Salute to Canada" programs on national television as he
did in 1981. Maybe on Canada Day, a congregation in English Canada

might sing the Canadian national anthem in church, something done only at great risk in French Canada. But all these expressions of patriotism in a religious atmosphere are mild compared to the zeal shown by Americans toward their own national symbols in a religious context.

In conclusion, Canada's place historically and geographically in relation to Britain and the US has permitted it to forge a unique culture, not quite British and not quite American. In the same way, Canadian Pentecostals and charismatics, although as Pentecostal as their British and American counterparts, have given a unique expression to their practical theology of the Spirit. It's not quite British and not quite American, but quite Canadian.

NOTES

1 Anderson, *Vision of the Disinherited*, 4.

2 Du Plessis, *The Spirit Bade Me Go*, 9.

3 Anderson, *An Introduction to Pentecostalism*, 190; McGee, "Missions, Overseas," 889–90.

4 McGee, "Shortcut to Language Preparation?," 122.

5 Anderson, *An Introduction to Pentecostalism*, 190.

6 For differences and similarities in the three distinct waves of Pentecostalism see Burgess and Eduard van der Maas, "Introduction," xviii–xxii; Synan, "Classical Pentecostalism," 553–5; Hocken, "Charismatic Movement," 477–519; Wagner, *The Third Wave*.

7 This term was first coined by Roman Catholic priest and theologian Killian McDonnell. See Robeck, "McDonnell, Killian," 853. For the major subgroups of classical Pentecostalism, Wesleyan, non-Wesleyan, and Oneness, see Synan, *Aspects of Pentecostal-Charismatic Origins*, 252.

8 See Creech, "Visions of Glory: The Place of Azusa Street in Pentecostal History."

9 Synan, "Classical Pentecostalism," 553. See Bruner, *A Theology of the Holy Spirit*, 58.

10 Anderson, *An Introduction*, 11–12.

11 See *Apostolic Faith* (Los Angeles), June-September 1907 and October-January 1908 issues in Corum, *Like as of Fire*.

12 Blumhofer, *The Assemblies of God*, 239–43.

13 Anderson, *An Introduction to Pentecostalism*, 191–3.

14 Ibid., 64–5.

15 Miller, "The Canadian 'Azusa'."

16 Aimee's first husband, Robert Semple, received the baptism in the Holy Spirit at the Hebden Mission. See Miller, "The Canadian 'Azusa'," 15.

17 Miller, "The Significance of A.H. Argue for Pentecostal Historiography."

18 Craig, "R.E. McAlister, Canadian Pentecostal Pioneer."

19 Ranaghan, *Catholic Pentecostals*, 266.

20 The first time the term Charismatic Renewal was used to refer to Pentecostals within mainline denominations was in an article in *Trinity*, the publication of the Blessed Trinity Society, in 1963. See Hocken, "Charismatic Movement," 480.

21 See Anderson, *Vision*, 3; Hocken, "Charismatic Movement," 477–9.

22 Anderson, *An Introduction to Pentecostalism*, 144–5.

23 Ibid., 91.

24 Ibid., 96.

25 Ibid., 89.

26 Ibid., 145.

27 Ibid., 147; Hocken, "Charismatic Movement," 477–8

28 Hocken, "Charismatic Movement," 477–8.

29 See Du Plessis, *A Man Called Mr. Pentecost*.

30 The first to document the beginning of the Charismatic Renewal in the Catholic Church were lay leaders Kevin and Dorothy Ranaghan. For a brief overview see Thigpen, "Catholic Charismatic Renewal."

31 See Ranaghan, *Catholic Pentecostals*.

32 Wagner, *The Third Wave*; Wagner, "Wimber, John," 1199–1200; Poloma, "The Spirit Movement in North America at the Millennium," 83–107.

33 Wagner, *The Third Wave*, 18.

34 Miller, "The Canadian 'Azusa'," 6.

35 Ibid., 5–29.

36 From the website of the Pentecostal Assemblies of Newfoundland and Labrador (http://www.paon.nf.ca/history.htm).

37 See Blumhofer, *The Assemblies of God*, 197–202.

38 Miller, "The Canadian 'Azusa'," 20–1.

39 Kulbeck, *What God Hath Wrought*, 6; Miller, *Canadian Pentecostals*.

40 Atter, *The Third Force*, 95; Craig, "R.E. McAlister: Canadian Pentecostal Pioneer."

41 Quoted in Miller, "The Canadian 'Azusa'," 21.

42 Besides the opposition manifested by the Hebdens to further structuring of the Pentecostal movement, much of their influence was lost on Pentecostal leaders because there seemed to be an undue emphasis on directed prophecy, that is, prophecy that would direct people into various ministries, including overseas missions. See Miller, "The Canadian 'Azusa'," 24.

43 Kydd, "Pentecostal Assemblies of Canada."
44 Reed, "Pentecostal Assemblies of the World," 965.
45 Kydd, "Pentecostal Assemblies of Canada," 961.
46 Reed, "Oneness Pentecostalism," 937.
47 Atter, *The Third Force*, 37.
48 Ibid., 37–8.
49 Kydd, "Pentecostal Assemblies of Canada," 961–2.
50 Kydd, "Canadian Pentecostalism and the Evangelical Impulse," 289–300.
51 Ibid.
52 Reed, "From Movement to Institution: A Case Study of Charismatic Renewal in the Anglican Church of Canada."
53 Reimers, *God's Country*, 18.
54 Ibid., 19.
55 Ibid., 23.
56 Ibid., 30. See also Popovici, "A Short History of the Catholic Charismatic Movement in Western Canada," unpublished paper cited in Reed, "From Movement to Institution," 6.
57 Reimers, *God's Country*, 70.
58 Prosser, "A Historical and Theological Evaluation of the Charismatic Renewal," 19–20. I rely heavily on his thesis as it is the best comprehensive study on the Catholic Charismatic Renewal in Canada, especially Quebec.
59 Prosser, "A Historical and Theological Evaluation," 23.
60 Prosser, e-mail message to author, 10 January 2005.
61 Prosser, "A Historical and Theological Evaluation," 24.
62 Ibid., 25. Cardinal Suenens was mandated by Popes Paul VI and Jean-Paul II to give pastoral oversight to the Catholic Charismatic Renewal worldwide. See Thigpen, "Catholic Charismatic Renewal," 465.
63 Prosser, "A Historical and Theological Evaluation," 26.
64 Ibid., 27.
65 Ibid., 28.
66 Ibid., 29–30.
67 See Swenson's chapter in this volume for more details regarding the emergence and decline of the Catholic Charismatic renewal.
68 Riss, *Latter Rain Movement*. See also Miller, *Canadian Pentecostals*, 261.
69 Riss, *Latter Rain Movement*; Miller, *Canadian Pentecostals*, 259–65.
70 Beyer, "Roman Catholicism in Contemporary Quebec: The Ghosts of Religion Past?"
71 Quoted in Bibby, *Restless Gods*, 16.
72 Di Giacomo, "La Vieille Capitale: son importance pour le pentecôtisme au Canada français dans les années 1970," 1.

73 Côté, *Les transactions politiques des croyants*, 32. The Catholic Charismatic Renewal attracted about 50,000 people to one of its rallies in the Olympic Stadium in Montreal in 1977. See the Canadian CCR website: www.renouveaucharismatique.ca/ccrc/ histoire_débuts.htm.

74 Much has been written about Quebec's Quiet Revolution and the fundamental transformation of Quebec society in the post-Duplessis era. Quebecers' self-designation of *Québécois* replacing the traditional *Canadien français* is symptomatic of this transformation. See Caulier, *Religion, sécularisation, modernité*; Comeau, *Jean Lesage et l'éveil d'une nation*; Dumont, *Genèse de la société québécoise*; Lesage et Tardif, *Trente ans de Révolution tranquille*; Linteau et al., *Histoire du Québec contemporain*; Thomson, *Jean Lesage and the Quiet Revolution*.

75 Useful in mapping Pentecostal growth worldwide, including in traditionally Catholic countries in Latin America are Cox, *Fire from Heaven*; Stoll, *Is Latin America Turning Protestant?*; Jenkins, *The Next Christendom*.

76 Jenkins, *The Next Christendom*, 234.

77 The challenge of charting numbers of adherents applies to Quebec as much as anywhere else. The consensus among scholars of religion in Quebec is that the evangelical population is about 1 per cent of the population with the Pentecostals constituting a little more than half that number. See Lougheed et al., *Histoire du protestantisme au Québec depuis 1960*, 123. A recent article, however, published by Christian Direction, a para-church service centre in Montreal, estimates that the percentage might be more like 17 per cent of the Quebec population if one counts those persons in mainline denominations who consider themselves evangelical (*"Est-ce le climat religieux du Québec est vraiment si unique?"*, article published in pdf format by Christian Direction, Montreal, Canada. n.d. n.a.).

78 Falardeau, *Essais sur le Québec contemporain*, 149.

79 Althouse, "The Influence of Dr. J.E. Purdie's Reformed Anglican Theology on the Formation and Development of the Pentecostal Assemblies of Canada," 15.

80 Ibid., 3–28.

81 Craig, "Robert Edward McAlister: Canadian Pentecostal Pioneer," 7–8.

82 Rawlyk, *Is Jesus Your Personal Saviour?*, 3–6.

83 Reimer, *Evangelicals and the Continental Divide*, 35. Reimer's is an insightful book comparing Canadian and American evangelicalism. He cautions us against stereotyping and analyses the evangelical world as a North American subculture and on the basis of geographical regions in North America. His sources are very valuable for further study on American-Canadian differences generally, but particularly with respect to evangelicalism of which Pentecostalism and charismatic Christianity is a major element.

2

Oneness Pentecostalism

THOMAS A. ROBINSON

INTRODUCTION

This chapter takes a critical look at the self-understanding and history of one branch of Pentecostalism, the non-Trinitarian segment that came to be known as the "Oneness" or "Jesus Name" movement.[1] This movement represents an unusual development within Pentecostalism and within Christianity, resurrecting a third-century controversy called modalism or modalistic monarchianism. After looking briefly at the tenets of modalism, I will examine the modern appropriation of modalist ideas in Pentecostalism and sketch the history of Pentecostal groups in Canada that espouse modalist, or Oneness, beliefs. Oneness Pentecostalism reflects a transition in Pentecostal belief and practice and its institutionalization distinct from Trinitarian views.

The modalist view holds that the Father, Son, and Holy Spirit are not distinctive entities within the Godhead but labels or modes of God, reflecting some aspect of God's character or God's revelation to humans. In early Christian theology, modalism sought to hold together two seemingly incompatible views. One was monotheism, which early Christians shared with Judaism, against the colourful polytheism of the Olympian gods and goddesses and lesser forces that characterized Greco-Roman paganism. The second belief was that Jesus was God in some substantial way, for early Christians prayed to Jesus, directed worship to Jesus, and spoke of Jesus much as Jews in the Old Testament spoke of God.[2] By the fourth century, the monarchian controversy had been squeezed off centre stage by the Arian/Nicene debate, which had developed somewhat out of the middle ground in the monarchian controversy. In the resolution of the Arian dispute, the Trinitarian position was formalized at the Council of Nicea. God was viewed as three "persons" in one being.[3] The creed shaped by that Council became a touchstone of orthodoxy from that time to the present. Not until the twentieth-century was modalism revived, although many forms of non-Trinitarian views in Christianity appeared from time to time. Other than the rejection of the Apostles' and Nicene Creeds, Oneness Pentecostals share little in their understanding of God with other non-Trinitarian groups.[4]

THE LANGUAGE OF RESTORATION

The claim by Pentecostals to a final and full restoration of apostolic Christianity is boldly reflected in the terms with which the early Pentecostals chose to identify and define themselves. One common label was "Full Gospel." Another was the term "Apostolic Faith."[5] Given how the early Pentecostals idealized the primitive Christian community, the claim to reflect the apostolic faith was just another way to assert the possession of the "full" Gospel, and both a way to assert restoration of cosmic and climactic proportions.

By making glossolalia a fundamental element in the restoration *and* by emphasizing other recent elements such as sanctification and healing as the essence of "apostolic" Christianity, Pentecostals found that they could write off most of Christian history as less than apostolic – less than the full revelation of God – for glossolalia and the recent emphases of the Holiness movement had not been a characteristic mark of most of Christian history. It thus became a Pentecostal stereotype to speak of church history as a decline from apostolic purity.[6] Most Pentecostals did grant that the process had started to be reversed through people like Luther and Wesley. Complete restoration was, however, available only in the Pentecostal revival.[7]

The sense of restoration that marked much of early Pentecostal preaching is reflected clearly in what was called the "Latter Rain," a term Pentecostals also used frequently to identify their movement.[8] The term comes from the Old Testament prophetic book of Joel,[9] where the author uses the term "latter rain" in his language of restoration. It referred to a particular pattern of the Palestinian agricultural cycle, in which there were two necessary rainy periods to assure good harvests: an early rain and a second, or latter, rain. Mixed with this imagery, the author of Joel used numerous striking images of restoration.[10] The attractiveness of Joel's message to Pentecostals did not stem merely from that book's theme of restoration. Most prophetic books of the Old Testament work with that theme. What made this book (rather than some other prophetic book with the theme of restoration and hope) so central to Pentecostals was the prior use of this book by the primitive Christian community to explain the phenomenon of glossolalia on the Day of Pentecost. According to Acts, when the first Christians were asked to explain the phenomenon of glossolalia, Peter quoted a passage from Joel. "This is that," Peter proclaimed.[11]

Most of early Pentecostalism's interpretation of Joel's restoration language misses the point of the story in Acts,[12] and it has resulted in Pentecostals using other images from the prophecies of Joel to emphasize the same division – granting to the twentieth-century revival the full essence of restoration that is supposedly only forecast by the events in the primitive church. Frequently sermons of Pentecostals employ the images of destruction in Joel (locust, cankerworm, and caterpillar) to describe what they assume to be a period of decay and decline from apostolic doctrine throughout most of church history. Then the Joel images of restoration are employed to illustrate the restoration that climaxes in the twentieth-century revival.

The classic sermon along this line was delivered by Canadian evangelist Aimee Semple McPherson. It has been frequently reprinted or used as a model. The destruction in Joel is taken to be descriptive of the church that failed to live up to apostolic fullness, and the restoration is taken to speak of the insights of people like Luther and Wesley, who were part of the restoration that culminated in the Pentecostalism of the twentieth century.

Many Pentecostals became disillusioned with the movement. John Walker, the editor of an account of the Azusa Street revival some forty years later, lamented that tremendous apostasy was not only to be found among the denominational churches, it was even to be found in "the most spiritual Pentecostal movements."[13] Walker went on: "It is evident that there is no movement in these last days that has accomplished God's purpose for this people. Every movement so far has utterly failed to unite God's people and bring them back to the perfect standard of the early church as described in the Book of Acts. God must raise up a new movement ... God must do a new thing; for all movements of the past have failed."[14]

Numerous groups within Pentecostalism have reflected similar discontent with Pentecostalism's failure to live up to its early claims, and they have usually turned in expectancy to some new movement that might usher in God's final act. Pentecostal historian Edith L. Blumhofer points out that "successive bursts of restorationist fervor have animated the Pentecostal worldview" from its beginning.[15] Some new groups began to use the label "Latter Rain" for themselves and deny it to the Pentecostals of the early years of the twentieth century. Walker, for example, called the Pentecostal revival of the early 1900s not the "Latter Rain" (as would have been claimed by these early Pentecostals), but the "Former Rain"[16] (what early Pentecostals described as the first-century Pentecostal experience). Walker claimed that "God has promised something more that we have not yet received, and that is what is called the Latter Rain."[17] Even Frank Ewart, one of the leaders in the early movement, spoke longingly some forty years after the Azusa Street revival: "Forty is a significant scriptural number, and many are expecting a great outpouring of the Spirit in more than Pentecostal effusion. The great revival of Joel has never yet been fulfilled, when the whole solar and physical system will be revolutionized."[18] Canada itself was the centre of the most influential effort to re-evaluate Pentecostalism, with "The New Order of the Latter Rain" developing in the Sharon Orphanage and Schools in North Battleford, Saskatchewan, in 1947–48.[19] Even more evolved schemes of restoration were proposed.[20] It seems that any revival might count as that last act of God – the anticipated Latter Rain – if it was recent and not yet discredited.

THE BEGINNINGS OF THE ONENESS MOVEMENT: THE "NEW ISSUE"

Such a sense of restoration and the quest for the final element in the recovery of apostolic truth caused Pentecostalism to be generally open to new ideas.[21] One can see that anticipation in a comment from Franklin Small, one of the early Oneness leaders in Canada. He spoke of Pentecostals being "in a receptive attitude to receive further revealed truth should it come."[22] Howard A. Goss, the general superintendent of the largest Oneness group, perhaps captures the atmosphere best. He said, "A preacher who did not dig up a new slant on some Scripture, or get some new revelation to his heart every so often; one who did not propagate it, defend it, and let it be known that if necessary, he was prepared to lay down his life for it, was considered slow, dull, and unspiritual."[23] In such an atmosphere, the radical ideas of modalism and water baptism in the name of Jesus at least had a chance for an initial hearing.

One of the most distinctive practices of Oneness Pentecostals is water baptism in the name of Jesus. Their use of this formula has come to represent a firm rejection of the traditional and near-normative Trinitarian formula of baptism ("in the name of the Father, the Son, and the Holy Spirit"). This novel baptismal practice was introduced early in the history of the Pentecostal movement,[24] and it constituted Pentecostalism's second major internal dispute.[25] Substantial numbers, particularly in Canada, followed this baptismal innovation in the early years of Pentecostalism. Indeed, many of the early leaders of what were to be major Trinitarian Pentecostal organizations were baptized in Jesus' name initially, including the first superintendent of the Pentecostal Assemblies of Canada (PAOC), the primary Trinitarian Pentecostal group in Canada.[26]

The emphasis on baptism in the name of Jesus is relatively easy to explain. It came about as a result of early Pentecostalism's intense focus on a short passage in chapter 2 of the book of Acts, where glossolalia is first mentioned in the Bible.[27] The event described there occurred on the Jewish feast of Pentecost, from which Pentecostals were to take their name. Concentrating on the biblical passage that most closely described their own experience, the attention of Pentecostals was drawn to the end of Peter's "Pentecost sermon." Peter commanded his listeners to repent and to be baptized in the name of Jesus Christ (Acts 2:38). The name of Jesus is used in other descriptions of baptism by the author of Acts,[28] and there is some indication that this formula was not uncommon in early Christian baptism.[29]

The use of the name of Jesus in the baptismal formula was initially discussed in 1913 at a camp meeting in Arroyo Seco, California. Robert E. McAlister, a Canadian evangelist, pointed out that baptism was regularly carried out "in the name of Jesus" according to the practice of the apostles recorded in the Bible. Many who heard this teaching became devoted to this emphasis. McAlister and fellow-evangelist Franklin (Frank) Small, also from Canada, started to preach this message, baptizing thirty people "in Jesus' name" in Winnipeg in 1913.[30] Bernard claims that these were the first baptisms in the name of Jesus anywhere in the world after the Arroyo Seco camp meeting discussions.[31] At first, the new message met with considerable success.

The issue of water baptism quickly came to a head in the US in meetings of the newly formed Assemblies of God (AG) in 1915 and 1916.[32] By this time, the issue of water baptism had grown from debates about the formula for water baptism into debates about the nature of God, with anti-Trinitarian views being expressed and aspects of modalism being proposed.[33] The modalist emphasis arose naturally. In the discussion of water baptism in Jesus' name, Pentecostals were confronted by an alternate baptismal command in the New Testament, where the titles "Father, Son, and Holy Spirit" are used as the formula for baptism (Matthew 28:19) – the standard formula of Trinitarian baptism. The question was how this command could be reconciled with the Acts' reports of baptism in the name of Jesus. Some concluded that the *name* of the Father, and the Son, and the Holy Spirit must be "Jesus." It was an easy step from there into modalism.

At the 1916 meeting of the AG[34] in St Louis,[35] the proponents of Jesus Name baptism lost the vote on water baptism. By early 1917, they had formed their own group, The General Assembly of the Apostolic Assemblies (GAAA), and by 1918 that movement had joined the Pentecostal Assemblies of the World (PAW), an older group that had accepted the Oneness position.[36] L.C. Hall, an American evangelist who joined the Oneness movement, recalls the label "'heretic' and other kindred epithets" being applied to the Oneness message during his 1915 campaign in Toronto.[37]

Numerous Oneness organizations sprang up, some because racial tensions led to division in the PAW. Two large groups, the Pentecostal Church Incorporated (PCI) and the Pentecostal Assemblies of Jesus Christ (PAJC), merged in 1945, taking the name United Pentecostal Church (UPC).[38] Segments of Oneness Pentecostals in Canada affiliated with the group.[39] Although UPC historian David Bernard maintains that there were no significant differences between the two groups in the merger,[40] Thomas Fudge has recently made the case for significant differences. Further, Fudge charges that such differences had a profound impact on Maritime Pentecostals in Canada. Both parties in the merger agreed in the use of the name of Jesus in baptism; both agreed on a modalist view of God. They disagreed on the significance of baptism.[41]

CANADIAN ONENESS HISTORY

Oneness Pentecostalism in Canada is diverse. It spans the spectrum. There are independent churches whose ministers are integrated into the larger religious life of the ministerial association of their cities, with the congregations sharing in joint efforts of the larger Christian and evangelical initiatives in their area. There are also independent churches led by authoritarian figures, which have been compared to Jim Jones and the like.[42] And, as one might guess, there is everything in between; from small village churches whose membership has never surpassed more than a handful to massive mega churches. There is another kind of diversity, that of geography. The histories of Oneness Pentecostalism differ quite substantially depending on whether one observes the Maritimes, the Prairies and the West, or Central Canada. Each has a different history. Except for the Oneness movement in Western Canada, Canadian Oneness Pentecostalism came to have unusually close ties to the UPCI, a major Oneness organization in the US.

According to Robert Larden, a former moderator and historian of the Apostolic Church of Pentecost (ACOP), the Oneness message initially was accepted by almost all Canadian Pentecostals.[43] Franklin Small claims that hundreds of thousands had been baptized by June 1915 and that "this new advance message was sweeping Canada and practically all Christendom."[44] In November of that year, L.C. Hall and George Chambers conducted meetings in Ontario, where hundreds were baptized in the name of Jesus.[45] Tyson claims that the "main contingency" of Pentecostals in Canada was rebaptized.[46]

In 1918, a conference was called for Ottawa with the purpose of establishing some formal organization of Pentecostals in Canada. Larden cites the minutes of the PAOC, which was the name adopted for the new organization. The minutes indicate that the group would work in conjunction with the Pentecostal Assemblies of the World (PAW), the largest Oneness American group.[47] This affiliation is frequently seen as further proof that the PAOC, now the largest body of Trinitarian Pentecostals in Canada, was originally Oneness in its doctrinal position.[48] The affiliation with the PAW was almost immediately reversed, however. The next year, by a vote of ten to seven, the PAOC changed its affiliation to the AG,[49] the large Trinitarian Pentecostal body in the US, although ministers were still allowed to baptize in Jesus' name.[50] Robert McAlister, one of the founders of the PAOC, had been associated with Oneness teaching in the initial years, but he reversed his position.[51] The matter of McAlister's change in affiliation is read by the different sides quite differently. Oneness Pentecostals view McAlister as someone who compromised, or worse.[52] Trinitarian Pentecostals see McAlister as someone who diverted Canadian Pentecostalism from the errors of modalism.[53]

Western Canada and the Apostolic Church of Pentecost (ACOP)

Franklin Small, one of the founding members of the PAOC, was clearly disillusioned with the change in affiliation to the AG. By 1920, the PAOC had dropped Small from its list of ministers. Small then took leadership in forming a new organization, the Apostolic Church of Pentecost (ACOP), gaining a Canadian charter in 1921.[54] Most Oneness Pentecostals in Western and Eastern Canada were affiliated with the ACOP in the early years. Oneness ministers in Central Canada generally remained affiliated with the PAOC until the 1940s, when Trinitarian belief was made a requirement for membership.[55]

One matter caused some dispute among ministers in the ACOP. Most Western ministers were Calvinist; those in Central Canada and the Maritimes were generally Arminian. Ralph Reynolds chaired a debate about the matter at the 1944 Newcastle Bridge Convention in New Brunswick, and he attributes this dispute to the separation of non-Calvinists from the ACOP.[56] Larden marks this year as the point of separation, although he notes that many Eastern Canada ministers continued to hold papers with the ACOP.[57]

The ACOP had particularly successful growth in Western Canada, notably on the Prairie Provinces.[58] In 1953, the Evangelical Churches of Pentecost and the ACOP merged. The Evangelical Churches of Pentecost were Trinitarian of sorts,[59] and the merger resulted in some changes to the Statement of Faith. The current statement speaks of "the eternal existence of one true God who is the Father, Son, and Holy Spirit," a statement that could be affirmed by both Trinitarian and Oneness members. It also affirms "water baptism of believers by immersion in the name of our Lord Jesus Christ."[60]

Central Canada

In Ontario and Quebec, Oneness and Trinitarian Pentecostals worked together within the PAOC for some twenty years. In 1940, the issue of water baptism and Oneness came to a head. Those who were not Trinitarian were asked to withdraw from PAOC membership.[61] The Oneness ministers then formed themselves as a district of the ACOP,[62] but that relationship was short-lived, in part due to the Calvinism of the ACOP. In 1947, most Oneness ministers left the ACOP and joined the UPC, as had the Maritime district a year earlier.

The Atlantic Provinces

Unlike Central and Western Canada, the Maritime Provinces had little contact with Pentecostalism in the first fifteen years of the Pentecostal movement. By the time Pentecostalism arrived in the Maritimes, both the PAOC and the ACOP (Trinitarian and Oneness bodies, respectively) were established, although neither group had made the Maritimes a focus of mission.[63] Pentecostalism in the Maritimes primarily was introduced from the US, particularly through churches and ministers in Maine. For the most part, that influence was Oneness. Initially Edgar Grant and John Deering helped to establish churches in the Woodstock area, and a number of churches sprang up both north and south of Woodstock along the Saint John River Valley of New Brunswick after meetings in 1917–18.[64] Stanley McConaghy reports that the novel elements of both Spirit Baptism and water baptism marked the earliest Pentecostal preaching in the area.[65]

More important to the modalist character of New Brunswick Pentecostalism was the fact that the leaders who had the greatest impact on the spread of Pentecostalism in the province were Oneness. In particular, these were Susan and Carro Davis, twin sisters from Macon, Georgia, a number of their earliest associates in Maine and New Brunswick, and one of their early converts, Samuel Steeves.[66] Steeves became a prominent voice of New Brunswick Pentecostalism. As the Maritime district leader of the ACOP, he established and led the first provincial Pentecostal organization, called Full Gospel Pentecostal Church. Perhaps most significant, he established the first Pentecostal Bible School (Emmanuel Bible Institute). Steeves' Bible School accounted for most of the formally trained second-generation Pentecostal preachers in the Maritimes. Since the Davis Sisters, Sam Steeves, and other early leaders were Oneness, most of the early churches in New Brunswick were Oneness,[67] and that influence is still visible in the dominant Oneness character of modern New Brunswick Pentecostalism. The Maritime Oneness churches (except for the Davis Sisters' church[68]) functioned within the ACOP until about 1944.[69] In that year, New Brunswick Oneness Pentecostals received a provincial charter under the name of the Full Gospel Church; this allowed them to hold church property. Most of the ministers continued to hold credentials, however, with the ACOP.[70]

Pentecostalism in Newfoundland and Labrador is largely Trinitarian, as a result of the work of Alice Garrigus, who arrived in 1910. It was not until the 1960s that Oneness Pentecostals in the Maritimes made

Newfoundland and Labrador a focus, and the efforts there have been largely unsuccessful. Only eight UPCI churches exist there after forty years of effort.

The UPC and Americanism in Canadian Oneness Pentecostalism

A major realignment occurred in 1946 when the Maritime Oneness group affiliated with the American United Pentecostal Church (UPC, later UPCI), which had been established a year previously.[71] Larden attributes this change in affiliation of Maritime Pentecostals to the fact that the ACOP was largely a Western Canadian organization, and that made fellowship between the two segments of the organization difficult.[72] The UPC had many churches in the Eastern States and thus offered closer contacts for Maritime Pentecostalism. At least one other factor played a role: the ACOP was Calvinist; Maritime Pentecostalism, influenced by Holiness tendencies, generally was Arminian.[73]

The relationship of the Maritime District with the UPCI lasted until 1967 when the district withdrew for a short time. The district rejoined in 1972, although several leading ministers refused to go along with that decision. Part of the discontent with the UPCI was the increasing emphasis that water baptism in the name of Jesus and Spirit Baptism, with speaking in tongues, was an essential experience of genuine conversion – a doctrine labelled "water-spirit" among Oneness Pentecostals. This view represented a narrower view of the church than many Maritime Oneness ministers held.[74] After an increasingly narrow view was passed at the annual UPCI conference in Salt Lake City in 1992, further Maritime ministers withdrew, including Raymond Beesley, who was Superintendent of the Maritime District at the time. Beesley had served over twenty-one years in that position, from 1974 to 1995.[75]

The success of Oneness Pentecostals in the Maritimes, especially in New Brunswick, is particularly striking. Bernard lists New Brunswick as having the fourth highest concentration of UPCI members in the world.[76] The UPCI have been far less successful in other areas of Canada, a situation lamented by Ralph Reynolds, one of the early Oneness Pentecostals. He blames the lack of a national office for the UPC in Canada as one of the reasons why the PAOC has established far more churches in Canada than have the Oneness groups.[77]

The ACOP is the only Oneness group that has its headquarters in Canada. Although it represented most Oneness Pentecostals in Canada at one time, the situation is much changed. The *nation-wide* membership of the ACOP is only about 14,000, in comparison to nearly that number in the UPC membership in the small province of New Brunswick alone.

CONCLUSION

Oneness Pentecostals number about 14 million worldwide, making them roughly the size of the Jehovah's Witnesses and the Mormons. In the US, Oneness adherents constitute about one-fourth of American Pentecostals. In Canada, although there was an early and widespread Oneness movement, Trinitarian Pentecostals have been considerably more successful, with the exception of the province of New Brunswick, which is the bastion of Oneness Pentecostalism in Canada. The Prairies had long had a strong presence of Oneness Pentecostals, but Trinitarian Pentecostals have had greater success there too.

Although Canadian Oneness Pentecostals had a history of co-operation with non-Oneness Pentecostals in the early period, under the influence of the American UPCI, Oneness Pentecostalism in Canada has become increasingly isolated from other Pentecostal groups and the larger Christian world. That situation is unlikely to change since fewer and fewer moderate voices can be found in the UPCI. Pentecostalism in Canada is now largely Trinitarian, as is generally the case of Pentecostalism worldwide.

NOTES

1 A number of other labels were applied to the movement. At first, it was widely called "The New Issue," but it is also referred to as "Apostolic" or "Jesus Only." The "Jesus Only" label is generally rejected by Oneness groups. See Bernard, *A History of Christian Doctrine*, 59–60.

2 For an examination of early Christianity's "Jesus devotion," see Hurtado, *Lord Jesus Christ*.

3 For a discussion of Monarchianism and the development of Trinitarian thought, see Brown, *Heresies*, 95–157.

4 Oneness adherents elevate Jesus to extremely high status; other non-Trinitarian groups tend to lower the status of Jesus, either to a human chosen by God (dynamic monarchianism and Unitarianism) or to an elevated creature of God (Arianism and the Jehovah's Witnesses).

5 Both Charles Parham and William Seymour, founders of Pentecostalism, took the name "Apostolic Faith" for their movements. After Parham became

discredited, Pentecostals began to prefer the name "Pentecostal" over "Apostolic." Today, the word "Apostolic" usually identifies Oneness groups, often Black or Hispanic. See Bernard, *A History of Christian Doctrine*, 34–5.

6 Ralph Mahoney, in introductory comments to the reprint of Aimee Semple McPherson's "Lost and Restored" sermon, said, "As we look back over Church history, we are dismayed over the spiritual condition that is found in the Church. Isaiah describes it in these words, 'From the sole of the foot even unto the head there is no soundness in it; but wounds, and bruises, and putrefying sores: they have not been closed, neither bound up, neither mollified with ointment. Your country is desolate, your cities are burned with fire: your land, strangers devour it in your presence, and it is desolate as overthrown by strangers (Isaiah 1:6–7)'. This graphic language accurately describes the condition of the Church through much of its history after the first century." See too Atter, *The Third Force*, 120; Brumback, "*What Meaneth This?*", 30, 276–81.

7 The mention of Luther and Wesley is fairly standard within Pentecostalism. Charles Finney and Evan Roberts, persons of considerable stature within the streams of American and Welsh revivalism respectively, are credible characters often added to the list. For example, Bernard, a Oneness historian, states: "The Pentecostal movement was a logical, scriptural extension of the ideas of the Protestant Reformation of the 1500s, the Methodist revival of the 1700s, and the Holiness movement of the 1800s. It was the next step in the restoration of apostolic doctrine and experience to professing Christendom." See *A History of Christian Doctrine*, 3.

8 Pentecostals were not alone in appropriating the term "Latter Rain" for the final world revival. An article by A.B. Simpson, founder of the Christian and Missionary Alliance, appeared in the Pentecostal paper the *Apostolic Messenger* (Winnipeg) 1, no. 1 (February–March 1908), 3. It was titled "What is meant by the Latter Rain?"

9 The book of Joel, along with the New Testament Book of Acts, played a significant role in determining the self-understanding of the Pentecostal movement of the twentieth century. See McQueen, *Joel and the Spirit*, 74–106. It is difficult to determine to what extent Joel shaped the primitive community. The Day of Pentecost sermon of Peter is the only explicit use of the book of Joel in the New Testament that approximates the way Pentecostals have used the book. There is one other reference to Joel in the New Testament (Romans 10:13), but it does not reflect Joel's distinctive imagery. The Apostolic Fathers show even less interest in Joel.

10 Dreams, visions, and prophecies are mentioned in Joel 2:28. Although glossolalia is not mentioned, the author of Acts clearly associates glossolalia with this restoration.

11 Acts 2:16. The phrase "this is that" became a popular refrain among early Pentecostals. Aimee Semple McPherson used the phrase as the title of her autobiography, *This Is That*.

12 According to the book of Acts, Peter used the section from Joel about the "pouring out of the Spirit on all flesh" to explain the occurrence of glossolalia on the Day of Pentecost. The twentieth-century Pentecostal use of Joel differs from the first-century church's use of the imagery in Joel, a point that seems to have escaped the notice of most Pentecostals. Pentecostals appropriated the term "Latter Rain" exclusively for their own revival, while describing the Day of Pentecost and the charismatic phenomena of the first century as the "Former Rain." Ewart states: "This palpable identification of the effect of the 'early rain' and the 'latter rain' upon the recipients, coupled the early faith once delivered, with the latter faith again restored, in all its fruitfulness, power and glory." See *Phenomenon of Pentecost*, 20. Again: "We surely received the 'Early Rain' at Pentecost" (25), and "this [twentieth-century] outpouring was the real counterpart of the 'early rain'" (29). Such was not the identification the author of Acts intended. The Day of Pentecost sermon was a proclamation of the presence of the long-hoped-for final restoration – the *latter* rain, not the *former* rain. The idea of climactic restoration was very much in the air in first-century Palestine, and the author of Acts actually alters the passage from Joel to emphasize the climactic nature of the restoration taking place on the Day of Pentecost. He uses the phrase "in the last days" (words not found in the book of Joel, but perhaps implied) to specify in the most unambiguous way the time of the restoration. What was occurring in Jerusalem was what had been promised by Joel (which clearly enough had an eschatological dimension). The much repeated Pentecostal phrase "This is that" was used in Acts for the first-century Day of Pentecost." "This" (the spirit-baptism on the Day of Pentecost) is "that" (Joel's foretold *latter* rain). Pentecostals try to reconcile the difficulties with their interpretation in various ways, the most common being an appeal to a dispensational framework of history. Sometimes the period between the apostolic age and the twentieth- century Pentecostal phenomenon is viewed as an age of apostasy and decline, a period during which God's time clock had stopped. In this way, the apostolic age and the twentieth century can be brought more closely together, and both may be associated with the "last days" of Peter's Pentecost sermon. Franklin Small, one of the earliest Oneness preachers in Canada, had a more cautious view. He claimed that the "last days" of Peter's Pentecostal sermon refers to all of church history, since a thousand years with God is as one day. See "Perplexed Christians," 2. More often than not, however, Pentecostals do not see any contradiction between these reconstructions, using elements from both without reservation.

13 Walker, *What Really Happened at "Azusa Street"?*, 82.

14 Ibid., 83.

15 Blumhofer, *Restoring the Faith*, 3.

16 Walker, *What Really Happened at "Azusa Street"?*, 84.

17 Ibid., 89.

18 Ewart, *Phenomenon of Pentecost*, 48. Later in the book, Ewart said, "There is not an organization in the entire religious world – Pentecost included, that is ready for this move of God in the end time," 89.

19 See Riss, *A Survey of 20th-Century Revivals in North America*, 112–24.

20 North American Pentecostalism is now spotted with scores of movements seeking some new experience beyond "baptism with the Spirit." Bill Britton argued for a third experience and used the Jewish feasts for support. There were three main feasts: Passover, Pentecost, and Tabernacles. Arguing that Passover represented salvation and Pentecost Spirit Baptism, he concluded that some new experience must exist to parallel the third feast, Tabernacles. See Britton, *Sons of God – Awake*, 25–38. Atter comments on these kinds of movements as they appeared in Canada. See *The Third Force*, 146–7. Blumhofer examines movements of this sort in *Restoring the Faith*, 203–21. The Toronto Blessing is part of this quest for restoration by thousands. See the chapter in this volume by Hunt.

21 Bernard, a Oneness historian, admits this connection: "the entire Pentecostal movement was based on restorationist thinking. Given this focus, it was only a matter of time until people began to realize that the apostles always baptized in Jesus' name and never spoke of God in the terms of fourth-century trinitarian orthodoxy, and further to see these points as doctrinally significant." See *A History of Christian Doctrine*, 60. Bernard points out that this view is held by Trinitarian historians as well, who see the Oneness development as "most zealously restorationist," as Blumhofer states in *The Assemblies of God*, 238.

22 Small, "Historical and Valedictory Account of the Origins of Water Baptism in Jesus' Name Only, and the Doctrine of the Fulness of God in Christ, in Pentecostal Circles in Canada." That does not mean that everyone accepted anything new. Quite the opposite. The majority of Pentecostals rejected the new Oneness teaching.

23 Goss, *The Winds of God*, 245. Fudge notes the "facetious irony" in Goss's comment. See *A Christianity without the Cross*, 64.

24 Parham baptized "in Jesus' name" by immersion in the first years of his ministry, but he reverted to the Trinitarian formula when the matter became a major controversy. See Bernard, *A History of Christian Doctrine*, 18–21. Bernard finds other examples of Jesus Name baptism in the earliest days of the

Pentecostal movement. Baptizing in Jesus' name did not necessarily identify one as a modalist. Parham, for example, was staunchly Trinitarian. See Robinson, "The Conservative Nature of Dissent in Early Pentecostalism: A Study of Charles F. Parham, the Founder of the Pentecostal Movement," 158–60.

25 The first major dispute was over whether Pentecostalism would retain the Holiness emphasis on sanctification as the "second work of grace," with "Spirit Baptism" as the "third work." This view was prominent in early Pentecostalism, largely because of the strong Holiness convictions of the founders of the Pentecostal movement, Charles Parham and William Seymour. William Durham, a Baptist minister from Chicago, argued for what came to be called "The Finished Work of Calvary," against the Holiness influence in Pentecostalism. Many had accepted his message by the time he died in 1912.

26 Bernard lists E.N. Bell (Assemblies of God), George Chambers (Pentecostal Assemblies of Canada), Aimee Semple McPherson (International Church of the Foursquare Gospel), and C.H. Mason (The Church of God in Christ). See *A History of Christian Doctrine*, 88. Others of note who were associated with the Oneness movement or Jesus Name baptism are listed in an appendix. Among them are William Booth-Clibborn, grandson of William Booth (the founder of the Salvation Army), George B. Studd (younger brother of missionary C.T. Studd), and Frank Bartleman, whose history of the Azusa Street revival remains a classic.

27 Speaking in tongues is mentioned in two documents of the New Testament. There are three references in Acts (2:4; 10:46; 19:6); in 1 Corinthians, there is an extended discussion over three chapters (12–14), with the primary discussion in chapter 14. One finds other references to the baptism of the Holy Spirit, which some Pentecostals connect to speaking in tongues.

28 Acts 8:16; 10:48; 19:5.

29 The language of various New Testament passages might be read that way: Romans 6:3; 1 Corinthians 1:13; Galatians 3:27.

30 Small's recollections on these events are recorded in his article "Historical and Valedictory Account." The material is reprinted in Ewart, *Phenomenon of Pentecost*, 94–102. The baptisms took place at the eighth annual Pentecostal Convention in Western Canada in November 1913. Although McAlister and Small baptized converts in the name of Jesus in 1913, it appears that those who had already been baptized in the traditional Trinitarian formula were not rebaptized at first. According to Tyson, the first rebaptism took place in 1914. See Tyson, *The Early Pentecostal Revival*, 171. Small was rebaptized in late 1915.

31 Bernard, *A History of Christian Doctrine*, 67, 87.

32 Tyson, *The Early Pentecostal Revival*, 173–6.

33 Small, "Historical and Valedictory Account," 1. The belief was not called modalism; often it was referred to simply as "the fullness of God in Christ."

34 The Assemblies of God was formed in 1914. Many who had accepted the message of baptism in Jesus' name were among the original members.

35 J.R. Flower, an opponent of Jesus Name baptism, was concerned that the modalist aspects of the developing theology would move Pentecostalism away from historic and contemporary Christianity. See Bernard, *A History of Christian Doctrine*, 77.

36 Tyson explains why the merger of the Oneness groups came about in chapters 8 and 9 in *The Early Pentecostal Revival*. Bernard notes that in the 1919–20 ministerial list of PAW, Canadian ministers were from British Columbia, Manitoba, Ontario, and Quebec. See *A History of Christian Doctrine*, 87.

37 Hall's comment appeared first in an issue of *Living Waters*. It was reprinted in Ewart's *Phenomenon of Pentecost*, 96, without reference to the specific issue of *Living Waters*. Not all issues of the early Pentecostal papers have survived.

38 Anderson, *An Introduction to Pentecostalism*, 49 notes that, as of 2004, the largest Oneness church in the world (and the largest Pentecostal group in China) is the True Jesus Church.

39 Most Western Canadian Oneness Pentecostals remained with the ACOP, though some joined the UPC: British Columbia (joined 1945) was part of Northwest District of the USA; Manitoba (1945) was part of the North Central District. Some areas of Canada that joined the UPC had their own districts: Maritime District (1946); Ontario District (1947). Some shifts in the boundaries of districts occurred over time, and more areas of Canada received their own districts: Atlantic District (1974), which included the Maritimes and Newfoundland; British Columbia District (1974); Canadian Plains District (1975), consisting of Alberta and Saskatchewan; Nova Scotia–Newfoundland District (1979); Central Canadian District (1988), consisting of Manitoba and Northwest Ontario; Nova Scotia District (1994); Newfoundland District (1994). See Clanton, *United We Stand*, 174–8.

40 Bernard, *A History of Christian Doctrine*, 98.

41 The PCI maintained that baptism in Jesus' name and Spirit Baptism were required for salvation. The PAJC members, somewhat under Durham's "Finished Work of Calvary" emphasis, thought conversion was assured at repentance. Fudge's book *Christianity without the Cross* is largely a presentation of the difficulties of that merger and the tensions and pressures to force the unique aspects of PAJC doctrine on former PCI members. The title of Fudge's book is provocative, capturing the primary criticism that many Oneness Pen-

tecostals have of the UPC. Fudge provides a good review of Durham's lasting influence on Pentecostalism.

42 In New Brunswick, Dana McKillop is the pastor of the Plaster Rock Pentecostal Church, a church that had been part of the UPCI but separated under McKillop's leadership. Court cases and legal challenges have made the press (Bob Klager, "Plaster Rock church as centre of controversy, lawsuit," *Telegraph Journal* (24 February 2001); "Plaster Rock church leader inspires fear, devotion," *Telegraph Journal* (5 March 2001).

43 Larden says that the Oneness message "was preached in practically every assembly in eastern Canada." See *Our Apostolic Heritage*, 88.

44 Small, "Historical and Valedictory Account," 1.

45 Bernard, *A History of Christian Doctrine*, 74.

46 Tyson, *The Early Pentecostal Revival*, 173.

47 The text of the resolution to establish the PAOC was printed in Small's paper *Living Waters*. The Oneness message was laid out in detail in that issue.

48 See, for example, Larden, *Our Apostolic Heritage*, 89. See, too, Small, "Historical and Valedictory Account," 1.

49 The PAOC became a district of the Assemblies of God, a union that lasted from 1920 to 1925. Some Western Pentecostals had already formed themselves into a district of the Assemblies of God in late 1919 (*Canadian Pentecostal Testimony* 2 (January 1921). See, too, Bernard, *A History of Christian Doctrine*, 92–3.

50 Larden, *Our Apostolic Heritage*, 89. The tolerance of Jesus Name baptism in the PAOC seems to have lasted until the 1940s.

51 In the first issue (December 1920) of the PAOC paper *Canadian Pentecostal Testimony* (later, simply *Pentecostal Testimony*), a brief, three-paragraph note was featured in the centre of the front page. It was titled "The Unity of God," and in it McAlister argued that the use of the word "one" in the Bible often indicated a compound unity, or a plurality.

52 It is common to see references to McAlister's baptism in Jesus' name and his Oneness position in histories of Pentecostalism written by Oneness historians. Ewart, who had a close association with McAlister in the early years, reprinted a report of McAlister's baptism and a letter from McAlister affirming a Oneness view in his 1947 history, almost thirty years after McAlister affirmed a Trinitarian position (*Phenomenon of Pentecost*, 98–9).

53 See, for example, Miller, *Canadian Pentecostals*, 65–6.

54 Larden, *Our Apostolic Heritage*, 90.

55 Anderson fails to note that Oneness Pentecostals in Central Canada remained in the PAOC for over two decades after the formation of the ACOP. See *An Introduction to Pentecostalism*, 49.

56 Reynolds and Morehouse, *From the Rising of the Sun*, 146–7.

57 Larden, *Our Apostolic Heritage*, 161. Reynolds also speaks of a similar debate at the 1938 Newcastle Bridge Convention, and marks this as the point of departure of Eastern Canada from the ACOP and the formation of a new eastern organization, the Full Gospel Pentecostal Church, in 1939.

58 Some Oneness ministers in the west left the ACOP to join the UPC.

59 The term "triunity" has been used for this group. See Anderson, *An Introduction to Pentecostalism*, 49.

60 The Statement of Faith is available at the ACOP website.

61 Reynolds and Morehouse, *From the Rising of the* Sun, 44–5. Small dedicated one issue of his paper to the history of the Oneness movement in Canada. See "Historical and Valedictory Account." In it, he addressed two articles from PAOC leaders that had appeared in the December 1940 issue of the *Pentecostal Testimony*. He also reprinted a report about Robert McAlister's baptism in Jesus' name and a letter from McAlister affirming a Oneness view of God. McAlister was an early and honoured leader of the PAOC who had at one time affirmed a Oneness position.

62 An ad in Small's paper in 1940 announced an ACOP camp meeting at Outlet, Ontario, *Living Waters* 1, no. 4 (April 1941), 8. Outlet Camp was a Camp started by Oneness preacher Clarence Cross in 1912. See Reynolds, *From the Rising of the Sun*, 109.

63 In 1926, Franklin Small held meetings for the Davis Sisters in Saint John. In 1928, Small travelled again to the Maritimes. He reports on his visit in "Our Trip through the Maritime Provinces," *Living Waters* 1, no. 1 (January 1930), 14–17.

64 For short biographies of Maritime Oneness Pentecostals, see Morehouse, *Pioneers of Pentecost*. For Deering, see 37–41; for Grant, see 68–72.

65 McConaghy, "Down Memory's Lane," 3.

66 Earl Jacques, Clifford Crabtree, Moody Wright, and Charles Flewelling were associated with the Davis Sisters at various times. All have a chapter in Morehouse's *Pioneers of Pentecost,* as do Sam Steeves and the Davis Sisters. More information is available on most of these individuals in Reynolds and Morehouse, *From the Rising of the Sun.*

67 Trinitarian Pentecostals were active in New Brunswick, too, but with less success. They had more success in other areas of the Maritimes. See Miller, *Canadian Pentecostals*, 155–83.

68 Although the Davis Sisters' church remained independent, from early on there was informal association with the ACOP. Franklin Small held meetings in Saint John with the Davis Sisters about a year after they started meetings

there. Small reports an attendance of 2,000 at a baptismal service. See "Our Trip to Eastern Canada," 6–7.

69 Larden, *Our Apostolic Heritage*, 161. Larden must have been referring only to the Oneness churches in the Maritimes, for there were various churches affiliated with the PAOC during this time.

70 Larden, *Our Apostolic Heritage*, 161.

71 In 1972, the UPC became the United Pentecostal Church International (UPCI).

72 Larden, *Our Apostolic Heritage*, 161–2.

73 Bernard makes the eternal security issue (Calvinism) the reason for the break between the Maritime and western elements of the ACOP. See *A History of Christian Doctrine*, 99. Although this was a factor, Maritime Pentecostalism was somewhat diverse, and although they would have rejected the idea of "eternal security," they disagreed as to how secure a believer was. E.P. Wickens, whose views tended to emphasize the security of the believer and whose earliest association with Pentecostalism was in Saskatchewan with the ACOP, was Superintendent of the Maritime District of the UPC from 1962–73.

74 Much of Fudge's *A Christianity without the Cross* deals with the situation in the Maritime Provinces.

75 Fudge, *A Christianity without the Cross*, 190, n279.

76 Bernard, *A History of Christian Doctrine*, 103. According to his figures, UPCI represents 1.1 per cent of the total population of New Brunswick. If one were to add the independent Oneness groups and Oneness groups still affiliated with the ACOP, the number of Oneness Pentecostals would increase. Based on the 2001 Canadian census data, 2.8 per cent of the population of New Brunswick is Pentecostal.

77 Reynolds and Morehouse, *From the Rising of the Sun*, 151.

3

Apocalyptic Discourse and a Pentecostal Vision of Canada

PETER ALTHOUSE

INTRODUCTION

A critical analysis of Canadian Pentecostalism must not only investigate the doctrinal articulations of the movement but must also flesh out the theological and social implications of those doctrines. The doctrinal statements are embedded in social discourse. In a perceptive study of moral reform in Canada, Mariana Valverde argues that scholars and social historians alike are in the process of revamping their methodologies, realizing that linguistic meaning does not reflect a pre-existing reality, but that reality is, at least in part, socially and linguistically constructed. Social discourse, symbolic systems, images, and texts participate in organizing social relations and inner feelings. Social discourse, as a function of semiotic analysis, is not a language separate from reality merely reflecting the world out there, but is a construct mediating between language and reality.[1] Valverde uses discourse analysis to probe the development of moral reform in Canada and how it shapes the moral character of the emerging middle class – negatively to prohibit certain moral vices, but positively to inform the bourgeoisie about how they should act, speak, think, and feel.[2] I want to suggest that the social discourse of early Canadian Pentecostalism is embedded in an apocalyptic rhetoric. In practice, early Pentecostals offered their criticism of the social situation in Canada, and in the world abroad, by means of eschatological imagery: the second coming, the tribulation, the antichrist, Armageddon, the day of judgment, etc. This should not be surprising since the role apocalyptic eschatology has played in the history of Christianity has had the dual effect of bringing hope and despair, reform and revolution.[3] Such has been the case in the development and institutionalization of Pentecostalism as it transitioned from a renewal movement to a number of denominational forms.

As important as Spirit Baptism was to the early Pentecostals, the initial impulse of the nascent movement was eschatological. In 1908, Mrs E.A Sexton proclaimed in the *The Bridegroom's Messenger*, "Jesus is coming! Jesus is coming! ... [T]he message of His coming is usually given in a 'new tongue' in the power of the Spirit."[4] An article in *The Pentecostal Testimony*, the official magazine for the Pentecostal Assemblies of Canada (PAOC) stated: "What is the purpose of the second coming of the Lord Jesus Christ? To many it is a feature of a program: just as salvation, the Baptism of the Holy Spirit, Divine Healing, the ministrations of the Holy Spirit among us, are features of a program ... *The second coming of the Lord Jesus Christ is not a feature of the program, but it is THE program.* The preaching of regeneration, the restoration of man back to God, the outpouring and the Baptism of the Holy Spirit upon believers, the working of signs and wonders and miracles in the earth, are features of this program, leading up to its grand and glorious fulfillment" (italics mine).[5]

The ability to speak in tongues was thought to empower the recipient to proclaim the "glorious fulfillment" of Jesus' imminent coming to establish his kingdom. At the same time, though, the eschatological message of early Pentecostals envisioned a world that was more equitable and just because it was a foretaste of the rule of Jesus Christ and anticipated the second coming. Early Pentecostal declarations of the end-times embodied within them criticisms of the present social order as fallen and corrupt and hinted at a better world to come, but one that would partially manifest itself in the material world of existence. Seldom did they articulate it in this manner, but the protest against the present and hope for the new can be traced in early Pentecostal writings, and these had real social implications.

My thesis is that the eschatological impulse in Canadian Pentecostalism led early Pentecostals to criticize the social situation in Canada, offering a countercultural vision based in their understanding of biblical Christianity, but that their political ambivalence delayed political activism and the transformation of Canadian society. While Pentecostals believe in personal transformation, their views of social transformation are nuanced within the context of the role of unions and politics in Canada. A number of strands will be drawn together throughout this chapter. The first is that the social agenda of early Pentecostals, both north and south of the border, was a continuation of the social agenda of the broader evangelical culture. This included a diverse continuum of conservative, progressive, and radical elements. The second strand investigates the similarities and differences between Pentecostalism in Canada and the US. The third strand suggests that understanding early Canadian Pentecostalism as fundamentalist in orientation is misleading.[6] Early Pentecostals were premillenarian and dispensational, but they articulated a doctrine of the latter rain, which asserted that the way a dispensation opens was the way it would close. Thus charismatic manifestations and healing were signs that Christ's kingdom was imminent. The last strand investigates how Canadian Pentecostal apocalyptic rhetoric both protested the social-political culture of Canadian society and contained within it the seeds for social action and transformation, even if this action was ultimately frustrated by the passive tendencies toward the political order. Finally, throughout this chapter I have limited my investigation of Canadian Pentecostalism to the PAOC. This is not to suggest that other forms of Canadian Pentecostalism are less worthy of investigation, but that this is my own limitation.

CONTEXT OF CANADIAN PENTECOSTALISM

The latter half of the nineteenth century, immediately prior to the emergence of Pentecostalism, witnessed an era of unparalleled co-operation among Protestant evangelicals. Evangelicalism cut across denominational boundaries and held common beliefs such as the atoning death of Jesus Christ for the sins of humanity and his resurrection to bring eternal life, the primacy of the Scriptures as God's Word and revelation, the experience of individual conversion and the subsequent social changes this brought to society as Christians lived out their faith in the world. As well, evangelicals exhibited a strong faith in God; a passion for divine truth; a holistic understanding of Christianity; impatience with intellectualism; a determination to evangelize society through missionary outreach, the establishment of confessional schools and Bible Colleges, temperance campaigns, and a concerted effort to influence the public agenda.[7]

Fostered primarily by revivalist sentiments, evangelicals emphasized the experiential nature of Christianity and promoted personal conversion. However, this evangelical zeal was not applied only to individuals and their personal hopes but to the whole of society. After 1850, and in earnest after Confederation in 1867, evangelicals intended to transform the "Dominion of Canada into the Dominion of the Lord."[8] Social transformation of Canada took on eschatological significance, in which evangelicals saw themselves as having a duty to work for the kingdom. As historian Robert Choquette argues, "This Canadian version of the Kingdom of God has significant nationalistic and millennial overtones, and sufficient symbolic power to provide the basis for the formation of a broad Protestant consensus and coalition. Not only the major Protestant denominations, but also a host of Protestant-oriented organizations such as temperance societies, missionary societies, Bible societies, the Lord's Day Alliance, the YMCAS and YWCAS utilize this vision as a framework for defining their task within the nation, for shaping their conceptions of the ideal society, and for determining those elements which posed a threat to the realization of their purposes."[9]

In this evangelical matrix, Methodists accentuated an instantaneous experience of conversion in which one was assured of forgiveness, followed by a realization of holiness, or entire sanctification, in which one is rid of any deliberate sin. Disagreement ensued over whether holiness was a process of moral growth and improvement following conversion or an instantaneous experience subsequent to conversion known as the "second blessing." Regardless, the implication of personal holiness was that Christians could work for social holiness, not only in order to cleanse society of social evils, but to transform the moral character of Canada.[10] Revivalism, prominent among Methodists, Baptists, and Congregationalists, fostered interdenominational co-operation and laid the groundwork for future co-operation on social issues. Presbyterians, who had been ambivalent about revivalism, embraced the revivalist sentiment following an interdenominational revival campaign in 1857–58, and low-church Anglicans embraced revivalism by the 1870s. Theological differences between Arminian Methodists and Calvinist Protestants (i.e., Presbyterians, evangelical Anglicans, and a variety of Baptists) were minimized in favour of the positive consequences of revivalism, in which true conversion created practical approaches for how to live one's life. Although revivalism was highly individualistic and embodied Victorian values of self-improvement, self-control, and self-reliance, it was also a public ritual that brought a community of people together regardless of denominational affiliation. It stressed both personal and social reform, providing impetus for political reform and humanitarian initiatives.[11]

Civic responsibility and religious service were integrated so that men of character could advance social moral values in society. Although excluded from positions of power, women banned together to form their own groups that raised church funds through socials, teas, and picnics, thereby making women essential to the fiscal health of the congregations and giving them new-found power within their respective denominations. Baptist, Presbyterian, and Methodist women's groups were important for the success of missionary endeavours from the 1870s on, giving their members an opportunity to exercise social power.[12] "The routine of missionary society meetings ... gave women a chance to take charge of their own social and associational life in the context of the congregation."[13]

As revivalism gained respectability across denominational lines, Protestants collaborated to claim their country for God and transform its social ethos, sparking various activist causes. "In transforming individuals into brothers and sisters in Christ, revivalism promoted a sense of community that naturally sought expression in collective action."[14] Evangelicals had now moved into the middle class and had more wealth for philanthropic causes. Following the biblical mandate, "Christians had a duty to extend compassion to those less fortunate than themselves: the poor, the sick, and, not least, the sinful. Thus soul-winning and humanitarianism went hand in hand. To improve others' material condition was good in itself, but to transform their moral and spiritual life was even better."[15] Sunday Schools became an outlet for social activism, as did the Young Men's Christian Association (1853) and the Young Women's Christian Association (1864). Men's groups cultivated church activism, whereas women's groups provided hostels for young women tempted by city pleasures. Other humanitarian organizations provided homes for the aged, orphanages for the abandoned, and relief for the poor.[16]

Evangelical concerns were evident in the political realm, particularly through the effort to enact law for Sabbath observance and temperance. Between 1850 and 1880 evangelicals lobbied various levels of government to close businesses and leisure activities, ensuring that workers would have at least one day of rest. Evangelicals also pushed government to enact laws prohibiting the consumption of alcohol, believing it to be a cause of many social ills. The House of Commons' late-night sessions often led to inebriation. The main concern, however, was that alcoholic consumption depleted family finances, making the escape from poverty more difficult, and was often involved in family violence. Evangelicals were not satisfied with voluntary abstinence; they wanted legislative clout. Both the Dominion Alliance for the Total Suppression of the Liquor Traffic and the Woman's Christian Temperance Union played key roles in securing provincial and national prohibition.[17]

In the first two decades of the twentieth century, the problem of labour became more acute as Christians from all spectrums witnessed the unjust labour practices of excessive working hours and minimal wages. The real problem here, as with temperance concerns, was the poverty that turn-of-the-century capitalism created. Richard Allen's classic work *The Social Passion*, which probes religious involvement in the rise of unionism in Canada, claims that the evangelical objective of winning the dominion for "scriptural holiness" encompassed social reform, as was demonstrated by the previous generation's involvement in the anti-slavery movement. In the latter half of the nineteenth century, evangelicals became more diffused as a more organic understanding of social thought emerged and the individual basis underlying evangelicalism shifted to a socially sophisticated view. The sense of divine immanence operating in revivalist movements was easily transferred to a sense of immanence in social reform. "The demand 'save this man, now' became 'save this society, now,' and the slogan 'the evangelicalization of the world in our generation' became 'the Christianization of the world in our generation.'"[18]

In part, the social gospel grew out of the social concerns of various groups inside and outside evangelicalism and across denominational lines.[19] Yet not all evangelicals wholeheartedly embraced the social gospel and some strongly denounced it as an abandonment of biblical Christianity. Allen deftly argues that involvement and reaction spanned across a continuum represented by conservative, progressive, and radical Christianity. He writes:

The conservatives were closest to traditional evangelicalism, emphasizing personal-ethical issues, tending to identify sin with individual acts, and taking as their social strategy legislative reform of their environment. The radicals viewed society in more organic terms. Evil was so endemic and pervasive in the social order that they concluded there could be no personal salvation without social salvation. Without belief in an immanent God working in the social process to bring his kingdom to birth, the plight of the radicals would surely have been desperate. Between conservatives and radicals was a broad centre party of progressives, holding the tension between the two extremes, endorsing in considerable measure the platforms of the other two, but transmuting them somewhat in a broad ameliorative programme of reform.[20]

The Great War represented a profound transformation of Canadian evangelical culture which continued to be concerned for the social problems plaguing society. Generally speaking, churches from most denominational stripes "greeted the war with heavy heart" but encouraged clergy, theology students, and parishioners to enlist. Many churches actively recruited, used their facilities as places for soldiers to relax away from home, and promoted victory bonds. The war was ascribed religious significance in order to give meaning to the human sacrifices and loss of life. The struggle for Europe's freedom was cast into redemptive terms and the war was viewed as God's battle. To participate in the war was "a supreme manifestation of faith, a supreme act of decision and sacrifice for Christ."[21] Yet a number of radical evangelicals, often though not exclusively of the Anabaptist persuasion, objected to the war on religious grounds. Prior to the war, strong pacifist sentiments existed in Canada, but faded at the onset of the war and as it progressed, to the point where in 1917 conscientious objection was frowned upon.[22] Among the reasons for pacifism was a belief that the war was a continuation of the imperialist endeavour and a phenomenon of late capitalism.[23]

Throughout the war social reform continued. The cause of prohibition reached its climax in 1915 and 1916 when Saskatchewan, Manitoba, Ontario, British Columbia, Alberta, and New Brunswick enacted prohibition laws. In 1918 the federal government terminated interprovincial trade of liquor. By the end of the war, and riding on the success of prohibition, Protestant evangelicals were looking to new issues. Laws were enacted on women's suffrage, workman's compensation and protective legislation. Provincial departments of labour and a fisherman's co-operative in Nova Scotia were created, and the Bureau of Social Research was established.[24] The heyday of evangelical social concerns and the social gospel coincided with the war.

Labour issues continued to be a problem in Canada, to the point where in June 1919 labour unrest reached its climax. On the one hand, trade union membership grew during the war to reach 380,000 in 1919. On the other hand, the causes of unrest included disparity between the cost of living and wages; the economic rehabilitation of returning soldiers; reaction to continued conscription, increased censorship, and the apprehension of conscientious objectors. The ban on strikes in October 1918 seemed particularly distasteful. However, in May and June 1919, the Winnipeg General Strike commenced, with sympathetic strikes in Brandon, Calgary, Edmonton, Prince Albert, Regina, and Saskatoon, and partial strikes in Toronto, Amherst, and Sydney. The issue was not industrial control but the right of metal workers to bargain collectively with agents of their own choosing.[25] Theological millennialism played a clear role in the strikes.[26]

The eschatology of the social gospel was predominantly post-millennial, in contrast to the emerging premillennialism of the new generation of evangelicalism. Throughout its history, evangelicalism was post-millennial in orientation, and the labour movement was in this tradition. Salem Bland, for instance, argued that the apocalyptic and premillennial views of the kingdom denied Jesus' humanity (and therefore human nature in general). The more conservative wing of evangelicalism, on the other hand, grew increasingly suspicious of the post-millennialism and modernist implications of the social gospel. Baptist theologian T.T. Shields, the fundamentalist, anti-unionist wing of the Presbyterian Church, and low church Anglican Canon Dyson Hague attacked the post-millennialism of the social gospel, believing it had substituted progress toward a better world for the return of Jesus Christ.[27]

Evangelicalism's social agenda and the growth of the social gospel paint in broad strokes the context in which Pentecostalism emerged. Pentecostals embraced much of the theological tenor of evangelicalism, emphasizing the primacy of Scripture, doctrine of atonement, a conversionist understanding of salvation, and pietistic holiness. They placed importance on revivalist campaigns and missionary endeavours, instituted Sunday Schools and Bible Colleges as models of training. The latter were to counter the excessive rationalization in university and seminary education, but also stemmed from an anti-intellectual tendency in evangelicalism as a whole.[28] Yet Pentecostals were also discontinuous with an older evangelicalism in its shift from post- to pre-millennialism, a shift occurring in segments of evangelicalism as well. Both Anderson and Dayton have investigated these changes, and I do not see a need to rehearse their conclusions here.[29] Rather, I want to explore the connections between Pentecostals and evangelicals with regard to their visions of a more just social order, embodied in their dissatisfaction with the values and structures of their time. In the next section I will demonstrate that Pentecostalism represents both a continuation of the evangelical social agenda, but also discontinuity, especially with many of the social gospel themes. However, even though early Pentecostals cannot be properly considered social gospellers, they had similar concerns regarding the problems of capitalism and impoverishment. While the social gospel wanted to make the world a more just place, early Pentecostal belief in tongues and healing as a prolepsis of the Second Coming embodied within it (albeit in embryonic form) material social implications for the transformation of society. For Pentecostals this was specifically understood as a vision of the kingdom that would not be fully manifested until the coming of the Lord. In the next section, I will suggest that some of the social discourses of Charles F. Parham and William J. Seymour, the initial leaders of the movement in the US, had social implications similar to those of evangelicalism and the labour movement. I will then turn to early Canadian Pentecostalism.

EARLY PENTECOSTALISM IN THE UNITED STATES: CROSS BORDER SHOPPING

The story of early Pentecostalism starts with Charles F. Parham, an antagonistic lay preacher in the Wesleyan Holiness movement who proclaimed the doctrines of holiness and healing and first articulated the doctrine that speaking in tongues is the sign of the baptism of the Holy Spirit. Parham adopted a premillennial dispensational structure for his eschatology, but modified it in such a way as to locate his theology of tongues within it. Believing that a dispensation opens and closes in the same manner, Parham argued that the glorious manifestation of the "supernatural gifts" in the apostolic period would also be manifested at the close of the dispensation of the church immediately prior to the imminent coming of the Lord.[30] His doctrine of tongues had immediate theological implications in that he believed that a recipient who was baptized in the Spirit could go to a different culture and supernaturally speak the language without prior knowledge or training. Parham also believed that the gift of tongues empowered the recipient for Christian service, to manifest the power of the Spirit in the church and the world.

Pentecostals have adopted some of Parham's beliefs but not others. For instance, the belief that one was supernaturally empowered to speak in another, unlearned language at will was repudiated, but Pentecostals still believe that at times the manifestation of tongues is another earthly language and can be understood. Important in this context, however, are the social implications of Parham's eschatology for the transformation of society.

According to Anderson,[31] early Pentecostal eschatology had revolutionary potential. It was a form of "anti-establishment Protestantism that was anticlerical, antitheological, antiliturgical, antisacramental, antiecclesiastical, and indeed, in a sense, antireligious."[32] It was also antidemocratic and antipolitical, attacking the status quo of dominant political systems.[33] Early Pentecostalism represented a protest against the dominant forms of Christianity and social-political realities in the world, with specific reactionary, radical content. Since Pentecostals were apolitical in practice, however, Pentecostalism's reactionary and revolutionary content lost out to more conservative tendencies.[34] This lack of specific action was due in part to the lack of any social or political power on the part of early Pentecostals. By and large, early Pentecostals were an oppressed group representing the underclass of American society. In the age of modernity, the people constituting early Pentecostalism were classified by Sheppard as neither pre-modern, modern, nor post-modern, but rather sub-modern. While living in a world that enjoyed progress, medical advancement, technological sophistication, and mass wealth, early Pentecostals had little access to these benefits.[35]

Parham's eschatology embodied a social-political protest with implications for social action, even though these protests were seldom pursued in a consistent manner. His eschatological rhetoric raised objections to American capitalism and nationalism. He predicted a cataclysmic class conflict between the government, the rich, and established churches on the one hand, and the masses on the other. Using apocalyptic rhetoric Parham claimed:

Capital must exterminate and enslave the masses or be exterminated ... In the death struggle ... the rich will be killed like dogs ... For a long time the voices of the masses have vainly sought for relief, by agitation and the ballot, but the governments of the world were in the hands of the rich, the nobles, and the plutocrats of the world, who forestalled all legislative action in the interests of the masses, until the wage-slavery of the world became unbearable; until the worm, long ground under the iron heel of oppression, begins to burn with vindictive fire, under the inspiration of a new patriotism in the interests of the freedom of the working class. Therefore, would it be considered strange if the overzealous already begin to use the only means at hand for their liberty – by bombs and assassinations to destroy the monsters of government and society that

stand in the way of the realization of their hopes? ... Ere long Justice
with flaming sword, will step from behind the pleading form of
Mercy, to punish a nation which has mingled the blood of thousands of human sacrifices upon the altar of her commercial and
imperialistic expansion.[36]

Evidently, Parham was critical of American capitalism for its quest for
profit at the cost of human misery. He was also critical of any attempt
to bring social justice through political action. Most striking, Parham
ensconces this criticism in apocalyptic imagery of divine judgment reminiscent of the final battle between the forces of God and the forces
of evil.

One might think that Parham would easily side with the social gospel,
which tried to alleviate the oppressive conditions of the working poor.
However, he was as critical of the emerging unionist movement as he
was of capitalism, once again with use of apocalyptic rhetoric. "While
we are not personally a member of any lodge or union, neither have we
aught against them, for if the church had done its duty in feeding the
hungry and clothing the naked, these institutions would not have existed,
sapping the life of the church ... " Parham credits both unions and lodges
for doing the charitable work of the church, or what the church should
be doing. However, he then slips into apocalyptic language and avers,
"Upon the ascension to power of an Anti-Christ, a worldwide union or
protective association will be organized by the fanatical followers, and
one will be compelled to subscribe to this union association, and receive
a literal mark in the right hand or forehead, or he cannot buy or sell."[37]
Even socialism was criticized for containing elements of the gospel and
elements of a fallen world. In a lecture entitled, "Christianity vs. Socialism: He [Jesus?] is a Christian, not a Socialist, but graduated from a
School of Socialism," he claimed that the "cry of socialism ... is the
heart-cry of Jesus."[38] Fear that the global, organizational structures of
unions would be a tool of the Antichrist made him suspicious of unions
and socialism, yet he thought aspects of socialist causes contained elements of Christian morality. Once again, Parham's protest is layered in
apocalyptic language. What is hinted at but left unsaid is that his real
fears are ongoing globalization and social rationalization.

Seymour likewise exhibited progressive and at times revolutionary
tendencies. He believed that the event of Pentecost as depicted in Acts 2
and the equalizing effect of tongues as the sign of the baptism of the
Holy Spirit could bring racial reconciliation, first in the church and ulti-

mately in American society. Seymour's African-American tradition not only included the study of the Bible, but also a "black folk Christianity" which sought freedom, equality, and community. Slavery, oppression, and injustice were identified as sin and freedom was not merely spiritual (i.e., the soul), but material – the whole person, body, spirit, and soul.[39] For Seymour, racial integration was an apocalyptic expectation. "The revolutionary desire for and expectation of a cataclysmic Second Advent of the Lord Jesus Christ to exalt the poor, the humble and downtrodden, put down the high and mighty and the oppressors and right every wrong" was core to Seymour's vision. Seymour believed that the baptism of the Holy Spirit and the equalizing sign of tongues would break down the barriers of race, gender, and nationality. The belief was confirmed by the Azusa Street revival, where Blacks and Whites, and indeed people of various ethnicities, worshipped together against the norms of American society at the turn of the twentieth century. Unlike Parham, who retained his racist attitudes and condemned the interracial character of the Azusa Street Mission, where "blacks and whites intermingl[ed] against every accepted custom of American society,"[40] Seymour included a statement in "The Doctrines and Discipline of the Azusa Street Apostolic Faith Mission of Los Angeles, Cal" that stated: "We find according to God's word to be one in the Holy Spirit, not in the flesh; but in the Holy Spirit, for we are one body. I Cor. 12:12–14. If some of our white brethren have prejudices and discrimination (Gal. 2:11–20), we can't do it, because God calls us to follow the Bible. Matt. 17:8; Matt. 23 ... Some of our white brethren and sisters have never left us in all the division; they have stuck with us. We love our white brethrens and sisters and welcome them. Jesus Christ takes in all people in his Salvation. Christ is all in all. He is neither black nor white, nor Chinaman, nor Hindoo [sic], nor Japanese, but God."[41]

According to MacRobert, Pentecostalism represented a revolutionary type of Christianity because it combined Adventist eschatology with racial integration. Early Pentecostals anticipated a cataclysmic end to this age initiated by God in the second coming, but they also saw themselves as agents of this "revolution." They believed that God's kingdom would be hastened by fulfilling the precondition of spreading the gospel throughout the world, a common assumption in evangelicalism.[42] For early Pentecostals, tongues, or more accurately xenoglossolia, was the means by which the evangelization of the entire world could be accomplished, but also a sign of hope for racial reconciliation and social transformation.

In the US, Pentecostals imbibed heavily of the diverse streams of evangelicalism, believing the coming of Jesus Christ and his kingdom was imminent, precipitated by a worldwide proclamation of faith in every corner of the world. Protests against industrial capitalism, urbanization, globalization, and rationalization of the social sphere suggest that Pentecostals tended to fit in more easily with some of the radical elements in evangelicalism rather than the more conservative elements of fundamentalism. Early Pentecostals did not embrace an apocalyptic vision of world destruction prominent in fundamentalism, but a more world-affirming vision of reconciliation under the reign of God, in which their Latter Rain eschatology, Spirit Baptism, and healing played a role in the redemption of the world. This approach allowed Pentecostals to be more critical of the social ills of the world, while holding that the solution was not predominantly political engagement but transformation that would come through the divine encounter. Unlike the social gospellers, early Pentecostals allied with an earlier brand of evangelicalism that believed evangelism and humanitarianism were two foci of the same gospel, and some went as far as seeing the very structures of society as part of the problem.

Thus strands one and three of my thesis – that the social development of Pentecostalism as a whole emerged in the context of evangelicalism, and that Pentecostal eschatology was more world affirming than the cataclysmic vision of fundamentalism allowed – have come together. What remains to be considered, however, is the relationship between Pentecostalism in the US and Canada with regard to their social protests, and how these protests were ensconced in apocalyptic rhetoric.

The development of Canadian Pentecostalism, including organizational formation, was influenced by evangelical and Pentecostal culture in the US (see chapter 1). Not only is cross border influence discernible (Pentecostals conducting meetings and establishing missions in Canada and the US), but strong institutional connections have existed between the PAOC and the Assemblies of God. Cross-fertilization from both sides of the continental divide also represented a continuation of nineteenth-century evangelical theology, values, and norms. Although Pentecostalism continued the evangelical social vision of humanitarian action and protests against social trends that devalued human existence, Parham and Seymour represented a radical protest of capitalism and racism respectively, even though the two were at odds concerning the issue of race. Yet the doctrine of Spirit Baptism and tongues was not only a sign of the divine-human encounter, but potentially signified equality of all people, regardless of class, race, or gender. "For there is no respect of persons with God (Romans 2:11)" and "There is neither Jew nor Greek, there is neither bond nor free, there is neither male or female: for ye all are one in Christ Jesus (Galatians 3:28)" were favourite verses quoted by Pentecostals, which, when combined with the Day of Pentecost account of Acts 2, created a powerful image for social reconciliation. What remains to be seen is whether or not Pentecostalism in Canada represents a continuity or discontinuity with the social protests of the more radical and progressive inclinations of Pentecostalism in the US.

SOCIAL DISCOURSE AND SOCIAL ACTION IN CANADIAN PENTECOSTALISM

For the most part, the thrust of the Canadian Pentecostal message in the first three decades was evangelistic, missionary, and eschatological, with the added emphasis of the baptism of the Holy Spirit with the initial evidence[43] of speaking in tongues. Spirit Baptism was believed to empower the believer for service and ministry in the church and the world, in decidedly social dimensions.[44] However, a perusal of the *Pentecostal Testimony*, the official magazine of the PAOC, hints at a variety of other social concerns. Early Canadian Pentecostals were concerned about and involved in the social agenda of the broader evangelical culture; they ran rescue homes, orphanages, soup kitchens, seniors' homes, soldiers' homes, etc.[45] These concerns were more pronounced in foreign missions than in Canada, in part because the evangelical church had made great strides outside North America. Ivan Kaufmann, a missionary to China, was concerned about the social evils in that country, in which "we are told nine-tenths of the city is taken up with opium traffic or smoking, white slavery and gambling,"[46] a sentiment echoed three years later in that "children cry as they are torn from their mother's side to go into a life of slavery or the houses of shame, which is far worse."[47]

These early pioneers were primarily responding to the Bible's message and working on the front lines of helping the poor, the downtrodden, the weak, and the widowed. Certain segments of early Pentecostalism were also pacifist in orientation, sometimes at the cost of imprisonment. J. Elmor Morrison was an interesting case in Canada, when during World War One he registered as a conscientious objector and was imprisoned in Kingston Penitentiary. In 1923, he and his wife Verent (Mills) travelled to South China as missionaries and in 1939 they travelled to Tsing Yuen to open a refugee camp, an orphanage, and a Bible Institute for Chinese Christians.[48]

One can even detect a concern for, but ambivalent attitude with regard to, more radical social issues such as labour and unionism. In 1920, James McAlister, R.E. McAlister's brother, wrote an article in the *Pentecostal Evangel* which revealed sympathies for the cause of unionism but ambivalence toward its revolutionary tendencies. These concerns were specifically couched in apocalyptic rhetoric: "Whilst our sympathies are with every just claim of labor for shorter hours and better wages, and whilst we support all that is good in Socialism as against the greed of capital and the crime of profiteering, we cannot but feel that Democracy [unionism?] is intoxicated with the wine of lawlessness, and is in danger of insensate deeds of violence which bring rivers of blood and a rain of tears" [postwar strikes?].[49] One notices that McAlister is sympathetic to the concerns of workers' rights and even the positive aspects of socialism, at least as they align with biblical values, and is critical of capitalism's concern for profit. However, he is unsympathetic to unionism. Not only is "Democracy" linked to the abuses of alcohol (a concern of the Temperance movement), it is also represented in apocalyptic imagery of "rivers of blood."

In 1933, Walter E. McAlister wrote an article which condemned child "slave" labour in the US, rhetorically commenting on a news report of "a shocking condition of affairs. Children work as many as fifty-four hours a week for the almost incredible pay of five cents a day. Domestic servants' wages are also found to be as low as one dollar a week." He connects this sorry state of affairs to a Legislature "which is dominated by industrialists." He then links this social problem to the "last days," as described in James 5:1–6 when "we are told of the fearful doom of the rich man who has heaped treasure together" so that "the hire of laborers ... is ... kept back by fraud."[50] Although McAlister's concerns were similar to evangelical views and even the social gospel, he reveals his ambivalence in failing to translate this problem into political action. He comments, "we are not to lend our efforts to revolution or strikes or labor upheavals ... The labor situation, the economic situation and the international relations of the various nations, has gotten out of control. The only permanent solution, to the world problems, is the coming of the Lord. All our efforts to patch things up must, of necessity, result in only a very temporary remedy at best."[51] The author of "The Promise of the Coming of the Lord" hints at the reason for this countercultural element in Pentecostal eschatology, claiming, "there will be no peace, no stable kingdom, no well-ordered government on the earth until Jesus comes … No matter how many times this world is patched up, no matter how men strive for fine, well-ordered governments, the time will come when they are to be overturned. And all the kingdoms of the world will become the kingdom of our Lord."[52] W.E. McAlister's criticism of the labour conditions in the us was far from conservative, but his passive attitude may be the result of a strengthening fundamentalist influence in the denomination.[53]

A countercultural social attitude that lacked specific social action appears to have been the norm in one segment of early Canadian Pentecostalism, but other segments were ambivalent and even antagonistic to political activity and the transformation of society. On the one hand, G.E. Smith rhetorically asked, "Should a Christian take part in the politics of the country?" to which he responded, "We believe not."[54] On the other hand, however, since the 1950s, a number of Pentecostal leaders have exhibited a more progressive attitude to politics and social action. From 1950 to 1973, four Pentecostals were elected to provincial parliaments: P.A. Gaglardi and Mrs Ethel Wilson (Social Credit), Everett I. Wood (NDP), and Raymond Edwards (Liberal). Gaglardi, Wilson, and Wood served as cabinet members in their respective legislatures.[55] A moral core was tantamount to good political and social action, as suggested by E.N.O. Kulbeck's advice: "In our Parliamentary system, if we want our vote to count in Ottawa, our final choice on how to vote will therefore be strongly influenced by the moral qualifications of the leader of the party, and his ability to form a government. For this reason a vote cast for a third party candidate, even though the local candidate is a good man, will be ineffective in Ottawa, except in an opposition role."[56] Even more interesting was the election of Sam Jenkins as President of the Marine Worker and Boilermakers' Union in 1955, while simultaneously active as a lay preacher and evangelist for the PAOC. Jenkins justified his unionist association by claiming that he was there to help the needy and reach union members for Christ.[57] Jenkins went as far as justifying breaking unjust laws. He commented, "I am my brother's keeper – against thieves, murderers, extortioners, and laws that discriminate against him. Therefore, I will join with him to fight a bad law. When I do so, I am helping to bear his burden, thus fulfilling the law of Christ."[58] If a law is unjust, claims Jenkins, "every nonviolent action I can take to break it, I will."[59]

Since the mid 1970s, the PAOC has adopted more conservative values while at the same time becoming more active politically. Constituents of the 1978 General Conference initiated a process to form a National Committee on Moral Standards and in 1980 established the Ethics and Social Concerns Committee to articulate its position on social issues and liaise with Parliament. In 1982, Hudson Hilsden was appointed as the chair of the committee.[60] A perusal of the documents reveals a morally conservative agenda on issues ranging from abortion, drugs, alcohol, and censorship to reproductive technologies, pornography, sexual orientation, and sex education,[61] though many of the issues remain within the overall evangelical matrix and humanitarian efforts such as famine relief are still a concern. Absent are the kinds of apocalyptic social rhetoric found among early Pentecostals, but the denomination has found a new strength in political activity. Yet Canadian Pentecostals have not adopted the stance of the social gospel and have generally maintained an arms-length relationship with social activists, seeing these groups as too socially radical. Pentecostalism as an organized body also refuses to take political sides, allowing constituents to make choices of conscience.[62] Curiously, a decade later the PAOC General Executive dissolved the Social Concerns Committee and "social concerns" was added to "evangelism" and "missions" as emphases in the ministries of the local church.[63] One official mentioned to me in conversation that the reason the Social Concerns Committee was disbanded was that the PAOC was unable to make any headway in the political arena and could therefore no longer justify the financial expense. Yet this overlooks the importance of having a voice in the political sphere, for the purpose of clarifying one's position, regardless of results. For all intents and purposes, the new force of political activity at the national level was dissipated into small pockets of concerned Pentecostals who lacked the resources of a national program.

Pentecostals today have settled for a fundamentalist dispensational eschatology that has taken a conservative stance with regard to the world, and consequently Pentecostalism in Canada has lost its countercultural voice. Pentecostals are now hesitant to condemn a society that values profit and privilege, possibly because Pentecostals are now members of the wealthy and privileged class.

At the beginning of this chapter, I proposed that early Pentecostals criticized many of the social values, norms, and structures of Canadian culture by means of an apocalyptic rhetoric, and offered a countercultural vision of the country, but that their ambivalence to political engagement seldom translated into political action. I have probed this thesis by exploring a number of strands. The first was the continuities and discontinuities between Pentecostalism and evangelicalism, both north and south of the forty-ninth parallel. Although some early Pentecostals exhibited more conservative social values, other Pentecostals continued the tradition of more radical and progressive social discourses, especially with regard to race, class, and labour. Even though they were suspicious of the program of the social gospel, Pentecostals shared some of the same concerns as the social gospel regarding the social direction of Canadian society. Yet, they believed the means to accomplish those ends were found in personal transformation through a call to proclamation and repentance, not social action.

The second strand was the relationship between Pentecostalism in Canada and the US, in which the countercultural voices of Parham and Seymour, who questioned the morality of capitalism's devaluation of the human being and the racist attitudes in society respectively, were picked up by certain segments of Canadian Pentecostalism. Humanitarian concerns such as the plight of the poor, orphanages, and old age homes were of concern to Pentecostals, but also the issues of fair wages, child labour, pacifism, and racist immigration policies. Some early Pentecostals were even willing to challenge the assumptions of capitalism, to suggest that elements of socialism were more faithful to the ideals of the kingdom.

Pentecostals both north and south of the continental divide tended not to address these social issues directly, but couched them in apocalyptic rhetoric. The third strand of my argument then insists that early Pentecostals did not fit easily into a fundamentalist dispensational eschatology that envisioned a complete desolation of the world order. If this were the case, then the countercultural voice envisioning a better society would be meaningless. Why work for a better world that will ultimately be destroyed? Instead, early Pentecostals proclaimed the Latter Rain eschatology that saw the baptism in the Spirit and the charismata as signs for reconciliation between people and races, as a glorious revival precipitating the coming of the Lord.

My final strand, which draws together the other three, insists that even though early Pentecostals in Canada embodied the seeds of social transformation, this was only in embryonic form and failed to translate effectively into political action. Aside from a few leaders who understood the implications of the movement's theology and attempted to effect social change, for the most part the discourse remained mere rhetoric and Pentecostals tended to reflect the dominant values of society. They have continued with humanitarian efforts, believing this is an integral part of the gospel. Consequently, what I have left unsaid up until now is that perhaps Pentecostalism's countercultural voice, even though frustrated by the lack of specific political action, might offer a means for contemporary Pentecostals to engage the public order and challenge the social structures that dehumanize life.

Admittedly, this investigation of the social aspects of Pentecostalism in Canada is more suggestive than definitive, poised between the methodologies of history and theology, and in need of further development. I have argued that early Pentecostalism in Canada and the US embodied a countercultural protest within its apocalyptic rhetoric that was not only a continuation of the broader context of the social agenda in evangelicalism, but was at times more revolutionary than conservative. However, early Pentecostal rhetoric seldom translated into social action, other than the humanitarian concerns that conformed to biblical principles. I have tried to map out a trajectory for the study of Canadian Pentecostalism that accounts for its social criticism and does not simply assume a fundamentalist-conservative orientation, seeing Canadian Pentecostalism as a diverse spiritual movement that has real tensions with historic fundamentalism.[64]

NOTES

1 Valverde, *The Age of Light, Soap, and Water*, 9–11.
2 Ibid., 23.
3 See McGinn et al., *The Encyclopedia of Apocalypticism*.
4 Sexton, "Editorial" as quoted in Faupel, *The Everlasting Gospel*, 20.
5 McDowell, "The Purpose of the Coming of the Lord," *Pentecostal Testimony* 4, no. 6 (June 1925), 4–5 (4); reprint of the *Pentecostal Evangel* (2 May 1925), 2; cf Faupel, "The Function of 'Models'," 66.
6 For the most part I have presupposed a non-fundamentalist understanding of early Pentecostalism, an argument I made in *Spirit of the Last Days*. I will not rehash those arguments here.
7 Choquette, *Canada's Religions*, 255–6.
8 Ibid., 231.
9 Ibid.
10 Valverde, *The Age of Light*, 10.
11 Clarke, "English-Speaking Canada from 1854," 283–5.
12 Ibid., 287–8.

13 Ibid., 288.

14 Ibid., 308.

15 Ibid., 309.

16 Ibid., 309–10.

17 Ibid., 310–11.

18 Allen, *The Social Passion*, 6–7.

19 Walter Rauschenbusch, the American credited with starting the social gospel, was not evangelical, but was disturbed by the misery he witnessed as a result of capitalism, and attempted to change the inequities.

20 Allen, *The Social Passion*, 17.

21 Ibid., 35.

22 Ibid., 47–8.

23 Ibid., 48.

24 Ibid., 39–40

25 Ibid., 87–8.

26 Ibid., 94–5.

27 Ibid., 227–8.

28 See Noll, *The Scandal of the Evangelical Mind*.

29 See Anderson, *Vision of the Disinherited* and Dayton, *Theological Roots of Pentecostalism*.

30 This eschatology was fully articulated by early Pentecostal D. Wesley Myland. See "The Latter Rain Covenant and Pentecostal Power" in Dayton, *Three Early Pentecostal Tracts*.

31 Anderson, *Vision of the Disinherited*.

32 Ibid., 214.

33 Ibid., 208.

34 Ibid., 208–9.

35 Sheppard, "Pentecostals, Globalization, and Postmodern Hermeneutics: Implications for the Politics of Scriptural Interpretation," 289–90.

36 Parham, *The Everlasting Gospel*, 28–30; as quoted by Anderson, *Vision of the Disinherited*, 209.

37 Parham, *The Everlasting Gospel*, 33–5; as quoted by Anderson, 210.

38 Goff, *Fields White unto Harvest*, 156.

39 MacRobert, *The Black Roots and White Racism of Early Pentecostalism in the USA*, 34–5.

40 MacRobert, *Black Roots*, 60.

41 Seymour, "The Doctrines and Discipline of the Azusa Street Apostolic Faith Mission of Los Angeles, Cal," (1915), 12–13, Assemblies of God Archives.

42 MacRobert, *Black Roots*, 80.

43 Note that the initial evidence did not become official AG doctrine in the US until the Kerr-Boswell conflict in 1918, but this doctrine was subsumed in the PAOC through its relationship to the AG.

44 See Althouse, "The Ideology of Power in Early American Pentecostalism," 99–118.

45 See, for instance, Chawner, "Fidadelphia, Stockholm, Sweden," *Pentecostal Testimony* 19, no. 2 (March 1938), 4; cf. Kydd, "The Pentecostal Assemblies of Canada and Society," 9–10.

46 Kaufmann, "Aggressive Work in China," *Pentecostal Testimony*, 5, no. 3 (March 1926), 5.

47 "News from South China," *Pentecostal Testimony*, 10, no. 4 (April 1929), 1.

48 Rudd, *When The Spirit Came Upon Them*, 149–50. Carman Clare Scratch also participated in government relief work in North China, Tibet, and Mongolia in 1945. Three years later he worked in an orphanage in Foochow. Rudd, 171–2.

49 *Pentecostal Evangel* (10 July 1920), 1; as quoted by Anderson, *Vision of the Disinherited*, 210.

50 McAlister, "The Cries of the Laborers," *Pentecostal Testimony* 14, no. 9 (October 1933), 6.

51 Ibid.

52 McDowell, "The Purpose of the Coming of the Lord," 5.

53 See Althouse, *Spirit of the Last Days*, especially chapter 1.

54 Smith, "Citizenship," *Pentecostal Testimony* 6, no. 1 (January 1927), 16.

55 Kydd, "The Pentecostal Assemblies of Canada and Society," 8–9.

56 Kulbeck, "Why a Christian Should Vote," *Pentecostal Testimony* (November 1965), 32.

57 Kydd, "The Pentecostal Assemblies of Canada and Society," 7.

58 Jenkins, "Breaking the Law," *Pentecostal Testimony* (September 1969), 28, as quoted by Kydd, "The Pentecostal Assemblies of Canada and Society," 11.

59 Jenkins, 4, as quoted by Kydd, "The Pentecostal Assemblies of Canada and Society," 11.

60 Miller, *Canadian Pentecostals*, 358.

61 Social Concerns: Positions/Resolutions, box RCI-10, file 2002–508, PAOC archives.

62 Miller, *Canadian Pentecostals*, 359.

63 Ibid., 400–1.

64 I would like to thank a number of people with whom I have discussed these ideas, including Ronald Kydd, John Stephenson, Jim Craig, and Brian Stiller. A special thanks to Marilyn Stroud at the PAOC Archives, who graciously located various sources.

4

Canadian Pentecostal Spirituality

RANDALL HOLM

INTRODUCTION

On 26 April 2002, at the age of 53 and in the midst of mid-life changes, author Charles Wilkins left his home in Thunderbay, Ontario and began walking to New York City – a distance of some 2,200 kilometres. Sixty-three days and a half million steps later, Wilkins arrived at his destination. Chronicling his pilgrimage in a book aptly entitled *Walk to New York*, Wilkins connects his readers with pastoral farm roads, urban interstate highways, ancient Aboriginal trails, and the CP Rail. Along the way he encountered bears, a bull moose, road kill, litter of every kind imaginable, and a series of encounters with a stellar cast of quirky characters. If, writes Wilkins, "my walk bore the earmark of the old-style spiritual journey, it did so largely, I would say, in its provision of the chance to reflect, to rediscover, and to re-arm against the pressures and pessimism that are so much a part of contemporary life."[1]

Wilkins is not the first person to draw a link between spirituality and walking. Arguably the earliest example of spirituality in recorded history is found within the Hebrew Bible. Long before the advent of the Law, as far back as Genesis 5, Enoch was singled out because he walked with God. Likewise Noah is described as a righteous man and spared the judgment of the flood because he walked with God. And Moses led the nation of Israel on foot, through a scarred desert, to their Promised Land. As a metaphor for spirituality, walking – "progress forward by lifting and setting down each foot in turn, never having both feet off the ground at once,"[2] has an ancient pedigree of transformation.

However, to talk of spirituality in the twenty-first century is to trudge through muddy waters. Spirituality, once a word conjuring primarily religious images, has found its way into the world of sports, business, medicine, and countless other professions. Whether by default or by design, as a descriptor, "spirituality" has come to trump virtually all other rivals designed to peer behind the veil and explore the values and practices of ultimate concern. From the playground to the boardroom, the word "spirituality" has suddenly surfaced as an indispensable component of essential well-being, all the while avoiding the charge of being naïve or prudish.[3] The diversity of such contexts frequently results in a definition of spirituality that is amorphous, ethereal, and aesthetic, escaping any concrete determination.

In contrast to such imprecision, when the church employs the term spiritual, it usually has in mind a distinct "cluster of values, beliefs and practices"[4] that marks the life of a person. In the Christian tradition a spiritual person is often a person of contemplative prayer and meditation on scripture. To paraphrase the Westminster confession, a spiritual person is one whose chief end is to pursue and enjoy God forever. That being said, Christian spirituality is not a separate entity unto itself. Within the Christian tradition, human spirituality is linked with the work and action of the Holy Spirit through individual lives both within and outside the life of the church. It is precisely God's Spirit working with and through the human spirit that is said to shape and transform one's spirituality – a spirituality that from the sixteenth century[5] onward, in the spirit of modernity, was generally expected to work nonetheless through the natural order of things. This was challenged when, at the dawn of the twentieth century, a new religious enthusiasm introduced itself. Identifying themselves as a repristination of the early church, these believers affectionately adopted the nomenclature "Pentecostal" (a reference to the events surrounding the birth of the early church) as their own. Born in a stable in the boroughs of Los Angeles,[6] these swashbuckling enthusiasts may have represented the socioeconomically disenfranchised,[7] but they enrolled in the "Holy Ghost School of progressive truth and supernatural power"[8] and anything seemed possible.[9]

There is no doubt Pentecostals, particularly in Canada, will not share all my conclusions. They are a suspicious lot when it comes to anything that smells of academia. "Academic" is not a ready adjective that Pentecostals use to describe a spiritual person. To the contrary, it is often employed to describe an activity that is antithetical to the work and aim of God's Spirit.[10] Narrative or testimony is the preferred method of Pentecostal historical self-interpretation. It is my hope, however, that in the end this analysis will resonate true for enough in the Pentecostal tradition of Canada that it will also shed some light for those on the outside looking in.

A WALK TO REMEMBER

On the eve of their centennial anniversary, Pentecostals around the world continued to distinguish themselves through their religious enthusiasm and ardent attempts to read the book of Acts both descriptively and prescriptively as the key for experiencing the signs and wonders of the Spirit – wonders which include, but are not limited to, praying in other "tongues," healing, prophesy, words of knowledge, and so forth. From a Pentecostal viewpoint not only should these experiences be normal as one opens oneself to the movement of God's Spirit, for many they are normative traits in the life of a Christian.

Early adherents were frequently reminded that the Holy Spirit cannot be "weighted, ticketed, or analyzed with the methods applied to the various 'religious bodies' in the world today. It stands alone, and stubbornly refuses to be categorized with any of them."[11] Pentecostals promoted themselves as a new dispensation of freedom that would not be held in the thralldom of church tradition. A motley group of freelancers, these early Pentecostals rallied around theological convictions that (a) Pentecostals were living in the last days; (b) because of the machinations of the Holy Spirit, Pentecostals were better equipped to live out the demands of a righteous Christian life; and (c) there was a symbiotic relationship between the infilling of the Holy Spirit or baptism of the Holy Spirit[12] and church health.[13]

If the Holy Spirit was the cause, spiritual was the effect. Early Pentecostals promoted a spirituality that was driven by the freedom of the Holy Spirit. They would not be guilty of resisting the Spirit as they yielded themselves as channels for the operation of the Spirit. Spirituality Pentecostal-style was promoted as a "cry for freedom." Pentecostals promoted themselves as by-products of the Latter Rain[14] while traditional church organizations were often disparaged as simply products of religiosity, "party spirits," "yokes of (ecclesiastical) bondage," that only intensify and perpetuate division.[15] Rhetorically, Pentecostals called for the end of "ecclesiastical hierarchies." The only leader required for true organization was Jesus himself, with the Holy Spirit being the impetus for fellowship.[16] In no way were they going to be guilty of restricting the free movement of the Holy Spirit, which was liable to "burst through anyone."[17] Individuals would be honoured for their God-given gifts and not for their pedigree, natural talents, or education.[18] Everyone was either a "Brother" or "Sister" in the Lord. And, as they felt called, were encouraged, by example, to step up and assume leadership roles in the church.[19] All were deemed equal.

In Los Angeles in the early part of the twentieth century, such utopian aspirations went with the territory. Over and against the triumphalist naturalism of the dominant culture, Pentecostalism posited a triumphalist supernaturalism that offered hope through the Holy Spirit for the majority not born of the right class, gender, or race. These Pentecostals were not simple holy rollers, too heavenly minded to be of any earthly good. Rather, they made their mark on society by transforming spiritual piety into social reform.[20]

Long on freedom and short on liturgy, early Pentecostals nonetheless pasted together a codified set of qualifiers designed in the spirit of modernism to repeat and perpetuate Pentecostal experience/spirituality for future generations.[21] Believers and seekers wishing to be initiated into the vocational work of the Spirit required a sign that would serve as the evidence of Spirit Baptism and would further assist believers in perpetuating the spirit of Pentecostalism. To this end, Pentecostals looked again to the book of Acts and drew a cause-and-effect link with the early church experience of speaking in other tongues. Tongues, an inchoate language often said to be the language of angels, became the sign or "initial evidence"[22] that one was baptized in the Spirit.

The church is certainly no stranger to signs of signification. Church history is filled with metaphors that point to divine realities beyond themselves. What distinguished the Pentecostal emphasis on the Spirit was its ability to transform tongues into a metonym that not only pointed to the Spirit, as a metaphor does, but shared in some way with its essence. As anthropologist Karla Poewe points out, metonyms enjoy an advantage over metaphors in that they are part of the same nature as the whole to which they point.[23] Therefore, the divine reality which is behind the metonym is not just an object to be studied and understood, as in metaphor, but an event to be shared and experienced.

Needless to say such an analysis is a sign in itself that Pentecostalism has sufficiently come of age in one hundred years to be the subject of serious scholarship in a variety of disciplines. Not the least it has given rise to its own self-critical analysis of Pentecostal spirituality. Russell

Spittler, a Pentecostal and the provost at Fuller Theological Seminary, has identified five values of Pentecostal spirituality. They include, but are not limited to, individual experience, where experience is felt rather than "telt"; orality, where history finds greater expression through story than theological treatise; spontaneity, where believers are compliant to the leading of the Holy Spirit; other-world-ness, where believers promote any activity that is said to have a lasting reward; and biblical authority, where adherents can cite chapter and verse in the biblical text for all decisions.[24] Complementing Spittler's comments, Harvard professor Harvey Cox identifies a primal dimension that is characteristic of Pentecostal spirituality. Cox says that Pentecostalism speaks to the "spiritual emptiness of our time by reaching beyond the levels of creed and ceremony into the core of human religiousness into what might be called 'primal spirituality,' that largely unprocessed nucleus of the psyche in which the unending struggle for a sense of purpose and significance goes on."[25]

Cox continues by observing such primal spirituality in speech, where Pentecostals "pray in the Spirit," perhaps in an unknown language; in piety, where Pentecostals encourage such religious expressions as dream, visions, and healing; and in hope, where Pentecostals wait in great anticipation for the visible return of Jesus Christ and the establishment of God's Kingdom.[26] On this latter point Pentecostal scholar Steven Land hangs the definitive core of Pentecostal spirituality. For Land, the nexus of such spirituality is revealed in the correlation of a distinctive apocalyptic affection for the Kingdom of God with the righteousness, holiness, and power of God, where the Spirit or the presence of God is the operating agent.[27] Out of such urgency for the Kingdom flow the core Pentecostal beliefs and practices.

In the year 2006 many Pentecostals worldwide remembered the birth of this distinctive outburst of Spirit activity. In particular, scholars will no doubt use this occasion to restate the contributions of Pentecostal doctrine and practice to the global church. I suspect, however, that among the rank and file of Pentecostalism, this milestone date has largely gone unnoticed. Such is the nature of Pentecostal spirituality. Whether it is driven by an apocalyptic urge for the Kingdom, or whether it manifests itself through primal experiences, Pentecostal spirituality seldom pauses to reflect on its own past as it is always moving forward to the next watershed moment. Such spirituality does not come without its challenges. Can a spirituality that feeds so directly off the immediacy of the Spirit, often at the expense of historical reflection, escape the marginalizing effect of the human spirit that too easily assumes that the divine and human spirit are working to the same end? In the absence of historical referents, can Pentecostals avoid creating a construct of God based on their elative feelings?

These indeed are some of the challenges Pentecostal spirituality faces following one hundred years of transition from movement to institution. However, in the last one hundred years the spirit of Pentecostalism has proved, if nothing else, to be extremely resilient in light of these challenges. Its resilience is due in no small measure to its adaptability to different cultural surroundings. In this regard, in what follows I will further elaborate on at least how one Pentecostal group, the Pentecostal Assemblies of Canada (PAOC), continues to develop and wrestle with its own spiritual identity. Established in 1919, the PAOC remains numerically the largest identifiable group of Pentecostals in the country of Canada.

WALKING BACK HOME

Canadians were also drawn to the new form of religious enthusiasm found in the US and throughout the world. On a regular basis, *The Apostolic Faith*, a newspaper-type publication produced by the Azusa Street Mission, home of the new revival in Los Angeles, reported spiritual outbreaks in Canada and other places, most of which had at least a casual link with Azusa Street. In a report on what many considered to be the Azusa Street revival of the north at the Hebden Mission in Toronto, we are told of Mr and Mrs Hebden, the founders of this mission, praying with other leaders to heal the sick and cast out demons. Mrs Hebden reports in November 1906 that she spoke in tongues in Toronto. "The Lord said to Mrs Hebden, 'tongues, tongues.' She answered, 'No Lord, not tongues, but power, power ...' They (the meetings) are heavenly. They are conducted informally. A stranger could scarcely discover who is in the lead. Christ is the Head. The Holy Ghost leads." And apparently the Holy Ghost was leading away from the perceived spirituality of the historic churches. Describing the atmosphere among those present at the Hebden mission, the reporter referred to a divine hush in the home. There is seriousness without rigidity, quietness without deadness and formality, joy and much praise without flippancy, liberty without licence. How anyone not right with God can come into these meetings and not become deeply convicted and how a believer can fail to enjoy them are conundrums. Pentecost has begun in Toronto.[28]

Pentecostalism was also taking hold elsewhere in Canada. One testimony described a crusade on 15 November 1907 in Winnipeg. "Twenty were baptized with the Holy Ghost and many were healed. The people brought handkerchiefs and aprons to be blessed as in Acts 19:12 and the Lord did wonderful signs through the simple faith of the dear ones that brought them. The Lord healed one young man of the tobacco habit, taking all the desire for the stuff away from him, through an anointed handkerchief, and he was saved in his own room. Demons were cast out of those bound by them."[29] While some came for healing and/or deliverance, others reported coming away with a new-found desire for service, writes Tom Anderson from Winnipeg. "I am here in Winnipeg and the glory of God is upon me. I can feel the Holy Ghost being and the cloven tongues of fire are burning from my head to the soles of my feet. I feel my nothingness and so unworthy to preach the Gospel, and my Heavenly Father so loving and kind to save such a wretched disgrace to humanity as I. God has his hand on poor me and has healed my body, opened up the way for service for me, got me into the harness, and I am getting fleshy and strong physically and realizing a channel for the Holy Ghost."[30] Far from being a metaphysical phenomenon sought for its own sake, healing was an opportunity to open oneself for service, service that would be accompanied ipso facto by the power of God. Whether the impression was accurate or not early Canadian Pentecostals captured a mood among many that the traditional church had grown too rigid, formal, joyless, and liberal. A Pentecostal spirituality, if nothing else, would invariably rectify such an imbalance.

By 1914, with the initial rush of Pentecostal enthusiasm waning in Los Angeles, most Pentecostals realized that their future depended on finding a way of institutionalizing their new-found freedom. For those like the Toronto Hebden Mission who refused such accommodation, demise quickly followed. The majority, however, found their way into any number of burgeoning new denominations/fellowships. The transition from renewal movement to denomination was well underway. The resulting landscape of Pentecostal churches was as variegated as it was colourful. Churches subdivided according to race, geography, doctrine, worship styles, and personalities. If the Spirit was the precursor to a new sense of unity among these churches, then either the Spirit was doing a poor job or individual agendas were supplanting the Spirit's work. In any event, while Canada and the US shared similar stories it was not long before notable differences began to emerge among the respective dominant denominations.[31]

As a child growing up within the PAOC, I observed that Canadian Pentecostal preachers rarely had the same sense of panache as did our American counterparts. Exceptions aside, when a church needed an evangelist who could convict "sinners" in their pews and elicit a response to an evangelistic appeal, they generally imported someone from the South. While Canadians have not suffered from a lack of good orators, Canadian Pentecostals have consistently preferred to borrow occasional excesses south of the border whence, I always suspected, they could return them in due season.

If the American experience of Pentecost could be likened to a sprint to the finish line in anticipation of the imminent return of Jesus Christ, Canadian Pentecostals have traditionally been marathon walkers – one step at a time. Ours is the journey in the wilderness with only a flash of the other world. To be a Canadian Pentecostal is to never have both feet off the ground at once.

In fact, Canada itself is a nation of walkers. We are not first in anything. Canadians generally prefer a wait-and-see attitude. Even our parliament is designed for much debate but little action, at least in the short term. We are a nation that gets more excited over the hobbling of a one-legged young man across Canada in search of a cure for cancer[32] than we do over any number of gold medals in an Olympic competition. Canada is a place where Revolutions are Quiet.[33] A recent national poll taken by the Canadian Broadcasting Corporation declared Tommy Douglas, the father of Canadian Medicare and the former leader of a social democratic party in Saskatchewan, the greatest Canadian of all time. Canada is a nation that would rather negotiate peaceful resolutions than flex its police or military force.[34] Socially, politically, culturally, the Canadian ethos is distinguished from the American – all of which has been amply documented elsewhere.

Therefore, it should come as no surprise that Pentecostalism and its accompanying spiritual ethos would develop asymmetrically from the US. In the US, in the spirit of enterprise and individualism, missionaries working in conjunction with denominational officials, in organizations like the Assemblies of God (AG), have historically always been required to raise their own funding support. Every so many years, missionaries are required to return to their homeland and canvas churches for pledges of support. This is a system that has been relatively successful, in part because it represents American entrepreneurship. In Canada, until very recently, overseas missions in the PAOC operated out of a general funding formula. Reflecting the social policies of the country, churches were encouraged to contribute monies to a national office who would then disburse these funds as need dictated.[35] This also reflects a transformation of Canadian Pentecostalism in relation to its institutionalization and transition from "fellowship" to denomination.

Again, in distinction to the American experience, Canadian Pentecostalism did not share the disenfranchised class dynamics of their southern counterparts. Many of the prominent early Canadian pioneers in the Pentecostal tradition were firmly entrenched in the middle-class values of the early 1900s. A.H. Argue, dubbed by many the greatest Pentecostal evangelist in Canada, left a very successful career in real estate in the early part of the twentieth century before becoming a full time evangelist. J.E. Purdie, Canada's first principal of a Pentecostal Bible College, was an ordained Anglican priest with advanced degrees in theology among his credentials (see chapter 5 in this volume). And many other pioneer Pentecostal leaders, such as A.G. Ward, G.A. Chambers, John T. Ball, and R.E. Sternall, had their beginnings in leadership with previously established denominations.[36] As a result, it should come as no surprise that while mainstream Pentecostals supported a Holy Spirit sponsored theology replete with speaking in tongues and other ecstatic giftings, they also maintained conservative, middle-class social values. Men were expected to bear the load of working and supporting their families. The privileged place of women was at home supporting their husbands.[37] While doctrinally similar to their American cousins, Canadian Pentecostals were in no hurry to ordain women to ministry. In Canada, the "End Times" urgency that fuelled much of the American Pentecostal revival was not so great that women could not continue to fulfill their "God-given responsibility and right" as homemakers. Exceptions to this rule were frowned upon.[38] While the PAOC shared a virtually identical doctrinal statement with American Pentecostals, they parted company on the ordination of women. Canada would not ordain women until a national conference vote in 1984.[39] And when they did, it was with the caveat that women would not be allowed to stand for an elected position on either a District or the General Conference.[40] Given the lengthy history leading up to such a change in judicial social policy, critics and supporters of the status quo had more than enough ammunition to claim that the denomination was simply acquiescing to feminist lobbyists within the denomination (see chapter 8 in this volume).

In the end, regardless of what position one takes on the issue of women's ordination, the rationale behind it reveals how Canadian

Pentecostals treat the issue of spirituality. On a spiritual level, Canadian Pentecostals could reluctantly accept women as preachers who, gifted by the Spirit, could speak forth an urgent message.[41] But they struggled to overcome the idea that such an "empowerment" by the Spirit could have a lasting residual effect in the person.[42] Or that the Spirit would contravene accepted middle-class social norms.[43]

TAKING A WALK ON THE WILD SIDE

Walking with one foot on the ground is a Pentecostal mainstay in Canada. But walking also implies that at least one foot is in the air. For Canadian Pentecostals that foot in the air has punctuated their walk in the park with an occasional walk on the wild side. Nearly fifty years after the Pentecostal movement landed in Canada, an outbreak of religious enthusiasm, led by brothers George and Ern Hawtin in November 1947 in the city of North Battleford, Saskatchewan, caught the attention of North America. The revival, dubbed by adherents as the "Latter Rain Movement," is said to have begun in a classroom at the Sharon Orphanage School.[44] The outbreak was marked by words of prophecy and what adherents called an effusion of spiritual gifts that could be transferred through the laying on of hands. Describing the chain of meetings that followed, George Hawtin testified: "Day after day the Word was taught, and then the signs followed its teaching. Morning, afternoon and evening, people were slain under the power of God and filled with the Holy Spirit ... We had been praying for a return of the days when people would be filled with the Spirit immediately when hands were laid upon them as they were at Samaria and Ephesus. It was our great joy one night to have two ladies walk up before the whole crowd and receive the Holy Spirit in this fashion. When hands were laid upon them one immediately fell under the power of God; the other began to speak in tongues as the Spirit gave her utterance."[45]

Reaction from the established Pentecostal tradition was swift and divided. People either bought into the new outburst of enthusiasm or rejected it as a faction vying for power, with an authoritarian leadership that negated sound biblical teaching with too much emphasis on prophecy. Attending one of the meetings, Pentecostal Richard Bombay reported: "It was like a continual convention with prayer, singing, preaching and many professed prophecies, most of them promising that God was going to do a 'new thing' that was way beyond the Pentecostal outpouring. I was acquainted with many who were there ... One of the first things that came to my notice was the great number of 'independents" present. Were they dissatisfied with their independence? It was also very apparent that there was a 'power struggle' for recognition as 'the apostle of the Latter Rain'."[46]

Outsiders to the Pentecostal tradition might easily conclude that, given a Pentecostal predisposition to at least a tacit Spirit theology, such occurrences should be expected if not desired. However, from a Canadian Pentecostal perspective, even if walking requires one foot in the air at all times there is no need to attract undue attention. In the end the so-called revival fizzled out – as perhaps all must do under the weight of their own pretensions – but not before dividing many Pentecostal churches. Even Pentecostals have their limits concerning how much spiritual enthusiasm is necessary or orthodox.

Almost fifty years later, Canada again garnished international attention hosting yet another Pentecostal romp into latter rains. This time in the city of Toronto, a small church affiliated with the Vineyard movement, a charismatic offshoot of Pentecostalism, became home to a spiritual renewal that has been affectionately dubbed the Toronto Blessing (see chapter 11 in this volume). Between the years 1992 and 1997[47] the Toronto Airport Christian Fellowship (TACF) Church became host to tens of thousands of people in search of a taste of transcendence. In the course of a service, participants could be seen exhibiting what appeared to be random acts of laughter, groaning, shaking, and on occasion barking like dogs. They could be sitting, standing, staggering as if they had too much to drink, or lying prostrate on the floor. With international attention it was not long before the nightly meetings attracted the media. Appearing on the Phil Donahue show, convert Janis Chevreau testified: "I was on the floor, and that began the laughter for about four hours ... There was an intense – I would describe it as joyfulness. I will just briefly tell you I'm a very uptight person. I'm not someone who has a lot of fun as a rule. I'm very serious about life, I saw the heavy side of it ... And to see me there (in that state of Spirit drunkenness) was absolutely a miracle in itself. But yeah, it's such an intimate time of having fun ... I would go home and literally that first night, there was such a joy that came over me. Our circumstances hadn't changed – and there were some hard circumstances we were in – I had a lot of pain, but it lifted right off. And I walked around for months with it lifted."[48] Chevreau's testimony was by no means isolated. As research for his book *Divine Hunger*, Peter Emberley, a professor of political science at Carleton University,

heard a familiar refrain when he asked participants at TACF, why are
you here? Respondents answered, "to be ravished; to be drunk in the
Holy Spirit"; "God's drawing me out of myself – like a meat grinder";
"Like a drug high, we are getting high on the Holy Spirit, It's like
never-ending intoxication."[49] Advocates likened such histrionics to
God's advertising signs. While the physical manifestations may not
have been an end in themselves, for some they were sacramental in that
they pointed to God's presence among them.

During the height of such activity, I was teaching at a prominent Pentecostal Bible college in the pastoral setting of Peterborough, Ontario, a
mere one and a half hour drive from TACF. Nightly carloads of students
from the college made the trek to Toronto, some in search of a "Pentecostal" experience, some out of desperate need, and some as simple
voyeurs. Reaction among students was mixed. Some were genuinely
touched as they expressed a new-found peace and/or freedom. Others
reaffirmed their commitment to enter into full-time pastoral ministry of
one kind or another. Yet for every student who testified that the spiritual exuberance witnessed at TACF was a blessing, others testified that it
was nothing more than a misguided maudlin exhibition that had more
to do with human desire on a shopping expedition in search of ecstatic
experience than with the work of the Holy Spirit. It was frequently
noted that if the experiences had a personal transformative component,
this did not spill over into social or civil change. In fact, the opposite
was frequently the case as the experientially elated often returned home
to a lukewarm reception, with friction and polarization between the
have's and have not's. In either case, a proverbial line in the sand was
drawn with people standing firm on each side of the debate.[50]

A LONG AND WINDING ROAD

Limning a Pentecostal spirituality is a difficult task. Indeed, even a
casual reading of Pentecostal history both in Canada and abroad
reveals a spotty past of internal squabbles and elitist triumphalism, all
unctuously defended in the name of Spirit freedom. Within the Canadian experience this has led to various corrective attempts to repristi-
nate the repristination. In Canada both the Latter Rain movement of
1948 and the recent Toronto Blessing stand in a perpetual line of
attempts at kick-starting the ethos of Azusa Street once again. Never
mind that the look and shape of each of these events is different and in
all probability has little in common with the early church.

As disingenuous as attempts have been to relate these various spiritual outbursts back to the second chapter of the book of Acts, they have nonetheless kept alive the "what meaneth this?" response of those early onlookers on the Day of Pentecost as they too wrestled with machinations of the Holy Spirit. To employ a metonym of my own, Canadian Pentecostals are *walkers*. Theirs is a walk that is coloured by the landscape and culture where they find themselves. At times it is brisk, with definite destinations in mind for the transformation of self and the world. At other times it slows to a crawl as adherents are simply trying to keep their blood flowing, and sometimes it is just plain silly. It is a walk that is easily distracted, as subscribers often venture off-road, to get away alone, to witness an aberration up close, or just for the thrill of the journey. And it is a walk with only provisional ends in sight. Even the Promised Land turns out to be just another walk. Along the path Pentecostals continue to stumble, get lost, argue over which path they should take, complain about the pacesetters, and debate the significance of the signs they discover along the road. Some would prefer to stay on the road and others pine for the chance to explore, but in the end it is just a walk with one foot in front of the other, with one foot in the air and one foot on the ground at all times.

NOTES

1 Wilkins, *Walk to New York*, 173–4.
2 *Oxford Reference English Dictionary*.
3 In 1999 the cover story of *Business Week* was dedicated to the growing practice of a secular spirituality in the workplace. Major companies are hiring urban shamans, chaplains, and other spiritual consultants in an effort to address employee well-being, better working conditions, and increased sales production. Conlin, "Religion in the Workplace," http://www.northernway.org/workplace.html (date accessed: 1 June 2005).
4 Spittler, "Spirituality, Pentecostal and Charismatic," 1097–1102.
5 There are many exceptions to this rule. While the Renaissance went a long way in advancing natural sciences, religious mystics, revivalists, and other groups living on the fringe maintained their presence as separate entities.
6 Known to historians as the Azusa Street Revival and the cradle of modern Pentecostalism, the revival was led by a self-taught Black man by the name of William Seymour and reached its apex during the years 1906–08. See Hollenweger, *Pentecostal Origins*.

7 See Anderson, *Vision of the Disinherited*.

8 Small, *Living Waters*, 82.

9 What follows is a personal reflection on the spiritual ethos of these thoroughly modern Pentecostals. In particular it will focus on one particular tradition within Pentecostalism, namely the Pentecostal Assemblies of Canada (PAOC). In part these reflections are those of an insider who was raised in a Pentecostal setting, completed undergraduate studies at a Pentecostal Bible College, and pastored Pentecostal churches. In part these reflections are as an outsider who completed graduate studies in a Roman Catholic university, who pastored a Presbyterian church, and is presently an Associate Professor in a non-denominational college. And in part this represents my personal *Walk in the Spring Rain* as I continue to stumble through my own search for spiritual connectedness.

10 It has been my experience that rank-and-file Pentecostals have no trouble in linking the stiff-necked Pharisees who were forever resisting the Holy Spirit of Acts 7 with the work of Pentecostal academia or otherwise. This is not to say that Pentecostals are not anti-knowledge. Knowledge is, after all, one of the gifts of the Spirit mentioned in Paul's letter to the Corinthians. Such knowledge, however, is understood to be of a supernatural nature that is revealed to an individual for specific uses. Presumably a spiritual person has access to such knowledge, but it is not acquired through extensive study; rather it is the product of prayer and yielding to the voice of the Holy Spirit.

11 Ewart, *The Phenomenon of Pentecost*, 9.

12 Although the noun construct "baptism in the Spirit" does not appear in New Testament literature, Pentecostals have drawn on various approximate phrases such as "baptizes with the Holy Spirit (John 1:33), "will baptize with the Holy Spirit" (Matthew 3:11; Mark 1:8; Luke 3:16), "will be baptized with the Holy Spirit" (Acts 1:5; 11:16) and "have been baptized in one Spirit" (1 Corinthians 12:13) to separate the Spirit's soteriological function from its vocational purpose and conclude that the latter effect is a second or in some cases a third work of grace on the part of the Spirit.

13 It is estimated that by the year 2005 global affiliated Pentecostals will number over 811million people. Burgess and van der Mass, *The New International Dictionary of Pentecostal and Charismatic Movements*, 287.

14 D. Wesley Myland, in a series of lectures, provided us a classic explanation for this concept. "If it is remembered that the climate of Palestine consisted of two seasons, the wet and the dry, and that the wet season was made up of the early and the latter rain, it will help you to understand this Covenant and the present workings of God's Spirit. For just as the literal early and latter rain

was poured out upon Palestine, so upon the church of the First Century was poured out the spiritual early rain, and upon us today is being poured out the spiritual latter rain." See "The Latter Rain Covenant and Pentecostal Power," in *Three Early Pentecostal Tracts*, 1.

15 Bartleman, "How Pentecost came to Los Angeles," 160.

16 Dayton, *Witness to Pentecost*, 59.

17 Ibid., 58.

18 Ibid.

19 Wacker, *Heaven Below*, 103–4.

20 In a comparative study between Black Power and early Pentecostalism, sociologists Gerlach and Hine concluded that both were movements of social transformation. See *People, Power and Change*.

21 From a sociological perspective such qualifications became essential in perpetuating the ethos of Pentecostalism. Theologically, however, the irony of assisting the Holy Spirit with such measures went largely unnoticed.

22 Early on, this evidence also became a requirement for ministerial credentials. Neither men nor women could be ordained into ministry if they could not state with assurance that they had been baptized in the Spirit with the evidence of speaking in tongues. As a young student attending a Pentecostal Bible college, I remember the angst-filled prayer rooms of earnest men and women seeking the gift of tongues in an earnest effort to qualify for Pentecostal ministry. One could not help but wonder what such spiritual gymnastics actually produced at the end of the day.

23 Following the work of Edmund Leach, Poewe defines metonymy in Pentecostal process as sign, index, and signal, where "A can stand for and indicate B while B is seen to cause A." See "Rethinking the Relationship of Anthropology to Science and Religion," 245 in *Charismatic Christianity*. In this case speaking tongues stands as evidence of the presence of the Holy Spirit while the Spirit is said to be the source of tongues.

24 Spittler, "Spirituality, Pentecostal and Charismatic."

25 Cox, *Fire from Heaven*, 82–3

26 Ibid., 81.

27 Land, *Pentecostal Spirituality*, 23.

28 "The Apostolic Faith" in Corum, *Like as of Fire*.

29 Ibid., 49.

30 Corum, *Like as of Fire*, 52.

31 In the US, the largest such denomination is the Assemblies of God and in Canada it is the Pentecostal Assemblies of Canada. They work as sister organizations freely transferring credentialed pastors to each other.

32 On 12 April 1980 Terry Fox began a one-legged "Marathon of Hope" as he
   hopped and skipped forty-two kilometres a day until his own cancer forced
   him to give up his journey near midpoint at Thunderbay, Ontario.

33 The Quiet Revolution is the name given a transformation in the province of
   Quebec during the 1960s where the Roman Catholic cultural synthesis virtually vanished as the church lost control of education and economic influence.

34 Cynics would suggest our present preference for diplomacy is due to the fact
   that the resources of our military force are too depleted to act as a deterrent.
   However, it must also reflect the fact that Canadians do not rate military
   power as a high priority in which they wish to invest their resources.

35 Since 2002 the PAOC mission department has begun to change its policies to
   reflect a modified American model. Missionaries are now required to raise
   their own support using what the PAOC calls a shared funding formula. Missionaries must find their own support, while the national office provides bud-
   getary assistance. It makes one wonder what exactly constitutes the sharing
   since missionaries are required to raise all their support. Time will tell if this
   new approach will survive given a Canadian perception of fairness.

36 There are exceptions to this rule, and by today's standards one might question the extent of some of their theological training, but nonetheless it is a
   factor that is often overlooked in the beginnings of Pentecostalism in Canada.
   Chief among those denominations that produced these early Pentecostal leaders were Mennonite Brethren in Christ and Christian Missionary Alliance. See
   Rudd, *When the Spirit Came Upon Them.*

37 D.N. Buntain, who served as the General Superintendent of the PAOC
   1937–44, was also the editor of the *Pentecostal Testimony.* Reflecting the
   mood of his day, he wrote, "The wife's real success is in the success of her
   husband." See "Marriage Misfits," *Pentecostal Testimony* (June 1954), 4.
   "How sad is the condition of that woman who, giving home, husband and
   children second place in her life, believes that she should be in the gaze of
   human eyes, leading and directing spiritual destiny to others, to the neglect of
   her home, and when it is too late to decide aright she finds herself alone, with
   only memories of that which she lost through her mistaken choice. She cast
   aside her veil and the sweetness of public applause, lost home and children in
   taking the wrong course and neglecting her first duty." See "Should Women
   Preach?" *Pentecostal Testimony* (1 Mar. 1939).

38 Buntain would have been surprised or even shocked had someone accused
   him of either chauvinism or discrimination. He was very sincere in attributing
   to women the "grander sphere." Writes Buntain, "In Christian lands women
   have realized what Christ has done for them, and have always been at the
   forefront ready to help in every Holy Ghost-led effort. Go into any congrega-

tion throughout the land and you will find women in the majority. Survey the Sunday Schools of any Christian land, and you will find the majority of the teachers are women. They are more open and responsive to the moving of the Spirit than men. Men have their part, but to woman as queen of the home and mother of the children, God gives an intuition, touch and power which men can never know. With Christ in control she becomes God's greatest agency in all the world." *Pentecostal Testimony* (1 Oct. 1944), 2.

39 For more information on the march toward ordination of women within the Pentecostal Assemblies of Canada see Holm, PhD diss., (Laval University, 1995). http://members.shaw.ca/rfholm/chapter7a.html (date accessed: 1 January 2005).

40 This was later changed during the General Conference in 1996. Presently the title ordination now grants women the same rights and privileges as their male counterparts in the PAOC – at least in theory.

41 In Pentecostal parlance, women were generally said to share a message while men preached a message.

42 One gifted and earnest spiritual leader within the PAOC who was wrestling with the concept of woman's ordination confided to me that he had no difficulty with women as spiritual leaders who could preach and teach as they were directed by the Spirit. But he did struggle with the notion of a woman pastor who would also be a fiscal advisor over a church. Business was better left to men as God directed. And so in 1984 women were finally ordained.

43 In fairness, these Pentecostal leaders sincerely believed these "social norms" were supported and enforced by the Bible. They would have difficulty accepting the fact that the Bible itself was written within a temporal social context. The irony lay with a Holy Spirit that could move mountains but was restricted as to what mountains it could move.

44 Since the motif "Latter Rain" was also prominently used fifty years earlier to describe the Azusa Street revival, this later version could be described as the Latter Latter Rain.

45 As quoted by Riss, *A Survey of 20th-Century Revival Movements in North America*, 115.

46 As quoted by Miller, *Canadian Pentecostals*, 263.

47 While it is generally recognized that TACF has returned to the normal ebb and flow of a regular church status, it is still a thriving assembly with scheduled meetings every night of the week except Monday. They include revival meetings and on Tuesday night what is called a "soaking meeting." "Soaking is intimate time spent with Jesus. It's you and I enjoying just being with Him. It's about returning to our first love ... From the beginning of the outpouring of the Holy Spirit at (TACF), John and Carol Arnott found that one significant

way of welcoming Him was by 'soaking' or resting in His presence. After ministering to the people who were flooding to the meetings, John and Carol would spend hours every night – up to 3am or 4 am – just lying on the church floor 'soaking' up the presence of the Holy Spirit. It is a practice they continue today, and one that is becoming more widespread." Their website can be found at http://www.tacf.org

48 As quoted by Poloma, "The 'Toronto Blessing' in Postmodern Society," 376.

49 Emberley, *Divine Hunger*, 42–9.

50 As for me, I deliberately chose not to attend. Given the emotion generated, it seemed wiser to weigh in from the outside without having to pick a side.

PART TWO

Aspects of the Canadian Pentecostal Experience

5

Pentecostal Theological Education: A Case Study of Western Bible College, 1925–50

BRUCE L. GUENTHER

INTRODUCTION

The charter creating the Pentecostal Assemblies of Canada (PAOC) in 1919 endowed the new corporate body with all the rights and powers for the following purposes and objectives: "a) to conduct a place of worship; b) to organize and conduct schools of religious instruction (colleges); and c) to carry on missionary work for the spread of the gospel and all such other operations pertaining to a regular denomination, such as the Church of England or Presbyterian Church of Canada."[1] Although the desire to establish a Bible school was evident among PAOC leaders as early as 1921,[2] it was not until 1923 that plans were approved by the Eastern District Conference to set up a series of "Itinerary [sic] Bible Schools in Eastern Canada."[3] These plans never came to fruition, although at least three other attempts were made during the early 1920s to establish Pentecostal Bible schools in different parts of the country. These short-lived attempts signalled the growing interest among Pentecostal young people and leaders in having a Bible school that was located in Canada. A number of young leaders had already begun attending schools in the US, but many others who expressed interest did not have the resources to do so. In August 1925 the General Conference of the PAOC met in Winnipeg; here it was agreed that a long-term "orthodox place of training to prepare candidates for Christian Ministry should be organized."[4]

Although it was agreed that this school should be located in Winnipeg, the understanding was that it would be only temporary until both

Eastern and Western Districts could set up their own regional schools. James Eustace Purdie (1880–1977) was appointed principal. Purdie knew nothing of the appointment at the time on account of his involvement in evangelistic and Bible conference work in Prince Edward Island.[5] Thus begins the story of Western Bible College (WBC), a story that offers a unique glimpse into the internal dynamics of a fledgling religious group struggling to establish itself in Canada.[6]

This chapter will examine the contribution of WBC to the development of the PAOC, a denomination that quickly became the largest and most prominent Pentecostal group in Canada. The school, along with six regional institutions that were subsequently patterned after WBC, played a significant part in training and deploying indigenous leaders, thereby facilitating the development of the denomination and its aggressive expansion across Canada during the twentieth century. The school functioned like a national theological training centre helping meet the needs of a denomination that was struggling both to design a workable organizational structure and to respond to internal anti-intellectual tendencies. Leaders within the school not only vigorously promoted missions and evangelism but also offered a more moderate theology that tempered some of the more extreme tendencies within the young Pentecostal movement. This extends into Canada Douglas Jacobsen's observation that the years 1930 to 1955 form a distinct period in the history of Pentecostal theology, an age of Pentecostal scholasticism characterized by logical organization and systematic completeness that sought to temper "the more radical claims of the movement's founders and to reframe the distinctive beliefs of Pentecostals in light of their compatibility with and place in the longer, larger, and broader 'catholic' Christian tradition."[7] Despite affinities, and some contact, with the larger world of fundamentalism, the school became a centre of influence within a Pentecostal religious world that was often isolated from other evangelical Protestants. The theological education and interdenominational ministry experience of some of the leading faculty at WBC helped lay the foundation for more open and co-operative relationships with other evangelical Protestants after 1960.

ORIGINS OF WESTERN BIBLE COLLEGE

The school was first known as Central Canadian Bible Institute; it opened on 16 November 1925 in the basement of Wesley Pentecostal

Church (later known as Calvary Temple) with an enrolment of thirty-two students. Its location in the booming metropolis of Winnipeg made the college equally accessible to students from Eastern and Western Canada. As the gateway to Western Canada, Winnipeg was, at the time, the third largest city in Canada and the most important metropolitan centre west of Toronto, with thousands of immigrants travelling through the city. The evangelistic ministry of the Argue family and their influence in establishing Calvary Temple, a congregation that served as a model for many other Pentecostal assemblies, helped make Winnipeg an important centre for Pentecostal evangelism and discipleship. Although the Pentecostal movement spread throughout many rural parts of the country, the focal points for the movement were cities.[8] Urban locations made the Pentecostal movement accessible to a greater number of travelling evangelists and missionary speakers. The urban location of the Bible schools enhanced the role played by urban congregations as strategic centres of influence.

The express purpose of the new school, as outlined in one of its first brochures, was "to train men and women for pastoral, evangelistic and missionary work at home and abroad."[9] The first three faculty members were Purdie, Kathleen I. Reid, and Daniel Newton Buntain, pastor of Wesley Pentecostal Church. Students were housed in several nearby residential buildings. Within two years the name was changed to Canadian Pentecostal Bible College. With the prospect of a student body of close to one hundred for the fall term of 1927, the school recognized that it had outgrown the basement of the church. It therefore purchased St George's Anglican Church and used this facility as well as Wesley Pentecostal Church. For the next several years, enrolment was consistently around 125. The school quickly established international connections; by 1928 enrolment had increased to more than 130 students, many of whom came from across Canada, the British Isles, and the US.[10]

The school temporarily closed its doors in 1930 so that it could relocate to Toronto, and its buildings in Winnipeg were sold. It was moved because the General Conference believed that Toronto was a more strategic location, closer to the larger PAOC population in the Eastern district (Ontario and Quebec). Here it operated for only two years before the effects of the Great Depression, the enrolment of a relatively small student body, and some tension between Purdie and A.G. Ward, R.E. McAlister, and G.A. Chambers, brought Canadian Pentecostal Bible College to a close once again.[11]

Meanwhile, with the sudden departure of the school from Winnipeg, students from Western Canada complained about the cost of annual travel to and from Toronto. As a result, a second Pentecostal college was started in 1931 called Western Bible College. It was led by Henry C. Sweet and once again used the basement of Wesley Pentecostal Church. When Canadian Pentecostal Bible College closed in 1932, Purdie returned to Winnipeg to become the principal of WBC, bringing with him the second- and third-year students from Toronto.[12]

The two ventures in Winnipeg, both of which were led by Purdie, represent the PAOC entry into the Bible school movement (hereafter WBC will be used to refer to both initiatives). Although leaders within the fledgling denomination were divided over the question of whether specialized training was necessary for ministers, it did not take long for the denomination to designate the school as its national school for training pastors. Despite the fact that it was operational for only twenty-five years until 1950, PAOC leaders are unanimous in identifying the school as the most influential Pentecostal institution in Canada in the first half of the twentieth century. It produced more than 500 graduates during its twenty-five years of operation.

As noted above, an important feature in the life and influence of WBC was its close relationship with Wesley Pentecostal Church.[13] The church was much more than simply the physical location of the school. It served as a giant object lesson for the Bible school students. The relationship with Calvary Temple enhanced the school's role as the "national" Bible school. The benefits were reciprocal: the energy and abilities of students and faculty supplied personnel for the various church ministries. As for most other Bible schools, providing opportunities for gaining practical experience in ministry was a priority, and the dynamic environment of Calvary Temple offered a perfect context for this. Students were involved in teaching Sunday school, engaging in various music ministries, preparing radio broadcasts, and taking a variety of roles in church services. Here they saw a vibrant and enthusiastic Pentecostalism in action. Involvement by young prospective ministerial candidates helped shape Pentecostal ministry in other urban contexts across the country.

Moreover, access to a large nearby facility and to music and radio equipment minimized capital costs for the school. Many church staff had faculty roles: Buntain taught at WBC prior to its move to Toronto; starting in 1937, Watson Argue, as well as his assistant Robert Sistig, both taught courses. WBC continued using the facilities of Calvary Temple until 1947 when the school moved into its own building just a few doors west of the church.

WBC officially closed its doors in 1950. The closure was precipitated by Purdie's resignation as principal as he wished to devote more time to itinerant preaching and teaching. During the 1940s student enrolments at WBC were consistently lower than they had been during the depression years of the 1930s. In part this was due to the absence of men, who were involved in the war effort; WBC enrolments did increase for several years following the war on account of returning war veterans, but by the end of the 1940s student numbers were once again in decline. Exacerbating the situation was the increased competition for prospective students on the part of newly organized regional schools.[14] By the end of the 1940s enrolment in some of the district schools was actually higher than at the Winnipeg school. Finding suitable accommodation was often a problem for students attending WBC; by the late 1940s, several of the regional schools had either built dormitories or converted buildings into student "hostels," making them a more attractive option. The Board of Governors, along with leaders of the Manitoba District of the PAOC, decided to merge the school with Bethel Bible Institute in Saskatoon. Pentecostals in Manitoba objected and wanted the college to remain in Winnipeg, but because a residential school model was preferred, and because the school in Saskatoon already owned a dormitory, WBC was moved to Saskatoon.[15]

AMBIVALENCE TOWARD FORMAL THEOLOGICAL EDUCATION

Despite the theological education acquired by many of the leaders involved in the early Pentecostal movement, they found themselves working with others who preferred a simple emphasis on the major Biblical "truths" along with a rather unsophisticated approach toward theology. Not everyone within the PAOC agreed that Bible schools were a good idea. Leaders were divided about the need for Bible schools and over the question of whether specialized training was necessary for ministers. Those opposed argued that the Holy Spirit would provide leaders with all the necessary resources; it is, after all, "God who makes preachers."[16] Like institutional structures, education was seen as a "manmade" innovation that hindered the leading of the Holy Spirit. Another common objection was based on the conclusion that the churches that had "lost out to God" had done so, at least in part, because their clergy had been "educated out of spirituality into deadness." The apostle Paul's words in 2 Corinthians 3:6 ("the letter kills but the Spirit gives life"), and Paul's presumed denigration of human wisdom in 1 Corinthians were regularly used to insinuate that theological education would inevitably result in such "deadness."[17] Still others who opposed Bible schools took a slightly different tack. The urgency of being involved in evangelism before the imminent return of Jesus Christ led some to question whether spending the time and money to go to Bible school was not in effect a waste.

Debates over the necessity of Bible school training were most intense during the first several decades following the formation of the PAOC, although a suspicion of higher education continued to linger for most of the twentieth century. The experience of Egbert S. Berry, a graduate in 1933, was commonplace. "On my way to College," he writes, "a Minister of the Gospel tried to dissuade me from my course. He believed that the only school necessary was that of experience. Looking over the years of my ministry, I have come to the conclusion that this would have been one of the biggest mistakes in my life. Because of the fundamental and Scriptural teaching received in the College, I have been spared many sorrows and escaped many pitfalls which come to the unlearned worker."[18]

Purdie, along with other PAOC leaders, regularly defended the validity and necessity of formal training. His articles generally exhibited a considerable degree of tactfulness and restraint, but occasionally a more vigorous directness is evident. For example, in 1939 Purdie wrote,

> The history of the Church proves that the majority of ministers who were most spiritual and most used in the salvation of souls were those who had tremendous doctrinal and theological convictions on the great verities of Christianity. Applying the foregoing to the present day evangelistic groups, we discover many colourless preachers who are earnest, but who have "a zeal without knowledge." ... Because they lack the true understanding of what they believe, their congregations suffer. The understanding of the truth in all its various angles not only makes us spiritually and intelligently free, but also provides the ground for true and pure thinking ... If we would stem the tide of Traditionalism, Rationalism and Mysticism, it behooves the Minister to be thoroughly prepared for his work. Hence the value of the Schools of the Prophets in the old Hebrew

days, and the Christian Colleges of training which have existed from early times.[19]

Many of those who rose to positions of prominent leadership in the denomination had the benefit of theological education prior to joining the Pentecostal movement and, as a result, recognized the long-term impact of a school devoted to the training of leaders in shaping the ethos and direction of a denomination. They saw the school as a necessary means for preserving and propagating their distinctive Pentecostal theology and as the means for moderating and stabilizing a tendency toward an excessive subjectivity and anti-intellectualism. The attitude on the part of denominational leaders vacillated between wariness and support. In an interview, Purdie describes the process by which support for theological education gradually prevailed:

> The ministers and people in the early history of the Pentecostal church were so preoccupied with the salvation of souls and the building up of the household of faith, together with days and nights of prayer, that with great victories in the spiritual realm they had not become conscious for a considerable time of higher education ... The Pentecostal church ... amid all the revivals ... [was] cautious as to how far she should go in exalting the intellectual ... This church was not opposed to any ministers of other churches that had intellectual attainments in higher education and degrees, as long as these men and women adhered to the Bible as the highest authority, and were in themselves real believers according to the New Testament, and essentially evangelical ... Pentecostals were not opposed to education when it was sound and true to the great theological settlement of the reformation ... Therefore they gradually saw the need of Bible colleges.[20]

On the occasion of WBC's twentieth anniversary in 1945, Purdie confidently asserted "that the discipline of sound study, which is so imperative for young men and women to have in these days of superficiality, together with our emphasis upon a life of prayer and devotion to the Lord Jesus Christ, has contributed much to the ministry of those that once sat in our lecture halls."[21] As the number of graduates increased, and as college-trained ministers and church workers spread across the country, assuming leadership positions within the denomination, the resistance toward education and Bible schools waned. The development of six additional regional schools by the PAOC during the late 1930s and 1940s confirmed the progress made in this direction.

THE THEOLOGICAL INFLUENCE OF WESTERN BIBLE COLLEGE'S CURRICULUM

Looking back some twenty years after WBC was started, Purdie identifies the two observations that prompted the unique design of the school's curriculum: "First, that while in the best and most evangelical Theological Colleges and Seminaries of that day, strong emphasis was laid upon the Bible as the infallible word of God, yet the student was not sufficiently familiarized with the actual content of the Holy Scriptures themselves; secondly, that while in the best Bible Schools on our continent, there were very good courses on the Bible itself, yet there was a lack of instruction in real Systematic Theology as taught in the best Seminaries. For these two reasons we drew up a course in which both elements of instruction are well-balanced."[22]

The curriculum was patterned after that of Wycliffe College, an Anglican Church of Canada seminary in Toronto, which was familiar to Purdie, and was recommended by Purdie as an internationally recognized "institution of high scholastic standing and of sound evangelical teaching balanced with real spirituality."[23] In addition to balancing systematic theology and biblical studies, efforts were made to balance "the deeper doctrinal, theological and historical subjects ... with the more practical such as Public Speaking, Pastoralia, Evangelism."[24] Courses were organized into four "fields" of study: theology, biblical studies, history, and practical theology. Throughout the history of the school, the area of theology remained almost exclusively the domain of J.E. Purdie. These four categories were expanded during the 1940s to include religious education, languages (Greek, Ukrainian, Hebrew, and Spanish),[25] and "the University Field of Opportunity," an option available to students who had attained "the required academic standing" (at least grade 12).

While the course of study at WBC was demanding by Bible school standards of the day, Purdie exaggerated the curricular superiority of the school when he described the academic program as "practically a Seminary Curriculum and of course very superior to the Bible Schools whose courses are mostly non-theological in character."[26] It was a program operating in makeshift facilities, without adequate textbooks, and with limited library resources. The tenuous financial situation of the college made it impossible to address these deficiencies.

The impact of the curriculum cannot be understood apart from the more general theological ethos among Pentecostals, which strongly emphasized dispensational premillenialism, prioritized evangelism and missions as the primary mandate of the church, and undergirded these two with an uncritical and sometimes even naïve approach toward the Bible and theology. Central to Pentecostal theological education was "the Book," the Bible, in which could be found inspiration and authority (and innumerable proof-texts). Human interpretations and opinions, that is, theology, were always to be regarded as secondary in importance to the Bible. To understand the Bible properly, students were instructed to read the Bible "prayerfully," not relying on "natural" reason for understanding.[27]

The missionary emphasis within the school was rooted in an evangelical conviction concerning the absolute necessity of the sinner's individual experience of salvation. "The propagation of the Gospel" was considered "the most noble cause of all."[28] Although D.N. Buntain affirmed that "every field in life is honourable," he simultaneously asserted, "there is no greater work among men than the training of leaders to go forth in full-time service as missionaries, evangelists, pastors and deaconesses."[29] The missionary emphasis was given a considerable degree of urgency by the belief in the imminent return of Jesus Christ and the belief that unrepentant sinners were destined for an eternal lake of fire. Current events, particularly prior to and during World War II, provided an abundance of signs indicating the imminent return of Christ. Theological debate faded into insignificance when compared to the urgency of evangelism and missions. Students met weekly to pray for, and learn about, the evangelistic needs of regions around the world. In 1945, a local chapter of the Foreign Missions Fellowship was organized among the students.

In addition to their studies, all students were involved in a myriad of activities designed to give them some practical experience in ministry. Students were expected to experience personally prayer, preaching, and evangelism. Each day began with a short, early morning chapel service. These services offered students the opportunity to practice leading services and speaking in public. One day a month was set aside for fasting and prayer. Each student was assigned to a specific ministry that included various evangelistic, children's, and youth activities at Calvary Temple, visiting hospitals and nursing homes, assisting at various

Pentecostal missions and churches in the Winnipeg area, and visiting house-to-house. The primary focus underlying all these activities was evangelism.

THE ROLE AND INFLUENCE OF FACULTY

Some of the most striking features of the faculty at WBC were the diversity of their denominational backgrounds prior to joining the Pentecostal movement, their extensive experience in professional ministry, and their relatively high level of academic qualifications. The experience and credentials of these diverse faculty members illustrate the ecumenical spirit that was present within the early Pentecostal movement. All were deeply committed to the project of designing and delivering a program of theological education to the Pentecostal movement. Their level of education was not typical of the majority of Pentecostals in the pew, or for that matter, of the majority of people in Canada. These individuals promoted a more moderate and less "sectarian" Pentecostalism, minimizing some of the anti-intellectual impulses within the PAOC more quickly than was possible in other Pentecostal groups such as the Apostolic Church of Pentecost. Their experience and education contributed to their success in establishing an institution for the training of ministers and church workers as early as 1925.

As was the case generally in the Bible school movement, the personalities and influence of several charismatic individuals shaped the unique ethos and direction of the institution. Although approximately fifty people were faculty or special lecturers at one time or another, this section will highlight the life and credentials of several who contributed most to shaping the ethos of the school. Unlike other denominational schools, to which faculty generally brought years of denominational familiarity and ministry experience, WBC was unique in serving a denomination that was less than a decade old. It is, therefore, helpful to examine the diversity of backgrounds that came together among the faculty of this school to create a tradition of theological education for the newly forged PAOC.[30]

After WBC ceased to exist in 1950, the former general superintendent (and co-founder of the school with Purdie), D.N. Buntain, remarked: "Knowing the movement as I do, I can say that Western Bible College under Dr. Purdie has done more to mould the character and shape the destiny of our movement than any other thing."[31] Accolades for Purdie abound,[32] and he has been dubbed the "Father of Canadian Pentecostal

Colleges." Purdie's role in shaping wbc in particular, and Pentecostal theological education in Canada in general during the first half of the twentieth century, can hardly be overstated.[33]

Purdie was born in Charlottetown, Prince Edward Island in 1880.[34] His parents were members of a low-church Anglican parish (St Paul's, Charlottetown) through which he was converted in 1899. Shortly after this experience he became a zealous lay worker in the Anglican church.[35] In 1902, Purdie began studies at the University of Toronto and Wycliffe College. He was ordained in 1906, and a year later graduated with a bd from Wycliffe. In 1909 he married Frances Emma Morrison whom he had met when she was a student at Wycliffe. They frequently worked closely together in public ministry. Her active role alongside her husband at wbc was formalized in 1935 with the title "Assistant to the Principal."

He first came into contact with Pentecostalism in 1911 in New Brunswick, but it was not until 1919 while serving as the rector of St James's Anglican Church in Saskatoon that, according to Purdie, "the infilling of the Holy Spirit ... manifested Himself in me by tongues flowing from my lips."[36] After his Pentecostal experience he began to invite Pentecostal speakers to his parish to introduce his parishioners to the new movement.[37] One such speaker was the young Walter McAlister, who helped establish Pentecostalism in Saskatoon. In 1920, Purdie moved to the us for a short time where he acquired more experience in revival ministry by assisting the fundamentalist Reuben A. Torrey. He thereafter used revivalist terminology and methods in his own services.

Purdie was respected and trusted by many leaders both within Pentecostal circles and within the broader evangelical world. He came to be regarded as one of the leading theologians within the young Pentecostal movement; as such, he was ideally suited to lead initiatives in the area of theological education. Despite the endorsement of Purdie by the General Conference, convincing the entire denominational constituency of the value of a theological education was a battle that lasted most of Purdie's lifetime. In his view, *both* evangelistic and teaching ministries were outlined in the New Testament.

On the basis of his own theological education and his ministry experience, he outlined seven factors necessary for creating a successful "divinity college." These factors included a doctrinal statement based on the acceptance of the Bible as "the completely inspired Word of God"; a company of well-trained teachers who will teach the statement of faith to others; the best possible curriculum that should be "scholarly, comprehensive, orthodox, thoroughly evangelical in every point of doctrine and such as the student himself can intelligently grasp"; a saved, Spirit-led student body; prayer on the part of faculty and students; a missionary vision; and a library of good books.[38] As his students became leaders and missionary pioneers, Purdie's views concerning the necessity of theological training as the means to stabilize and guide the young movement were vindicated. In spite of the fact that he published relatively little, devoting himself instead to preparing lecture notes and extensive preaching, Purdie "has to be acknowledged as the primary figure in mediating theology to several generations of the Pentecostals."[39]

Despite his considerable abilities and achievements, several anomalies surround Purdie. His educational background, along with his own reading, gave his frequent emphasis on the need for "well-trained" faculty credibility. Because of his constant concern for defending the academic reputation of WBC, it is difficult to understand why he pursued arrangements with institutions that did not have a good academic reputation. Recognizing the correlation between academic credibility of an institution and the credentials of faculty, Purdie tried to ensure that all of his faculty were "lettered." Toward this end Purdie negotiated an arrangement with Central University (Indianapolis) so that WBC graduates with a high school diploma could, with no extra work, obtain a ThG (Graduate in Theology) degree. Virtually everyone on faculty during the mid–1940s who did not already have an academic degree was given a ThG (mischievously referred to as "thugs"). These arrangements did not produce the desired result; recipients of the ThG discovered later that very few other institutions were willing to recognize its validity. Although Purdie was given a DD *honoris causa* by the Reformed Episcopal Seminary (Philadelphia) in 1936, a year later he expressed a desire to obtain a PhD with minimal effort from Central University, the same institution from which he negotiated the infamous ThG degrees.[40] In view of the attitudes of some within the denomination toward higher education, and despite a General Conference Resolution in 1936 explicitly discouraging the use of titles such as reverend or doctor, it is difficult to understand Purdie's ongoing expectation that people address him as "Dr Purdie."[41] Although the ThG degrees did not bring the kind of academic respectability and recognition for which Purdie had hoped, he was nevertheless the first Bible school principal in Canada to even consider the possibility of negotiating transfer credit into a university degree program, a process that he initiated as early as

1937. The ThG's notwithstanding, the faculty were (generally speaking) more academically qualified than most within the Bible school movement. By the mid–1940s, approximately one-third of the faculty had both a bachelor's degree and an advanced degree in theology.

Purdie's influence extended well beyond the institutional walls of WBC and into the PAOC. As early as 1931, a National Bible School Committee was put in place "for the supervision of all Bible school matters, including the curriculum, and general policy of all Canadian Bible Schools" endorsed by the PAOC.[42] The Committee, made up of Purdie, Buntain, A.G. Ward, John McAlister, and J.W. McKillop, was formed in response to the emergence of a new Pentecostal school in Winnipeg in 1931, the temporary closure of Canadian Pentecostal Bible College in Toronto in 1932, and the subsequent merger of these two ventures. After having established a "national" school for training ministers, and having approved a course of studies along with a process for approving ministerial candidates, the prospect of additional schools that might dilute these standards prompted the General Conference to instruct this Committee to write and distribute a National Bible School policy that would ensure a level of consistency within all PAOC schools. The General Conference warned that any students attending a school that did not meet its standards would not be eligible for ministerial credentials within the PAOC.[43] Beginning in 1948, the committee was led by Purdie for almost a decade together with the principals of the other PAOC Bible schools.

Purdie's role as both a theologian and an educator within the denomination led to the request by the General Conference in 1951 that he prepare a catechism. *Concerning the Faith* contained 300 questions and answers to be used in the formal instruction of Pentecostals. It represented Purdie's attempt to demonstrate the consistency of Pentecostal ideas with the historic Christian creeds. Although his strongly held views concerning premillennialism stood at odds with the prevailing amillenialism among Anglicans, Purdie's Anglican roots are clearly evident and at times are in tension with the non-creedal, non-confessional approach toward doctrine that is common within Pentecostalism. In a movement predisposed toward Arminian theology, Purdie offered a more moderate Reformed theology.[44] Throughout his Pentecostal ministry, Purdie preferred to use the Keswick expression "infilling of the Holy Spirit" instead of the usual Pentecostal expression "baptism of the Holy Spirit."[45] In opposition to certain Holiness movement influences, he denied that this "infilling" of the Holy Spirit could be a second work of grace; it is instead given by God for power and liberty in service.[46] In his catechism, the Lord's Supper and baptism are "sacraments" rather than mere "ordinances."[47]

Purdie's influence also extended beyond Pentecostal boundaries. Throughout his life he maintained contact with other Anglicans; he never did relinquish his membership in the Anglican Church, or even his practice of wearing a clerical collar.[48] During his tenure at WBC, he continued to preach at numerous interdenominational ministerial associations across the country, seminaries, and conferences. After the closure of the school in 1950, Purdie continued an itinerant evangelistic and healing ministry that lasted well into the 1970s.

Another notable figure in the life of WBC was Henry Charles Sweet whose involvement enhanced the credibility of both the school and the wider Pentecostal movement. Invaluable were his contacts with a broad network of people and denominations. He taught at WBC at various times beginning in 1931 until its closure in 1950. Sweet's life and ministry were characterized by a truly remarkable ecumenical breadth, a love for learning, an ardent premillennialism, and lifelong success as an evangelist.[49]

Sweet's early childhood was spent in England where he was raised in the Bible Christian Church, which merged with the Methodist Church in 1886. His family immigrated to Manitoba when Henry was a young teenager. It was not until he was twenty-one that "he became sure of his regeneration by the Spirit of God."[50] As opportunities became available he conducted services in the Salvation Army and Baptist Church at Morden, Manitoba. Following his graduation from the University of Manitoba, where he obtained a BA in Moral and Mental Philosophy, he attended both Colgate Theological Seminary and Crozer Theological Seminary, where he earned a BD. He subsequently attended the Evangelical Theological Seminary (later known as Dallas Theological Seminary) and was awarded a ThD in 1928.

He was ordained by First Baptist Church in Chester, Pennsylvania in 1897 and until 1904 ministered in various Baptist churches across western Canada. In 1904 he joined the Presbyterians. His association with the Pentecostals began around 1914, during his time as the minister of a Union Church (made up of Presbyterians and Methodists) in Conquest, Saskatchewan. Within a year he became actively involved with the Pentecostals on a more frequent basis in Winnipeg. Conflict within the broader Pentecostal movement spilled over into the PAOC during the early 1920s; for at least a short time, Sweet was aligned with the new

Apostolic Church of Pentecost.[51] Why he did not remain with the Apostolic Church of Pentecost, and why he never officially joined the PAOC, is not clear. At about this time, Sweet started what turned out to be a three-decade relationship with Bethel African Methodist Episcopal Church, a Black church in Winnipeg.

In 1928 he joined the faculty of the fledgling, transdenominational Winnipeg Bible Institute. Sweet's tenure was short-lived; he was abruptly dismissed in 1930 after the Board drafted a policy requiring faculty to support their affirmation that "the school was not Pentecostal, that it was not in sympathy with Pentecostal demonstrations on its premises."[52] Within weeks Sweet, along with several of his students, formed the new WBC.[53] Within a year, Canadian Pentecostal Bible College in Toronto closed, and Purdie arrived back in Winnipeg. Purdie's insistence that he be the one to lead the Pentecostal school strained relations somewhat, but Sweet nevertheless continued to teach homiletics and New Testament courses at WBC. Despite his dismissal from Winnipeg Bible Institute, he continued to preach periodically at the independent Elim Chapel, the centre of a fundamentalist network in Winnipeg, during his time as a faculty member at WBC.[54]

Like Purdie, D.N. Buntain was born in Prince Edward Island. His family moved west, and after studying at both Brandon College in Manitoba and Wesley Methodist Theological College, he was ordained into the Methodist ministry.[55] During the early 1920s, Buntain's church joined the Pentecostal movement. Wesley Pentecostal Church not only became the birthplace for Canadian Pentecostal Bible College in 1925 but also became one of the eminent assemblies in the movement. Buntain became the general superintendent of the PAOC in 1937, a position he held until 1944. He then moved to Edmonton, Alberta where he became the pastor of Edmonton Tabernacle. In 1947, he again became involved in theological education by starting Canadian Northwest Bible Institute in Edmonton.

While Buntain was not as academically inclined as Purdie or Sweet, he helped them shape the ethos of the school (and the PAOC) in other ways. Kydd observes the significant social impact they had by helping the young movement relate to the larger society. All three were open to co-operation with other evangelical groups. In part, Buntain's efforts to keep the Pentecostal movement from being too narrowly parochial came from his experience as a Methodist when he served as secretary of the Ministerial Association in Winnipeg.[56] Although the student population, and the Pentecostal movement at large, was by no means a monolithic blue-collar group, students at WBC were expected to learn about social graces and etiquette, as well soteriology.[57] He encouraged Pentecostals to run for public office and convinced the denomination to respond to a League of Nations report by participating in an outcry against slavery in 1934. Like Purdie, he encouraged Pentecostals to overcome their fear of education and of Bible schools, but he did so on pragmatic grounds. "The world today with all its schools and books," he wrote, "has no place for an ignorant man. There was a time when it did not matter much whether a man had education or not, for nobody else had any. But it is different today. If we are going to capture the educated, cultured people, and lead them for God, we must be cultured, trained and fitted."[58]

More than most other evangelical Protestant groups in the first half of the twentieth century, the Pentecostals encouraged the participation of women in ministry. Although the denomination agreed that both women and men are called to prophesy and preach, they did not permit women to become "elders" in their congregations. Despite this restriction, a significant number of women, about 40 per cent of the faculty, taught at WBC.

One of the founding faculty members was Kathleen Reid, whom Purdie recruited in 1925. She had earned an MA from Edinburgh University and, as an Anglican missionary, had eleven years of teaching experience at a college in India. Gladys Lemmon abandoned her plans to pursue a teaching career after a miraculous healing from terminal lung cancer and instead became actively involved in the Pentecostal movement. She was one of the first students to enrol in Canadian Pentecostal Bible College in 1925, and one of the first to graduate, and was the valedictorian of the graduating class of 1928. After graduation she joined the faculty, a position she maintained for twenty-three years.[59] In addition to being the dean of women for several years, she taught New Testament, church history, and missions' courses and served as the national director for the denomination's Women's Missionary Council. Hanna (Mooney) Sweet, wife of H.C. Sweet, was an older sister of the well-known Canadian activist and suffragist Nellie McLung. Following a distinguished career in education, teaching in the public school system in Winnipeg from 1915 to 1937, she joined the WBC faculty on a part-time basis. Eleanor L. Siemens was on faculty from 1940–48. During this time she developed the area of Christian education, which included arranging formal affiliation with the Evangelical Teacher Training Association.

The composition of the faculty of WBC illustrates the diversity of denominational and educational backgrounds that was present within the early Pentecostal movement in Canada, and its ecumenical nature. This background made it possible for WBC to develop a curriculum that was, at least during the 1930s and early 1940s, more rigorous than most Bible schools in Canada. Furthermore, it enabled the school to challenge anti-intellectual tendencies within the denomination and to encourage the young group to build relationships with other denominations.

THE INFLUENCE OF WESTERN BIBLE COLLEGE WITHIN THE PAOC

Despite its inauspicious beginnings and meagre resources, WBC played an integral role as the PAOC's de facto national theological training school. The school was never an autonomous enterprise; it was an institution explicitly designed to serve the needs of a denomination that was struggling to draft a workable organizational structure and to deploy personnel for aggressive expansion. The school helped the young denomination develop indigenous leadership. The objectives of the school were to nurture Pentecostal youth in their faith and to train PAOC leaders, skilled in evangelism and expository preaching. The actions and activities, therefore, of alumni are important for understanding an institution's ongoing influence. A list included in the college newsletter, *The Gleaner,* identifies more than 335 alumni who were engaged in some form of professional ministry in 1950 (in total around 700 students attended the college).[60] It is safe to say that more than half the students who attended WBC did eventually get involved in professional ministry.[61]

The opportunity to study at WBC significantly reduced the number of prospective Pentecostal leaders studying in the US. In 1938, E.N.O. Kulbeck appealed to former students to support the newly formed Canadian Pentecostal Bible College-Western Bible College Alumni Association, warning that "of our young folks who go to the United States to study, of those who go into full-time work, it is doubtful if fifty percent of them will return to Canada."[62] Purdie had good reason for consistently reminding denominational leaders about the strategic importance of the Bible school ministry for the growth and development of the denomination: more than 70 per cent of alumni involved in professional ministry were active in Canada. Not surprisingly, in view of the emphasis on missions within the WBC environment, a significant proportion of those involved in professional ministry chose to go overseas as missionaries. By 1950 more than fifty of the school's alumni had entered missionary service in Africa, China, India, British West Indies, South America, Palestine, and Labrador. By 1971 this number had increased to seventy-eight who were serving in twenty different countries.[63]

What is perhaps more remarkable is the number of alumni who served as teachers within educational institutions. Some of the best students were encouraged to continue their theological studies. Several students – Gladys Lemmon, Earle Cairns, Alvin C. Schindel, L.T. Holdcroft, and J.C. Scott – were recruited almost immediately after graduation to teach at WBC. Although Lemmon stayed at WBC, the other four went on to assume positions of leadership in other schools. Former faculty members and graduates played a vital role in the six regional schools started during the late 1930s and 1940s. In 1950 about 8 per cent, or twenty-six people, were involved in teaching at a Bible school, college, or seminary. By 1971, Purdie estimated this number to have increased to around seventy – almost equal to the number of persons who had served as overseas missionaries.[64]

By the end of World War II, the number of Pentecostals in Canada had increased from approximately 500 in 1911 to over 57,000. The number of PAOC churches had grown to 300, with 190 ordained ministers and 52 missionaries. By 1960 membership had increased to over 142,000. Without the leadership personnel supplied by WBC and the regional Bible schools, the denomination would not have been able to sustain its remarkable rate of growth in Canada, nor its missionary activity around the globe.[65]

After a decade of having only one PAOC Bible school in Canada, other districts began to organize their own schools. As noted previously, WBC served as a model for these regional schools. In 1935 George R. Hawtin started the Saskatchewan Bible School for Pentecostal Workers in Star City. Within two years it was moved to Saskatoon where it became Bethel Bible Institute (in 1961 its name was changed to Central Pentecostal College).[66] In 1939 Ontario Pentecostal Bible School (later known as Eastern Pentecostal Bible College, and now called Master's College and Seminary and located in Toronto) was started.[67] Four more schools were started during the 1940s including a Bible school in Victoria in 1941. Originally located at the Glad Tidings Tabernacle, the British Columbia Bible Institute moved to North Vancouver in 1951. In 1962 this school was renamed Western Pentecostal Bible College, and in 1974 it moved to its present location in Abbotsford, British Columbia (it is now known as Summit Pacific College).[68] In 1941 the Institut Biblique Bérée was established in Montreal by Mme L. Bellemare of Montreal and W.L. Bouchard from Providence, Rhode Island. Although it was designed more as a school for training lay workers, its three-year French-language curriculum was nevertheless modelled after that used by their English-language counterparts. The Maritime Bible School, first located in Truro and then Halifax, started in 1944. It lasted only three years. Students were then encouraged to attend the school in Ontario. In 1946, D.N. Buntain was instrumental in starting Canadian Northwest Bible Institute (later known as Northwest Bible College, and now called Vanguard College) in the facilities of Central Tabernacle in Edmonton. After the closure of WBC in 1950, none of the other schools emerged to take over WBC's former role as the central, national school. Instead, each school focused, with remarkable success, on serving the needs of its own district.

More than a few of Purdie's graduates became involved in these regional schools. One informal estimate offered by the editorial committee that produced a history of Western Pentecostal Bible College suggested that seventeen of the school's personnel traced their academic background to Purdie's classroom.[69] When L.T. Holdcroft, a former student and teacher at WBC, became president of Western Pentecostal Bible College in 1968, the presidents of all four English-language PAOC Bible colleges were alumni of WBC, including Herbert Bronsden at Eastern Pentecostal Bible College, Alvin C. Schindel at Central Pentecostal College (Schindel had taught at both WBC and Eastern Pentecostal Bible College), and John Cooke at Northwest Bible College.

The influence of WBC was extended through the regional schools in other ways as well. The "Standard Curriculum" for all PAOC colleges was virtually a duplicate of the curriculum used at WBC with faculty often using mimeographed notes they had received at WBC.[70] Furthermore, a considerable number of the articles published in the *Pentecostal Testimony* during its first several decades of operation came from faculty and alumni of the school. WBC shaped the emerging ethos of the PAOC through the sermons and pastoral influence of its alumni, the publications and itinerant ministry of its faculty, and the role of alumni within regional Bible schools.

NOTES

1 Letter from J.E. Purdie to Col C.D. McPherson, 25 August 1943, Purdie Papers, Central Pentecostal College Archives (hereafter CPCA).

2 "Report of the General Conference," *Pentecostal Testimony* (November 1921).

3 Miller, *Canadian Pentecostals*, 202–3.

4 Purdie, "What God Hath Wrought: Historical Sketch of the College, 1925–1950," 2.

5 Ibid.

6 This article is condensed from a more extensive and detailed chapter in Guenther, "Training for Service," 221–67.

7 Jacobsen, "Knowing the Doctrines of Pentecostals," 90–1.

8 This was observed by Atter as early as 1937. See "The Pentecostal Movement." In 1941 the Pentecostal membership was almost evenly divided between urban and rural members. See Jaenen, "The Pentecostal Movement," 129–35. The movement was significantly more urban than many other emerging evangelical Protestant groups during the first half of the twentieth century.

9 *Central Canadian Bible Institute, 1926–1927*, CPCA.

10 *Gleaner*, 1.

11 Miller, *Canadian Pentecostals*, 207.

12 Financial reasons initially prevented the Purdie family from moving to Winnipeg from Prince Edward Island in 1925 when the school first began. In 1929, the family finally did move only to learn shortly after that the school was being relocated to Toronto. While Purdie followed the school to Toronto, apparently his family did not, prompting some to suggest that for Purdie the move may have been perceived as temporary from the outset. See Althouse, "The Influence of Dr. J.E. Purdie's Reformed Anglican Theology on the Formation and Development of the Pentecostal Assemblies of Canada," 21; and Craig, "'Out and Out for the Lord': James Eustace Purdie, An Early Anglican Pentecostal," 43).

13 Along with the evangelistic ministry of A.H. Argue, which was headquartered in Winnipeg, a series of Charles S. Price evangelistic and healing services during the 1920s did much to attract attention to the Pentecostal movement in Winnipeg. In 1937 Watson Argue, son of A.H. Argue, became the pastor of Wesley Pentecostal Church. He not only continued the tradition of aggressive evangelism that had characterized the assembly but also added the new innovation of regularly scheduled, live radio broadcasts. In order to accommodate the increasing size of the congregation, the large First Baptist Church on Cumberland Avenue was purchased in 1938. It was renamed Calvary Temple – apparently at the suggestion of Price. During the 1940s, Sunday evening services regularly filled the 1,600 seat auditorium to capacity; it became the largest PAOC assembly in Canada.

14 Purdie, "What God Hath Wrought," 4.

15 Peters, *The Contribution to Education by the Pentecostal Assemblies of Canada*, 28.

16 A.C. Schindel, interview with Bruce Guenther, 2 December 1997. See also the comments by Pierce, *The Gleaner*, 12; and Miller, *Canadian Pentecostals*, 201–2.

17 The same dynamic is described by Blumhofer in *The Assemblies of God*, 110.

18 "Since I Left Bible College ... " *Western Bible College Yearbook*, 1939–40, 21.

19 "The Need for Preachers with Convictions," *Western Bible College Yearbook*, 1938–39, 3.

20 See Peters, *The Contribution to Education by the paoc*, 24.

21 *The Portal*, Twentieth Anniversary Issue, 1944–45, 3.

22 *The Portal*, 1946–47, 4.

23 Letter from J.E. Purdie to Central University, 16 November 1937, Purdie Papers, CPCA.

24 J.E. Purdie, "The Principles of Our Balanced Course," *Western Bible College Yearbook*, 1938–39, 3.

25 Courses in Ukrainian and Spanish were offered in an effort to accelerate students into cross-cultural evangelistic ministries. The Ukrainian department was started in 1944 in conjunction with the Russian and Eastern European Mission (Chicago).

26 Letter from Purdie to Central University, 16 November 1937, Purdie Papers, CPCA.

27 See comments in Mervil Jackson's class notes (Mervil Jackson Papers, CPCA).

28 *Western Bible College Yearbook*, 1938–39, 24.

29 *Rejoice*, 136.

30 A complete list of faculty can be found in Peters, *The Contribution to Education by the paoc*, 173.

31 *Jubilation*, 11.

32 See the *Pentecostal Testimony* (June 1970), 5; and *The Gleaner* (April 1950), 6–8.

33 Miller, "Portraits of Pentecostal Pioneers: J.E. Purdie," *Pentecostal Testimony* (February 1987), 22–4; and Letter from Earl Kulbeck to Donald Klan, 6 July 1977, Pentecostal Assemblies of Canada Archives, Mississauga, ON (hereafter PAOCA).

34 Detailed information about Purdie's past was recorded by Gordon Franklin in 1973 through an extensive series of interviews (see J.E. Purdie, Interview by Gordon Franklin, 1973, CPCA; and Craig, "James Eustace Purdie, An Early Anglican Pentecostal").

35 "Principal of the Western Pentecostal Bible College for Thirteen Years," *Pentecostal Testimony* (May 1938), 17.

36 "My Own Pentecost," *Pentecostal Testimony* (June 1970), 9. Purdie acknowledges the significant influence of various Holiness movement writers, most notably Phoebe Palmer.

37 Prior to his Pentecostal experience Purdie established a pattern of inviting prominent fundamentalists to preach in his parish, including William Evans from Moody Bible Institute, Rowland V. Bingham, founder of the Sudan Interior Mission, and the Congregationalist preacher, G. Campbell Morgan.

38 "Factors that Make a Divinity College," *The Portal*, 1943–44, 3.

39 Kydd, "The Contribution of Denominationally Trained Clergymen," 26, 28. See also Althouse, "The Influence of Dr. J.E. Purdie's Reformed Anglican Theology," 3–28.

40 Letter from Purdie to Central University, 16 November 1937, CPCA. In addition to his BD from Wycliffe College, Purdie eventually received a BA from Temple Hall College and Seminary (1946), and an StD from St John's University in India (1950).

41 At least some denominational leaders felt that this did more to hinder than help his promotion of WBC (A.C. Schindel, Interview with Bruce Guenther, 11 December 1998).

42 *1932 Yearbook, Constitution and Bylaws of the Pentecostal Assemblies of Canada* (London: PAOC, 1932), 38.

43 This committee did not meet regularly. In 1946 the national committee on Bible schools and colleges was activated with Purdie as chairman, Charles Ratz as secretary, and the Bible college principals as the other members. In 1956, this committee was re-constituted and given the mandate to formulate and administer the "National Standard for Canadian Bible Colleges."

44 This did not go unnoticed by other PAOC leaders. Earl Kulbeck suggests that Purdie's influence gave the denomination "a certain texture which makes it unique in the Pentecostal world" (Letter from Earl Kulbeck to Donald Klan, 6 July 1977, PAOCA).

45 This is also evident in Western Bible College's "Standards of Faith" that reads "We believe in ... the infilling of the Holy Spirit as an essential equipment for service."

46 Purdie, *Concerning the Faith*, 44–6. See also "Christianity and the Holy Spirit," *The Gleaner* (April 1950), 22–4.

47 *Concerning the Faith*, 71–2. These hints of Anglicanism within the PAOC catechism are identified by Stronstad, "Dr. J.E. Purdie and Western Bible College," unpublished paper, 1974, Purdie Papers, CPCA.

48 Kydd, "Pentecostals, Charismatics and the Canadian Denominations,"
224–5. Purdie maintained a role as Honorary Assistant at St Margaret's
Anglican Church in Winnipeg, occasionally preaching and helping with communion (Letter from J.E. Purdie to J.E. Harris, 18 August 1952, Vancouver
Bible Institute Papers, Baptist General Conference Archives, Edmonton, AB).

49 See Kydd, "H.C. Sweet: Canadian Churchman," 19–30.

50 "Sweet Memories," *The Portal*, 1948–49, 4.

51 Larden, *Our Apostolic Heritage*, 92–3. He was not only one of the signato-
ries on the group's application for a federal charter in 1921, but he was also
elected to a three-year term as a presbyter in the new movement.

52 Kydd, "Canadian Pentecostalism," 297; Hildebrandt, "A History of the Winnipeg Bible Institute and College of Theology from 1925–1960," 37–8; and
Hindmarsh, "The Winnipeg Fundamentalist Network, 1910–1940: The
Roots of Transdenominational Evangelicalism in Manitoba and Saskatchewan," 312.

53 See Sweet, "The Founding of the Western Pentecostal Bible College – 1931,"
29 April 1931, PAOCA.

54 Kydd, "H.C. Sweet: Canadian Churchman," 28.

55 See Buntain, *Why He Is a Pentecostal Preacher*.

56 Kydd, "The Contribution of Denominationally Trained Clergymen," 24.

57 Ibid., 23. See Buntain's remarks about the "cultural refinement" that WBC
"stamped" upon its leaders. *The Gleaner* (April 1950), 11.

58 "EC," *Pentecostal Testimony* 20, no. 7 (1 April 1939), 3. Kydd demonstrates
how Buntain's organizational experience and ability, which he developed during his time with the Methodists, greatly helped the early development of the
PAOC. Buntain justifies the use of efficient organizational structures with the
same kind of pragmatism with which he defended education. See "The Contribution of Denominationally Trained Clergymen," 31–2.

59 "The Dean of Women," *The Portal* (1946–47), 7.

60 *The Gleaner* (April 1950), 28–32.

61 The student body mirrored the remarkable diversity that made up the denomination. The close-knit college environment mixed students who were urban
and rural, rich and poor, male and female, and from various denominational
and national backgrounds. In most years, the women enrolled outnumbered
the men. Over the years students from more than twenty different countries
and more than twenty different denominations attended WBC (see *Western
Bible College Yearbook*, 1942–43, 3). Bible schools were sometimes mischievously referred to as "bridal schools." This dynamic was certainly evident at
WBC; it is worth noting that 40 per cent of the people on the alumni list of
1950 were married to someone who had also attended the school.

62 "Our Fellowship," *The Gleaner* (May 1938), 3. Canadian Pentecostals were often resentful when their young leaders accepted positions in the United States, yet ironically they encouraged scores of their graduates to go to virtually every other country.

63 *The Gleaner* (April 1950), 14; and *The Gleaner* (November 1971), 1.

64 *Pentecostal Testimony* (June 1970), 4

65 Miller, *Canadian Pentecostals*, 214.

66 Controversy over control surrounded this school from the outset culminating in Hawtin's departure in 1947. Loyal students followed him to North Battleford, Saskatchewan where he established Sharon Bible School, which became the headquarters for the Latter Rain Movement. The near loss of one of their Bible schools prompted the PAOC to strengthen the link between their schools and the denominational organizational structure. See Miller, *Canadian Pentecostals*, 260–5; and Riss, *The Latter Rain Movement of 1948 and the Mid-Twentieth Century Evangelical Awakening*.

67 The school was preceded by several annual six-week programs run by Gordon F. Atter at Cobourg, ON. The first was held in 1937 with twelve students. See *The Gleaner* (May 1938), 5.

68 One of the reasons given for the necessity of a school in British Columbia was the growing attractiveness of local "non-Pentecostal" schools. See *Jubilation*, 11. Because of the strong anti-Pentecostal sentiments in non-Pentecostal schools, attending almost always resulted in the rejection of Pentecostalism and the permanent loss of these young people (Letter from Earl Kulbeck to Donald Klan, 6 July 1977, PAOCA).

69 *Jubilation*, 11.

70 Lynn, *Truth Aflame*, 34.

6

Scripture in the Pentecostal Tradition:
A Contemporary Reading of Luke-Acts

MARTIN MITTELSTADT

INTRODUCTION

An unprecedented global and trans-traditional deluge of the Spirit during the past one hundred years has led various historians and theologians to write of the twentieth century as the "century of the Spirit."[1] Noted American missiologist Ralph Winter, when speaking of the shape of contemporary Christendom, states, "both at home and abroad, a more enthusiastic worship centered trend is surely taking place – the Pentecostalization of the church."[2] This rapid transformational impact of Pentecostalism has not passed by Canada. Methodological factors such as the mechanisms of church government, catechesis, and missionary strategies are surely substantial. Social historians would identify the movement's impetus as an ongoing reaction to nineteenth-century assertions that a mature humanity had outgrown the need for "religion." The recognition that Pentecostalism was the fastest growing stream throughout twentieth-century Christendom caused Harvard Professor of Religion Harvey Cox to reverse his view of a dwindling church in a "post-religious" secular age and now speak of the emergence of Pentecostal spirituality as a manifestation of the "unanticipated."[3]

While these and other factors have their place in analytical history, Pentecostals believe the primary strength of the movement is found in the shape of an upper room revival experience analogous to the events recorded by Luke on the Day of Pentecost. In this chapter, I examine this facet of Pentecostal self-understanding, specifically, the function of

Luke's treatment of the upper room in shaping classical Pentecostal theology and praxis.[4] I centre my attention on why Luke-Acts is not only a favourite but also an essential text for Pentecostals and their understanding of transformation. First, I argue that Pentecostals demonstrate continuity with traditional Judeo-Christian hermeneutics. Continuity, however, does not mean that Pentecostals interpret or appropriate the text in the same ways as these traditions. Second, I propose that a proper understanding of Pentecostalism must include an awareness of specific interpretive emphases that shape and define the unique nature of Pentecostal theology. These two sections offer hermeneutical clarity for understanding the internal logic of Pentecostalism. Third, I consider current cultural and ecclesial concerns in light of a Pentecostal approach to Luke-Acts at a time when one movement, the Pentecostal Assemblies of Canada (PAOC), wrestles with issues surrounding its transition from a renewal movement to a highly bureaucratized denomination. Finally, I suggest ways for ongoing dialogue between Lukan interpretation and current concerns among Pentecostals.[5]

WHY LUKE-ACTS?

The very name "Pentecostal" is well suited for the environment of Luke-Acts. While the expansion of the Pentecostal movement brings increasing exegetical diversity, Pentecostalism is noted for its accent on what Hendrikus Berkhof calls the neglected "third element," beyond the *duplex gratia* of justification and sanctification, namely, Spirit Baptism.[6] Pentecostal pioneer Charles Parham argued that contemporary Christian experience "should tally exactly with the Bible" and specifically with the oft neglected second chapter of Acts. He concluded that the empowerment for witness provided for the disciples on the Day of Pentecost should be experienced in contemporary Christendom to the same measure. Early Pentecostals would follow Parham's initial exegetical impulse and declare a sharp distinction between conversion to Christ and the post-conversion experience of Spirit Baptism.[7]

The rationale for this belief was found throughout Luke-Acts via Bible studies, sermons, and devotional works. The Lukan narratives were important because they provided Pentecostals with both a strong motivation for pursuit of the Spirit and a biblical pattern for contemporary believers. As "people of the book" Pentecostals are not guilty of criticisms often levelled against them, such as a propensity to excessive personal revelation that supersedes Scripture.[8] On the contrary, Pentecostals have held Scripture in high regard, emphasizing biblical inspiration and authority as the foundations for interpreting implications for Holy Spirit experience. For example, Canadian Pentecostal pioneer, A.G. Ward stated:

> I feel we must not fail to recognize that as a movement grows numerically and new departments are opened up, of necessity it must be carried on in the most efficient business-like way. We have certainly outgrown some of our former policies and methods of conducting affairs, and now we must either make the necessary changes and improvements or be forced into retrogression. As a movement, we have remained on the cutting edge of evangelistic outreach and growth because of our creative methods to meet the changing needs of society with the unchanging gospel of Jesus Christ. We have been open to the voice of the Spirit as He has led us into new ways of responding to the challenges of the day. At the same time, we have stood faithfully upon the Scriptures as our only authority in matters of faith and practice.[9]

Thomas Zimmerman, former superintendent of the Assemblies of God, also cites reverence for the Word of God as a primary reason for the Pentecostal explosion. His analysis of the revivals recorded in biblical history demonstrates a similar starting point: "The revivals under Asa (2 Chron. 15:8–19), Joash (2 Chron. 24:6), and Hezekiah (2 Kings 18:6), as well as those under Josiah, Zerubbabel, and Nehemiah, were attributable largely to the fact that these Old Testament leaders insisted on a renewed commitment to the Mosaic documents, especially Deuteronomy."[10] For Pentecostals like Ward and Zimmerman, the exemplary lives of biblical leaders serve as a model for contemporary believers. A primary characteristic of the use of Scripture in the Pentecostal heritage is a simple, natural, and reverential use of the words of Scripture both in the nourishment of personal piety and in setting a mandate for mission as a primary agenda for the church. Pentecostals settle especially upon the narratives of Acts as a foundation for such a contemporary renewal of the church.

While Pentecostals enjoy a rich interpretive history built upon the narratives in Luke-Acts, a sense of exegetical authenticity came via the monumental work of the Canadian Roger Stronstad. Written originally as a master's thesis for Regent College in 1975, *The Charismatic Theology of St. Luke* has served as a foundational and enduring Pentecostal

contribution to the interpretation of Luke-Acts.[11] Building on the earlier work of British evangelical I. Howard Marshall, Stronstad interprets Luke-Acts on its own terms and not according to what Paul writes
in his letters.[12] He insists that historical narrative, such as Luke-Acts, is
homogenous and offers, in addition to historical purposes, legitimate
didactic and theological purposes. While Pentecostals are not alone in
these approaches to Luke-Acts, Stronstad provides the first Pentecostal
attempt to furnish a comprehensive interpretation of Luke's theology of
the Holy Spirit. He argues for a legitimate experiential theology based
on historical precedent, the teaching of Jesus, and the teaching and
preaching of the apostles. In short, Jesus teaches that the Father would
give the Holy Spirit to those who ask (Luke 11:13; 12:1–12) and
instructs the disciples to pray that they might receive the Holy Spirit
(Luke 24:49; Acts 1:4–5, 8). In obedience to Jesus' command, Luke
records that the disciples and ensuing followers of Jesus receive the fulfillment of these programmatic prophecies (Acts 2:1–4). The Acts 2
"Pentecost narrative" and several ensuing Lukan reports of the outpouring of the Spirit in Acts serve as historical precedents for contemporary reception and experience of the Spirit (see Acts 8: Samaritan
Pentecost; Acts 9: Paul; Acts 10: Cornelius' household; Acts 19:
Ephesian Pentecost).

While Stronstad offers the first enduring scholarly defence of a Pentecostal interpretation of Lukan pneumatology, this understanding was
already firmly entrenched in Pentecostal spirituality via countless devotional and homiletical exhortations.[13] The official organ of the Pentecostal Assemblies of Canada (PAOC), the *Pentecostal Testimony*,
regularly highlights this understanding. In 1951, an unidentified writer
serves as an example: "Each of us as individual Christians, however,
would do well to read again the book of Acts to see how the Holy Spirit
actually operated when He first took His place in the lives of those who
received Jesus Christ as Saviour. Then we would do well to lay aside all
preconceived notions as to how we think He ought to operate, and ask
the Lord Jesus Christ to show us exactly how He wants the Holy Spirit
to operate in us. In this exercise we would do well to follow the scriptural injunction 'to tarry' – taking time before God in order to be so
completely yielded to His will."[14]

Similarly, Aaron Lindford reflects on the events of the Day of Pentecost and correlates the validity of scriptural authority and historical precedent:

And of this baptism Peter says, "This is that." The experience they had just received was in harmony with the words of the prophet Joel. The baptism of the Holy Spirit is not merely pragmatic, it is dogmatic. True Pentecost is doctrinally sound. The "thisness" of experience and the "thatness" of exposition go together. We must not stress the "thisness" at the expense of the "thatness" – that borders on existentialism, making subjective feeling the criterion. Nor must we emphasize "thatness" and omit "thisness" – that is arid dogmatism. We must have both: an experience that has for its centre the grace of God, and for its circumference the revealed word"[15]

Linford's emphasis upon the Pentecost narrative as paradigmatic for contemporary experience must not be missed. I will return to this component of Pentecostal interpretation in section two.

CONTINUITY WITH JUDEO-CHRISTIAN HERMENEUTICS

Before examining how various emphases of a Pentecostal reading of Luke-Acts might find a place in broader Christendom, it is prudent to connect Pentecostal interpretive methodology to the larger Judeo-Christian tradition. For Pentecostals, their primary interpretive approach stands in harmony with the hermeneutical methods of Judaism and Catholicism. In order to trace this continuity, it is useful to consider the work of Russian literary critic Mikhail Bakhtin. According to Bakhtin, when reading and analyzing a text, there is neither a first nor a last word, nor are there limits to the dialogic context. Thus, meanings born in the dialogue of past centuries ought never to be finalized, that is, ended once for all. Instead, they must always be renewed in the process of subsequent, future development of the dialogue. At any moment in the development of a dialogue, there are suspended masses of forgotten contextual meanings, which at certain moments of the dialogue's subsequent development are recalled and invigorated in renewed form in a new context. If Bakhtin is correct, if no text is absolutely dead, then no individual sees the world of a theological concept in all its fullness, much less how it might be expanded by future thinkers. Thus, readers engage the still unfolding insights of others to complement and enlarge their own.[16]

Nowhere is this idea better captured than in the Judaic tradition. When examining the Talmud, readers soon notice that the Hebrew

Scriptures do not offer the final homiletical word. Instead, the scripture text is assumed to be ambiguous and incomplete. On any given Talmudic page, the smallest portion is the Scripture text with additional concentric circles of commentary. These circles provide a clear picture of Jewish hermeneutic: Rabbis writing on the margins of the Scripture served as active commentators and participants breathing continuous life into ancient texts.

The history of Catholic interpretation reveals a similar methodology. While rigorous biblical exegesis is a well-known hallmark of Catholicism, Pentecostals often bemoan Catholic emphasis on the dual role of Scripture and tradition as co-informants of the Church. This misunderstanding might be clarified by setting Catholicism alongside its Judaic ancestry. For Catholics, the biblical text is ever living, speaking forth from generation to generation and offering life and meaning to the Church through the continual efforts of the Church's thinkers.[17] In Bakhtinian fashion, this practice runs parallel to Judaism. For Catholics, as for Jews, tradition continues to write its history "on the margins" of the biblical text.

Like Jews and Catholics, Pentecostals also employ a rigorous emphasis on Scripture with a Bakhtinian disposition. As people of the book, Pentecostals struggle to bring the implications of Luke's ancient text into the present. In continuity with Judaic and Catholic methodology, Pentecostals believe thoroughly in the continuity of interpreting the biblical story. Just as the Talmudic commentary invigorates the Scriptures for Judaism and just as tradition enlivens the ancient texts for Catholicism, so also Pentecostals analyze the drama of biblical narrative in successive generations through the life of the Spirit. Scripture is not to be treated as mere propositional truth but expounded and brought to life through the playful interaction between the text and the present life of the Spirit. Since Pentecostals recognize themselves in the text, they conclude that the Spirit-life described there is available and accessible to contemporary believers. This interplay between Scripture and contemporary Pentecostal experience then includes believers as "living texts."[18] It is the biblical narratives that provide meaning; the "big stories to tell us what is real and significant, to know who we are, where we are, what we are doing, and why ... it is the story that constructs the ideal and defines the sacred."[19]

In the *Pentecostal Testimony*, Karel Marek comments on "Acts Chapter 29" with a subtitle stating, "In case you hadn't noticed recently there are only 28 chapters recorded in the Book of Acts in your Bible."[20] In his opening paragraph, with vintage Pentecostal exhortation, he declares, "I've frequently heard of churches with a desire to 'write' Acts chapter 29. Is it not the dream of every preacher? Is this not what the world needs to see?"[21] To encourage a person/ church in the writing of Acts 29, Marek weaves a connection among three words in Acts: witness, Pentecost, and prayer. In order to write additional chapters to Acts, Pentecostals must start and continue with Acts 1 – the prayers in the upper room. Witness according to Acts chapters 2–28, of course, is impossible without Pentecost (Acts 2) and there is no Pentecost without prayer (back to Acts 1). As "living texts," Marek calls Pentecostals to a renewed posture for reception of a contemporary "Day of Pentecost" and the ensuing empowerment. Canadian pioneer A.G. Ward writes in *My Personal Experience of Pentecost*, "After receiving the Baptism of the Holy Sprit I found that the Bible was like an entirely new book to me. Floods of light from the eternal hills broke upon it. I realized that the same Holy Spirit, who in the days of long ago inspired holy men to write the Holy Scripture, had come into my heart to enable me to understand their real content ... Another blessed result of the incoming of the Comforter to my heart has been that I have learned to cultivate the faculty of sacred imagination and to realize the Unseen."[22]

A lengthy portion of Ward's testimony is also cited by Gloria Kulbeck in her early history of the PAOC.[23] Kulbeck uses Ward's story as an exemplary "Pentecostal testimony." His account is but one example of a crucial component of the oral and written theology of practice of the Pentecostal community in which personal stories of the life-giving Spirit enliven Pentecostals to mirror the biblical experiences and power of first-century followers of Jesus. For Pentecostals, testimony, alongside doctrinal discourse, is a legitimate source of doctrine, echoing Jewish Talmudic practice and Catholic Tradition. The presence of the Spirit working in the life of an individual believer generates testimony, witness, and thanksgiving to God. Doctrine sets certain parameters for Pentecostals, but "faith" understood as a body of beliefs would never be the first definition given in a Pentecostal lexicon. For Pentecostals, the Bible is a story read into their lives and their lives into that story. It is no accident that the original and official publication of the PAOC, the *Pentecostal Testimony*, is so titled. In continuity with the Judaic and Catholic traditions, it is reasonable to speak of the innumerable testimonies as examples of Pentecostal "midrash."[24] This signature homiletic emphasizes for Pentecostals a convergence of the Scriptures with contemporary experience and makes available the power for ongoing prophetic ministry and healing to a broken world.

PENTECOSTAL EMPHASES: APPROPRIATING THE TEXT IN UNIQUE WAYS

In light of this continuity with historic Christianity, it is important to remember that all Christian traditions read a partial vision of the Scriptures through their own lenses. This fractional reading might be best described as a "canon within the Canon" in which a distinctive within one tradition might lead to the ability to see certain motifs with clarity while others are missed partially or entirely. It is with this in mind that I examine, from a social historical perspective, specific Pentecostal emphases deduced from their reading of Luke-Acts.

A Restoration Movement

Pentecostalism is certainly one of the most notable and successful restorationist movements in history. According to the tenets of restorationism, history is providential, moved forward by supernatural guidance from creation to an imminent final consummation. Driven by a nineteenth-century surge of restorationism, Pentecostals embraced the belief that the end of the world was at hand and that God's governance of history is intimately tied up with human response. Early participants were certain that God had called them to bring about a worldwide revival to prepare men and women for the Lord's coming. While they were not certain as to the exact time and place of this return, they were convinced this timing depended somewhat on human responses.[25] In light of this perception, Grant Wacker proposes that two creatively connected impulses served as the driving forces of early Pentecostalism. The primitivist is a powerful backward quest to forego all human-made traditions in order to imitate the first-century church under the rule of the Holy Spirit. The complementary pragmatic impulse, nevertheless, highlights Pentecostals' eagerness to engage any method necessary in order to accomplish the movement's purposes.[26]

Interpretation of Luke-Acts is central to the advancement of this initiative. For Pentecostals, the standard-setting New Testament church is Luke's idyllic community emerging from the Day of Pentecost. The emerging community continues daily to heed the instruction of the apostles, abide in prayer, and share astonishing harmony that includes the breaking of bread and care for the needy (Acts 2:42–47). Further, the now Spirit-filled community witnesses many signs and wonders by the apostles, a specific fulfillment of Acts 1:1 where Luke states that his second volume is a continuation of "all that Jesus began to do and teach." As restorationists, Pentecostals expected this New Testament church to be restored to its full vitality just prior to the return of Jesus Christ. The experience of the Holy Spirit by the apostles and others, described in the book of Acts, became the sign of "the last days" as prophesied in Joel 2:28–32 and first experienced in Acts 2:17–21. The Acts 2 narrative came to be called the "Former Rain" and complements the current Pentecostal outpouring deemed the "Latter Rain." The fulfillment of the last days' outpouring of the Spirit calls for the convergence of an intense eschatological expectation and reliance upon the Holy Spirit's power to usher in the final consummation of God's kingdom. The Day of Pentecost (Acts 2) is preceded by the ascension of Jesus (Acts 1:6–11), locating the coming of the Spirit in eschatological perspective. That is, the coming of the Spirit provides empowerment for witness before the coming of the kingdom at the return of Jesus. The former rain on the day of Pentecost inaugurated the last days, and the current latter rain is the culmination of the last days.

A Missiological Movement

In continuity with many restoration movements, Pentecostals are intensely missiological. The connection between the two is immediately apparent. In Luke-Acts, the emerging community, filled with the Spirit and now in the last days, launches an impressive push to proclaim the gospel to all people (Acts 1:8). In prime Pentecostal fashion, the Canadian Rev. David Slauenwhite provides a bridge linking Luke's first-century missionary mandate to the contemporary Pentecostal mission: "The marks of a Pentecostal church are therefore clear. Prayer is our atmosphere and is done in the Spirit with intercession for souls. Holy living is our calling, through a Spirit-filled life meant to be a witness that Jesus saves. Preaching is our method, under the anointing of the Spirit, with an evangelistic intent. Manifestations of the Spirit's presence and demonstration of His giftings are expected and encouraged, so that we may effectively reach others with the gospel."[27] Slauenwhite's comments link the harmonious Acts community with the contemporary mandate for missions and Pentecostal prescription for growth. Accordingly, the spiritual life of the believer and the activities of the church are to be realized on a supernatural plane. Believers are to be led by the Spirit, and the church is to be directed by the Spirit. Signs and wonders such as healings, miracles, and answers to prayer should accompany proclamation of the gospel. Moreover, inspired utterances will be given and should be expected through the Spirit for the encouragement of the church. Divine direction will be received through a Spirit-guided administration.

Luke repeatedly highlights the concord between the Holy Spirit and the emerging leadership. For example, it is by means of a vision that the apostle Peter overcomes his hesitancy to evangelize a Gentile household (Acts 10–11). After witnessing extraordinary results, Peter defends his actions by recounting the Spirit-led direction compelling him to obey and proclaim the gospel to Gentiles. Jewish leadership embraces Peter's testimony and rejoices in what God is doing among the Gentiles (Acts 11:18). Later, in the church at Antioch, prophets and teachers thrust Barnabas and Saul into a Gentile missionary campaign. While it would have undoubtedly been desirable to retain Paul and Barnabas as their chief ministers, leadership responds to the direction of the Holy Spirit: "Set apart for me Barnabas and Saul for the work to which I have called them" (Acts 13:2). In the crafting of his story, Luke conveys the work of the Holy Spirit alongside human leadership in providing details for directing mission strategy.

Once again, first-century methodologies reflect contemporary Pentecostal strategies by way of the convergence of the primitivist and pragmatic impulses. The same "biblical pragmatism" noted above characterizes Pentecostal mission strategy. The prominence given to the role of the Holy Spirit does not diminish the human response to complete passivity. On the contrary, the need for creative and Acts-like engagement of all mental, physical, material, and spiritual powers in the planning and execution of God's work is expected. Through the ministry of the Spirit, Pentecostals attempt to mirror the apostles in an active effort to take the gospel to all people. The Holy Spirit has a strategy for each age and place. J.E. Purdie, a pioneer in Canadian Pentecostal education, illustrates well the role of the Holy Spirit in mission activity. He states: "With the vision glorious, may not the Church press forward to greater and more far-reaching practical work both at home and abroad! There are unique openings and opportunities to enlarge and extend the borders of the Church through good, sane, aggressive and definitely planned continuous evangelistic work, and to push forward today and take new lands for God. To do this effectively, we must have the vision borne in upon us by the power of the Holy Spirit Himself."[28] As people of the Spirit, Pentecostals long for passionate empowering and strategizing ministry that extends and enlarges first- century mission.

CURRENT CONCERNS

In conjunction with the idea of a "canon within the Canon," there is evidence of emerging concerns within Canadian Pentecostalism. While the previous section demonstrates that a Pentecostal reading of Luke-Acts encourages closer inspection of Luke's contribution to a life of the Spirit, recent scholarly and pastoral analyses are exposing lacunae that warrant attention. As Pentecostals (and members of any other tradition) continue to define their distinctive, there is a natural tendency to sharpen the focus on primary and debated areas and, in so doing, overlook other emerging concerns signalling a movement in transition. This is undoubtedly evident by way of the mixed messages currently received concerning egalitarianism and social justice. It is probable that ecclesiastical concern for the rights of women and other minorities is partly in response to cultural developments in the last half of the twentieth century. How Pentecostals respond to these issues will be crucial as they move through a process of transition and transformation.

An Egalitarian Movement

The missiological compulsion of Pentecostals draws further strength through a conviction that the Holy Spirit acts powerfully in all Christians. Accordingly, Stronstad argues that Pentecostals ought to enlarge the Reformation axiom of the priesthood of all believers (including women) to one that would encourage "the prophethood of all believers."[29] Through his analysis of Luke-Acts as the story of an eschatological community of prophets, Stronstad calls for a contemporary prophetic community centred not primarily upon individual experience but upon world-centred vocational service.[30] A look at the early history of the movement demonstrates that Pentecostals embraced an initial egalitarian impulse, specifically a hospitable home for women in general and for women preachers in particular.

Affirmation of this position is found in Luke-Acts by way of numerous stories concerning ministry by women from all levels of society ranging from prostitute to social matron and pietistic worshipper to pragmatic housekeeper. Though Pentecostal women often faced formidable ecclesiastical and social hurdles, biblical characters such as Elizabeth, Mary, Anna, Lydia, and Priscilla led Pentecostals to consider opportunities for women that they might not enjoy in other denominations. Further motivation for the contemporary role of women was also found in the Pentecost narrative. Luke notes that several of the 120 followers present on the Day of Pentecost were women (Acts 1:14) and affirms that everyone receives the Holy Spirit (Acts 2:4). When Peter begins to explain the events to the onlookers, his quotation of Joel 2:28–32 (in Acts 2:17–21) asserts that the deluge of the Spirit is upon young and old and men and women alike. With biblical assertion in hand, contemporary applications became possible: "God Almighty is no fool ... Would He fill a woman with the Holy Spirit – endow her with ability – give her a vision for souls and then tell her to shut her mouth?"[31] The irony of this statement is its polemical tone. And in the first half of the twentieth century, women were often accorded opportunities to preach. Herein lay the tension: while Pentecostals affirm the role of women in theory, women often receive mixed signals when they attempt to enact God's call.

Women in Pentecostalism continue to assert their call to preach and to serve publicly while remaining in congregations where they are told to be submissive to male leadership and serve at male discretion. At first glance, this is remarkably puzzling, but certain socio-historical factors cannot be overlooked. Throughout the last century, Pentecostals listened to broader religious and societal trajectories – various non-egalitarian arguments stemming from presuppositions about fixed gender roles, women as the weaker sex, and the doctrinal positions of evangelical denominations – which continue to divide many Pentecostal churches.[32] Further, when positive change might have been possible in the wake of the feminist movement, the reverse became the norm: Pentecostals dug in their heels and opposed the "evils" of feminism and asserted female submission (see chapter 8 in this volume).

Contemporary Pentecostal women, consequently, continue to make their way through mixed messages. While they remain active, believing that their work as Christian women matters in the church and this world, many women lack the ecclesiastical affirmation necessary to encourage further efforts. It is here where a reading of Acts by some Pentecostals is like a prophetic voice for the current day, calling for renewal, indicating how far the movement has moved through the process of transition and institutionalization. The filling of the Spirit levels access to the privilege of preaching and affirms that a pneumatic spirituality and ministry is available for all people. Since the same Holy Spirit is actively at work in the woman as in the man, the experience of Pentecost means that a new day has arrived. Pentecostal women ought to be able to live their lives in light of the Lukan narratives embracing not only baptism in the Holy Spirit but their prophetic calling.[33]

A Social Justice Movement

Over the second half of the twentieth century, as Pentecostals came under increasing attack for an indifference to social concern, a growing body of Pentecostal literature began to address social ethics and social justice. A theology of social concern was needed to support Pentecostal participation in these spheres.[34] As a result of scholarly efforts, Pentecostals are now involved with the poor for social renewal in unobtrusive ways and have initiated major social reform programs and institutions. While Pentecostals exhibit a greater social consciousness, these efforts are seldom given proper theological reflection as part of everyday pneumatic spirituality.[35]

Before proceeding to Luke-Acts, it is important to recall the reason for this indifference. First, there is no denying the fact that in the formative years of the movement eschatological fervour blurred the meaning of social improvement (see chapter 3 in this volume). As restorationists expecting the imminent return of Christ, Pentecostals typically saw social service and social action as meaningless human work in light of the need to preach redemption to masses. The temporary benefits which might accrue from limited involvement in social justice would be negligible in contrast to urgent evangelistic ministry. In other words, the results of such social work would be unnecessary in light of the imminent establishment of God's eternal kingdom where God would order perfect justice for all. Furthermore, only evangelistic ministry ushers in the return of Jesus, and only evangelistic ministry prepares people for God's eternal kingdom.[36] Second, the earliest Pentecostals were not strong proponents of social justice for the simple reason that they often found themselves among the marginalized. Canadian historian Ronald Kydd remarks: "When Pentecostalism was young we did not have an outreach to the poor, we were the poor! We just reached out to ourselves and we were reaching the poor!"[37] However, as the Canadian population increased and the economy improved following World War II, Pentecostals experienced significant upward mobility, losing the label of marginalization. Unfortunately Kydd's rejoinder offers little consolation: "Since then we have become the rich and we still do not have any approach to the poor."[38]

While Pentecostals claim a pneumatic theology of ministry that asserts identification with the mission of the church as portrayed in Acts, further efforts to emulate consciously and theologically the essential ethical character of the kingdom of God are warranted. When surveying Luke-Acts, the reader notices that Luke gives significant emphasis to the "already-present" kingdom of God being experienced in the early church. The power of the Holy Spirit initiates a new redemptive order of life in Jesus Christ amidst the old social order. This new order includes conscious attempts to create *koinonia* and to overcome the moral biases and cultural prejudices inherent in the old social order by forming an inclusive community of men, women, slaves, free, rich and poor, Jew and Gentile. Jesus teaches that where God reigns a new redemptive society is formed in which strangers are incorporated into an affirmative community; peace is made with enemies, injustices are rectified, the poor experience solidarity with the community, generous sharing results in the just satisfaction of human needs in which no one suffers deprivation, and all persons are to be treated with dignity and are deserving of justice because they share the status of God's image-bearers. [39] Such actions and social practices that embody love, justice, and *shalom* constitute the normative moral structure in a social ethic reflective of God's kingly rule, a rule defined at Pentecost.

Kydd echoes these ideas in his analysis of Luke 4:14–21. While Pentecostals long to follow Luke's presentation of Jesus under the anointing and power of the Spirit, Kydd laments that imitation of Jesus is often reduced to mere proclamation. Instead, Jesus stands as the fulfillment of Isaiah's prophecy: "The Spirit of the Lord is upon me, because he has anointed me to bring good news to the poor. He has sent me to proclaim release to the captives and recovery of sight to the blind, to let the oppressed go free, to proclaim the year of the Lord's favour" (Luke 4:18–19). This programmatic prophecy is repeatedly fulfilled not only through the life of Jesus but also through the emerging community. Jesus and the apostles offer holistic redemption. As Kydd says: "In Luke 4 Jesus proclaimed that He would take the gospel to the streets. He went to the big and the small, the rich and the poor, He went to the broken. You and I are called to these people. If we are filled with the Holy Spirit He will show us those people and He will help us to understand what needs to be done. I believe that He will give us the courage, perseverance, the love to hang with those people until the grace of God becomes a reality of their lives."[40]

According to Kydd, Pentecostals, as people of the Spirit, need to make the direct link between Spirit and the spirituality of living Spirit-filled lives, not the least being in the arena of social ethics. Even a cursory inspection of Luke-Acts draws attention to Luke's special concern for the poor, the marginalized, and the helpless. The life of the Spirit is not limited to inspiring a certain speech but it also calls for the intended effect of such speech.[41] Jesus does not merely project salvation, freedom, peace, and justice as eschatological hope but emphasizes their present "today" reality (Luke 4:21; 19:9). As Pentecostals affirm a life of active eschatological expectation, continuity between God's present reign and the reign to come will "guarantee that noble human efforts will not be wasted."[42]

CONCLUSION

This assessment of Scripture in Pentecostalism offers evidence of a movement significantly directed by a focused reading of Luke-Acts. First, Pentecostals are drawn to Luke-Acts by a desire to imitate the community vividly described by Luke and to continue the story into contemporary life. Such a reading of Luke-Acts might best be summarized as a search for a paradigm of mission.[43] Through experience of the Spirit, Pentecostals embrace a restorationist pursuit of the "latter rain," that is, a restoration of the church to its first-century power. Whether through devotional reading or preaching of the biblical text, there is a desire to make the same Scriptures effective in contemporary ministry as a continuation of the pattern of Jesus and the early church. Thus, the Holy Spirit anoints Jesus from the beginning of his ministry, and Jesus thereby accomplishes his mission. In Acts, the Pentecost narrative records the transfer of the charismatic Spirit from Jesus to the disciples. The same Holy Spirit that had earlier anointed Jesus as a new messiah now anoints the emerging disciples to perpetuate his mission and ministry. The disciples thus become the successors to the earthly charismatic Christ, continuing "all that Jesus began to do and teach" (Acts 1:1).

In continuity with the first-century community, contemporary Pentecostals covet similar enabling transference of the Spirit as the means for continuing Jesus' own mission to the contemporary world. Second, as a restorationist community desiring life in the Spirit, it is in continuity with the narrative of Luke-Acts that Pentecostals attempt to exhibit the same missiological zeal as the first Christians. As people of the Spirit, Pentecostals desire to duplicate the missionary success of the first-century church. Finally, scholars and pastors within Pentecostalism are beginning to note that the movement, now into its second century, needs further maturation as it moves through a process of transition. I have addressed two areas of concern deriving from my own reading of Luke-Acts, which are central issues for Pentecostalism in Canada.

NOTES

1 See Synan, *The Century of the Spirit.*
2 Winter is the founder and director of the US Center for World Mission. This observation is part of our recent email correspondence and is used with his permission.
3 The titles of two prominent works by Cox convey his change. The earlier position is articulated in *The Secular City* and his recent position in *Fire from Heaven.*
4 I use the term "Pentecostal" to refer to those who share in the experience of Spirit Baptism in the classical sense. I distinguish between Pentecostals and charismatics, the latter being those of the renewal movement beginning in the late 1950's in mainline denominations. Charismatics usually did not form their own new denominations but remained within their established Protestant, Catholic, and Orthodox traditions. For excellent summaries of Pentecostal and charismatic traditions see Lederle, *Treasures Old and New* as well as various articles in Burgess and van der Mass, *New International Dictionary of Pentecostal and Charismatic Movements.*
5 The largest classical Pentecostal denomination in Canada is the Pentecostal Assemblies of Canada (PAOC). Born, raised, and first credentialed in the PAOC, I write as a sympathetic yet critical insider of this classical Pentecostal position. I am currently ordained with the Assemblies of God (US), a sister denomination.
6 Berkhof, *The Doctrine of the Holy Spirit*, 90.
7 See Parham, *The Life of Charles F. Parham*, 52. For bibliographical data on later influential defences of Spirit Baptism see Williams, "Baptism in the Holy Spirit."
8 Early Pentecostals regularly found themselves defending their continuity with historic Christianity. In the following example, McAlister, "Our Distinctive Testimony, Replying to Rev. James McGinlay, Pentecostal Church, London" *Pentecostal Testimony* 13 (March 1932) responds to a critic by placing the

movement in continuity with Christendom before highlighting the distinctiveness of Pentecostalism: "I want to first state that the Pentecostal people do not magnify the speaking in tongues. You will attend this place for months at a time and never hear the subject mentioned. You will find in this place that the virgin birth of Christ, the centering around the Lord Jesus Christ in His vicarious death is mentioned a hundred times here for every once that the matter of tongues is mentioned. Notwithstanding this fact, we believe that tongues have a place in the Scriptures and all we ask is to give it the place that the Scripture gives it, no more and no less" (13).

9 A.G. Ward to J.W. McKillop, December 18, 1935, Four *Papers of the General Secretary* (PAOC Archives).

10 Zimmerman, "The Reason for the Rise of the Pentecostal Movement," 9.

11 Revised and published in 1984 by Hendrickson Publishers, Stronstad's work remains in print to the present day. Stronstad is a member of the faculty of Summit Pacific College (Abbotsford, BC).

12 See Marshall, *Luke: Historian and Theologian.*

13 See Kydd, *I'm Still There! A Reaffirmation of Tongues as the Initial Evidence of the Baptism in the Holy Spirit.* Kydd's work preceded Stronstad and served as a more popular tract with a scholarly bent intending to combat the challenges of an evangelical hermeneutic. In contrast to Pinnock and Osborne, "A Proposal for the Tongues Controversy," 8, who state that Acts is "weak methodologically and exegetically. Didactic passages must have precedence over historical passages in establishing doctrine," Kydd calls into question any distinction that elevates didactic texts above historical ones in matters of doctrine and practice.

14 Author Unidentified, "Signs and Wonders: Can the Present Church Fight the Increasing Antichristian Forces with Less Power than the Apostles of Old?" *Pentecostal Testimony* 32 (June 1951), 6.

15 Lindford, "The Initial Sign," *Pentecostal Testimony* 54 (September 1973), 3.

16 See Bakhtin, *Speech Genres and Other Late Essays,* 170; Coates, *Christianity in Bakhtin,* 29.

17 See Johnson and Kurz, *The Future of Catholic Biblical Scholarship.*

18 Suurmond, *Word and Spirit at Play,* 22–3. Smith, *Moral, Believing Animals,* 65, speaks similarly of living narratives as "a form of communication that arranges human actions and events into organized wholes in a way that bestows meaning on the actions and events by specifying their interactive or cause-and-effect relations to the whole."

19 Smith, *Moral, Believing Animals,* 67, 77.

20 Marek, *Pentecostal Testimony* 70 (December 1989), 24–5, is a retired educator of the PAOC.

21 Ibid, 24. According to Land, *Pentecostal Spirituality*, the Pentecostal story may also be framed by the ongoing metaphor of journey as a powerful language of transcendence, crossing over and moving beyond. While there is a constant recognition that we are not yet what we ought to be, this metaphor of journey evokes adventure, courage, and daring. For Pentecostals, the life we are called to is one where we seek to live in continuity with the first-century Christian communities hoping to transform and embrace the neighbourhood, the society, the world. Concerning this motif in Luke-Acts, see Filson, "Journey Motif in Luke-Acts."

22 Ward, *Pentecostal Testimony* 37 (May 1956), 7.

23 Kulbeck, *What God Hath Wrought*, 30–1.

24 Yong, *Discerning the Spirit(s)*, 134, also writes of the importance of a holistic understanding of human religiosity and that the Pentecostal experience "demands interpretation of the experiential dimension of spirituality over and against an emphasis on textuality in religious life." Pentecostal spiritualities reflect the conviction that Pentecostals experience God through the Spirit and are expressed in liturgies that are primarily oral, narrative and participatory. On the importance of testimony in Pentecostal liturgy, see Albrecht, *Rites in the Spirit*; and Ellington, "The Costly Loss of Testimony," 48–59.

25 Cerillo and Wacker, "Bibliography and Historiography of Pentecostalism in the United States," 392.

26 Wacker, *Heaven Below*, 11–15.

27 David Slauenwhite is a former district superintendent of the Maritime district of the PAOC and remains an active writer and preacher. See *Fresh Breezes: An Historical Perspective on the Pentecostal Assemblies of Canada*, 12.

28 Purdie, "The Vision Glorious," *The Gleaner* 11 (April 1950), 20.

29 See Stronstad, *The Prophethood of All Believers*.

30 Ibid., 123. Stronstad's use of the prophetic extends beyond an utterance gift to a lifestyle that is essentially vocational.

31 Frey cited by Wacker, *Heaven Below*, 169.

32 On this issue see Faupel, "Whither Pentecostalism?," 9–28. He argues persuasively that the emergence of Pentecostalism as a subgroup of evangelicalism increasingly encourages a silencing of the voices of women.

33 See the excellent defence of Pentecostal women in ministry by Gill and Cavaness, *God's Women*.

34 Moltmann, *The Spirit of Life*, 186. Moltmann asks where are the "charismata of the 'Charismatics'" in the everyday world, in the peace movement, in the movements of liberation, in the ecology movement."

35 See Tennant, "Tallying Compassion." In an interview with Cnaan, *The Invisible Caring Hand*, 56–9, the myth that mainline churches are more involved

with social services than evangelical churches is dispelled. Both spend an equal amount of resources in this area.

36 See Dempster, "Christian Social Concern in Pentecostal Perspective: Reformulating Pentecostal Eschatology," 51–64. Dempster, a Canadian Pentecostal, is president of Vanguard University in Costa Mesa, California.

37 Kydd, "To See Is To Be Called," *Pentecostal Testimony* 77 (January 1996), 11.

38 Ibid.

39 Examples include Luke 1:17; 7:22; 19:1–10; Acts 2:42–47; 4:32–37; 6:1–7; 11:27–30.

40 Kydd, "To See," 11.

41 See Wenk, *Community Forming Power*; Mittelstadt, *Spirit and Suffering in Luke-Acts*.

42 Volf, "On Loving with Hope: Eschatology and Social Responsibility," 29.

43 This approach is not exclusive to Pentecostal scholarship. In fact, with the emergence of literary criticism, careful scholarship on paradigmatic imitation of Lukan narratives continues to increase. Consider the following works: Mattill, "The Jesus-Paul Parallels and the Purpose of Luke-Acts: H.H. Evans Reconsidered;" Praeder, "Jesus-Paul, Peter-Paul and Jesus-Peter Parallelisms in Luke-Acts: A History of Reader Response;" Kurz, "Narrative Models for Imitation in Luke-Acts;" Kurz, "Open-ended Nature of Luke and Acts as Inviting Canonical Actualization."

7

Native Pentecostalism in British Columbia

ROBERT K. BURKINSHAW

INTRODUCTION

In most parts of Canada, Pentecostalism did not become a movement of significant proportions among indigenous peoples. Nevertheless, it did become a force of some numerical significance in the period after 1950. The 2001 census reported that nearly 19,000 or 3.4 per cent of the nation's "Registered/Treaty Indians" identified themselves as Pentecostal. Those numbers signified that Canada's status Indians were nearly three times more likely than the general population (1.24 per cent) to identify themselves with Pentecostalism.[1] In that same census, just over 35,000 of all people in Canada who claimed some Aboriginal origins also claimed to be Pentecostal.[2]

Pentecostalism developed some strength in native communities from Quebec westward to British Columbia and it took several forms. In the far North, ongoing revivals led many Inuit to embrace a charismatic version of Anglicanism or to meet in Full Gospel house churches;[3] in other regions the Foursquare Church or independent Pentecostal congregations took root. In even more communities the Pentecostal Assemblies of Canada (PAOC) established congregations. By 1986, the PAOC, Canada's largest Pentecostal body, reported 108 native congregations nationwide.[4]

Despite the significant numbers, very little scholarly attention has been paid to Pentecostalism among Canada's first nations peoples.[5] This study will focus on British Columbia and the establishment of the PAOC among its first nation communities over the latter half of the twentieth century. The dual purpose will be to describe basic elements of that development and to attempt to provide some explanations for it. Furthermore, this chapter illustrates the nature of transition for the PAOC and especially its view of mission and Aboriginal culture in Canada.

NATIVE INITIATIVE AND LEADERSHIP

In the late 1930s, the BC conference of the PAOC began to express official interest in the "logging, mining & fishing camps & many small towns and settlements" along the 7,000 miles of BC coastline, and by 1941 it had launched a "gospel boat" ministry.[6] At first no specific mention was made of ministry to native peoples but within several years the conference approved a motion that "an investigation be made relative to the possibility of the Home Missions department of the Province granting extra funds to help support work among the British Columbia Indians."[7] Very quickly the denomination acted on this recommendation; several additional gospel boats were added and "native evangelism" became a significant line item on the conference Home Missions department budget.[8]

A few native converts were reported by the late 1940s and a small native congregation developed at Alert Bay, on a small island off the northeast coast of Vancouver Island. However, in the early to mid 1950s, Pentecostal revivals began to spread rapidly among BC's coastal natives. Numerous reports of significant outbreaks of revivals in various native communities along the coast created considerable interest and enthusiasm in the PAOC. First-hand accounts suggest that revival began in, and then spread from, Alert Bay, where John Nygaard, PAOC missionary with the gospel boats, was based. The revivals included spontaneous prayer meetings in homes, large crowds in a church building, long services full of spirited singing and testimonies of conversion and healing.[9] The provincial superintendent travelled to northern Vancouver Island in April 1954 to witness the revival himself. He reported that he observed "the grace of God in a mighty visitation among the native people and my heart was glad." In Alert Bay, following a service for unresponsive "whites," eager natives packed the church for a revival service. At Quatsino, on northern Vancouver Island, nearly the entire village crowded into a revival meeting, which lasted late into the night. At Gilford Island, over 200 filled a large community hall for an Easter Rally that featured lively singing, preaching, prayers for healings, and testimonies. In a packed house meeting on Village Island, the old-time Pentecostal superintendent noted that the fervency "carried me back to my earliest recollections of the Pentecostal visitation." In another house meeting, on nearby Tournour Island, the service lasted until 2 am because of the number responding in repentance, including a boatload of people who had left the meeting earlier, "but the burden of sin was so heavy they turned the boat around and came back and surrendered to God."[10] In the northwest coast region of the province, a PAOC missionary noted that the Pentecostal message was being well received in the city of Prince Rupert and on "nine or ten" native reserves in the region.[11] Another rejoiced in responsive crowds as high as 400 and "a mighty move of the Spirit of God" at Pentecostal meetings.[12] In Kincoleth, a primarily Anglican reserve, fifty to seventy people were reported coming to the altar at services every night.[13]

Evidence suggests that these revivals were characterized by a great deal of native initiative, despite the PAOC's official interest and its investment in personnel and finances in outreach to natives. Outbreaks of Pentecostal fervour often appeared to be more spontaneous rather than the result of organized PAOC outreach. John Nygaard noted the tremendous impact in Alert Bay in the early 1950s of natives travelling to Vancouver to the Oral Roberts evangelistic and healing crusades. Upon return home, it was their enthusiasm and new commitment that helped spark widespread interest in Pentecostalism and led to overflow meetings and significant responsiveness.[14]

Native initiative expressed itself as numbers of converts became involved in evangelistic activities undertaken without any PAOC leadership. Indeed, Nygaard even initially opposed the fervent street meetings led in Alert Bay by accordion-playing Sarah Sampare. She persisted despite his displeasure, stating that "God led her to do it," and soon Nygaard became more positively inclined, especially after observing the favourable impact of her preaching upon both native and white people.[15]

In a manner reminiscent of the spread of Methodism among the Tsimshian of the north coast in the nineteenth century, groups of enthusiastic native Pentecostal converts travelled to other villages on evangelistic missions.[16] In the 1954–55 period, groups led by native evangelists travelled by boat from Alert Bay to surrounding villages in the waterways around Vancouver Island and reached as far south as Courtenay, approximately 250 kilometres distant.[17] In the spring of 1954 approximately forty young native men from Alert Bay, led by native evangelist Stacey Peters, travelled in two fish boats to Campbell River to hold Pentecostal singing and testimony services among the natives living in that area. As a result, dozens of natives reportedly crowded into the town's PAOC church "to seek deliverance from sin."[18]

The PAOC superintendent reported enthusiastically on the positive impact of these spontaneous groups as they travelled "from island to island setting revival fires burning."[19]

On the central coast, the origins of the Bella Coola native Pentecostal church, for many years one of the largest and most stable native congregations in BC, can be traced to largely native-led revivals which broke out in late 1954 and early 1955. Stacey Peters led a group of recent converts by boat about 300 kilometres north from Quatsino to hold services in Bella Coola. Large crowds attended the meetings and the first reported to respond to Peters' message of conversion was chief Johnny Moody. Upon the public declaration of his new faith, a large number in the crowd followed his lead.[20] Marion Johnson, a young PAOC missionary working in the Norwegian settlement of Hagensborg, about twelve miles inland, helped in the meetings. Subsequently she played a key role in organizing the native converts into an ongoing PAOC congregation, but she was not responsible for organizing or leading the revival.[21]

As these reports indicate, native evangelist preachers figured prominently in the spread of early revivals. Stacey Peters hailed from Quatsino and testified of being both healed of a serious leg injury and converted at meetings at Vancouver's Broadway Pentecostal Tabernacle. He travelled the province, preaching to native congregations wherever he found them, especially at canneries up and down the coast. A number of observers described him as a highly effective "pioneer preacher" who was able to gain a great response from native congregations.[22] While he did work with the PAOC, he always remained independent.[23] In addition to Peters, a number of native preachers worked on the BC coast. Harry Hunt, a Second World War veteran, notorious as a drinker and fighter in his home town of Alert Bay, was converted in the early 1950s revivals. After studying at the PAOC Bible College in North Vancouver for three years he entered an evangelistic ministry in BC that took him all over the province and beyond.[24] His "athletic style of preaching" often led to large-scale conversions, and healings were frequently reported at his meetings.[25] In 1958, after just a few years of full-time preaching, he carried a notebook in which he had recorded the names and addresses of over 1,000 converts.[26] The PAOC was very interested in having him join their ranks because of his effectiveness. In 1962 Nygaard reported continuing co-operation with Hunt, "the spiritual tide is still high. Bro. Hunt ... gathered from here (Bella Coola) and Bella Bella an invasion colony and invaded Klemtu, which is about 4 hours by boat from Bella Bella. The results were gratifying. They recorded 52 decisions."[27] However effective he was in helping the PAOC at times, Hunt always remained independent during more than forty years of preaching.[28]

In the late 1950s, brothers George and James Kallappa, young Makah from Neah Bay, on the Olympic Peninsula of Washington, were encouraged by the independent Faith Temple in Victoria to begin preaching on the west coast of Vancouver Island. Both were recently converted alcoholics and gifted preachers who shared many cultural and linguistic similarities with bands living immediately across from Neah Bay on the Straits of Juan de Fuca on the coast of Vancouver Island. They met with considerable responsiveness in a number of isolated communities, including several in which relatives of theirs resided. In Bamfield, for example, all of the ninety people cramming the largest building available came to the altar at the end of the service. Congregations developed in small settlements such as Ucluelet, Bamfield, Ahousat, and Nitinaht. The Kallappa brothers soon joined the PAOC and went on to play significant roles in native churches in the province for much of four decades. James served as pastor in a number of native churches in BC, was very involved in training of native leaders, and eventually became director of Native Evangelism for the PAOC in BC. Because of an extensive ministry in Alaska and Arizona, George spent less time in BC but, by all accounts, was one of the most sought after evangelists and rally speakers in the province."[29]

The revival on the north coast also depended to a large extent on native preachers. In 1959 native lay preacher Paul Clayton reported on a week of meetings. "I've been having wonderful times in the service of my Lord. I went up to Kincoleth ... The whole village had a wonderful time except just a few people who did not come to the services."[30] At Kitkatla, William Gladstone, a native lay preacher, reported revival in which about "45, mostly young people, received the fullness of the Spirit."[31]

While native people often took the initiative in revivals on BC's coast, they also frequently sought and welcomed assistance from the PAOC. In 1952, Paul Mason, a young man from the Kitkatla reserve in the northwest region, wrote the BC PAOC office, identifying himself as secretary of the Native Revival Hour, a native radio ministry based in Vancouver. He wrote to thank its superintendent for sending a gospel boat to the fishing grounds and canneries in the summer and to request their return the following summer "to continue Gospel work in the canneries." He concluded, "That as a young man of Kitkatla, I am very much concerned about my people in this great North West – so this is by way of appreciative acknowledgement of your kindness in sending Bro. and Sister Dearden among us at this time."[32] Similarly, at a service of welcome in the Anglican church in Kitkatla in 1954, a lay reader asked the PAOC superintendent for a "resident ordained minister to help them walk in the way of righteousness."[33] Four years later, the PAOC Northland field director reported, "We also visited another reserve where the Natives are earnestly desiring services, but, Brother and Sister Williams find they cannot manage this due to lack of finance and adequate transportation."[34] The people of Clo-oose, a village on the west side of Vancouver Island, reportedly asked the PAOC missionary to move to Clo-oose and provided a house which was suitable both for the family and for holding services."[35]

INCREASING LEADERSHIP ROLE OF THE PAOC

Native initiative and leadership in the revivals continued for a number of years, but increasingly the PAOC and its missionaries began to play more significant roles, both in organizing PAOC congregations in native communities and helping to spark revivals. For example, in the winter of 1957–58, Marion Johnson, the PAOC worker organizing the native congregation in Bella Coola, was invited to hold services in Bella Bella, several hours away by boat. A number of Bella Coola people assisted her and the meetings in Bella Bella met with conversions on a large and dramatic scale. The annual report of the director of the Gospel Boats ministry to the denomination declared:

Sister (Marion) Johnson, the Mother to the Indians, leads the way and truly is a spiritual mother ... Her family is no small number, and the revival is incredible, for since last October till now, approximately 80 souls have bowed at Calvary and found a cleansing stream ... The astounding part is the young people – a gang of 18 boys and girls is broken up. The leader, Joe, is 19, a notorious character of such calibre so that he has put a gun to his throat and asked if any dared to pull the trigger. In court he threatens, "sentence me and you will pay the fare when I get out." Such a weapon of fear he wields that no one dares to do anything with him. God has saved him, and also baptized him with the Holy Ghost. The secretary also is saved and many of the gang. The village of Bella Bella is much relieved at the change which has come over these lives.[36]

Within a few months, that combination of native initiative and PAOC leadership led to a further cycle of outreach. In response to an invitation from the isolated village of Klemtu, Marion Johnson travelled with thirty new converts from Bella Bella and they were officially welcomed by the chief councillor and the United Church elders at a banquet held in their honour. They were given the use of the church and a generous offering to cover their expenses. Johnson reported, "There was a moving of the Spirit of God in conviction and about 20 persons were saved ... The Klemtu people were amazed at the change in the Bella Bella young people and were deeply stirred as they listened to them testify and pray."[37]

Although welcomed in some communities, the Pentecostal revivals faced stiff opposition in other villages, especially from the long-established mainline churches and their membership. PAOC leaders tended to attribute the opposition to defensive church leaders who, accustomed to nearly exclusive religious authority in their area, were protecting their historic "turf." In 1953, John Nygaard created a stir at the BC conference when he reported that some leading Anglicans in the Alert Bay area were pressuring the Department of Indian Affairs to withhold "government relief money" from seniors who continued to attend Pentecostal services.[38] A decade later, he described that pressure as a move "to banish us and every Pentecostal believer off all the islands."[39] Although that particular situation appeared to be resolved quickly,[40] opposition continued.

In 1959, in response to news of large numbers being baptized and joining the Pentecostals at Kitkatla, C.W. Lynn, PAOC officer, commented: "In all these areas we face bitter opposition from other churches. Few Natives attend these formal services, fewer have any experience with God, most all are blighted by drink and stuck in the gumbo of sin, but it would seem that these church leaders would rather have it that way than for the Pentecostal message to come with deliverance and reality. Let us pray for such a sweep of the power of God as will lift whole Native villages into the fullness and glory of New Testament Christianity and free them from the ecclesiastical Pharaohs who frighten them into submission."[41] Lynn elaborated further on the situation that same month in a letter to the PAOC headquarters in Toronto in which he commented on a resolution passed by the BC district. That resolution had stated: "Whereas our Pentecostal message is accepted on some of our Native Reserves across Canada, Be it resolved that this Conference recommend to the General Executive that they appeal to the Department of Indian Affairs at Ottawa for Dominion-wide recognition to minister on Indian Reserves."[42]

In his letter to C.M. Wortman urging action by the national office, Lynn wrote, "This seemed to us to be a very important Resolution. We continually meet up with a situation where either the Anglicans or the United or the Catholics seem to feel that they only have an exclusive right to hold services on Native Reserves ... I think it is time that the Government awakened to the fact that there are others interested and able to labour to improve the lot of the Indians of our country."[43] Such efforts did lead to official recognition of the PAOC. For example, in 1962, the PAOC minister in Chemainus, Vancouver Island, rejoiced in gaining the legal right to perform marriages. He reported: "We feel this event constitutes a milestone in our ministry here: helping these dear Indian folk understand that we, in the sight of God *and* the Law, have the authority to perform marriages; giving them a greater sense of security in the Gospel we preach; and imparting to them more boldness to exercise the religious freedom that is rightfully theirs."[44] However, significant opposition continued for some time longer. In 1962, PAOC workers on Kuper Island, a largely Roman Catholic reserve just off the east coast of Vancouver, reported that "The home on the reserve in which we held our Bible Club is now closed to us. There is a continued attempt being made to halt the work of the Gospel on this reserve.[45] From Massett, on the Queen Charlotte Islands, in 1963 it was reported, "Yet while the Lord has been moving in the services, the Devil has been fighting too. The air has been let out of our tires, rocks have been thrown and broken the back windows, and the wiring has even been all pulled out from under the dash in our jeep."[46] The following year, field director Nygaard commented, "At Masset we found nothing new. The same old war raged as we have always faced. I would say fiercer, perhaps ... "[47] James Kallappa, who preached in most of coastal BC, agreed that the most serious opposition he observed was from the Anglican church in the Massett area in the early 1960s. He felt that Anglicans, fearful of decline, were "intimidated" by Pentecostals and afraid of losing members in large numbers.[48]

Some native converts felt that fellow native mainline church members, more than church leaders, led the opposition to their conversion. Bruce Brown, self-described alcoholic and drug addict before his conversion in the early 1960s during the early days of Pentecostalism on the Queen Charlotte Islands, experienced significant opposition from fellow band members, including some of his own family. Even though he had not attended Anglican services for years and even though his destructive lifestyle changed subsequent to his conversion and he became very useful to the band as a leader, his conversion was not welcomed by all. He believed that people's traditional loyalty to the church and their concern for the "religious unity of the village" caused them to oppose both his conversion and his efforts to lead a small Bible study group.[49]

Despite such opposition, by the mid to late 1960s, it was clear that the PAOC had established itself as a major presence in a number of communities in BC's coastal region. It was conducting regular services in twenty-six communities; a number of congregations had become well established, with several owning their building. In the north, congregations formed in Prince Rupert, Masset, Hazelton, Kispiox, and Kitwancool. Three hundred people attended the dedication of the newly acquired building at Kispiox in 1962[50] and that year the PAOC pastor of the native congregation in Hazelton reported "after five years of energetic ministry, the number of Natives who are embraced in the Pentecostal Fellowship in the general area run into the hundreds."[51] On the central coast, Bella Bella and, especially, Bella Coola, became centres of Pentecostalism. Bella Coola, the first native congregation to gain its own building, was formally organized as a legal entity in 1965 and was able to support itself financially and to make contributions to PAOC funds.[52] It continued as a centre of revivalism. In 1966 it was reported, "Sunday night we had a great visitation from heaven; we had to move to a hall (Moore hall), and we were packed in until we didn't have much room to work around the altar. Monday night, the last night of the rally, we moved into a larger hall, and they counted 400 – many of whom had to stand the whole service."[53]

PAOC institutional development was perhaps most evident on Vancouver Island where the denomination was able to build on some earlier Pentecostal work. In the late 1940s, the Alert Bay native PAOC congregation became the PAOC's first native church in BC.[54] Its roots were in a tiny independent Pentecostal group started by several Apostolic women preachers from Vancouver around 1930. The Foursquare denomination had developed a native congregation at Fort Rupert but withdrew in 1947, allowing the PAOC to begin a congregation there in the early 1950s.[55] PAOC congregations formed quickly in nearby areas in the northern part of the island at Quatsino, Port Hardy, Coal Harbour, and Gilford Island (in which every child between the ages of three and eleven years reportedly attended the PAOC Sunday school). In addition, regular services were conducted in many smaller villages.

As an alternative to the summer camp meeting grounds, which had become a mainstay of Canadian Pentecostalism, North Isle Native Pentecostal Camp in Fort Rupert at the north end of Vancouver Island was built in the 1950s. Because of the summer fishing season, most native Pentecostals were unable to attend summer camp meetings and thus they and PAOC workers built the North Isle camp which was able to accommodate Thanksgiving and Easter native rallies which drew hundreds from surrounding areas.[56]

In the mid-island area, native initiatives led to the formation of the West Coast Indian Fellowship in 1964, a native-led organization which formally affiliated with the PAOC.[57] Its main function was to organize regular rallies and camp meetings and it included groups of native Pentecostals in Bamfield and Port Alberni, which had originated with the work of independent evangelists. It also included congregations in Chemainus and Nanaimo which had been founded by the Mattaniah Indian Mission, an organization begun in the mid 1950s by Carl Miller of Seattle. With the assistance of college interns, they had developed a circuit ministry which included up to fourteen villages. The summer highlight was a vacation Bible school, which involved up to 450 children on eight reserves.[58]

In 1964 the BC PAOC district formalized the leadership of its native work by creating the full-time position of field director for Native Evangelism. Long-time Gospel Boat worker and pastor of native congregations John Nygaard was appointed to the position for a two-year trial period. In 1966 the position and appointment was made an ongoing one.[59] Obviously, the denomination was encouraged by the developments. The BC superintendent summarized in February 1965, "During the past years, it has been very evident that it is God's day of visitation to our Indians of B.C., as well as other places. The revival has spread from village to village until a goodly number of points are found with congregations."[60]

By the late 1960s and the 1970s in BC, reports of opposition from mainstream churches continued but with reduced frequency. Apparently many came to terms with the PAOC and examples of co-operation began to appear. For example, in 1971 in Queen Charlotte City, a United Church building " built more or less as a community project" was offered for use to the PAOC and it was reported that "the people who form the building use committee gave the impression that they sincerely hoped we would feel free to use it."[61] In the Northwest, PAOC churches began to participate in the local funeral custom in which all local church groups make presentations of gifts or play or sing music to the family of the deceased. "When it comes to death, we forget about denominational lines and try to support the people." [62] In the spirit of generosity reminiscent of potlatching, the bereaved families raised large sums to help defray costs of church groups, including PAOC groups, which had travelled long distances.

In the late 1960s and the 1970s reports of revivals continued, but with reduced frequency. Several new congregations were begun but native evangelism director Nygaard expended most of his energy in constructing church buildings for native congregations in a number of small communities.

In that period the PAOC also identified three urban centres as of particular strategic significance for its native outreach; Prince Rupert on the north coast, Nanaimo on Vancouver Island, and Vancouver. Prince Rupert was called "hub of the wheel; the center of many villages" and was the centre of much of the commercial fishing activity on the coast in which so many natives were employed.[63] As early as 1963, C.W. Lynn stated, "I am sure that we will all agree that a Revival Centre in Prince Rupert, where we have hundreds of Natives who have tasted Pentecostal blessings, is just as purposeful as a Revival Centre in any other city of the world."[64] Similarly, Nanaimo was considered the "hub of the island." Vancouver, with its tens of thousands of native residents, was considered of special importance.

In 1965 the BC district passed the following resolution: "Whereas there are many Indians converging on Vancouver from various points, and Whereas an increasing number of native students are attending High School and University in Vancouver, and Whereas the home church ties of these people are thus severed, and other organizations are seeking to draw these people away from their Pentecostal faith: Be it resolved that an Indian Revival Centre in Vancouver be given immediate consideration by the district executive."[65] Because of the strategic importance of these three centres and because of the considerable fluidity of the native population, with a continuous flow back and forth from isolated reserves to the city, the PAOC was prepared to give greater assistance to these "revival centres" than it was to congregations in smaller centres. When strong leadership was in place such a strategy paid off with regular attendance often well over one hundred people. However, frequent instability of both leadership and of the local population also led to these centres sometimes falling into decline, even temporary closures.

Dynamic new leadership of PAOC native ministries under Peggy Kennedy, following the retirement of veteran John Nygaard, led to renewed expansion of the PAOC in the 1980s. Eleven new churches and ministry sites opened in that period. Significantly, seven of the new churches and ministry sites were in the province's interior (Merrit, Williams Lake, Burns Lake, Prince George, Fort St James, Penticton, Salmon Arm), a region in which the native population had been largely untouched by Pentecostalism. It was also significant that two of the new churches, in Victoria and Prince George, were in larger urban centres with substantial transient native populations.[66] The Vancouver native church reopened after a hiatus of several years when it began to draw large crowds, especially to its Sunday evening services. In 1988, Canadian Native Bible College, a two-year program designed to train native Pentecostal pastors, opened in Vancouver. Its enrolment reached twenty-five in its first years of operation.[67]

Numerically, Pentecostalism seems to have hit its highest point by about 1990. The 1991 census revealed that 6,180 people who claimed at least some Aboriginal origins in BC identified themselves as Pentecostal, a higher number than in any province except Ontario. In terms of those listed as registered or "treaty" Indians, 3,165 (4.1 per cent) identified themselves as Pentecostal. Of natives who lived on reservations, the percentage was even higher, at 5.2 per cent, or 1,660.[68] Highest was in the heavily populated Vancouver Island and Central Coast census district in which 985, or 10.6 per cent of reserve residents were Pentecostal. In that district the number of Pentecostals varied widely; from zero on some reservations, especially on the southern end of Vancouver Island to 130, or 67 per cent, of the 193 residents of the Quatsino reserve on the north end of the island. In between were the Nanaimo area reserves (70 Pentecostals of 479 residents – 15 per cent), Alert Bay reserves (115 of 617 – 15 per cent),Bella Bella (180 of 1,104 – 16 per cent) and Bella Coola (180 of 705 – 26 per cent). The second highest concentration of Pentecostals on reserves was in the equally populous North Coast census district, where 430 or 5 per cent identified themselves as Pentecostal. On the Kitwancool reserve, long responsive to Pentecostal revivals, 140, or 45 per cent of 308 residents listed themselves as Pentecostal. In other regions of the province, a few isolated smaller pockets of Pentecostal natives were found but, overall, only about 2 per cent or fewer of their smaller reserve populations identified themselves as Pentecostal.

While the overall number of native Pentecostals was not extremely large, the figures gain in significance when viewed against the backdrop of decline among the mainline Christian denominations on the reserves. In 1951, nearly 98 per cent of all on-reserve natives in BC identified themselves as either Roman Catholic (58 per cent), Anglican (21 per cent), or United Church (19 per cent). By 1991, that total had dropped dramatically to 72 per cent – Roman Catholic (44 per cent), Anglican (13 per cent), and United Church (15 per cent). Apparent secularism was the biggest "winner" in that period on the native reserves with those declaring no religious affiliation rising from negligible numbers to 12.5 per cent in 1991. In addition, just over 2,300 British Columbians identified with "Native Indian or Inuit" religions that year. That census does not allow any kind of geographic breakdown of those identifying with that form of religion. It is clear, however, that Christianity was facing a renewed challenge from forms of Aboriginal spirituality. In such a context of declining affiliation with mainline Christianity and increasing challenges to it, the appearance and growth of Pentecostalism is more noteworthy and raises significant questions.

ACCOUNTING FOR PENTECOSTALISM IN NATIVE COMMUNITIES

Why Pentecostalism was able to take root and grow among native British Columbians in that period is one of the most important of such questions. Certainly Pentecostalism was also growing in the general population in the same period, but not nearly to the same extent as among native people. On the census of 1991, 2.1 per cent of all British Columbians labelled themselves as Pentecostal, one of the highest rates of any province in Canada. However, that was much less than half of the proportion (5.2 per cent) found on native reserves in the province and one half the proportion of the 4.1 per cent of status/treaty Indians in BC who called themselves Pentecostal. Thus it seems reasonable to look for explanations that are unique to native communities.

Dombrowski found that in southeast Alaska a socio-economic explanation helped to account for Pentecostal expansion. He noted that new converts were drawn from the ranks of those who were on the margins of village society, who were most affected by the economic dislocations of the 1960s and 1970s.[69] His findings certainly fit well with a long-established historiography regarding the spread of Pentecostalism elsewhere in the world.[70] However, marginalization does not seem to have been the case in the areas of greatest Pentecostal strength in BC. It indeed was true that most native communities experienced a lower standard of living than the provincial norm, but there is no evidence to suggest that converts were drawn from the margins of native society. Instead, in all the regions of Pentecostal strength, at least some band councillors, even chief councillors, either lent their support to Pentecostalism or themselves became Pentecostal.

In the late 1950s, Pentecostals seemed rather surprised by the warm welcome band leaders accorded them on Vancouver Island. From the north end of the island, it was reported that "Chief Speck of Turnour Island has been filled with the Spirit ... it has made a marvellous change in his life. At a Native Brotherhood meeting recently, John (the missionary) was invited to open with devotions and for the banquet was privileged to sit with the councillors and the Chief at the table!"[71] At Bamfield on the west side of the Island, it was reported that "Sister Marion Johnson has been welcomed by the Natives at Bamfield. The chief sent a special invitation when he heard she was at Port Alberni."[72] Several years later, missionary Mary Scholey wrote from Bamfield: "I had a very encouraging letter from the Oheat Chief Councillor from Port Alberni, commending us for the work done in the reserves; he mentions that the band meetings have taken on a new tenor since the people have been changed by the Bible teaching, and the arguments and quarrels have ceased. He invited me to meet with the Council and to attend the band meetings; and to keep them informed of special church meetings so their business sessions would not keep any of the people from attending services."[73] In Nanaimo Chief Baldhead personally helped build the Nanaimo Native Church and spoke at its dedication, urging the Pentecostal pastors to visit his people.[74] In Quatsino, several strong leaders of the native Pentecostal church were also respected leaders in the community.

In Bella Coola, not only was the first public convert chief Johnny Moody but several lay leaders of the congregation served on the band council. Ten years after the conversion of Chief Moody, Chief Lawrence Poudlus and his wife were reported converted to Pentecostalism in 1964 and had their five children dedicated in a Sunday morning service.[75] In that community, rather than being considered marginalized economically, Pentecostal natives came to be regarded by the manager of the Canadian Fish Company as "highliners, choice fishermen." Because they had stopped drinking following their conversion, he felt they were more effective fishermen who presented far fewer problems than he usually experienced with fishermen. To show his gratitude he provided a fishing boat each season for many years for use by missionary Nygaard, who needed to supplement his family income for six weeks each summer.[76]

In the northwest region, strong leaders in the local Pentecostal churches in Kincolith, Kitwancool, Massett, and Metlakatla also became leaders in their communities.[77] Throughout the coastal region, band councils gave permission to PAOC congregations to use buildings and land owned by the band, and a number of councillors hosted meetings in their own homes.[78]

A much more satisfying explanation for the spread of Pentecostalism among BC natives lies in the affinities between native views of spirituality and the spiritual perspective of Pentecostalism. Historians of worldwide Pentecostalism frequently note Pentecostalism's ability to resonate with the underlying spirituality of many societies that have been resistant to Western rationalism. For instance, Gaston Espinosa's study of the growth of Pentecostalism among Latin Americans suggests that its preachers' "charisma-laden message tapped into the worldview of popular religiosity with its tremendous emphasis on divine healing and the spirit world."[79] Canadian United Church historian John W. Grant provides a similar explanation, ascribing Pentecostal successes, at least in part, to the fact that the "charismatic approach has affinities with Indian concepts of communion with the spirits ... "[80]

Historian Susan Neylan's penetrating study of nineteenth-century Christianity and missionaries among the Tsimshian of BC's north coast suggests a similar explanation. She asserts that the Tsimshian took an active role both in responding to and spreading Christianity in the nineteenth century because of some striking compatibilities of spiritual outlook between themselves and evangelical Protestantism. Not only did the Tsimshian view the world in essentially spiritual terms, but their concepts of spiritual transformation, the acquisition of spiritual powers, and the responsibility to attain their more than human potential all made them more attentive to Christianity, particularly in its more revivalist forms.[81] With her explanation in mind, it is not surprising that the nineteenth-century spread of Methodism along the BC coast, especially as preached by indigenous evangelists, has been described as "marked by signs and wonders and by spiritual contests reminiscent of the earlier conversion of Europe."[82] In the mid-twentieth century, Pentecostalism, with its intense focus on spiritual experiences and gifts, appealed to many on the BC coast in a similar way.

Indeed, in the 1950s and 1960s, evangelists noted a special appeal of Pentecostalism to older natives who recalled fondly the long lost days of Methodist revivalism.[83] The mainline Methodist (United Church) and Anglican missions had long lost most of the revivalist fervour which had marked their earlier days. Although it would be difficult to classify those denominations as thoroughly liberal, they had adopted twentieth-century norms sufficiently that Harvey Cox's analysis contains some relevance for their native ministries. Cox argued, "Liberals tried to adjust to the times but ended up absorbing so much of the culture of technical rationality that they no longer had any spiritual appeal."[84] Native preacher James Kallappa explains that a liberal, rational approach was foreign to most natives. "The gifts of the Spirit were so appealing to the Natives ... They wanted 'life,' not the 'deadness' of the mainline denominations ... They want and need 'the anointing.'"[85]

BC natives were especially attracted to Pentecostalism's claims of spiritual sources of physical healing. They frequently experienced work-related accidents and suffered a high incidence of diseases such as tuberculosis. Further, they seemed unwilling to separate the spiritual and the physical aspects of life and evidenced little of the skepticism toward faith healing so characteristic of Western society. They were "traditionalists" of the type which Harvey Cox notes: "History shows that the norm in most of the cultures of humankind ... has been the complementarity of religion and healing, not their separation. It has only been very recent, and mainly in the West, that the two have been so utterly divorced."[86]

Long before Pentecostal missionaries actively began working among BC natives, first nations people expressed considerable interest in the practices of healing within Christianity. The Indian Shaker Church, which combined Christianity with elements of native religion and placed considerable focus on physical healings, appealed to a number of native people in southern BC in the first half of the twentieth century. While remaining much stronger in Washington State, in which it originated, and in Oregon, there is evidence of interest and activity among natives in British Columbia. Soon after the turn of the century, small groups of Shakers appeared in up to about a dozen communities on Vancouver Island and in the adjacent Gulf Islands and in several communities near Vancouver.[87]

Larger numbers were attracted to evangelist and faith healer Charles S. Price, whose 1923 meetings made Pentecostalism well known in the province. His massive rallies in Victoria and Vancouver drew crowds up to 15,000 that overflowed the largest arenas in both cities and touched off significant controversy in the press and in the churches.[88] News articles make clear that native people travelled long distances to attend these meetings. The *Vancouver Daily World* reported on 19 May 1923, "tonight will be a remarkable one at the arena when Dr. Price will seek to cure 60 Indians who have arrived here, chiefly by boat, from many parts of the province. He stated this morning in conversation that many Indians, including a chief, had been cured of cancer and other diseases at Victoria under his influence."[89] In 1924, Price returned to Victoria and Vancouver. Controversy over claims of healings and his encouragement of "speaking in tongues" reduced overall attendance, but participation by natives did not seem to decline. In an article entitled "Indians Come to Hear Evangelist," the *Victoria Daily Times* reported on 3 May 1924: "It was a healing meeting and Indians from the reservations in many parts of the Island congregated in the Auditorium."[90] There is no evidence that natives returning to their reserves from the Price meetings established Pentecostal congregations. However, it is possible that the significant native participation in those rallies influenced the strength of native Pentecostalism a generation later on Vancouver Island and in other coastal areas.

A major and direct impetus to the outbreak of Pentecostal revivals in the 1950s, as was mentioned earlier, came from native people returning from Oral Roberts' healing meetings in Vancouver, Seattle, and even further afield. In 1953 an Alert Bay area chief went to Oral Roberts' meetings in Seattle and brought back recordings received from Roberts. Local people eagerly came to attend meetings in which the recordings were played. In those meetings, people claimed to be healed and converted, including the chief's daughter.[91] Some natives went even greater distances to pursue healing, sometimes with considerable local significance. In 1957 it was reported that a man from Bella Bella "who had been listening to Oral Roberts' program and reading his magazine decided to go to his campaign for prayer as he was afflicted with a serious heart ailment. Travelling by air all the way to New Mexico, he was not only saved but wonderfully healed and is anxious for the Full Gospel message to be upheld in this village."[92] Several months later he was one of the people of the village who helped arrange meetings with Marion Johnson from Bella Coola which resulted in significant Pentecostal revival over the next months in Bella Bella.[93]

Radio broadcasts, to which coastal natives frequently listened on their battery powered radios, played a leading role in their familiarity with healing evangelists. Pentecostal elder Beatrice Scow remembers being impressed by the impact of a healing evangelist, "Brother Ralph," of Seattle. A tuberculosis patient at the Nanaimo Indian Hospital in 1951–52, she recalls that the majority of her fellow patients in the very large ward listened regularly to his broadcasts. Although not yet a convert herself, she was much moved as she observed nearly every native patient bowing in prayer, with hand laid on the radio, as the evangelist prayed at the end of the broadcasts. Scow herself was led to seek conversion by the radio preaching of W.E. McAllister of Broadway Pentecostal Tabernacle in Vancouver.[94]

Oral Roberts was perhaps the best-known healing evangelist among native British Columbians but other healing evangelists, including Don Moore, Len Lindstrom, Jimmy Swaggart, and Max Solbrekken, were able to draw large crowds from native communities over the decades. For example, in 1987 the denominational newsletter reported: "Hundreds of Native people from around the District and the western provinces gathered in Vancouver for the Jimmy Swaggart Crusade, May 29–31. On the Crusade Sunday, over 125 visitors found their way to Vancouver Native Church for a tremendous day of ministry. Part of the significance of the Crusade was seeing such a widespread provincial Native response – another indicator of the growing tide of revival in our land."[95] In more recent years, international healing evangelist Max Solbrekken, based in Edmonton, Alberta, frequently draws very large crowds of native people to large rallies in Prince Rupert.[96] The evangelist's website features several stories of healing by native people in the northwest part of the province.[97]

While natives found very attractive the large, often spectacular meetings of big-name healing evangelists, their local Pentecostal services also frequently featured prayer for physical healing. Native pastor Bruce Brown states that healing prayer and prayer for deliverance were "way more common in native churches than in white PAOC churches."[98] Monthly reports from the pastors and missionaries over the decades bear out his observation. Stories of healings figured quite prominently nearly every month and often were accompanied by reports of increased responsiveness in the community. Some of the stories were quite dramatic. From Hazelton, in 1957 it was reported:

During the service one of the Chief's daughters collapsed in the home and one of the boys came running to tell the parents. We went to pray for this little girl and when we got to their home there were about a dozen native folk praying, I mean praying. We went in and Bro. Williams and I knelt at the bedside, I took hold of her hand, it was cold. I could feel no pulse and the father said to me he thought she was dead. So we prayed, claiming the promises of God and the finished work of Christ, and as we finished praying I noticed the eyelids flicker, then slowly the eyes opened, color came into the face and the little girl sat up as her mother embraced her. The little girl raised her hand and said, Praise the Lord.[99]

In 1966 John Nygaard reported on an Easter Rally at Fort Rupert.

Sunday night was a memorable night when God moved in a way that neither Sister Meyer (evangelist) nor any of us had ever seen. A little baby was attacked as Sister Meyer was preparing to bring the message. The little tyke stiffened and turned colours. A sister tried to apply mouth to mouth respiration, which failed. Death was very present as the father took the child in his arms and brought it to the altar. Oh how they prayed – and the little thing cried again as the Galilean walked among us for the rest of the evening. Wandering ones came home and found rest as the Holy Spirit tugged away at their hearts. Others received the precious Baptism in the Holy Spirit ... To some poor souls, "God is DEAD" but to our Indians, God is very much alive.[100]

While Nygaard's statement may have bordered on both paternalism and triumphalism, it no doubt was accurate in the sense that it highlighted the desire of many natives for a form of Christianity that was compatible with their essentially spiritual world view.

Consideration must also be given to other areas in which compatibility existed between Pentecostal culture and the culture of BC coastal natives. Native culture on the BC coast has been described as an "events-oriented" culture in which large group events, spanning a number of days and involving large groups of people and often considerable travel, took precedence over routine schedules. Rather than putting their money into houses, savings, or insurance, natives placed high value on travelling with friends to events or in hosting events and providing generous feasts.[101] Pentecostal meetings, especially the rallies and camp meetings which took place a number of times a year, fit well into such a culture. Once the fishing season was completed, large-scale rallies, usually called the Thanksgiving rally, took place. A number of revival meetings would usually take place over the winter and, before people left for the fishing season, Easter Rallies were held. The meetings often lasted for days and included extended singing, emotional sermons, altar calls, testimonies, and prayers for salvation, healing, and deliverance and were followed by generous meals. Sometimes mass baptisms of converts took place.[102] People often travelled considerable distances to attend the meetings and, as a consequence, the crowds frequently far exceeded the capacity of church buildings so that band community halls were often used. Family ties often proved important, especially when the group travel involved evangelistic meetings on a reserve without a Pentecostal congregation. Often one or more members of the travelling group had relatives in the village to which they travelled, thus providing legitimacy to their activities.[103]

In addition, music provided common cultural ground between natives and Pentecostals. Cox notes that music has been one of the keys to the spread of Pentecostalism worldwide.[104] On the BC coast this was especially true because of a strong musical tradition, involving choral groups and bands, which had developed, at least partially, as a result of the extensive music training in residential schools.[105] The informal and extended nature of Pentecostal services provided both an outlet for a great deal of the musical talent as well as liberty and freedom in the services, including dancing. A remarkable number of native Pentecostal music groups sprang up, sporting names such as the Gospel Harmonizers (Bella Coola), the Gospel Heralders (Bella Bella), Quatsino Indian Village Choir, the Kitwancool Orchestra, and the Burning Bush (Kispiox). They travelled extensively, helping to draw crowds to evangelistic services and rallies.[106] Observers frequently commented on both the outstanding quality of the music and the enthusiasm of the participants.

A further explanation relates to the timing and context of the initial surge of Pentecostal revivalism in the 1950s and 1960s. In that period a type of "spiritual vacuum" was developing in many native communities for two basic reasons. Mainstream Christianity was no longer fulfilling the same role that it had for several generations of natives and traditional native spirituality was not seen as an option by most people at that time. Rodney Stark and Roger Finke make the point that as religious groups decline, other groups step up to take their place. The market for religion is always high. The suppliers will on occasion change.[107]

By the early twentieth century, most native reserves and villages had come to adopt almost exclusively either Roman Catholicism (largely in the interior but also in some coastal areas), Anglicanism (north coast, northern Vancouver Island, and several pockets in the interior) or Methodism, later United Church (Vancouver Island, central and northern coast).[108] Census reports indicate that on very few reserves did more than a handful of natives adhere to a branch of Christianity different from that of the majority and in a great many cases, 100 per cent of the residents of the reserve indicated the same denominational preference. However, in addition to the decades-long decline of the revivalism which had been so attractive to native people, a waning of enthusiasm among the historic churches for native ministry seemed to be prevalent, especially in the United and Anglican denominations. Canadian mission historian John Webster Grant notes that for much of the twentieth century, many missions of the mainstream churches "had become little more than holding operations." As early as 1916 "the Methodists reported that their missionaries were dying off and that younger men were showing little eagerness to replace them. In succeeding years their missions tended to be filled by new graduates always looking towards greener fields or by veterans for whom no 'better appointments' were available." Anglican missions, which never fully recovered from the withdrawal of the Church Missionary Society, suffered shortages of priests and missionaries.[109] The situation was similar to that of nearby southeast Alaska in which the older churches were finding it increasingly difficult to maintain existing congregations.[110]

Even when services could be maintained, attendance on reserves was often not very high. Numerous reports indicated that large numbers on many reserves rarely attended church.[111] The majority of natives in BC continued to identify themselves with their historic denomination, at least nominally, but for many, enough of a spiritual vacuum was created by the decline of these churches that they readily welcomed Pentecostal revivals.

Also in the 1950s and 1960s, native traditional culture and spirituality were no longer viewed as a viable option for many. It appeared simply inevitable that traditional first nations culture and religion would soon disappear and, consequently, that there was no future in retaining their past. The integration of native people into mainstream society was the favoured approach, culminating in the federal government's White Paper of 1967. Large numbers of BC natives, often the product of missions and of residential schools, seemed to accept the inevitability of the decline of their heritage. A 1987 study of Bella Coola noted that a process of "mainstreaming" had long been underway in that village. "Many changes occurred in the year 1933 as one of the Nuxalk chiefs reportedly told the people they must forget their Indian ways, language and culture, and become like white men. That year the chiefs stopped going to the petroglyphs for ceremonial and 'community planning' purposes and the first children were sent to residential school."[112] In 1954, a white visitor to Kitlatka, in the northwest, commented favourably on its progress toward assimilation: "this is a large village and quite up-to-date."[113] Similarly, in nearby Bella Bella a new PAOC minister remarked in the early 1960s, "Things are so very different here than they were in the N.W.T. [North West Territories]. The people are so much more advanced as well as hungry for the Word of the Lord."[114] So weak was loyalty to traditional spirituality that Pentecostal converts and PAOC evangelists and ministers report virtually no opposition to their work stemming from loyalty to native spiritual traditions in the 1950s and 1960s.[115]

The weakening of the mainline churches and traditional religion in that period removed the customary spiritual resources to deal with severe social problems, particularly the abuse of alcohol and its attendant problems, which were severe in many areas.[116] Pentecostalism's promise of deliverance from alcoholism proved attractive to many and stories of being set free from drinking problems figured at least as largely in native Pentecostal testimonies as did stories of physical healings.[117] Indeed, reports from the churches frequently mention people attending "who sought deliverance from alcohol."[118] An Oral Roberts song, often reported to be the favourite in native services in BC, alludes strongly to personal deliverance from alcohol:

> I was nearing despair, when He came to me there
> And He told me that I could be free
> Then He lifted my soul out of Satan's dark snare,
> When He reached down His hand for me.
> *Chorus*
> When he reached down his hand for me
> When he reached down his hand for me
> I was lost and undone without God or His Son
> When He reached down His hand for me.[119]

The religious/spiritual/social situation in a number of native communities was succinctly summed up in the comment of an elderly native woman, reported by a PAOC pastor: "We have lost our song long ago. But you Pentecostals – you have a song!"[120]

As attractive as Pentecostalism proved to be for many BC natives, numerical decline set in during the 1990s. In the 1970s and 1980s some inroads into major urban centres and in the province's interior were made but growth never matched the almost spontaneous expansion of the 1950s and 1960s. By the 1990s a number of forces combined to reverse the upward trend for Pentecostalism. The number of congregations declined from a high of 26 to 22. The census of 2001 reports an even steeper decline in numbers. On the reservations, the proportion listed as Pentecostal fell from 5.2 per cent to 3.0 per cent of the population, and among all registered/treaty Indians, the proportion fell from 4.1 per cent to 2.3 per cent. Potentially even more serious than those declines of 40 per cent, half or more of the native churches were without pastoral leadership, and deep discouragement replaced the formerly positive reports. Aboriginal ministries director James Kallappa provided a stark report to the 1999 district conference: "Aboriginal Ministries could possibly be facing the darkest hour in its history. With its decrease in attendance, declining finances, lack of pastors, sickness, burnout, the necessity of closing churches, insubstantial leadership and the possibility of selling one of our buildings has brought with it discouragement and frustration to many."[121]

In some ways the decline was predictable. It was one example of many out of a long Christian history of revivalism transitioning to institutionalization and routinization, with an attendant loss of enthusiasm and vitality.[122] However, as is always the case, unique factors were at work. With some notable exceptions[123] native Pentecostalism in BC experienced particular difficulty in adjusting once the fires of revivals died down. Ironically, some of the same cultural forces which aided its expansion in the 1950s and 1960s contributed to its decline.

NOTES

1 Statistics Canada, 2001 Census, "J3046: 2001 Target Group Profile of the Registered/ Treaty Indian Population in Canada." (prepared for the writer on request by Statistics Canada).

2 Statistics Canada, 2001 Census, "J3030: 2001 Target Group Profile of Aboriginal Origins Population (Single and Multiple Responses)" (prepared for the writer on request by Statistics Canada).

3 See "Northern Church Grows and Matures" and "New spirit sweeps the Arctic," in *Christianweek* 14, no. 4 (16 May 2000).

4 Pentecostal Assemblies of Canada, World Missions Communications, November 1986. The terms used to refer to Aboriginal peoples vary and are in flux. While "Aboriginal" is currently used, the term "native" was employed by the people Burkinshaw interviewed.

5 See Grant, *Moon of Wintertime*, where he gave little more than passing reference to Pentecostalism.

6 Minutes of 11th district conference of British Columbia PAOC, 27 July 1938 and 14th district conference, 18 July 1941

7 17th district conference, 4 July 1944

8 17th district conference, 5 July 1944 and subsequent conference minutes. It usually hovered around 10 per cent of the total home missions budget for the conference.

9 Interviews with Sarah Sampare, Fort Rupert, BC, 30 October 2004 and Beatrice Scow, Alert Bay, BC, 29 October 2004. Both lived on the Alert Bay reserve at the time and both became leaders among Pentecostal natives.

10 PAOC, BC District, Circular letter No. 4 (May 1954).

11 Circular Letter, May 1954.

12 Circular Letter, June 1954.

13 Circular Letter, March 1954.

14 Nygaard, *Beyond the Hammer and the Sword*, 58–60.

15 Sampare interview, 30 October 2004. This is the only example of native women taking the lead in preaching in this period that I could find. White women preachers became well accepted in many communities but native women were better known for the strong, but usually informal, leadership role they played in the home prayer meetings and in the congregations that formed.

16 Neylan, *The Heavens Are Changing: Nineteenth-Century Protestant Missions and Tsimshian Christianity*, 58–9.

17 Scow interview and Sampare interview.

18 Circular Letter, May 1954.

19 Ibid.

20 Sampare interview and Nygaard, *Beyond the Hammer*, 82–3.

21 Nygaard, *Beyond the Hammer*, 82–3 and Circular Letter, March 1955.

22 Interview with Dave Bauman and Merv Bowden, Chemainus, BC, 24 September 04 and Sampare interview. Stacey Peters was Sampare's nephew.

23 Sampare interview.

24 "Tribute to Harry," Carnegie Community Centre Newsletter, 15 September 2003; Nygaard, 60, George Kallappa to R. Burkinshaw, 22 July 2004 and Bauman and Bowden interview.

25 Circular Letter, March 1958, May 1962 and interview with Randy and Cheryl Barnetson, Vancouver, 5 February 2004.

26 Bauman and Bowden interview.

27 Circular Letter, June 1962.

28 Bauman and Bowden interview.

29 Based on a survey of Circular letters from 1960s into 2003; interview with James Kallappa, 30 March 2004, Neah Bay, WA, unpublished notes compiled by James Kallappa and interview with George Kallappa, 7 and 8 April 2004, Anahim Lake, BC.

30 Circular Letter, January 59.

31 Circular Letter, February 59.

32 Circular Letter, August 1952.

33 Ibid., May 1954.

34 BC District Conference sectional and departmental reports 1958, Northland section field director's report, A.F. Kennedy.

35 Circular Letter, September 1963 .

36 BC District Conference sectional and departmental Reports, Gospel Boat field director's report, 1958.

37 Circular Letter, March 1958. Despite reports of successful evangelistic forays into Klemtu, the PAOC never established a church there. This appears to be because not all natives who experienced Pentecostal revivals left their own mainline denominations and became Pentecostal. Many continued to affiliate with their denomination but also attended Pentecostal meetings from time to time. John Webster Grant notes that the native practice was to attend services of various denominations rather indiscriminately. "Exclusivism has never been the Indian way." Grant, *Moon of Wintertime*, 213.

38 The conference passed the following resolution, "Whereas ... our missionary from Alert Bay, Rev. John Nygaard, has reported that adherents of his church have been refused government relief money, in what would appear to be discrimination against our Pentecostal Indian folk, that this conference go on record as requesting our District Superintendent, if necessary, to contact the Indian Commissioner in Vancouver, urging him to do all in his power to correct this unfortunate situation." Minutes of 26TH Annual conference, 19 May 1953. The Scow and Sampare interviews confirmed that some elderly Pentecostals felt threatened that they would lose their benefits.

39 Circular Letter, July 1964.

40 "Your Supt. went with John (Nygaard) to see the Indian Commissioner in Vancouver, and had a very satisfactory interview with him about our work among the Indians." Circular Letter, June 1953.

41 Circular Letter, May 1959. The comments appear to be those of the superintendent. It is possible, however, that he was simply passing on, or paraphras-

ing, comments of William Gladstone, the native lay preacher who wrote the report of the baptisms.

42 Minutes of the 1959 BC District Conference, Resolution #11.

43 C.W. Lynn, BC Supt., to Dr C.M. Wortman, Toronto, 20 May 1959.

44 Circular Letter, July 1962.

45 Ibid.

46 Circular Letter, January 1963.

47 Circular Letter, July 1964.

48 J. Kallappa interview, 30 March 2004.

49 Interview with Bruce Brown, Langley, 4 February 2004.

50 Circular Letter, March 1962.

51 Ibid.

52 BC District Conference, 1966, Report of the Native Evangelism and Gospel Boats and chart; Churches' giving to Western Pentecostal Bible College, May 1965 to 20 April 1966. Adult, baptized membership was 35, growing to 47 in 1967. BC District Conference, 1967 Report of Native Evangelism and Gospel Boats.

53 Circular Letter, May 1966.

54 The small congregation had been mixed native and non-native previously but, following the appointment of John Nygaard as pastor in 1946, it became primarily a native church. See Klan, "Pentecostal Assemblies of Canada Church Growth in British Columbia from Origins until 1955," 167–8.

55 Klan, "Pentecostal Assemblies of Canada," 167–9.

56 Nygaard, *Beyond the Hammer*, 164–74.

57 "Suggested Working Agreement between The British Columbia District of the Pentecostal Assemblies of Canada and The West Coast Indian Fellowship," 1964. Copy in conference files, WPBC archives.

58 Fellowship News, January 1984 and Nygaard, *Beyond the Hammer*, 176–9.

59 BC Conference Minutes, 1966.

60 Circular Letter, February 1965.

61 Fellowship News, March 1971.

62 J. Kallappa interview.

63 BC District Conference, 1971, Report of Native Evangelism and Gospel Boats.

64 Circular Letter, July 1963.

65 BC District Minutes, 1965, Resolution #10.

66 BC District Conference, 1990, report of Native Evangelism co-ordinator.

67 BC District Minutes, 1988, Resolution #8 and BC District Conference, 1989, report of Native Evangelism co-ordinator.

68 For the purposes of this study, several large reserves surrounding Kelowna, Vancouver, and Victoria have been eliminated because the majority of residents on those reserves are not native but live on residential lands leased from the bands.

69 Dombrowski, "Against Culture," 295–324.

70 Anderson, *Vision of the Disinherited*.

71 Circular Letter, March 1958.

72 Circular Letter, November 1960.

73 Circular Letter, May 1965.

74 Fellowship News, January 1970 and October 1971.

75 Circular Letter, January 1964 and July 1968, James Kallappa interview.

76 Nygaard, *Beyond the Hammer*, 89–94. It would be a stretch to argue from this that PAOC growth was enhanced by a special relationship to industry. This particular incident came several years after the initial revival brought most of the conversions at Bella Coola. Other practices, such as lumber companies donating material or selling lumber at discounts for PAOC churches, were not unusual but were commonly provided for other denominations as well. Indeed, Nygaard needed to make a special visit to Vancouver in order to persuade forestry company McMillan Bloedel to give the customary 25 per cent discount for lumber for church construction to the PAOC. Nygaard, *Beyond the Hammer*, 84.

77 J. Kallappa interview; Brown interview; Nygaard, *Beyond the Hammer*, 126.

78 E.g., Circular Letter, May 1954 and October 1963, Fellowship News, October 1968 and July/August 1994, 1978 District Conference, report of Native Evangelism and Gospel Boats, 1988 District Conference, report of Northwest Northlands Section, 1992 District Conference, report of Native Ministries.

79 Espinosa, "El Azteca: Francisco Olazabal and Linto Pentecostal Charisma, Power, and Faith Healing in the Borderlands," 613.

80 Grant, *Moon of Wintertime*, 202.

81 Neylan, *The Heavens*, 27–44; 268–9.

82 Grant, *Moon of Wintertime*, 133.

83 Interview with Peggy and Jack Kennedy, Vancouver, 24 February 2004. See also Hollenweger, "Methodism's Past in Pentecostalism's Present," 169–82.

84 Cox, *Fire from Heaven*, 105.

85 J. Kallappa interview.

86 Cox, *Fire from Heaven*, 108.

87 Ruby and Brown, *John Slocum and the Indian Shaker Church*.

88 See Burkinshaw, *Pilgrims in Lotus Land*, 100–20

89 *Vancouver Daily World*, 19 May 1923, 3.

90 *Victoria Daily Time*, 3 May 1924, 9.

91 Circular Letter, April 1953.

92 Circular Letter, August 1957.

93 Circular Letter, December 1957.

94 Scow interview.

95 Fellowship News, July/August 1987.

96 Telephone interview with Dan Starlund, Terrace, BC, 21 June 2004. Rev. Starlund serves as presbyter of Aboriginal ministries in BC.

97 As of 22 July 2004, the website – www.mswm.org/miracle – featured testimonies of healing by a man from Kitwancool and by one from Kitsagulka, both in BC's northwest, in addition to several others from BC's northwest. In addition, the website included a lengthy tribute to Jack Williams, long-time PAOC minister to natives in the Hazelton, Kispiox, Kitwanga, and Kitwancool region.

98 4 February 2004 interview.

99 Circular Letter, March 1957.

100 Circular Letter, June 1966.

101 G. Kallappa interview.

102 Seventy-five were baptized at the Easter Rally at the Fort Rupert Campgrounds in 1959. Circular Letter, April 1959.

103 G. Kallappa interview.

104 Cox, *Fire from Heaven*, 121.

105 According to Grant, "as late as the 1950s running a church choir or band was said to carry more prestige in British Columbia than holding office in a community-oriented organization" *Moon of Winterime*, 174. J. Kallappa interview.

106 Dombrowski points to a similar dynamic in southeast Alaska. He notes enthusiastic singing, active congregational participation in the selection of songs, and playing of instruments (tambourines or shakers). Meetings could be quite long, especially in revival services. "Many people in the village point out that this sort of participation was true of early church membership throughout the region, and the Salvation Army bands of the various villages were always well supported and very popular though this is not the case today. Still many Southeast Natives, even those who do not now attend church, can sing traditional hymns," 269–70.

107 Stark and Finke, *Acts of Faith*.

108 Whiteheand, *Now You Are My Brother* provides a helpful map of the various mission stations, iv.

109 Grant, *Moon of Wintertime*, 197–8.

110 Dombrowski, "Against Culture," 265–6.

111 Interviews with Brown, Kennedy and Circular letter, May 1959.

112 Walmsley, "Changing the Future: A Social Development Plan for the Nuxalk Nation." March 1987.

113 Circular Letter, May 1954.

114 Circular Letter, November 1966.

115 All interviewees, Brown, J. and G. Kallappa, Kennedy's, made the same point.

116 "Bella Bella is a pitiful sight these days, when the liquor rights were given the natives in July, it meant war on our natives here. With fishing so good in these parts, it meant such an influx of fishermen and liquor and more liquor ... " Circular Letter, November 1962. Bamfield, "Had another funeral last week, a little baby of an unsaved drinking family. How terrible is their grief!" Circular Letter, March 1963.

117 All interviews and Nygaard, *Beyond the Hammer*, 85 and 98–9. Dombrowski, describes a similar theme in testimonies in Pentecostal services in southeast Alaska. "Perhaps the most common theme, though, is alcohol. Drinking problems are common in many villages, as are problems with drugs. Few villages have bars or even liquor stores, and many are ostensibly 'dry,' but all have bootleggers who buy out of the village and resell locally at greatly inflated prices. Most testimonies involve a confession of being a former 'hard drinker,' and of having hurt spouses, children, friends and neighbours as a result," "Against Culture," 279.

118 Circular Letter, October 1964.

119 BC District Conference, 1965, quoted in Report from the Director of Native Evangelism.

120 Home Missions narrated slide presentation, Peggy Kennedy, produced 13 December 1983.

121 1999 District Conference, Aboriginal Ministries report.

122 Grant describes such declines of Christianity at various points in time among natives in Canada, *Moon of Wintertime*, 92–3.

123 The Bella Coola church, with strong native lay leadership, exhibited considerable stability for many years.

8

Ministering Women in the Pentecostal Assemblies of Canada: A Feminist Exploration

PAMELA M. S. HOLMES

INTRODUCTION

One of the notable characteristics of the early Pentecostal movement in Canada, including the Pentecostal Assemblies of Canada (PAOC), was the number of women involved in various ministries. The early copies of the *Pentecostal Testimony,* the official publication of the PAOC, and the minutes of the initial meetings to organize the PAOC mention several women who were actively pursuing full-time ministry in Canada and overseas. The ministry of these women seemed to be welcomed and endorsed by their male counterparts. The ability of the fledgling movement to make "space" for women within its ranks at a time when such involvement would be controversial was significant.

One woman in particular, Ellen K. Hebden, was instrumental in the emergence of the Pentecostal movement in Canada. After emigrating with her husband, James, from England, she directed, either in partnership with James or alone during his absences, what has been called the "Canadian Azusa," that is, the East End Mission or Hebden Mission in Toronto, Ontario. Having received the baptism of the Holy Spirit on 17 November 1906 she was possibly the first person in Canada to have spoken in tongues, apparently without contact with William J. Seymour's American Azusa Street Mission or previous teaching on the matter.[1] Five months later, approximately eighty others, including her husband, had prayed in tongues. Shortly thereafter, six additional congregations were established in Toronto[2] and it was clearly reported in William Seymour's publication *The Apostolic Faith* that Pentecost had come to Toronto.[3] By the end of 1910, there were fourteen new congregations in Canada most of which were associated with the Hebdens. As well, of the fifteen overseas missionaries – seven of whom were women[4] – mentioned in a list compiled by George Chambers shortly before the PAOC became organized, all had been at least briefly connected with the Hebden Mission. Ellen Hebden also published the first Pentecostal periodical, *The Promise*. Toronto had become the "Canadian Jerusalem" in the sense that many early Pentecostal leaders considered the city a key location that must be visited, with the Hebden Mission the foundation for the city's ministries.[5]

In the early years of Pentecostalism in Canada, many other women were actively involved. Several women ministered as pastors, often pioneering new works. Alice Belle Garrigus from Boston started the Bethesda Mission in St John's, Newfoundland. From there the work expanded eventually forming the Pentecostal Assemblies of Newfoundland.[6] The Davis sisters, Carro and Susan, first started a church in Fredericton, New Brunswick in 1923 before moving on to found works in Saint John and Moncton. From the Saint John church several other assemblies were established throughout New Brunswick, Nova Scotia, and Prince Edward Island.[7]

Women were not only applauded for starting new works but also raised up as a positive model to emulate, as when John McAlister praised the "splendid little church Sister Beck built on her farm about five miles from Mawer, Saskatchewan."[8] Many women worked alongside their husbands as pastors. One such woman was Lillie Myrtle McAlister, wife of R.E. McAlister, who was himself a prominent leader instrumental in the establishment of the PAOC.[9]

Some lay women worked alongside their lay husbands or other nonclergy men in pioneering work. In Maxim, Saskatchewan Mabel Hurlbut ministered with her husband, Charles. Mabel had formerly worked with Carrie Judd Montgomery.[10] "Brother and Sister" Wills worked in Calgary, Alberta.[11] One woman, Mrs Adams, is reported to have opened a small mission work on Lonsdale Avenue in North Vancouver in 1915 with the help of her son Leslie.[12]

Occasionally women were called on to fulfill pastoral responsibilities when a man was not available. For example, Miss Laura Arnold is reported in the March 1921 *Pentecostal Testimony* as filling in for Brother Sternall in Kingston during his absence.[13] Mabel Cunningham ministered at first with her husband in St Catharines and Parry Sound. However, after her husband's death in 1925 she agreed to assume the duties of pastor in

Parry Sound and other assemblies. In July of 1925 she was "set apart for the work of the Lord by the brethren" at the London conference. She also served as an evangelist working with Ray and Joyce Watson in the Maritimes and in later years with her daughter, Jean,[14] earning her the title of "the Aimee Semple McPherson of Canada."[15]

Some women started new works only to be replaced when a pastor or pastoral couple was called. For example, by 1909, Mrs Martha Perry and her daughter, Mrs Olive Peterkin, were reported as faithfully and successfully witnessing to the Pentecostal expression of the faith in Parry Sound. Later, Rev. and Mrs George Wills were called as pastors and a building was erected by 1912.[16] Mrs Henry Snyder and Mrs George Stewart, who were expelled from their church in Vineland in the Niagara Peninsula after visiting Toronto and returning home Spirit baptized, held meetings in local homes and an unused school building. This became the nucleus of one of the earliest Canadian Pentecostal churches pastored by A.G. Ward (1908–09).[17]

Several women ministered as evangelists. Some were single women, like "Evangelist Miss Ethel Lee" who advertised her services in the *Pentecostal Testimony*. Others, like Sister Black, ministered alongside their husbands. One particularly well known evangelist was Zelma Argue whose ministry helped to establish the fledgling PAOC. Born in Winnipeg, Manitoba, she was ordained as an evangelist with the Assemblies of God in the US and eventually pastored in Los Angeles, California. However, in her earlier years she was active in the Canadian movement, often travelling with and assisting her father, A.H. Argue. As early as December 1920 she was publicly acknowledged in the first published issue of the *Pentecostal Testimony* and by the March 1921 edition of the same periodical was recognized as an evangelist in her own right.[18] Several articles by Zelma Argue were printed in the early *Pentecostal Testimony*.

Many women ministered as overseas missionaries and their activities were mentioned in various issues of the *Pentecostal Testimony*. Several were single – Miss Ethel Bingeman in West Africa oversaw a "mission station"; Sister Cora Haist of China; Miss Lettie Ward in China who "taught a class of Bible Women"; Miss Elsie Feary from Caracas, Venezuela where a new chapel had been opened; Florence Stock in North China reported that there were "over 27 single women missionaries ... only two young men and a few married couples"; Sister C. McCloud in India; Martha Hisey and Miss Kirsch in Liberia; Blanche A. Appleby in South China; Miss Katie Builder in India; Miss Gollan in Liberia, West Africa; Miss Brown in an overcrowded Jerusalem where over a thousand immigrants a month were arriving; Miss Anna Sanders in Mexico where the Catholic "priests warn the people against us."[19] The list could go on and on. One woman who must be mentioned is Sarah Weller, from Parry Sound, who went as a missionary to India in 1911, where she died from malaria and was buried in 1918 before the PAOC was organized.[20]

Still other women ministered alongside their husbands on the mission field. For example, the July 1921 issue of the *Pentecostal Testimony* includes a letter from Marion Wittick Keller of British East Africa. She claims that the work there was trying but going well as she labours with her husband. Dr and Mrs C.M. Wortman from London, Ontario worked together in the "Rest Home and the anticipated Maternity Home" in Argentina as well as the proposed Bible school; Brother and Sister Taylor were to be found in Africa; Brother and Sister James in China; Mr And Mrs Paul Andersen in India; Brother Bailey and his wife in Venezuela; Mr And Mrs Joseph K. Blakeney, missionaries to the Belgian Congo; George C. and Abbie Slager in China; Brother and Sister Watt in India.[21] Again the list could go on. It is obvious that the early Pentecostal movement in Canada was extremely mission-minded, with women actively participating in this area of ministry.

This brief survey indicates that women were active in various areas of public ministry within the fledgling Pentecostal movement in Canada and made significant contributions in the pioneering and establishing of the PAOC. Both the numbers of women and the types of ministry they exercised suggest that the early Pentecostal movement was an egalitarian one, in practice, if not in theory. On the surface it appears that women performed the same functions as men without any interference or objection from the men.

THE LATTER YEARS: EXPLANATIONS AND ANALYSIS

Although women were noticeably welcomed and involved in different ministries both in the years directly preceding the organization of the PAOC and on into its youth, as the institution matured the participation of women declined so much that by 1974 the question was asked as to why there were "fewer women today who profess to have a call ... than in earlier years." [22] While it has been suggested that the problem resided within the women themselves, a closer look at the available data hints at a more complex situation.[23]

Prophetic versus Priestly

Several explanations have been given to explain the decline in the numbers of ministering women within Pentecostalism. One, by the late Gerald T. Shephard and Charles H. Barfoot, explores the results of the shift within religious communities from an early, informally, and relationally organized state with a charismatic and prophetic style of leadership to an institutionally authorized style of priestly leadership. Within this schema the concept of a "personal call" becomes the "decisive element" which distinguishes a prophet from a priest. A prophet appeals to direct, personal revelation and charisma in defining and legitimating both calling and authority. In contrast, a priest is defined by and has legitimate authority based on allegiance to a particular religious tradition.

The early classical Pentecostal movement demonstrates evidence of this shift having occurred. In the early years evidence of Spirit empowerment and gifting when claiming to have a "call" was essential. In fact, the only distinction between clergy and laity was this calling. As the movement developed, however, the "priestly" aspects of calling took precedence and ministries became graded, with men holding the most prestigious positions.

This pattern is particularly noted within what has been called the religion of the lower classes, described as recognizing equality for women because of the prophetic and supernatural powers given by God. Nevertheless, the apparent equality of the sexes is overshadowed by the monopoly of men in religious functions, especially the administration of sacraments (or in the case of some Pentecostals, ordinances). As a result, the early freedom of gifted women is quickly eclipsed by the coexisting patriarchal assumptions and practices.[24]

That these patriarchal assumptions and practices existed alongside egalitarian impulses within the early Canadian Pentecostal movement is readily illustrated. Even though women did not hesitate to exercise their right to live out their calls to ministry, they still deferred to available, qualified men. For example, in March 1921 Miss Ethel Bingeman, reporting on the "Christmas Convention and Annual Meeting" held in Liberia, noted that among the twelve missionaries present, there were two couples, one man, and seven single women. After the four-day convention where "several were saved and filled with the Holy Ghost," Brother Garlick, who was reported as having only recently arrived with his wife, was the one to baptize the new converts.[25] Sheppard and

Barfoot, quoting Weber, state: "Only in very rare cases does this practice [equalization of the sexes] continue beyond the first stage of a religious community's formation, when the pneumatic manifestations of charisma are valued as hallmarks of specifically religious exaltation. Thereafter, as routinization and regimentation of community relationships set in, a reaction takes place against pneumatic manifestations among women, which come to be regarded as dishonorable."[26] This pattern existed within the early years of the Pentecostal movement within Canada. Ellen Hebden, an influential and foundational figure in the emergence and initial spread of Pentecostalism, particularly within central Canada, was against organization of any kind.[27] Therefore, when it came to the organization of the PAOC, the Hebdens absented themselves. Ellen Hebden's prophetic ministry, whereby she directed individuals – many of whom later became leaders in the organized PAOC – to particular areas of ministries under the influence of the Spirit, came under scrutiny and was deemed suspicious. In the process, "Sister" Hebden was disempowered and sidelined.[28]

As the "routinization and regimentation of community relationships" took place, the rest of the women were systematically disempowered. Although many women were present in at least some of the early organizational meetings[29] when the PAOC was originally charted on 17 May 1919, the "first or provisional directors" of the corporation were all male.[30] In their "Memorandum of Agreement" dated 26 April 1919 these men decided, among other matters, that the PAOC was to be an organization primarily consisting of and controlled by ordained Elders and Pastors all of whom were to be male.[31]

The constitution was soon put into practice. In November 1919 two men, Elder Bruce Freeborn and Harry Law, were recommended for ordination. In comparison, Miss L. Arnold and Mrs A. Lindsay were recommended for Missionary credentials, Mrs Parker was recommended for a Deaconess Certificate and William Parker and Brother and Sister L. Lowen were recommended for fellowship certificates. If the women had any objections or comments regarding their omission from ordained ministry or from leadership positions within the new institution, they were not recorded in the minutes.

While women's ministries within the new organization were still welcomed and affirmed, such ministries were to be exercised within a patriarchal hierarchy.[32] The effect was oftentimes confusing. For example, in 1949 letters were exchanged between Rev. J. Roswell Flower from Springfield, Missouri and Dr C.M. Wortman, the General Secretary of the PAOC, regarding the ordination of Mrs Hazel Argue, Richard Fleming May, and Margaret C. May.[33] Dr Wortman informed Flower that Rev. Richard Fleming May was ordained on 15 February 1938 while Mrs Margaret C. May and Hazel Argue were granted the credentials called a "Ministerial License for Women" (May on 1 August 1945; Argue on 28 April 1949). Dr Wortman went on to explain,

> we have two grades of credentials for women. One is a deaconess and more or less corresponds to a probationer minister, the other is the status of ministerial license for women which corresponds in qualification to the standing of an ordained minister although we do not have a regular ordination service when these credentials are granted. We do not refer to this grade of minister as "an ordained minister" but the qualifications are very similar. A woman must have Bible School training and several years of independent proven ministry before she becomes eligible to apply for these credentials.
>
> One of our problems here is in regard to women who hold a Ministerial License and then are married and in their married life do not actually carry on an independent ministry. As a rule however, they are jealous of their status and are unwilling to be classed in any other way than as a Licensed Minister even though they may only help their husbands to a small degree in the work.
>
> I am not sure in my own mind whether your ordination for women is exactly the same as for men or not. However, I believe it would be quite in order if you wished to recognize our grade of Ministerial License for Women as the equivalent of a man's ordination.
>
> In the past we have sometimes laid hands upon the women in a special service at the time of their receiving their credentials but it is not understood as a general thing that they are formally ordained as the men are. Then too, in their ministry if they are engaged independently they usually refer the matter of ordinances of the church to men if possible.
>
> Then again, our governments do not recognize these women as eligible to perform marriage ceremonies as ordained ministers ... [34]

I am not certain how Flower sorted this out but Wortman seems to be saying that this Ministerial License for Women is closer to that of men's ordination, in fact could be viewed as the same as the men's ordination only that women cannot legally officiate at weddings and women were encouraged to step aside and allow a qualified man to preside for the ordinances. No wonder the women jealously guarded this status, considering the effort that went into attaining it and the ambiguity in practice surrounding it. It is interesting to note that here is an instance of women actually objecting to the possibility of being "demoted."

By August 1925, when the western conference was deciding to affiliate itself with the eastern-based PAOC, the leadership was all male. When it was decided that the Western Council would be dissolved "with the view of bringing all Canada into one body" it was decided that "Provincial Districts with equal representation in the general body" would be established. The leaders of these Provincial Districts elected at this conference were also all male. When it was noted that "the majority of missionaries already on the foreign fields are women and sufficient funds are not yet forthcoming to send all those who offer themselves to the field" it was resolved that "when new recruits offer themselves, men have first consideration ... " With the large percentage of women involved in missionary work, this was a significant and restricting shift in strategy. Again, there is no recorded objection by women to this shift.[35] A patriarchal, hierarchical, priestly organization had firmly supplanted any earlier egalitarian, Spirit-empowered prophetic impulse.

An article in the August 1925 *Pentecostal Testimony* reported on the above meeting where four women were granted Deaconess Credentials.[36] Entitled "Qualification of Ministers" and addressed to "fellow- workers in the Gospel ministry," the article referred to women only as examples of error, such as the "lady who arose" in a church service to advocate for a Saturday Sabbath. The lady was compared with "that wicked woman, Jezebel, who called herself a prophet, to teach and to seduce" and described as a harsh and critical "lady" who had threatened a "good shaking" to the minister who indicated that he "was glad that woman" was not his wife. In contrast, reference is made to a "Brother preacher" and to "each young man entering his seminary to study for the ministry."[37] With all authority being given to men as leaders, ministers, and models while women were being systematically demeaned and demoted, women's involvement in ministry started to decline.

Anti-cultural

David G. Roebuck has claimed that anti-culturalism explains some of the declining numbers of ministering women within Pentecostalism.

Anti-cultural tendencies increased with a growing relationship with evangelicalism and its promotion of patriarchal order. As society began to expand roles for women during the 1920s, culminating in the rise of feminism by the 1960s, Pentecostal churches reacted strongly against such expansion. Women were soundly and often reminded where their scripturally based place was – in the home and in submission to men. Many women would find it difficult to reconcile their call to ministry with the institutional restriction on that call, a difficulty further compounded by the corresponding battle between traditionalists and feminists within church and society generally.[38] Therefore, the number of women found in ministry within Pentecostal churches declined.

That an anti-cultural stance was operative within the early PAOC is evident in an article by Zelma Argue in the July 1922 *Pentecostal Testimony* entitled "Two Types of Women Described in the Bible." Argue insists that "Young women of 'Pentecost,' Spirit-filled and consecrated to God" should obtain their standards and ideals from the "unchanging Word of God" rather than from "the world" which was understood to be "ripening for Anti-Christ."[39] The writing of such an article demonstrates that early PAOC members were aware of and negatively concerned with the changing behaviour of women in their time. It is, therefore, not surprising that churches were often started by women only to have an ordained male called by the congregation as soon as it was financially feasible.[40]

This anti-cultural stance, particularly as it involved women, continued to be manifest. In 1975, Gordon Upton mentioned the "paradox which exists between our fellowship and the world in general" regarding the declining numbers of women in congregational ministry. He wrote: "The Women's Liberation Movement is focusing attention upon the role of women in business, politics, and society in general and has been eminently successful in engendering wide-spread acceptance of female leadership in these areas. In spite of this the trend has been moving in the opposite direction in The Pentecostal Assemblies of Canada as far as lady preachers and evangelists are concerned."[41] This anti-cultural attitude continues to be present even among the women. As late as 1991, Shirley Flewitt, a retired minister, wrote in an article "Mentors to Many" of the many women who had influenced her life and thanked the *Pentecostal Testimony* for "highlighting women's place in the ministry." Then she added, "I am not a women's lib advocate and do not feel any need to protest, go on the march or whatever to secure a place. God does have a place in His program for women ... And He doesn't need extremists to promote His plan."[42] The changing behaviour and roles of women within society, particularly as they manifested in a feminist agenda, were strongly opposed.[43]

AUTHORITY ISSUES

The Spirit's/God's Authority

Roebuck insists that the primary reason for the decline of women in ministry within Pentecostalism involved "the limitations on authority that are inherent in the doctrine of Spirit baptism combined with the anti-culturalism of Pentecostalism."[44] In his view, Spirit Baptism, while encouraging the practice of preaching, never included a concept of authority granted for women. As it was the Holy Spirit who was in control when one was baptized, authority was understood to be centred in the Spirit and not the women. The women were only vessels which the Spirit equipped and used in order to assist in evangelizing the world before Christ's return. While women's influence may have expanded beyond the domestic realm and into the world in order to evangelize, this expansion included witness but not governmental authority. As Pentecostalism became institutionalized, various Pentecostal groups found scriptural support for excluding women from leadership positions within their governing bodies.

This factor can also be found within the PAOC. In the early days of Pentecostalism, whether or not one was qualified to minister – whether preaching, teaching, evangelizing, or something else – was based on the prerogative of the Spirit. As the Spirit was understood to be the one who gifts people for ministry within the church and the Spirit could gift whoever the Spirit pleased, leadership was determined on the basis of gifting. When it came to women, "in the early Pentecostal movement, having the 'anointing' was far more important than one's sex"[45] or being part of an organization. A high premium was placed on the immediate experience of being guided by the Holy Spirit. This meant that women as well as men were free, in fact had an obligation, to follow the call to preach the gospel. If questioned about their involvement in ministry, it was not uncommon for women to appeal to God's leading and affirmation of their call and their obligation to be obedient to it. This attitude can be seen in the words of Blanche A. Appleby when she signs her correspondence regarding her work in South China reported in the December 1922 issue of the *Pentecostal Testimony*, "*Yours in*

His bonds," which implies that she was a slave for God with no choice but to do the Master's Will.[46]

Spirit Baptism was understood to equip and empower anybody, including women, to minister in fulfillment of prophecy found in Acts and Joel. An example of this egalitarian assumption can be found in the writings of Zelma Argue. In her 1920 article entitled "Your Sons and Your Daughters" she does not defend the rights of women to minister. Rather she defends the rights of young people to prophesy. Gender isn't the major concern for Zelma in this article – youthfulness is. Argue simply acknowledges that women have been "conceded the right to prophesy, to minister" based on Acts 2:17, 18 and Joel 2 while defending the rights of the young to do likewise. She exhorts the youth, "Young people of Pentecost, get the vision! Let the fire of the Holy Ghost burn within you … 'For yet a little while and He that shall come will come, and will not tarry.'" It was the emphasis on the imminent return of Christ, that these were the last days, which gave the Acts and Joel passages pre-eminence with their affirmation of empowerment for everyone.[47]

By 1927, eight years after the PAOC was chartered, Mrs J.S. Still repeats similar arguments in the same periodical and uses them to directly defend women's right to preach in an article entitled, "Should Women Preach the Gospel?"[48] In her opinion, opposition to women preaching was demonic. That everyone, including women, was expected to be a "soul-winner" was understood by the men as well. R.E. McAlister writes in the PAOC periodical in October 1921 that "It is the privilege of every Minister of the Gospel – of every Christian man and woman, boy and girl, to be a soul-winner."[49]

The Scripture's Authority

When Christ did not return as immediately as expected, the original impulse to view everyone as a soul-winner who could potentially be empowered for and involved in a preaching ministry was seriously undermined. As the movement organized for a longer stay on this earth, institutional concerns surfaced and eclipsed the earlier emphases. Other teachings of Scripture regarding male headship, such as Ephesians 5, 1 Timothy 2, and Titus 2 began to come explicitly into play as increasing attention was focused on corporate authority and how it might function. Although the early Pentecostal movement was deeply concerned about obeying the promptings of the Spirit, the determination to be faithful to the authority of Scripture was also of great concern. And

Scripture not only indicated in Acts and Joel that in the last days all would be empowered to witness in an egalitarian model of ministry, it also seemed to teach that men and women were to be in a male head-ship-female submission relationship to each other based on Ephesians, 1 Timothy, and Titus. One way to reconcile the apparent contradiction was to insist that the Bible's teaching on male headship takes precedence over the other passages and experiences of the Spirit. Therefore, a woman's claim to have been called by the Spirit to a ministry or leadership position must be understood as having a limited sphere of practical operation. This appears to be the solution for the PAOC.

As long as the movement remained relationally related and organized, questions of male headship/female submission could play themselves out on individual and local levels, remaining relatively hidden. However, once the PAOC was incorporated as an organization, the biblically based theological tension that directly pertained to the prophesying women in its midst received increasingly more attention as the biblical passages legitimating male headship were emphasized and applied.

However, the confusion created by such seemingly conflicting guidance from such an authoritative text among people who take the Scripture and the role of the Spirit and their own obedience to God very seriously was not resolved. Two papers which were written in response to a request by the "National Committee on the Role of Women in the Church" in 1975 illustrated the two major, conflicting, dominant positions taken during this period. Based on her review of Scripture, Grace Brown concluded that men and women were equal before God. Therefore, women who were in charge of music, Christian education, or youth work within a local congregation deserved to be called "Pastors" like their male counterparts.[50] Based on his review of Scripture, G.R. Ewald concluded that, although he had voted for the ordination of women because they were already doing the job, he thought that women should remain in supportive roles. In his understanding, even though "Reverend" was not a scriptural term, women should only be granted the title "Deaconess."[51]

During the period of 1976–84 when prolonged and passionate debates regarding the ordination of women raged, studies and committees were established more than once to research the biblical stance on ordination and women in ministry.[52] At the General Conference in 1988, four years after the decision to ordain women was made, a private member's resolution was presented to rescind the decision on the grounds that it "violates our belief in the authority, supremacy and sufficiency of Scripture in all matters of faith and practice." Although it was defeated,[53] the question of the correct biblical stance remained.

In contrast to articles written by Argue and Still in the 1920s which affirmed ministry for all, including women, based on the understanding of a latter rain outpouring of the Spirit, an article by another woman in ministry in the 1980s illustrates the changes that had occurred, not only in the denomination, but also in the mindset of women in ministry. In 1988, Margaret Gibb, who is described as pastoring Greenfield Park Pentecostal Church, near Montreal, along with her husband Robert, wrote in the July issue of the *Pentecostal Testimony*, "Pentecostal women in our nation hold firmly to the *Biblical principle of male leadership and headship*" (emphasis mine).[54] She places this position in contrast to the "feminist message of women's rights for power and authority" which "has fallen on deaf ears, as far as our women are concerned." Yet she argues that *"God is calling women today to give aggressive, dynamic spiritual leadership in our local churches."* God calls but Scripture dictates. Gibb suggests that what the church needs is a role model in the form of "pastors' wives, women in leadership, lay women in the local church who will give strong *spiritual* (emphasis hers) leadership." What that spiritual leadership might entail and how it differed from men's denominational leadership is not clear. Instead, Gibb's primary concern regarding women in ministry appears to be, in contrast to Argue and Still, not a latter rain outpouring but the issue of male headship and the feminist challenge to that male headship. No longer was it a world that needed evangelizing so much as an organization that needed protecting. After seventy years the emphasis had clearly changed in women's writings although the underlying confusion regarding the Spirit's/God's authority remained.

Institutional Authority: Men in Charge

One institutional concern evident in the original charter of the PAOC and the minutes of conference meetings in the first few years centred on the issue of authority. Within a short period of time, various ministries were placed under the authority and direction of the incorporated entity known as the PAOC. In practice, that meant that the General Executive of the denomination, all men, exercised authority over the various ministries on a national and international level, while local pastors, increasingly male as ordination was denied women, exercised authority at the local level. Although many of these concerns were of a practical and financial nature,[55] the decision-making power was being deliberately concentrated in the home office back in Canada which was under male leadership. "Evangelists," whether male or female, were placed in submission to "Pastors" at the August 1925 Western District conference.[56] Clearer lines of institutional authority were being established in order to resolve difficulties which had arisen. These difficulties, although not caused by women, directly affected them as many of them were evangelists.[57]

Whereas in the beginning God's Spirit was understood to be the one who had the authority to empower people to minister, as the movement institutionalized and made the transition to an organized denomination, this authority shifted to the men in leadership through the conferring of various levels of ministerial credentials including ordination and administrative positions. Before Pentecostalism was organized, women did not have to concern themselves with questions of credentials, ordination, or national leadership. However, once the movement was organized a decision was made that ministering women were not to be ordained or to hold positions of authority over men. The effect, intentional or not, was to disempower on a practical and organizational level the women whom God had empowered and called.

This movement toward institutionally disempowering women was noticeable as soon as the women were barred from leadership and ordination, without their objections, and granted the secondary status of being a Deaconess. The status of these Deaconesses was further demoted when the Ministerial License for Women was established. Even those women who met the requirements for the Ministerial License were reminded that their authority to live out their call was based on the recognition that it was the Spirit who called them. However, that call by the Spirit was not to override the biblically based rights of men within the organization.[58] If a qualified, presumably Spirit-called and ordained man was present in any ministering situation, he pragmatically took precedence over a Spirit-called and credentialed woman. Of course, this submitting of a credentialed woman to an ordained man was easy to regulate in that the denomination effectively barred women from officiating at weddings and funerals and discouraged them from presiding during the ordinances if a man was available. At the same time, while women were warned not to overstep their bounds and usurp authority over men, the role of women within the home was being idealized. As the mothers of men, women were told that they had a "grander sphere" of responsibility and privilege.[59] Nevertheless, by 1950 women who held the Ministerial License for Women were allowed to vote in the General Conferences.[60] By 1960, they were allowed to officiate at weddings within their own pastoral charge.[61]

The institutional exercise of authority over women sometimes illustrated the dangers of patriarchal ideology and practices not being acknowledged or addressed. By the late 1920s the issuing of Deaconess Certificates for women was such standard practice that a "Deaconess Uniform approved by the Conference" was suggested. This uniform was a dark blue dress with white collar and cuffs topped off with a hat.[62] The attention to detail by the PAOC regarding how ministering women should be dressed is noticeable in the announcement regarding a new 1929 "Deaconess hat." Although the new hat was considered an improvement on the "old hat of 1928," the old hats would still be considered "satisfactory."[63] Later a pin labelled "PAOC Deaconess" was added to the uniform.[64] This interest in a uniform for women in ministry seems unusual in a denomination which did not approve of clerical garb. Such an interest may have stemmed from a concern to validate women's involvement by assigning women an outfit which, while distinguishing them from non-ministering women, might at the same time have been seen as in keeping with the sombre suits of male ministers. Such an interest may have arisen from counter-cultural concerns regarding the new-found freedom of women of the flapper generation. Or it may have been an effort, unconscious and controlling, to produce a particular image for Christian women as sober, serious, and chaste.[65] Regardless, while there is no written record of women deaconesses objecting to the dress code imposed on them, the degree of control over ministering women – right down to the details of which hats they must wear – is illustrative of the changing role of women in the PAOC.

Telling, also, is the reaction to the organization of a "Women's Missionary Council (WMC)" in September 1944 to encourage prayer, to promote missionary work, and to assist "in any co-operative work which may have the endorsation (sic) of the Movement from time to time." While women had been meeting informally since 1915, in 1942 the Manitoba District Conference, perhaps influenced by the example of Nellie McClung, took the lead in preparing a "resolution sponsored by the ladies, to be presented to the General Executive that year." Alberta followed suit. A National Director was appointed in 1944, Mrs Ethel (Bingeman) Jamieson, one of the earlier mentioned missionaries to Liberia, West Africa who had taught in two Bible Colleges and developed a network upon her return to Canada.[66]

Marion Parkinson who writes an account of these proceedings does not explain why it had taken almost thirty years for this particular type of ministry by women to have been formally recognized. She relates that intentional efforts were taken to reassure the men that the women were not attempting to usurp their authority. She also notes that women were directly taught that male headship was the norm. The male-instituted and maintained "chain of command" was to be "respected and honoured."[67]

Nor does Parkinson speculate on why the newly formed WMC was "squeezed into what might have been at one time a 'cubby hole' for 'what nots' in the basement ... about four feet square without windows" even though it was a clear demonstration of the indifference, lack of value, or disdain placed on women and their ministering efforts within the institution. Parkinson does, however, acknowledge that, while seeking "the stamp of approval" of "the brethren" was encouraged by a few superintendents and leaders who "did all they could to 'put a word in for the ladies,'" some congregational pastors refused to have an organized women's group and other district superintendents were against the idea.[68]

It wasn't until 1978 that the name of the "Women's Missionary Council" was changed to "Women's Ministries' in recognition that "the ministry" of women "across the Dominion of Canada is becoming increasingly varied, involving the lay woman extensively."[69] With the reaction of some of the leading men to lay women's organizing for ministry, it is not surprising that women seeking equal recognition with men were in for a difficult and prolonged battle with the movement.

Ordination of Women

A second institutional concern, which increased in prominence as the organization matured, focused on the issue of ordination. As ordination implied authority, the two became entwined. During the 1970s when discussions were held regarding women's ministries in the PAOC, the authority of men and the concurrent submission of women surfaced as being of real concern. One report clearly connected the issues of institutional authority and ordination when it stated, "Women have always been excluded from the status of ordained clergy in the PAOC, since ordination makes one eligible for election to every office within the church, whether on district or national levels, as well as conferring the right to use the title 'Reverend.'"[70] Even though women had been actively involved in the early years, the PAOC, legally formed in 1919, did not begin ordaining women until 1984.

In the mid 1970s, when the number of women involved in ministry within the PAOC was in such serious decline that[71] commissions were started to study the matter, the 1974 General Conference put forth its first resolution to ordain women. The resolution was defeated, by failing to receive the required two-thirds majority vote.[72] Again in 1976, a similar motion was promptly defeated by a show of hands. A 1978 report commissioned by the General Conference regarding the ordination of women stated, "The PAOC makes ordination to the full Christian ministry, not only the formal recognition of the call of God upon a person who has fulfilled certain requirements of study and probation, but also makes *the office of the ordained minister the highest recognition accorded to spiritual leaders within the Fellowship*"[73] (emphasis mine). However, this "highest recognition" was to be denied women.[74] Again in 1980 a resolution to ordain women was defeated.[75]

It was not until 1984 that the PAOC voted "overwhelmingly in favour" of ordaining women by a "90 per cent majority" after a great deal of discussion. Randal Holm claims that the definition of ordination became a significant factor in this turn of events, more significant even than biblical backing. Holm cites a report given by David Boyd at the conference which insisted that "*ordination confers nothing!* It is simply a recognition of the call of God and the consecration of that person to that call to certain types of ministry*" (emphasis mine).[76] Once ordination had been stripped of its institutional authority, the majority of the delegates were satisfied.

Notably, the fact that the motion was "Carried" was not included in the original minutes. A note by a "Margaret" and a "Hilda" with an initialled "o.k." pointed out this omission and asked "Should this not be added in the typed and signed Minutes in the book in the safe?" This note was added to the minutes.[77] Nevertheless, ordained women were not eligible to serve at the district or national leadership level. Their exercise of institutional authority over men continued to be limited.[78] Women who had served the church for years were almost immediately ordained.[79] The grassroots response to this 1984 decision to ordain women was mixed. Some enthusiastically endorsed the decision while others vehemently opposed it.[80]

In 1994, a delegate at the General Conference expressed concern that there was "no enabling legislation to allow women to be candidates for certain elected offices."[81] In 1998, as part of the "International Office

Redesign," representation on the General Executive was opened up to women. In addition, an approved resolution on "gender inclusivity" stated explicitly that "The Pentecostal Assemblies of Canada provide for gender inclusivity in all matters relating to the credentialing process and qualifications of candidates for the elected offices of District and General Executives, and that to implement this the General Constitution and By-Laws be reworded where necessary by the General Executive to provide for such." [82] Women were finally and officially deemed eligible for leadership positions at the district and national levels. This materialized at the 44th General Conference in 2000 when Lillian Douglass was elected to the general executive on the second ballot. Gender inclusivity was also approved for local church constitutions.[83] After a long, drawn out battle, due to a restructuring of the denomination, women were finally and officially occupying the leadership positions they had long been denied.

The news of the latest advances by women into leadership within the General Executive was accepted with a relative lack of fanfare or fuss. The September 2000 issue of the *Pentecostal Testimony* said nothing. A short, two line paragraph in the "Editorial" of the October 2000 *Testimony* coupled with a picture "Introducing the General Executive" near the end of the same edition, announced the event to the constituency.[84] Two months later in the December issue, Lillian Douglas, "the first woman elected to serve on the general executive" was again mentioned within the context of her appointment to the "Premier's Advisory Council on Health."[85]

MINISTERING WOMEN IN THE TWENTY-FIRST CENTURY

With the 1998 reorganization of the denomination which allowed ordained women access to leadership positions at the national and district level, time will tell whether or not women's involvement in ministry and leadership within the PAOC once again increases. The failure to address the underlying tension between the authority of the Spirit, the authority of Scripture, the authority of men, and the authority of the organization, coupled with a pragmatically practiced anti-culturalism, could continue to limit women's involvement in ministry and leadership.

Perhaps a review of, and return to, Pentecostal particularities might be helpful. Within Pentecostal thought and practice is the realization that anyone who submits to the "Will of God" can be empowered for service to the church and the world. Authority, therefore, becomes embedded in God's Spirit alone and not in the charismatic figure exercising certain spiritual gifts. It is God who is in charge and the Spirit, like the wind, blows where she wills.

Perhaps also a return to the Pentecostal practice of "discerning the Spirit" is in order. While supposedly a regular practice in Pentecostal circles, rarely has anyone dared to ask what "spirit" is being manifested in a community where patriarchal assumptions and hierarchical practices silence and restrict Spirit gifted and called women and men. And what "spirit" is being manifested when Scripture is appealed to in order to undermine the Spirit's authority?

Perhaps, in the meantime, the PAOC may proceed in the same way that Pentecostals have always proceeded – seeking to discern which way the Spirit is blowing by paying attention to what and whom the Spirit is blessing and empowering. Denominational concerns, while important, must become secondary to the Spirit's agenda. God calls, equips, and empowers people, as individuals or as institutions, as they respond in obedience to God's will and God's way. Perhaps that might be an appropriate ordering of authority while the biblically based theological tension is being resolved and culturally based ideologically assumptions are being uncovered.

NOTES

1 Hebden, "How Pentecost Came to Toronto," 1–3. See also Seymour, *The Apostolic Faith*, 4; George C. Slager, letter to W.E. McAlister, 24 March 1954, PAOC Archives, Mississauga, ON.

2 Miller, *Canadian Pentecostals*, 39–40, 42.

3 Seymour, *The Apostolic Faith*, 1.

4 Rogers, "And Your Daughters Shall Prophesy," 21.

5 Miller, *Canadian Pentecostals*, 41, 43–44.

6 See Janes, *The Lady Who Stayed*.

7 Parlee, "Carro and Susie Davis," *Pentecostal Testimony*, (December 1987), 16–17.

8 *Canadian Pentecostal Testimony* 9 (october 1921), 1.

9 She is described as being "actively engaged in the work" for about ten years, nine of them as a co-labourer with her husband. "She took an active part in the meetings, chiefly as leader of the song service, and also in the altar work, occasionally giving forth the Word of God." *Canadian Pentecostal Testimony*, 2 (February 1921), 1.

10 Miller, *Canadian Pentecostals*, 89.

11 Cadwalder, "Report from the West," *Canadian Pentecostal Testimony*, (Janunary 1923), 2.

12 Miller, *Canadian Pentecostals*, 95.

13 *Canadian Pentecostal Testimony*, (March 1921), 1.

14 *Pentecostal Testimony*, (September 1938), 19–20.

15 Miller, *Canadian Pentecostals*, 139.

16 Ibid., 51.

17 "Memories: The Story of 75 Years in Vineland," anniversary brochure, Vineland Pentecostal Church, 1983, PAOC Archives, Mississauga, ON.

18 *Canadian Pentecostal Testimony*, (January 1923), 3; (September 1921), 4; (December 1920), 1; (March 1921), 1, 4.

19 Ibid., 1; (December 1921), 3; (September 1921), 4, 5, (April 1921), 2; (December 1922), 1; 2:6 (June 1922), 1; (January 1923), 5; (May 1921), 3; (June 1922), 4.

20 Miller, *Canadian Pentecostals*, 51.

21 *Canadian Pentecostal Testimony*, (July 1921), 1, 2; (September 1921), 4; (December 1922), 1, 3; (February 1921), 3; (December 1922), 4; (November 1922), 1.

22 Handwritten Minutes of Ministry of Women Committee Meeting held in Toronto on 17 January 1974 found in the PAOC Archives.

23 Theoretically, I draw upon the works of Barfoot and Sheppard and Roebuck for their specific analyses of women and Pentecostalism. Readers should be aware of the growing literature on women and religion which is beyond the scope of this paper. For example, see Lawless, *Handmaidens of the Lord*; Nesbitt, *Feminization of the Clergy in America*; Chaves, *Ordaining Women*.

24 Barfoot and Sheppard, "Prophetic vs. Priestly Religion: The Changing Role of Women Clergy in Classical Pentecostal Churches," 3–4.

25 *Canadian Pentecostal Testimony*, (March 1921), 2.

26 Barfoot and Sheppard, "Prophetic vs. Priestly Religion," 3–4 refer to the work of Weber.

27 Hebden, *The Promise* (October 1909), 1 and (March 1910), 1.

28 Miller, *Canadian Pentecostals*, 44.

29 *Minutes of the General Meeting of the General Assembly of the Pentecostal Assemblies of Canada* held at Kitchener, ON. 25–28 November 1919, 1.

30 See the first page of the *Charter Issued to the Pentecostal Assemblies of Canada*, 17 May 1919, "By-Law Number 23."

31 "Memorandum of Agreement," 26 April 1919 forming part of the Original Charter issued to the Pentecostal Assemblies of Canada, 17 May 1919, 1–3.

See also *Minutes of the Annual Meeting of the Eastern District Council of the Pentecostal Assemblies of Canada*, 11–13 October 1922, 1–2.

32 *Minutes of the Third Eastern District Conference* held at Toronto, Ontario, 29 July to 1 August 1924, 3–4.

33 Copy of letter to Dr C.M. Wortman, General Secretary-Treasurer, PAOC from Rev. J. Roswell Flower, General Secretary, Assemblies of God, 6 June 1949, PAOC Archives.

34 Copy of letter to Rev. J. Roswell Flower, General Secretary, Assemblies of God from Dr C.M. Wortman, General Secretary, PAOC, 22 June 1949, PAOC Archives.

35 *Minutes of the Annual Conference of the Western District Council of the Pentecostal Assemblies of Canada* held at Wesley Church, Winnipeg, Manitoba, 12 August to 16 August 1925, 2, 4–5.

36 Ibid., 5.

37 "Qualifications for Ministry," *Canadian Pentecostal Testimony* (September 1925), 10–12. "Acknowledgement," *Canadian Pentecostal Testimony* (October 1925), 8 indicates that it was an address by Pastor A.G.Ward of Toronto at the Eastern District Conference.

38 Roebuck, "Go and Tell My Brothers", 1–2.

39 Zelma Argue, "A Personal Talk to Pentecostal Young Women: Two Types of Women Described in the Bible," *Canadian Pentecostal Testimony* (July 1922), 2–3.

40 H.M. Cadwalder, "Report from the West," *Canadian Pentecostal Testimony* (January 1923), 2. "Western Canada Section," *Canadian Pentecostal Testimony* (May 1925), 6. *Canadian Pentecostal Testimony*, (November 1925), 8.

41 Gordon Upton, "Submission to the National Committee Investigating 'The Ministry of Women in the Pentecostal Assemblies of Canada," June 1975, as found in PAOC Archives, Toronto, ON, 5.

42 Shirley Flewitt, "Mentors to Many," *Pentecostal Testimony* (October 1991), 21.

43 It is unfortunate that Pentecostalism takes this anti-cultural stance. Particularly as it pertains to the role of women in all areas of life, there is within Pentecostalism a solid basis for articulating empowerment for women (and others) that would provide a parallel to secular feminist ideology. Perhaps it's time Pentecostals moved beyond attacking to developing a constructive alternative.

44 Roebuck, "Go and Tell My Brothers," 5–9.

45 Blumhofer, *The Assemblies of God*, 137.

46 *Canadian Pentecostal Testimony* (December 1922), 1.

47 *Canadian Pentecostal Testimony* (December 1920), 3, 4 (March 1921), 3. See also *Canadian Pentecostal Testimony* (December 1921), 4; *Canadian Pentecostal Testimony* (August 1922), 1; *Canadian Pentecostal Testimony* (March 1921), 2.

48 J. S. Still, "Should Women Preach the Gospel," *Canadian Pentecostal Testimony* (June 1927), 6.

49 *Canadian Pentecostal Testimony* (December 1921), 2.

50 Grace Brown, *Women in Ministry: Prepared by Grace Brown for the paoc as part of a study on the position of women in the church as ministers*, 6 June 1975, PAOC Archives.

51 G.R. Eward, *An Examination of the Scripture on the Role of Women in the Church: As requested by the National Committee on the Role of Women in the Church*, May 1975, PAOC Archives.

52 *Minutes of the 30th Biennial General Conference of the Pentecostal Assemblies of Canada*, 19 to 24 August 1976, 17–19, 23.; Rev. Jack Ozard, Chairman, *Committee on 'Women in Ministry' – Report to the 1986 Conference, Western Ontario District, paoc*, PAOC Archives, 1, 4.

53 *Minutes of the 36th Biennial General Conference of the Pentecostal Assemblies of Canada.* 1988, 42. See also Holm, "Ordination of Women," *Pentecostal Testimony* (May 1992), 6.

54 Margaret Gibb, "A Woman's Place in Ministry," *Pentecostal Testimony*, (July 1988), 10–11.

55 *Canadian Pentecostal Testimony* (January 1921), 1; (April 1921), 3; (December 1922), 2.

56 *Minutes of the Annual Conference of the Western District Council of the Pentecostal Assemblies of Canada* held at Wesley Church, Winnipeg, Manitoba, 12–16 August 1925, 2.

57 Holm, "Organizational Blues: The Struggle of One Pentecostal Denomination with the Bugbear of Institutionalism," 8.

58 D.N. Buntain's article "Should Women Preach and Teach," *Pentecostal Testimony* (March 1939), 3.

59 Buntain, "The Christian Wife," *Pentecostal Testimony* (December 15, 1940), 3.

60 *Minutes of the General Conference of the Pentecostal Assemblies of Canada*, 1950.

61 *Minutes of the General Conference of the Pentecostal Assemblies of Canada*, 1960.

62 *Minutes of the General Conference of the Pentecostal Assemblies of Canada*, 1928, 42.

63 R.E. McAlister, General Secretary-Treasurer, PAOC, *Notice to Deaconesses*, no date, PAOC Archives.

64 *Minutes of the General Conference of the Pentecostal Assemblies of Canada*, 1935, 107.

65 *Canadian Pentecostal Testimony* 4 (March 1921), 2.

66 Parkinson, *A Dream Now a Reality: A Story of the Women's Missionary Council* (Toronto, ON: PAOC Archives, n.d.), 1–6.

67 "New & Views" in *Women's Missionary Council Handbook*, 11th ed. (Toronto, ON: PAOC, 1944, 1976), 11, 13–14, 22.

68 Parkinson, *A Dream Now a Reality*, 6–14.

69 *Minutes of the 31st Biennial General Conference of the Pentecostal Assemblies of Canada*, 24–29 August 1978, 18.

70 "Report of General Conference Committee Re: Ordination" (1978), 2, PAOC Archives.

71 Gordon Upton, "Submission to the National Committee," 1, 4.

72 *Minutes of the 29th Biennial General Conference of the Pentecostal Assemblies of Canada*, 23–27 August 1974, 4–6.

73 *Report on Ordination as commissioned by the 1978 General Conference*, PAOC Archives.

74 *Minutes of the 31st Biennial General Conference*, 21–2.

75 *Minutes of the General Conference of the Pentecostal Assemblies of Canada*, 1978, 1980.

76 See Holm, "A Paradigmatic Analysis of Authority within Pentecostalism," 6–7.

77 *Minutes of the 34th Biennial General Conference of the Pentecostal Assemblies of Canada*, 1984, 10–20 and photocopied note overlaid on page 20. See also Holm, "Ordination of Women," *Pentecostal Testimony* (May 1992), 2.

78 *Minutes of the 35th Biennial General Conference of the Pentecostal Assemblies of Canada*, 1986, 5, 29. See also the *paoc General Constitution*, By-law 3, election of officers, Section 1, Qualifications a) Executive officers, By-law 14, District Conference, Section 9, Elections, (a) Qualifications, 3, PAOC Archives.

79 *Pentecostal Testimony*, (November 1996), 23.

80 See for example Bob Skinner's article, "An Idea Whose Time Has Come," *Pentecostal Testimony* (December 1984), 1ff. And the "Reader's Response" *Pentecostal Testimony* (March 1985), 8. *Minutes of the 36th Biennial General Conference of the Pentecostal Assemblies of Canada*, 1988, 15, 16, 31, 32.

81 *Minutes of the 41st Biennial General Conference of the Pentecostal Assemblies of Canada*, 1994, 41.

82 *Minutes of the 1998 Biennial General Conference of the Pentecostal Assemblies of Canada*, 1998, 3–4. "36 Resolutions," appended to the *Minutes of the 1998 Biennial General Conference of the Pentecostal Assemblies of Canada*, 1998, 4–5 as compared with the *Minutes of the 1998 Biennial General Conference of the Pentecostal Assemblies of Canada*. 1998, 5, 7, 16–17.

83 *Minutes of the 44th General Conference of the Pentecostal Assemblies of Canada*, 2000, 21, 23, 27 and "Proposed Amendments," 7.

84 *Testimony* (October 2000), 3, 26.

85 *Testimony* (December 2000), 17.

PART THREE

Institutionalization and Globalization

9

Denominational Charismatics – Where Have They All Gone?
A Canadian Anglican Case Study

DAVID A. REED

INTRODUCTION

Signs of a new expression of Pentecostal spirituality in the mainline churches were beginning to emerge in North America as early as the late 1940s. The traditional Pentecostal emphasis on the "outpouring" of the Holy Spirit – called baptism in the Holy Spirit – and the gifts of the Spirit, especially healing, were beginning to seep into the wider Christian world. This spillover was not initiated by the Pentecostal denominations that were by now becoming increasingly organized and institutionalized. The carriers were predominantly newly formed independent Pentecostal ministries such as the healing evangelists (e.g., Oral Roberts, William Branham), and the Full Gospel Business Men's Fellowship International. Episcopalian Agnes Sanford, through her Schools of Pastoral Care, was instrumental in introducing the Pentecostal experience of Spirit Baptism to the mainline denominations.[1]

But it was Dennis Bennett, rector of St Mark's Episcopal Church, Van Nuys, California, who popularized these stirrings into a movement. Through the influence of parishioners who reported to him that they had received the Pentecostal experience with speaking in tongues, Bennett personally experienced Spirit Baptism in November 1959.[2] The following April he publicly announced his experience, which led that summer to *Time* magazine running two articles that heralded the beginning of a new movement. This new spiritual trajectory expanded in a surprising direction in 1967 when the Pentecostal experience spread to a group of Roman Catholic students and teachers at Duquesne University and the University of Notre Dame respectively.

The movement impacted the historic churches during this formative stage in important ways. By 1977 an ecumenical charismatic conference held in Kansas City brought together over 50,000 leaders and people from every major Christian tradition. Early expectations of a new and greater wave of renewal were, however, unfulfilled. Instead of a springboard, Kansas City became the high-water mark of the first and formative phase of the movement. Even Episcopal charismatic writer William DeArteaga states that, "by 1980 that fresh outpouring had ended, though few wanted to admit it."[3] Catholic charismatic scholar Peter Hocken provides the more nuanced conclusion that the 1977 conference closed the formative period of the movement, during which time the constitutive elements of charismatic renewal had become embedded within the institutional structures of all the major denominations. The second phase, 1977–87, would be a period of consolidation.[4]

This was the beginning of what soon became known as the *charismatic movement*, a stream of Pentecostal-type spirituality that was becoming embedded within the historic churches. Those who chose to remain in their churches were eventually called *denominational charismatics*. A distinctive feature of this denominational stream is that, unlike the older Pentecostals who were often forced out of their denominations at the turn of the century, a remarkable number of charismatics remained in their churches. While the movement was spreading rapidly throughout these historic churches, it was also forging another stream of *independent charismatics* – churches and ministries that hold no denominational affiliation but relate to and co-operate with one another.

CANADIAN ANGLICAN BEGINNINGS

Charismatic renewal in the US spread rapidly throughout the country and across the Canadian border. In 1960, Gordon Scovil, an Episcopal priest from Van Nuys who by now had experienced Spirit Baptism visited his brother, a priest in British Columbia's Diocese of Caledonia.[5] Under Scovil's initiative the experience began to spread, with St Andrew's Cathedral in Prince Rupert becoming a small centre for the renewal. Though the bishop permitted the charismatic gathering, he did not allow mention or teaching of the experience in public worship.

It did not take long before the new movement became divisive and distrustful of traditional authority. The dean of the Cathedral, George Patterson, was soon caught up in the new experience and eventually resigned to join the Pentecostals. With no model to guide this new spiritual experiment of grafting Pentecostal experience onto traditional church life, the gains initially made were squandered on the loss of credibility. That loss was felt in one young priest who was initially attracted to the movement and experience, Douglas Hambidge, who was later to become bishop of the Diocese of New Westminster and archbishop of British Columbia and Yukon. Hambidge recalls that he initially saw hope in the charismatic experience for revitalization of personal faith, but soon became disillusioned with the disruption that accompanied the movement in the diocese. Consequently, he withdrew from further involvement.

Another story with a different strategy and happier outcome emerged a few years later. John Vickers had been in business for most of his life.[6] But in 1963, at age sixty and living in Victoria, British Columbia, he was ordained a priest in the Diocese of British Columbia (Vancouver Island). Early in his parish ministry, he embraced the charismatic experience through the ministry of Dennis Bennett, by then rector of St Luke's in nearby Seattle.

A decade later, in June 1973, Vickers initiated a bold move to introduce renewal throughout the diocese.[7] He gained support from the bishop and diocesan synod to organize a two-week mission with Dennis and Rita Bennett. Their mandate was to introduce the charismatic renewal to every parish in the diocese. The benefits were many: every person and parish was given the opportunity to learn about the renewal, it was presented with the full support of the bishop and synod, and renewal beliefs and practices were seeded through numerous small groups forming in parishes.

Equally significant was the formation of the only Anglican centre for renewal in Canada. When Vickers was required to retire from parish ministry at age 70, Bishop Gartrell appointed him the first director of the newly formed Anglican Renewal Centre (1974–81), located at St Saviour's Church, Victoria West. The purpose was to guide, teach, and provide wholesome resources in charismatic renewal. The Centre, with its weekly Friday evening services, a stream of renewal speakers, and Vickers' wise leadership, left an important legacy in the diocese. It modelled renewal for Anglicans, provided a spiritual home for those

attracted to charismatic spirituality, and contained an otherwise potentially divisive movement within the Anglican fold. During those years,
no clergy or leader from this diocese left to join the Pentecostals.[8] As
one priest, Ivan Futter, observed, the Centre was "successful in keeping
renewal in the Anglican Church; there was not a major defection of
Anglicans going to the Pentecostal church."[9]

Vickers' own gifts were well suited for his new appointment – he was
a "powerful preacher" with a bent toward teaching, was committed to
the healing ministry, and enjoyed the confidence of bishops.[10] A distinctive emphasis of Vickers' ministry that shaped charismatic renewal in
the diocese and Western Canada was his strong belief that healing is an
integral aspect of renewal.[11] Also, parishes throughout Western Canada
embraced Agnes Sanford's Schools of Pastoral Care and the healing
ministry of the Order of St Luke. Finally, a life-long and devoted Anglican, Vickers had no interest in taking on battles of protest but remained
focused on a positive presentation of the purpose and benefits of being
blessed and empowered by the Holy Spirit.[12] The role of the Centre had
run its course and was closed by the bishop in 1985. While there have
been skirmishes and the renewal movement is not particularly large, the
influence of Vickers and Bennett is still evident in the diocese.[13]

The appointment of John Vickers to the renewal centre gave him an
influence and platform that quickly led to a stream of invitations to
speak and lead missions across Western Canada and as far east as
Ottawa. This not only spread the message and experience of charismatic renewal, it also drew in a new generation of leaders and laid the
foundation for a more organized stage of the movement. That stage was
the formation of an organization for the promotion of charismatic
renewal. The American Episcopalians had already held their first meeting of charismatic clergy in February 1973, which resulted in the founding of Episcopal Renewal Ministries.[14] In 1978 Charles Alexander,
rector of St James, Calgary, and John Vickers initiated the formation of
a regional organization, Anglican Renewal West, at a meeting in
Brooks, Alberta.[15] In 1983 a national body, Anglican Renewal Ministries, was formed, modelled after the renewal organizations in the UK,
US, and New Zealand. With some reluctance, in 1986 western leaders
yielded to the urging of Episcopal and eastern Canadian charismatics,
and integrated their ministries into the new national body.[16] Anglican
Renewal Ministries (ARM) Canada continues its mandate to provide
leadership and resources for renewal and outreach within the Anglican
Church of Canada.

By 1990 the Canadian charismatic movement was more than two decades old; it had spread across the country and was visible in congregations and conferences. It was well into its second generation. By then pronouncements could be heard about the state or the future of the movement, even its demise. The mass worship events, the prayer and praise services in local congregations, seemed to have faded in numbers and intensity. Where had all the charismatics gone? What impact did the charismatic movement have on the general church? In what ways did it illustrate an institutional transition?

In 1990 I embarked on a cross-country research trip in an effort to identify the presence, beliefs, and practices of charismatic Anglicans. Further, I wanted to understand how the movement was consolidating in Canada and what the future might hold for charismatic Anglicans. Reflecting on my findings since then, I have come to some other conclusions about the role of renewal within the church.[17] I will return to this point later.

Who Are These Charismatic Anglicans?

As I investigated charismatic renewal in the Anglican Church in 1990 I discovered some very interesting facts about the role of renewal in the church, for the participants and the institution. Interestingly, charismatic Anglicans found a home in the church in the 1980s, making significant contributions to the institution. While charismatic Anglicans were not getting any younger, there were signs that the movement was transitioning once again. I will return to this point later. Specifically, I discovered that charismatic Anglicans had a demographic profile similar in most aspects to that of the general active Anglican population with the majority of respondents being women and aging. The clergy were even older than the laity. The middle-age movement was also liturgically "middle-of-the-road," with over half of laity and clergy preferring this designation to low or high church.[18] Some personal comments from the respondents expressed the sentiment of many when they described themselves as "catholic evangelical charismatics." Charismatic Anglicans, though traditionally orthodox in doctrine and morals, broke with conservatives in their strong support for the contemporary liturgical rite in the *Book of Alternative Services*. Charismatic Anglicans indicated that their interest was less on liturgical form than on the provisions for greater involvement by the laity, personal or local expression, and spiritual experience.[19]

Charismatic Anglican clergy accounted for about 20 per cent of the active clergy pool either through a charismatic experience or influence of charismatic spirituality. There were also a good number of clergy who sympathized with the movement even though they did not identify with it. Regionally they were strongest in Western Canada. It was estimated that about 30 per cent of Anglican parishes in Canada had been influenced by the charismatic movement.[20] Adding that about 17 per cent of the bishops reported having had a charismatic experience, it is not unrealistic to suggest that Barrett's estimate of 18 per cent for Episcopalians is a conservative figure for the whole body of Canadian Anglican charismatics.[21]

Lifelong Anglicans made up most of the charismatic Anglicans with the majority of lay people active in the Anglican Church for more than twenty years. Most lay converts came from sister mainline churches, primarily United Church of Canada and Roman Catholic. Few came from Baptist and Pentecostal traditions. Therefore, though the charismatic experience may have once been exclusively in the Classical Pentecostal tradition, the renewal was clearly a movement within the church. Except for an inclination toward the evangelical and middle-of-the-road to low church traditions and a preference for the *Book of Alternative Services*, charismatics reflected the rank and file of active Anglicans in age, gender, history, and liturgical preference.

The type of experience most common in my findings fit the classical Pentecostal view in which glossolalia accompanied the experience at the time or shortly thereafter. This was true for the laity and the clergy. However, charismatic Anglicans did not believe that glossolalia was a necessity or a requirement for one to be a charismatic. Nearly half the clergy preferred to speak of glossolalia as a kind of appropriation or release, probably reflecting the influence of British Anglican and evangelical-charismatic writers like Michael Green and David Watson.

Charismatic Anglicans described how their experience impacted their lives through personal spirituality, especially by an increased love for Christ, Scripture, and worship. Many responded that they gave more time to the church through social concerns, especially compassion for the poor and needy and sharing their faith with others. Clergy reported that, next to personal spirituality, they desired to witness to others about Christ. Far from being transitory and ephemeral, such definite spiritual experiences can be determinative motivators in changing outlooks, attitudes, and behaviour. The overall results indicated that the primary contribution of the renewal movement was to infuse Anglicans with a meaningful experience of God, significant enough to reorder attitudes and practices. Though a charismatic experience for many Anglicans was controversial, the results were rather traditional in that, they strengthened and reinforced their commitment to the church. At least initially, their personal experience translated into personal involvement, measured by the significant increase in giving of time and money. Potential for evangelism was strong, especially among the clergy. Charismatic experience is a distinct expression of Christian spirituality that has significantly intensified a love for the primary Christian sources of spiritual strength – prayer, Scripture reading, and corporate worship. Overall, however, most charismatic Anglicans were more activist than contemplative.

While the charismatic renewal in the 1970s brought much tension in the church, with many charismatics leaving, the 1980s saw charismatic Anglicans stay, making significant contributions with high levels of involvement. This factor also had the effect of stabilizing the church. This important finding illustrates another transition within a mainline church as it encounters charismatic renewal. The transition is largely related to a growing acceptance and appreciation of charismatic renewal by the bishops as well as the sense that charismatics were welcomed in the church.

In summary, the findings revealed that a significant number of charismatic Anglicans regarded the Anglican Church as their spiritual home. The majority of charismatics who had chosen to remain or make their spiritual home in the Anglican Church felt for the most part supported by the institution and its leaders. For many who may have faced the prospect of changing affiliation because of their charismatic experience, the choice to remain may have been a more cherished one. While they were committed to the institution and even its agenda, they continued to seek recognition of their presence and a positive response to their spiritual agenda.

The volatile period of the seventies produced casualties from the mainline churches with many leaving to join the classical Pentecostal denominations and independent charismatic congregations. Twenty years later the sifting period was over, resulting in a sizable segment of active Anglicans identifying with charismatic experience and practice. They were not only present but generous in support and active in ministry and leadership. While many "burned out on experience" during the previous decade, by 1990 these charismatics were firmly oriented to service within the institutional church.

The decisive factor in the personal changes and the motivation for service was the charismatic experience. The more definite the experience – a crisis experience accompanied by glossolalia or another charism – the greater the personal change, motivation, and commitment. The charismatic experience resulted primarily in revitalizing the spirituality of these Christians and provided them with the motivation and charisms to serve. Their greatest potential for contributing to the institutional church was in the areas of spiritual experience in faith and worship, lay ministry, compassionate caring, evangelism, and the ministry of healing.

AN UNCERTAIN FUTURE?

The tension between established institutions and movements of unrest and protest within them is not new. Movements of reform and revolution have been slaughtered at the hand of the institution's executioner. They have also redrawn the face of religions and nations. But as sure as the sun rises, movements live to face a challenger in whose face they see a contemporary rendition of themselves as they attempt to perpetuate the vision for which they so valiantly fought generations earlier. Agreed, most tensions are less bloody, and many are necessary for the healthy survival of institutional life. The church in its institutional form is no exception. While a sequel to the original study summarized here has not been conducted, this is an opportunity a decade and a half later to reflect on changes and challenges for the future.

The formative stage of the modern charismatic movement, the outward swing of the pendulum as it were, culminated with the Kansas City conference in 1977. It had entered the new territory of Christian spiritual experience, growing out of grassroots yearnings for a meaningful encounter with God. The second or "Consolidation" phase spanned the next decade. According to Hocken, since 1988 the charismatic movement has been moving forward in the third stage that he calls "Globalization and Turning Outward."[22] Many charismatics are downplaying their distinctive, dropping the label "charismatic," focusing more on co-operation with their churches, or merely being assimilated into the larger institution without making a difference. On the other hand, the expanding evangelical world, formerly resistant to things charismatic, has been penetrated deeply by the renewal movement. The most rapid and visible growth is in Africa, Asia, and Latin

America and within the stream of Independents who happily wear the charismatic label.

Two phenomena in the 1990s made a particular impact on the charismatic movement. One was Alpha, an evangelistic course for spiritual seekers, originating from an evangelical-charismatic parish, Holy Trinity, Brompton, in London, UK.[23] Its global popularity has resulted in more than six million people having taken the course. Though it was designed as an evangelistic tool to reach the unchurched, its attraction for regular churchgoers suggests that many mainline Christians believe, but have lost the ability to articulate their belief, especially in ways that are compelling to others. Because of Holy Trinity's identification with renewal, Anglican charismatics were early supporters and promoters of the program. As they turned to Cursillo in an earlier generation, they now find in Alpha a highly compatible vehicle for satisfying their passion to evangelize. Unlike Cursillo, the Alpha course incorporates a one-day retreat that focuses on receiving the empowering presence of the Holy Spirit in ways that are familiar to those in renewal.

The second phenomenon was the Toronto Blessing, a "spiritual refreshing," that was ignited in a small Vineyard church plant in suburban Toronto in early 1994 and burst on the international scene almost immediately.[24] Ironically, its influence among Anglicans came circuitously through a personal contact in Holy Trinity, Brompton, where the revival took root and spread throughout the global Anglican network (see chapter 11 in this volume). The accompanying phenomena shifted from the familiar glossolalia of an earlier generation to uncontrollable laughter, bodily spasms, and falling down. The primary attraction seems to have been a spiritual refreshing for tired believers and burned-out leaders, especially those who had been in charismatic ministry. Two major ripple-effect spin-offs followed from Toronto: Holy Trinity, Brompton, and the "Pensacola Outpouring."[25] Charismatic Anglicans, like others, found in this new wave important ingredients for adapting charismatic identity and mission for the future.

Many of the contributions of the charismatic movement to the church evident two decades ago are still valid. In a tradition that holds ordained priesthood in high esteem, a countervailing emphasis on the *ministry of the laity* is to be applauded. As my 1990 research shows, the degree and depth of lay involvement and support by Anglican charismatics is significant, especially when one considers that many of the parishes in which they serve are likely small and rural. Contempo-

rary praise music has continued to enjoy an increasingly wide acceptance in the church and has contributed to vibrant Anglican worship.
The present concern is not the presence of praise music but the poor
quality that has been increasingly evident throughout the 1990s. Healing ministry is now commonplace in many non-renewal parishes
throughout the church.

In 2001, ARM Canada made an effort to fill a void in national
renewal leadership by appointing the retired bishop of Brandon,
Malcolm Harding, as itinerant "Ambassador" for renewal to the
church. To date, he has visited twenty-four dioceses conducting parish
missions, clergy retreats, and leadership training courses; teaching on
Evangelism and Discipleship; and speaking at diocesan synods. His
assessment of the state of the renewal movement in the Anglican
Church is that it is not waning: "There is still a growing thirst at the
grass roots level for renewal teaching." He observes that many of the
earlier congregational centres of renewal are still thriving, and "there
are new pockets as well as long time established pockets of renewal all
across the country."[26]

There is at least one flagship charismatic parish in nearly every diocese
and often many more at some stage or with some expression of renewal
in their congregational life. What is less clear is the present average age of
those who identify with the renewal movement. The 1990 research
revealed that the movement reflected the greying demographics of the
wider church. In a review of clergy, men and women, who are taking
leadership in parish renewal, Harding observes that a number of them
belong to the younger generation. But what has not yet emerged is a
young leader of the stature of John Vickers or Charles Alexander.[27]

The ARM Leadership Training seminars are well subscribed, though
the lay training sessions are presently better attended than the clergy
events. This corroborates other observations that charismatic spirituality is in many ways a popular movement that speaks to and provides
spiritual nourishment and empowerment for the laity. Harding's teaching includes such themes as personal encounter with the Holy Spirit,
healing, and personal gift identification. Leadership training gives
attention to congregational life – including leading a parish into
renewal, managing conflict, cell group ministry, equipping the whole
body for ministry, and discipling lay leaders. Harding's ministry and
ARM in general reflect a conclusion of the 1990 study that evangelism is
at the very least a prime motivation and by intent the ministry of preference.[28] While there is evidence that charismatics and renewal congrega-

tions are generous and compassionate in response to the needy, there remains a lacuna in articulating a vision and mission for social justice.

One of the significant events of the 1990s that in part redefined the role of Anglican charismatics was the formation of a coalition of orthodox-minded Anglicans called Anglican Essentials Canada. It began at a conference held in Montreal in June 1994. The three constituting bodies – Anglican Renewal Ministries of Canada, the evangelical Barnabas Anglican Ministries, and the Prayer Book Society of Canada – produced a joint document called the Montreal Declaration of Anglican Essentials.[29]

The significance of this coalition is that Anglican charismatics are for the first time represented in the church as a *political body*. It is noteworthy that many of them, especially clergy, would not be counted in this coalition were it not for the renewal movement. As noted earlier, most charismatics self-designated as "middle-of-the-road." This means that the majority was not previously identified or ideologically aligned with other strong orthodox bodies such as the evangelical or Anglo-Catholic. The clergy in particular were representative of the broad, liberal churchmanship that in the 1960s was the most theologically equivocal and spiritually vacuous. It was this constituency with which the charismatic renewal was most effective.[30] In other words, without the renewal movement, most charismatic Anglicans that now represent approximately 20 per cent of active Anglicans in Canada simply would not be in the Essentials coalition. The charismatic movement, therefore, has brought to the orthodox table a sizable body of now orthodox Anglicans.

As the church and renewal movement together look to the future, they are faced with two challenges. First is the development and deployment of renewal-oriented clergy for parishes. It became evident in the 1990 study that parish renewal in many places suffered from lack of stable and long-term leadership. There are a number of possible reasons for this. One is the rural character of Canadian parishes. Many congregations are small and rural resulting in frequent turnover of pastors and lack of continuity required for building a renewal-oriented congregational identity. Bishops in northern and rural dioceses often complain of the difficulty in attracting clergy to these remote regions. Unlike large population centres where the faithful can choose from a variety of congregational options and large congregations can provide a range of worship styles, rural parishes are too small for variety and the distance to the next parish too great. Whether a charismatic leader will consider this situation an opportunity for or barrier to developing charismatic ministry depends largely on the person.[31]

The distinctive character of Canadian regional identity, the vastness of the land, and the demographic clustering of population discourages the kind of mobility from one region of the country to another that one observes, for instance, in the US. This in turn, combined with the structure of episcopal authority in Canada, tends to discourage easy movement across diocesan boundaries and inhibits to some degree the deployment of renewal clergy to parishes seeking that kind of ministry.[32]

Finally, the 1990 study highlighted the scarcity of clergy equipped to lead renewal-oriented parishes. The problem is similar to the lack of evangelical priests in the Canadian church. One reason is likely that, unlike England with no fewer than seven evangelical theological schools, there is not a similar ethos in Canadian Anglican theological institutions.[33] Charting the direction for leadership education into the twenty-first century will need to be a co-operative effort.

The second challenge will be to examine the popular view within the renewal movement that the Spirit moves in "waves." While it is the work of historians and sociologists to trace stages of development and decline in movements, it is a spiritual and theological task to discern the movement of the Spirit in the processes of history and the church. The observer can follow the emergence of sub-movements that have appeared within the broad sweep of Pentecostal history. Following the first wave called classical Pentecostalism, the charismatic movement – with a different focus and in a different ecclesiastical place – became the second wave. The new trend in the 1980s away from the crisis experience of Spirit Baptism with speaking in tongues to "signs and wonders" and "power evangelism," defined what C. Peter Wagner called the Third Wave.[34] The Toronto Blessing and the ministry of David Pawson in England are candidates for the fourth wave.[35]

There are two possible interpretations of the function of waves in a movement. One is what may be called charismatic wave-waiting. This is the temptation in some charismatic circles to reduce the Spirit's sphere of activity to creating revivals. Admittedly, these waves are to be cumulative and eventually designed to produce a renewed church, and perhaps even the return of Christ. But this approach also encourages passivity, as the faithful wait for the next wave to appear. A more serious objection is that it encourages a diversion from holistic ministry in the world. While evangelism is a form of outreach, wave-waiting tends to understand evangelistic activity as pulling people out of a world that has no redeemable qualities left in it. The degree to which this tendency in charismatic circles applies to Anglican charismatics is for them to judge.

An alternative interpretation is that these waves represent periodic recalibrations or adjustments of a movement that is now far more comprehensive and complex than initially estimated. The global Pentecostal-charismatic movement is unsurpassed in the church's history for its growth to over 500 million in less than a century. Given the speed of cultural and global change, the worldwide scope of the movement and its innate cultural adaptability, the waves may simply be those visible moments – about once a decade – when the movement now wrapped around the globe partially remakes itself for the next phase. Like turning around an ocean liner, the direction will be discerned only after reviewing the cumulative effect of a series of waves. This in no way implies that each successive wave is progressively better than previous waves or that it is a simple linear movement from one stage to the other. Rather, we may be observing the multi-faceted, complex phenomenon of a movement globally connected by a common experience of God while simultaneously interacting with cultures that are legion. Only the next generation with a longer trajectory from which to view this series of waves will be qualified to assess more accurately their nature and function.

Revitalization of the church is a long and complex process. So says Martin Robinson, British church growth expert and student of evangelical revivals. He outlines five phases of a revival movement, all in dynamic relationship with one another: (1) unusual and extraordinary phenomena, (2) the emergence of new denominations, (3) the renewal of the historic denominations, (4) some expression of social engagement with the wider society, and (5) the global impact of the modern missionary movement, including the presence of Christian immigrants in the West.[36] Robinson believes that these markers are only partially fulfilled in the present evangelical-Pentecostal/charismatic movement. He further observes that the historic churches are showing few signs of being revitalized, and social vision among the renewed is still weak.

Canadian charismatic Anglicans continue to be open to the unusual phenomena that springboard each new wave. Through no fault of theirs, the Anglican Church shares with most historic churches in North America the sad report of little change. The primary social involvement of Anglican charismatics at present is the public and ecclesiastical debate over same-sex blessings, as expressed through the work of the Essentials organization.[37] Though this may be judged to be a worthy social cause, the action is primarily by the nature of the case a negative one. While the 1990 study revealed charismatic Anglicans were carrying out compassionate ministry quietly, there is opportunity for visionary leadership to initiate a visible and public social ministry as both compassionate act and compelling witness to the gospel.[38] If Richard Lovelace's comment is correct – that while revival is a sovereign work of God, the nurturing and maturing of its effects are given to humans – then there is still much to be done. That mandate belongs to those who have tasted the new wine afresh, but it is surely not theirs alone to bear.

NOTES

1 See Hocken, "Charismatic Movement," 477–519.

2 Bennett, *Nine O'clock in the Morning*.

3 De Arteaga, *Quenching the Spirit*, 56. De Arteaga does point out, however, the conviction of Richard Lovelace, an evangelical Reformed observer of revivals, that revivals begin as a sovereign work of God but are sustained only as the human instruments move beyond personal piety to "the area of social action and concern."

4 Hocken, "Charismatic Movement," 485.

5 The following account of the first contact by Canadian Anglicans with the charismatic movement is provided by Douglas Hambidge, now retired Archbishop of New Westminster, BC. Phone interview, 27 September 1990.

6 Interview with John Vickers, Victoria, BC, 3 October 1990.

7 Vickers recounted the process in a privately published paper, "The Anglican Renewal Centre – How It All Began" (Victoria, BC: Privately published, n.d.). Canon Neil Robinson chaired the Programme Committee that planned the visit, and personally accompanied the Bennetts throughout the diocese; interview, Victoria, BC, 1 October 1990. Bennett's first visit to the diocese was to St John's, Quadra, in 1962. But it was the 1974 mission, culminating with a four-day seminar on the Holy Spirit at Christ Church Cathedral, Victoria, that led to the establishing of the renewal centre; see Ed Hird, "Anglican Pioneer in Renewal," *Anglicans for Renewal Canada* (Summer 1992).

8 Robinson, interview.

9 Futter, interview, Victoria, BC, 7 October 1990.

10 These leadership qualities in Vickers were identified by then priest at St Saviour's, Tony Essex; interview, Victoria, BC, 4 October 1990.

11 Futter, interview. This more robust embrace of the healing ministry contrasts somewhat with the ministry of "Terry" Fullam, whose influence was stronger in the east. While Fullam embraced the healing ministry, he did not empha-

size it either in his parish ministry at St Paul's, Darien, CT, or his itinerant teaching ministry.

12 This was evident in Vickers' observation – gracious still – of another renewal leader whose ministry, Vickers believed, had been harmed by his preoccupation with fighting the New Age movement; interview.

13 The presence of the renewal movement in the Diocese of British Columbia, including renewal-oriented parishes, is attested by the Rt Rev'd Malcolm Harding, former Bishop of Brandon, MB, and current itinerant teacher or "Ambassador" for Anglican Renewal Ministries Canada; phone interview, 26 July 2005.

14 See C.M. Irish and C.B. Fulton, Jr., "Acts 29 Ministries."

15 Charles Alexander, interview, Metchosin, BC, 1 October 1990. Alexander eventually inherited the mantle of charismatic Anglican leadership from Vickers, though in both cases their influence was limited primarily to Western Canada.

16 This decision was vigorously resisted by some western leaders, including Charles Alexander and then bishop of Calgary, Morse Goodman. Since Canada is geographically large and identities are primarily regional – unlike American identity – it was feared that grassroots network and fellowship would be lost. In its short history, A.R. West had focused primarily on conferences for fellowship and teaching. The vision of the national organization was to provide more structure and resources, such as a magazine. Also, Alexander pointed out that the smaller Canadian parishes, unlike their American counterparts, did not have the financial resources to release their leaders for itinerant ministry. A brief history of Anglican Renewal Ministries is provided by Alexander in *Anglican Renewal Ministries*. Also see Bibby, *Anglitrends*.

17 The research was originally conducted during a sabbatical from Wycliffe College in the fall of 1990. The project was further supported by a grant from the Association of Theological Schools. The research method involved both written surveys and personal interviews. I visited twenty-three of the thirty dioceses in Canada, with phone interviews to key persons in the remaining seven. Travels took me from Halifax to Victoria, distributing surveys to laity, clergy, and bishops, each slightly different, and interviewing key individuals. Each survey provided space for personal comments, which provided additional feedback and insight. Over 1,100 surveys in total were distributed. The results of the study are based on data received from 471 laity (representing 62 per cent returned), 102 clergy (69 per cent) and 25 bishops (75 per cent). Donald Posterski, Director for Church Relations of World Vision International, provided invaluable assistance in the development of the research method and survey instruments. See Reed, "From Movement to Institution."

18 The "high" and "low" designations within Anglicanism represent theological and liturgical tendencies toward the Catholic and Protestant traditions respectively.

19 The expectancy of a conscious spiritual experience in corporate worship is a defining feature of Pentecostal-charismatic spirituality; see Baer, "Quaker Silence, Catholic Liturgy, and Pentecostal Glossolalia – Some Functional Similarities," 150–64.

20 *Anglican Church of Canada Confirmation Questionnaire*, 3.

21 Barrett, "Statistics, Global," 825.

22 Hocken, "Charismatic Movement," 500.

23 See Hocken, "Alpha Course," 312, and www.alphacourse.org.

24 Originally affiliated with the Vineyard movement begun by charismatic leader John Wimber in California, the church was dismissed from the fellowship and is now the independent Toronto Airport Christian Fellowship.

25 See Poloma, *Main Street Mystics*. The "Pensacola Outpouring" occurred at the Brownsville Assembly of God Church in Pensacola, Florida, and therefore is sometimes referred to as the "Brownsville Revival."

26 Malcolm Harding, electronic letter, 27 July 2005.

27 Harding, electronic letter, 9 August 2005.

28 See the Vision Statement of ARM: "Renewing the church to reach the world for Jesus," www.cyberus.ca/~arm/index2.htm.

29 The Montreal Declaration is posted on the website: www.anglicanessentials.org/fusion_pages/index.php?page_id=2

30 This profile is in marked contrast to the British experience in which the renewal movement attracted such leading evangelicals as David Watson, Michael Harper, and Michael Green.

31 One charismatic priest in the Diocese of British Columbia viewed it as an opportunity: since there was no other Anglican congregation within miles, members would still attend because there was no alternative, even if they did not like it. In contrast, a charismatic priest in New Brunswick refrained from introducing distinctively charismatic elements in the liturgy for precisely the same reason; he did not want to place undue hardship upon unhappy parishioners who would be constrained to travel twenty-five miles to the next Anglican parish. These two approaches, however, may be dictated as much by east coast/west coast culture as personality.

32 During the 1990 study, one priest recounted having watched a successful twelve-year renewal-oriented parish ministry in a rather remote area quite literally evaporate within a year under the leadership of his successor, a priest who unmaliciously had no experience or interest in charismatic renewal.

33 Wycliffe College in Toronto continues to be the only identifiable "evangelical" Anglican theological college in Canada.

34 See Wagner, *The Third Wave.*

35 Pawson, *The Fourth Wave.*

36 See Robinson and Smith, *Invading Secular Space*, 13–16.

37 The unfortunate consequence of the debate in the Diocese of New Westminster was the departure of seven congregations to form the Anglican Church in New Westminster. Having changed its name to the Anglican Communion in Canada, the number has now grown to fourteen congregations. See: www.acicanada.ca.

38 Here one thinks of the anti-slavery movement by British parliamentarian, William Wilberforce, and the Clapham Sect.

10

The Canadian Catholic Charismatic Renewal

DONALD S. SWENSON

INTRODUCTION

There is substantial evidence that charismatic renewal in the Canadian Catholic Church emerged as a potentially vibrant movement in the late 1960s but entered into a significant decline beginning around 1975. Since then, this renewal movement has been nearly absent from the Catholic Christian landscape. In this chapter I will account for the rise and decline of the Catholic Charismatic Renewal (CCR) with reference to several theoretical views. More specifically, I will review Finke and Wittberg's thesis that the Roman Catholic Church has been able to provide for renewal and revival within its circle without sacrificing unity.

ROMAN CATHOLICISM AND RENEWAL

Finke and Wittberg argue that the Roman Catholic Church has been able to provide for renewal and revival within its circle without sacrificing unity.[1] They use the church-sect dichotomy to provide a conceptual schema for their historical analysis of the cycle of revival movements within the Roman Catholic Church. A better term than *revival*, perhaps, is *movement of renewal*.[2] Wach's central concept, a "protest within," refers to a reform movement without the separatist impulse of the sect.[3] There is a long tradition of dissatisfaction with the "way things are" within the church, emerging protestation against the reification of sacred symbols, ritual, and ethos, and a subsequent movement for change. A second term Wach uses is *ecclesiola in ecclesia*. The literal meaning is a "little church within the large church." The term has several advantages for conceptualizing a movement of renewal within the Catholic Church. It attends to a collective "protest within" by the group defining itself using renewal language in relation to the ecclesiastical body. It also clearly distinguishes the renewal movement from the secessionist protest that sometimes occurs among Pentecostals.

The second author who adds to our understanding of renewal movements is Hill.[4] He developed the concept of *revolution by tradition* to account for the "'innovative' nature of tradition," which Weber, in paying less attention to the normative element within traditional authority, failed to explore as a potential source of social change. A revolution by tradition can be described as an attempt to realize in the present or in the immediate future a basis for authority which has the sanction of a precedent. The relevant tradition claims to have "always existed" but to have been neglected or usurped by those at present in positions of authority with the result that the latter can no longer claim legitimacy. He adds that renewal movements represent a "tradition whereby different groups within a single overall tradition may stress different aspects of that tradition by giving a differential emphasis to particular historical periods."[5]

Finke and Wittberg review a number of male- and female-revival movements within the Catholic Church that have been a common feature both of Eastern and Western Catholicism since the fourth century. Even though they have faced papal and episcopal opposition, their success has been due, in part, to their appeal not to an innovation of doctrine or practice, but a return to a pristine past: the life of Jesus, the communal example of the early church, the insights of the Church Fathers. However, like Protestant sects, these religious orders undergo an endless cycle of birth, transformation, rebirth, and, often, extinction.

Finke and Wittberg give the following examples: the early ascetic-desert movement common in Egypt and Northern Africa from about the third to the sixth century; the genesis and rise of the Benedictine Era from the sixth to the thirteenth century and the monasteries which were characterized by common ownership of property, prayer, work, and obedience to the Abbot or Abbess; the rise of the mendicant orders from the thirteenth to the sixteenth century which stressed poverty and itinerant preaching; the "apostolic orders," men or women dedicated to a common cause (education, nursing, care for indigent children, or evangelism) yet under the authority of the papacy, from about the sixteenth century through to the middle of the nineteenth. From this time to about 1965, there continued to develop new congregational orders in Ireland, France, Poland, Spain, Belgium, and Bavaria. A pattern of growth and decline has been exhibited and is summed up in Finke and Wittberg's observation: "It is accordingly clear that examples of durability are exceptional and religious orders tend to follow a path of gestation, consolidation, expansion, stabilization, decline, and extinction, with the entire cycle lasting usually somewhere between 250 and 350 years."[6] Finke and Wittberg explain that the success of renewal movements is related to three important factors: their ability to market the faith, presentation of innovative activities, and separation from the host society.

Spreading the faith was a feature central to renewal movements. Benedictine monks of the sixth century brought Christianity to the Anglo-Saxons of Britain; the Irish monks journeyed to Scotland, the Anglo-Saxon monk, Boniface, spread the Gospel to the Germans in the eighth century, the Franciscans were missionaries in Mexico in the sixteenth century, and the Jesuits, among other orders, to a lax Catholicism in Europe in the sixteenth century.

The members of many of these orders were also very creative, thus attracting new members to the movement. They introduced innovations in music, worship, preaching, education, retreats, spiritual direction, and ministry to children. A key to their success (and perhaps central to why so many declined when others did not) is that they adapted the faith to the local context which called for new ways of doing things.

The third reason for their popularity is that there was a clear division between the renewal group and the outside culture with its secular values. For example, all religious orders have accepted celibacy in contrast to married life. Further, their accent on a simple life that illustrates Jesus' "Sermon on the Mount" is in radical contrast to the pursuit of power, money and the "good life." My thesis is that the modern charismatic renewal in the Catholic Church is a continuation of these patterns of renewal and revival within Catholicism. The next section will document its emergence and its apparent demise with reference to the events surrounding Catholic renewal in Canada and the US since the 1960s. What follows is a description of several renewal groups, how they emerged, organized, dealt with internal dilemmas, and eventually declined. In the conclusion I will make some comments about the current state of renewal movements and the future of renewal for the Catholic Church.

THE EMERGENCE AND DECLINE OF THE CANADIAN
CATHOLIC CHARISMATIC MOVEMENT

The Catholic Charismatic Renewal (CCR), according to O'Connor, has a number of precursors or roots that help explain the modern renewal in the Catholic Church.[7] He cites several popes, a number of theologians, various religious-social movements, and the Second Vatican Council (1962–65) as precursors to the movement. During the nineteenth century, for example, the German theologians Moehler and Scheeben composed several treatises on the Holy Spirit and wrote of the role of the Holy Spirit in Church life, the place of the Holy Spirit in the personal life of the Christian, and the gradual rediscovery of the charismata of the early Church.[8] Other theological reflections included the Trinitarian indwelling within the Christian, the Holy Spirit uniting Catholics with the Father and the Son, and the revalorization of charismata that included teachings that these gifts, especially prophecy, were permanent endowments of the Church and not restricted to early Christianity. In 1897 Pope Leo XIII published an encyclical letter, "On the Holy Spirit," wherein he encouraged the Catholic faithful to appreciate the person of the Holy Spirit, to be open to the gifts of the Holy Spirit,[9] and called on every Catholic congregation to prepare for the feast of Pentecost by a novena of prayer.

Concerning the specifics of the renewal movement in the Catholic Church in the 1960s, O'Connor documents five aspects that provided fertile soil for the movement. First, there was a liturgical movement which focused the Church on the central mysteries of the Christian faith (the incarnation; Jesus' ministry, death, and resurrection; and Pentecost) and encouraged lay participation. Second, during this time there was also an emphasis on biblical renewal which was theological and experiential. Theologians updated interpretations of the Scriptures using historical methods and archaeological findings. Renewal of biblical study was particularly important to lay Catholics, enabling them to listen attentively to and ponder the Scriptures. Third, the lay movement extended ecclesial giftedness and ministry beyond the ordained clergy. The fourth movement, the ecumenical movement, encouraged Christians to be aware of the scandal of disunity they were presenting to the world and to dialogue, pray, celebrate, and love each other. The last movement, the Mystical Body movement, prompted the release of another encyclical, *Mystici Corporis*, by Pope Pius XII in 1943. It consisted of a valorization of the presence of the Holy Spirit throughout the whole Church (lay and cleric), emphasizing the vital communion of the faithful with one another in Christ. Pius XII wrote: "Christ is in us through his Spirit, whom he gives to us, and through whom he acts within us in such a way that all divine activity of the Holy Spirit within our souls must also be attributed to Christ ... This communication of the Spirit of Christ is the channel through which those gifts, powers and extraordinary graces, found superabundantly in the head as in their source, flow into all the members of the Church."[10] Together these various aspects within the Church acted to make Catholics open to the charismatic emphases of renewal.

Another major event, the Second Vatican Council (1962–63), is considered by charismatic Catholics to be the most important factor in the emergence of the CCR. It is striking that Pope John XXIII, the initiator of the council, compared the council to a *New Pentecost*. For a period of time before the council commenced, John XXIII encouraged all Catholics to pray that the Holy Spirit would renew his wonders. O'Connor noted that the document on the Church mentioned the Holy Spirit 258 times. He also considered that this document was the Magna Carta of the CCR. Along with this, the ecumenical tone was striking. The council pointed out that Christians of other denominations are linked to the Catholic Church through the Holy Spirit and receive gifts, graces, and sanctifying power. Finally, what is also most interesting is that, after much debate, charismata are accepted as vital for the growth and maturity of the Church. The document on the Church includes this statement: "Allotting his gifts 'to everyone according as he will' (1 Cor. 12:11), he distributes special graces among the faithful of every brand. By these gifts he makes them fit and ready to undertake the various tasks or offices advantageous for the renewal and upbuilding of the Church, according to the words of the Apostle: 'The manifestation of the Spirit is given to everyone for profit' (1 Cor. 12:7). These charismatic gifts, whether they be the most outstanding or the more simple and widely diffused, are to be received with thanksgiving and consolation for they are exceeding suitable and useful for the needs of the Church."[11]

O'Connor finishes his analysis of the background to the CCR by acknowledging Pope Paul VI as the *Pope of the Holy Spirit*. He noted that this pope spoke repeatedly of charismata, acknowledged that the Holy Spirit animates and sanctifies the Church, unifies God's people, is the source of a perennial Pentecost, anoints the faithful with prayer and all sorts of gifts, and pours divine love into all hearts. Pope Paul VI notes: "This is what the Church needs. She needs the Holy Spirit. The Holy Spirit in us, in each of us, and in all of us together, in us who are the Church."[12]

While these movements and events played a preparatory role for renewal, the CCR can be traced to a small prayer group which began in 1966 when three college professors, and the wife of one, met in Duquesne University, Pittsburgh, Pennsylvania. The setting was ecumenical. A Presbyterian woman shared her experience of the baptism of the Holy Spirit and the professors responded with openness to renewal. Shortly after, another centre for renewal emerged in South Bend, Indiana where some University of Notre Dame students went to a local Assemblies of God church. A common effect of these contacts was the establishment of charismatic prayer groups. The movement spread from here but also appeared to grow spontaneously in other parts of the US in such cities as Cleveland, Boston, Orlando, Los Angeles, St Louis, and New York. Many clergy joined, as well as members of religious orders such as the Augustinians, Basilians, Benedictines, Capuchins, Dominicians, Franciscans, Holy Cross Fathers, Jesuits, Josephites, Marionists, Mercedarians, Passionists, Redemptorists, White Fathers, Sisters of the Immaculate Heart of Mary, Daughters of the Blessed Elizabeth, Sisters of Mercy, Sisters of Charity, and the Franciscan Missionaries.[13] The Canadian connection occurred when Catholics attended renewal meetings in the US and then came back to organize prayer groups for renewal. An editor of a prominent magazine devoted to the CCR, the *New Covenant*, comments on these events at Notre Dame and Duquesne: "[they] triggered the explosive growth of the Charismatic Renewal in the Catholic Church ... It signaled a new phase in Church history; explicitly Pentecostal phenomena began to occur among groups of Catholics who saw no need to leave their Church in order to grow in the life of the Spirit."[14]

It was estimated that about 200,000 Catholics were involved in renewal groups around 1972 based on the numbers of Catholics attending the annual conference at Notre Dame, the circulation of the *New Covenant*, and the fact that 20,000 copies of a manual on how to be baptized in the Holy Spirit had been sold during the previous eighteen months.[15] Of the 60,000 Catholic clergy in the US in 1972, about 1,500 or 2–3 per cent were active in this renewal movement.[16] A more modest figure was presented by O'Connor in 1973 wherein about 37,500 Catholics were part of prayer groups in the US and Canada.[17] He cites the source from the Communication Centre in South Bend,

Indiana which tracked the number of prayer groups in the two countries. Yamane estimates that at its peak the CCR encompassed hundreds
of thousands and made contact with as many as four to seven million
Catholic Christians.[18]

The CCR took, primarily, three forms from the early years of the
1970s: informal prayer groups, retreat weekends, and more formalized
prayer communities. Martin, a lay leader in the CCR, calls the first one
fellowship.[19] The second type Martin terms intermittent renewal fellowships occurring in the context of retreats, conferences, or the teaching setting but without a long-term commitment beyond a designated
period of time. The third form, the prayer community, was termed by
Martin *Covenant Communities*. What follows is an account of informal prayer groups and covenant communities and the role they played
in renewal.

Covenant Communities

The elements present in the covenant community called for a total commitment of the participants to each other and to the belief that Jesus is
Lord. The relationships within the community were strong and enabled
the members to respond to each other's needs. The term covenant also
related to the fact that the relationships involved going beyond the level
of acquaintance. But the community was not to be considered a frater-
nity or a sorority. The bond for the participants was a common belief
that Jesus is the Lord of the community, the head, and that this draws
the members together in the spirit of Jesus.

The covenant community was further characterized by the following
elements: participants were well known to each other; they made a covenant with one another; there was present a hierarchy of leaders; and the
community had extensive involvement in the larger charismatic movement. Most communities were ecumenical in nature with a significant
number belonging to the Catholic Church but also engaging with the
wider Pentecostal and charismatic renewal in the Protestant churches.
Entrance into the community was preceded by extensive teaching on
renewal and the role of the community. I had the opportunity to study
one such community in Ann Arbor, Michigan during this time.[20] There
were approximately thirty communities that were offshoots of this one.
Communities developed in Eastern Canada, the Eastern seaboard of the
US, Ohio, Texas, New Mexico, Oregon, Louisiana, the Philippines, Tai-
wan, Mexico, and British Honduras. In the early 1970s, there were an

additional two communities in Western Canada which were not the direct offshoot of the Ann Arbor community.

The social structure of the community varied. Frequently, single persons lived in a household with the head of the community being the person who owned the house. Discipline was fairly strong and the whole community was involved in regular prayer, Bible study, and instruction. The Ann Arbor community (called the Word of God) began with a small prayer group of four in 1967. Slowly numbers were added and many became interested in new directions for the Christian life. By 1973, this community grew to encompass 1,200 committed members.[21] The gift of prophecy was central to the growth and development of the community. The participants waited to hear the "Lord speaking" through individuals often to encourage the group in Christian maturation and growth. The socialization process involved "Living the Life in the Spirit Seminars" that lasted for twelve weeks. This was followed by a twenty-two week study period on the meaning of living in a covenant community. Thereafter, people were invited to make a public covenant including a commitment to live the Christian life, be a member of the Word of God Community, respect the order of the community and share in the financial support of the community. The polity of the community consisted of lay elders called "Coordinators," who, in turn, govern other coordinators of smaller units. The smaller units met once a week in a prayer meeting setting. The whole community met several times a month in a common celebration.

As mentioned, leadership was hierarchical and strong. One of the beliefs was in the "charisma of office," meaning that the power to lead or to function does not lie within the person but in the "office of leadership." Leaders in the communities made the case that within the Catholic tradition one did not necessarily need to be ordained to lead.[22] This was especially evident in the monastic movement wherein most of the elders were not ordained. This same rationale was used in the Word of God community and in other covenant communities justifying lay people performing the role of elders.

The religious experience of the Word of God Community centred on building the communal nature of the group. There were challenging personal demands. When members failed, they were called to repent and to seek forgiveness, often in a public setting. The main outreach of the community was not through external involvement but, rather, by being a witness to the larger church community and the world around them through renewal. Leadership issues became controversial, especially the role of women in the communities when the traditional role of men and women in marriage and the family were discussed. One of the coordinators published a major study of the roles of men and women intended to justify the traditional role of men as leaders.

Another objective in writing the manual on gender roles was to restore Christian, male-female social relationships. Yet, these issues over the roles of women and men in renewal communities illustrate that the communities were institutionalizing very quickly. The transition from a renewal movement to an institutionalized group is one of the dilemmas renewal groups experience, as Finke and Wittberg identify. The gender dilemma included several elements. First, there was a sense that brother-sister configurations should be accented wherein people relate to each other in a spirit of care and service and not as candidates for special one-to-one relationships. Second, it was thought that in marriage, a man and a woman were partners with complementary roles. Clark writes: "The husband should be the head of the family. He should care for and protect his wife. He should provide for her clarity in what is expected of her, and he should provide a steadying and ordering influence on her emotional life ... The wife in turn should support her husband. She should serve him freely, not equating this service with something beneath her dignity. She should be a loyal partner whom he can count on as part of his own person. If a Christian family life is working well, the husband should not love his wife in the same way she loves him, but there should be a complementary aspect to their love."[23] There appeared to be a balance between freedom and control. Members were encouraged to live out their Christian call in a personal way as well as to be submissive to the community authority and the ecclesial hierarchy.

Early in the 1980s, a major schism occurred between two branches of Covenant Communities, one centred in the Word of God and the other, the People of Praise in South Bend, Indiana. The People of Praise continues to the present with many extensions in other parts of the US and Canada. One such extension is in Saskatoon, Saskatchewan. However, the Word of God community and its extensions have been disbanded.

Styled after the Word of God community, another covenant community emerged in Western Canada named The Love of God Community. Petroski, in a case study of this community, outlined in detail its history, its special characteristics, and its decline.[24] The genesis of the community was constructed as an informal prayer group in May of 1969 with the group growing rapidly in the following years to number about

250 members with an annual income of over $90,000 by 1976. In the latter years, there were five employees with business offices and assets of $48,000. In the historical analysis that follows, Petroski divides the community's life-course into five periods, discussed here in the Canadian context.

Ecstasy and Enthusiasm

Shortly after the initial beginnings in Duquesne, a group of people from a prayer group at Notre Dame University, Indiana, visited a lay congregation in Combermere, Ontario and shared their experience of the baptism of the Holy Spirit. A priest of that congregation was assigned to the Marian Centre in Regina, Saskatchewan. From his leadership, a charismatic prayer group emerged with its first public prayer meeting held in the library of the Regina Archdiocesan offices in 1969 with nineteen members in attendance.[25] The prayer group was unique in that members had an experiential encounter with Jesus through the power of the Holy Spirit and expressed themselves through the gifts of the Holy Spirit, especially speaking in tongues and the gift of prophecy. Petroski writes: "Those attending these early meetings experienced such fascination and enthusiasm that they could hardly wait for each meeting to commence."[26] Further, participants were open to share their personal hurts and pains and to be prayed with for the healing of these wounds. In addition, they experienced what many sociologists of religion describe as an experience of belonging and empowerment.[27] Petroski comments: "this sense of excitement and joy was the fact that through this experience everyone was given a deep sense of success and belonging, feelings that many could never have probably attained in their natural societal milieu."[28]

A Growing Sense of Mission

Within several months of the initial events, several members of the group were invited to convents and monasteries to participate in prayer days, days of recollection, and retreats, and to accompany numerous Pentecostal ministers to their churches, camps, and assemblies. The impact of the community extended as far as Vancouver, Calgary, Edmonton, Saskatoon, and Moose Jaw. In the spring of 1970, sixty members were regular attendees and the group moved to a larger facility in the diocesan centre. As numbers grew, leadership issues emerged and a "Core Group" was organized to work out the theology behind the baptism of the Holy Spirit and the charismatic gifts. This too illustrates how the movement became institutionalized, shifting from the experiential to a formal explanation for what the members of the community had experienced.

The In-Between Years

In the fall of 1970, the priest of the community was transferred to another part of Canada and what ensued is what Weber termed "a crisis of leadership." The second leader, already a member of the core group, assumed leadership but was unable to provide social order and stability in the prayer meetings. The group became more introspective and concerned with such matters as general group behaviour and theological orthodoxy. It was during this time that a break occurred within the group when a local Pentecostal pastor rebaptized a Catholic member of the prayer group which was contrary to the established ethic within Catholicism that water baptism is a once-in-a-lifetime occurrence. Essentially, the initial ecumenical nature of the group was weakened, raising another dilemma of institutionalization for the Catholic renewal movement.

In December of 1971, the prayer group was renamed "Emmanuel" claiming inspiration of the Holy Spirit. This "naming" coincided with the dilemma of numbers: many new people felt alienated as the community gained new members. A solution was to sub-divide the group into several cell groups who would meet in more intimate settings followed by a larger group meeting on a weekly basis. Further, it was thought that more formal education was needed to initiate new people into the group, and a series of teachings called "Life in the Spirit Seminars" began. Along with this, an informal covenant was signed by forty-two people in the fall of 1972 to renew support for the community.

The Word of God Community

From this time on, there grew to be more contacts with the Word of God Community in Ann Arbor, Michigan. From these contacts, members were encouraged to "sing in tongues," sing with enthusiasm, praise out loud, and learn more about a more formal covenant. The core-group concept was discontinued and a new order of leaders was constructed around "head-coordinators." Petroski commented that this process occurred with little or no input from the larger prayer group and no internal consensus from among the three coordinators.

Still, the infrastructure of the community developed apace. A large hall was rented to accommodate growing numbers. A music ministry was established. Offices were rented and an appeal for donations made along with the formulation of an official religious society for tax deduction purposes. In comparison, the later experiment was modest: single women and men moved into the homes of family members.

The turning point for the community, according to Petroski, seems to have been the adoption of the covenant idea that came from the Ann Arbor community in the spring of 1974 when thirteen members signed the document. After this event, struggle and disillusionment followed. Members seemed to participate on a legal basis and did so out of duty but not conviction. It was also during this time that a "sub-community" meeting was initiated to meet the needs of those who were not part of the "covenant community." Petroski makes a very interesting observation. Those who attended the sub-community meetings appeared to be thriving while those who made a covenant agreement were floundering.

Decline and Disestablishment

Subsequent signs of decline occurred in 1976 when the first coordinator resigned. Thereafter, a nominal Board of Directors became more active in the community. An attempt was made to involve more people in the decision-making process but the covenant community ceased to meet and the members' agreements were suspended. To shore up interest and commitment in the rest of the community, questionnaires were handed out to get input, various psychological techniques in the cell groups were tried, and the construction of a new pattern of meeting was established. The group also faced other problems when in the winter of 1976 the boiler in the building owned by the community was broken and it was too costly to repair. Public meetings were discontinued with members only meeting in cell groups, following the resignation of the coordinators.

Petroski attempted to explain the rise and decline of this community in the light of dissonance theory and the theology of Jacques Ellul.[29] Dissonance occurs when the gap between the expectations of the leaders and the experience of the members widens. The community then attempts to counteract this dilemma by re-establishing the purpose of the Church and thus restore it to an experiential reality. Petroski writes: "The community had no profound appreciation of its objectives and tended to stumble over its conscious ideals which because they were religious, led it into a further identification with those of the predominant collective culture. Thus, because of its lack of clarity in addressing its objects, the efforts of the community were co-opted by the larger society and denatured by the resulting dissonance and despair."[30]

Informal Prayer Groups

The second form that renewal took within the Catholic Church was the informal prayer group. As indicated above, the prayer group was the genesis of the community and it was the most common type of the CCR wherein participants came together about once a week to sing, praise, listen to teachings, pray, and enjoy fellowship. Leadership tended to be informal and both women and men were active in this kind of leadership. Various roles were assigned to participants such as leading in song and praise, offering personal reflections on the meaning of a scriptural text, praying over others for physical or emotional healing, and taking responsibility for the physical maintenance of the space.

Participants were expected to have a personal relationship with Jesus Christ, evangelize, study the Scriptures, manifest the gifts of the Holy Spirit especially glossolalia, prophecy,[31] and healing, show forth the fruit of the Holy Spirit, be committed to live a fuller life of the Spirit of Jesus and a life of service to others. Another pattern was the commitment to be faithful to the parish that they were a part of and to work toward unity with each group as well as across them.[32]

There existed a strong emphasis on the unity of the Church, an adherence to the Church hierarchy, a focus on sacramental life, and a continued belief in the specific tenets of Catholicism such as the communion of the saints, the recognition that Mary is the sinless and virgin mother of God, the real presence of Jesus in the Eucharist, and the Pope as the sign of Catholic unity within the renewal movement. A concomitant characteristic of the CCR was an awareness of the place of obedience to the local bishops with the bishops acting as a *linkage unit* between the movement and the hierarchy of the Church.[33] Many dioceses appointed a priest to be this link between members of the renewal and the Church hierarchy. There was also frequent counsel by priests to encourage renewal members to remain within the Catholic Church and serve the local church. One such priest writes: "To all who receive, I ask that they stay in their churches to become a leaven in the bread. For if they truly have the Holy Spirit, then by their fruits others will know Him – and will catch His fire as the dry grass before the wind-driven flames on the prairie."[34] This quest for linkage was not just a one-way street, though. While the leaders of renewal looked to stay connected with the Church, the bishops also encouraged it. In 1969, for example, the National Conference of Catholic Bishops in the US not only endorsed but encouraged the renewal movement to develop while maintaining a strong link to the Church. Their cautionary note was that the movement should be pastored in such a way as to avoid extreme emotionalism and to guard against the mistakes of the original Pentecostal movement which frequently led to schism and division.[35]

These linkage units went beyond the diocesan and national level to the Vatican. Beginning in 1972, a dialogue started between the Vatican Secretariat for Promoting Christian Unity with delegates from the Roman Catholic Church, the Pentecostal churches, and those from the neo-Pentecostal movement which included those from the Catholic, Protestant and Anglican communions.[36]

Two authors expressed great hope for the CCR. McDonnell, a priest-theologian, wrote: "The goal of the charismatic movement is not to import the movement into the church where it will be tolerated. Rather its end is a church which is renewed charismatically and no longer needs a separate movement."[37] Byrne, a lay elder, commented: "As part of the overall renewal of the Church in our generation, the Lord is awakening among Catholics a consciousness and awareness of the role of the Holy Spirit which for too long had become for too many a matter for theologians or mystics, these Catholics are experiencing the powerful presence of the Holy Spirit in their daily lives."[38] He also states: "The Charismatic Renewal is an amazing reality today. It is a powerful force which God seems to have unleashed in our midst. It is a historical and sociological phenomenon which in a short time has already demonstrated its power and appeal."[39]

Around the end of the 1970s and the beginning of the 1980s, there began a significant decline of the movement. Prayer group after prayer group dissolved so that in Calgary only a handful of prayer groups existed. The only Covenant Community that continues to meet is in Saskatoon and its numbers have also declined.

There are few published studies on the institutionalization of renewal in the Canadian Catholic Church. One that is salient is a case study of the movement in the context of new religious movements in Montreal from 1973 to 1978. The study involved up to seven graduate students from Concordia University. Francis Westley was the principal investigator and the author of the published work.[40] The project investigators were not primarily interested in Catholic renewal (their concern was with new religious movements) but they used data from the CCR as a comparison and a contrast with these movements. The researchers visited several Catholic renewal groups and conducted interviews with the participants. Westley categorized the various types of groups in Montreal to be small English speaking, large English speaking, and small Francophone groups. Three groups were studied that reflected each type. As with the larger CCR, the participants emphasized the Holy Spirit and the charismatic gifts.

Westley contrasts the CCR with the new religious movements on two fronts: healing and the integrated self. The gift of healing was highly valued in the prayer groups, including both the healing of the mind and of the body that was channelled not only through the clergy and nuns but also through lay people. The origin of the healing did not come from the participant but from God. She documents several stories that illustrate the process.[41]

> In the healing the Father took me in his arms. The Father blotted the pain and the negative effect it had had in my life. My innocence was restored to me and it set me free.

> I had a hard childhood. I had no mother. I cried to bed about it and was jealous of others who had a mother. I went through the experience of memory healing. I walked with God and forgave everyone who had hurt me. I remembered even things that I had forgotten. It was very beautiful. I felt very good after.

> I was on retreat. During mass everyone stands around the altar. All of a sudden a Sister G. said "someone is sick." I was having heart trouble ... I couldn't speak but I put up my hand. I was sitting and she was standing beside me. She put her hand on me ... so did the others ... in about four minutes praying over me the pulse went right back to normal. This is a charismatic gift. When you are in the group you can feel the pain of someone else.

Westley interprets these case stories as providing evidence for a theme of unity. To be healed is to forgive. Healing is a process that involves a transformation of negative memories and a new attachment to fellow members of the renewal. These experiences are also linked to group identity.

Another characteristic of renewal for its participants is the experience of "an integrated self" or, in evangelical Protestant terms, being "born again." There is a sense of homecoming, rebirth, of coming to oneself in the divine presence. It is, as Westley notes, an identity forming process: a new person in a new relationship with the divine and with others. She writes: "The 'I was lost but now I'm found' theme is so common to this type of group that is has become another cliché."[42]

Westely completed her study in 1978 and does not address the decline of the movement. Around that time, she conducted an interview with a prominent Pentecostal leader from Quebec. The leader's impression was that the single most critical factor that led to the movement's decline was that the Quebec bishops were fearful of ordinary Catholics deviating from traditional Catholicism and set about to control the movement from above. The net effect was that many of these Catholics left the Church and joined the classical Pentecostal denominations. Eventually, the groups dissolved and the Montreal renewal movement became a short-lived phenomenon of the recent past. For more on the CCR in Quebec, see chapter 1 in this volume.

CONCLUSION

All is not lost in the demise of the CCR. Many members became renewed in their spirits and went on to serve in their parish communities and worked on committees, engaged in liturgical activities, and the like. Another development is the use of the Alpha Program among Catholics that includes charismatic elements but is much more holistic in its approach toward ecclesial renewal. Many Catholic parishes in Canada are now using the program for renewal. A third remnant in Western Canada is the "Live-in." This is a program where organizers invite Catholic Christians for a weekend where they are introduced (or reintroduced) to Christianity in a dynamic and personal way. The downside is that there is very little follow up. The last example is St Michael's Catholic Community in Calgary. The pastor was involved in the CCR for many years but found that it did not bear fruit for parochial renewal. He began to introduce parishioners into praying Scripture using *Lectio Divina*[43] as a method. This has been combined with the Alpha Program which has been a carapace for about 1,000 parishioners. From this program, about 300 people have formed small cell groups called "Home Groups" aimed at renewal. For the last twelve years, this parish community has been a vibrant sign of hope for

renewal of the local Catholic Church. Locally, there have been gatherings wherein Catholics, Pentecostals, and evangelical Protestants have
met to celebrate together including the Global Day of Prayer. In the
Calgary edition of the 2005 Global Day of Prayer, a local Catholic
priest was on the planning committee and the Calgary Catholic Bishop
was one of the leaders in prayer.

On the official front, Catholic and Pentecostal theologians have been
meeting from 1970 until 2003.[44] These meetings have been sponsored
by the Pontifical Council for Promoting Christian Unity with several
Pentecostal denominations. The first phase (1972–76) of these meetings
and the second phase (1977–82) focused on the understanding of both
traditions in their confessional identities. Perspectives on *koinonia*
(community, church, or fellowship) were the topic of the third phase
(1985–89). The theme of the fourth phase (1990–97) was evangelization, proselytism, and common witness. The last phase thus far (1998–
2003) focused on Christian initiation and the baptism of the Holy
Spirit. Each focus has resulted in a final report under the name of that
particular focus. Thus, there are genuine signs both on the theological
and practical level of interchange, dialogue, and nascent signs of
unity.[45] While renewal played an important role for many in the Catholic Church, the institutionalization of renewal communities and their
ensuing decline in Canada illustrates the various tensions of transition
for Pentecostal-charismatic Christianity. Still, if Finke and Wittberg are
correct, renewal will take other forms within the Catholic Church.

NOTES

1 Finke and Wittberg, "Organizational Revival from Within: Explaining Revivalism and Reform in the Roman Catholic Church," 154–170.
2 Swenson and Thompson, "Locus Theologicus and Constructing a Sacred
   Past: Charismatic Renewal among Catholics as a Movement of Renewal;"
   Wach, *Sociology of Religion*; Hill, *The Religious Order*; Swenson, *Society,
   Spirituality and the Sacred*.
3 Wach, *Sociology of Religion*, 173.
4 Hill, *The Religious Order*.
5 Ibid., 107.
6 Finke and Wittberg, "Organizational Revival from Within," 160.
7 O'Connor, "The Hidden Roots of the Charismatic Renewal in the Catholic
   Church."

8 Ibid., 172–5.
9 There is no mention of charismata.
10 Cited in O'Connor, "The Hidden Roots," 181–2.
11 *Constitution of the Church*, section 12 and cited in O' Connor, "The Hidden Roots," 185.
12 *L'Osservatore Romano* 12:81 (7 December 1972) and cited in O'Connor, 188.
13 O'Connor, *The Pentecostal Movement in the Catholic Church*.
14 See Martin, "About This Issue," index.
15 Ibid.
16 Swenson, "The Charismatic Movement," 95.
17 O'Connor, "The Hidden Roots."
18 Yamane, "Charismatic Movement," 80–2.
19 Martin, "Covenant Communities," 140–60.
20 Swenson, "The Charismatic Movement."
21 Petroski, "Professed Religious Ideals and Realities," 33.
22 Clark, *Unordained Elders and Renewal Communities*.
23 Clark, *Man and Woman in Christ*, 649.
24 Petroski, "Professed Religious Ideals and Realities."
25 The locus is symbolically important for the identity of the CCR that envisions itself as   being linked to the Roman Catholic Church.
26 Petroski, "Professed Religious Ideals and Realities," 17.
27 These are two substantial functions of religion that Durkheim outlines. See *The Elementary Forms of the Religious Life*.
28 Petroski, "Professed Religious Ideals and Realities," 21.
29 See Ellul, The *Presence of the Kingdom*; and Ellul, *The Technological Society*.
30 Petroksi, "Professed Religious Ideals and Realities,"100.
31 It had come to be interpreted within the Pentecostal, neo-Pentecostal and the CCR that a person is inspired to speak words of love and encouragement to a prayer group or a prayer community.
32 Bennett, *The Holy Spirit and You*; Byrne, *Threshold of God's Promise*; Ranaghan, *As the Spirit Leads Us*; Williams, *The Era of the Spirit*; Christensen, "Pentecostalism's Forgotten Forerunner."
33 Swenson, "The Charismatic Movement."
34 Orsini, "When I Let God Come Near," 18–19.
35 Zaleski, "Report of the American Bishops".
36 Secretarius, *Ad Christianorum Unitatem Fovendam* (The Vatican: Citta Del Vaticano, 1971).
37 McDonnell, "Catholic Charismatics," 210.
38 Byrne, *Threshold of God's Promise*, 30.

39 Ibid., 22.

40 Westley, *The Complex Forms of the Religious Life*.

41 Ibid., 69–70.

42 Ibid., 79.

43 An art of prayer that goes back to the sixth century under the leadership of St Benedict. It was and is the prayer form of the Benedictine Religious Order. People are encouraged to read the Scriptures on a daily basis, memorize a small text from that reading, and then ruminate on it all day long as the Psalmist counsels (Psalm 1).

44 See "Pontifical Council for Promoting Christian Unity" http://www.prounione.urbe.it/dia-int/pe-rc/i_pe-rc-info.html.

45 The Pentecostal/Roman Catholic dialogue has produced a growing literature. See Del Colle, "Theological Dialogue on the 'Full Gospel': Trinitarian Contributions from Pope John Paul II and Thomas A. Smail," 141–60; Del Colle, "Pentecostal/Catholic Dialogue: Theological Suggestions for Consideration," 93–6; Robeck, "Pentecostals and Ecumenism in a Pluralistic World," 338–62; Moltmann and Kuschel, *Pentecostal Movements as an Ecumenical Challenge*.

The "Toronto Blessing" – A Lesson in Globalized Religion?

STEPHEN HUNT

INTRODUCTION

As is relatively well documented, Pentecostalism has for many decades been associated with expressions of ecstatic and esoteric Christianity. Glossolalia, divine healing, words of knowledge, and prophecy are included among some of the distinguishing features of the movement – whether designated "classical" or neo-Pentecostal – which have spread through many quarters of the world.[1] Nonetheless, from early 1994 the phenomenon that was to circle the globe for some five years, associated primarily with the so-called "Toronto Blessing," appeared to have become more extreme and bizarre. The "Blessing," as it was more colloquially known, swept through thousands of churches worldwide, indifferent to denominational allegiance and cutting across evangelical networks. Its point of departure, so to speak, has been commonly designated to be that of a previously insignificant church situated close to Pearson International Airport, the Toronto Airport Vineyard Church.

Relatively few scholarly works have charted the origins, development, and eventual disappearance of the Toronto Blessing nor offered explanations for its appeal in largely Pentecostal or charismatic circles. This chapter, written approximately a decade after the Blessing seemingly first emerged, attempts to reflect on aspects of a quite remarkably abstruse set of events. The main concern will be to explore the Toronto Blessing "movement," as it can rightfully be designated, in terms of contrasting theories of globalization. This paper will suggest that it can largely be comprehended and appraised as a "package" of esoteric phenomena that was exported from Canada to diverse parts of the world albeit for a relatively fleeting period of time. The chapter will nonetheless suggest that the erstwhile account of the "actors" involved, and of not a few sociologists as well, that the Blessing somehow "started" at one charismatic church in Canada and that the phenomena associated with it were subsequently disseminated globally, constitutes a gross simplification of events which, in reality, developed over a protracted period of time.

There is little by way of academic works directed toward describing the phenomena associated with the Toronto Blessing, and even fewer have attempted to explain them. Those which do attempt to explain range from fairly sympathetic sociological accounts in the form of ethnographic studies[2] to fairly strong theological critiques.[3] Most, however, provide first-hand descriptions of the Blessing and its associated bizarre manifestations. The most obvious distinguishing feature was uncontrolled if not hysterical laughter during church services and later specially organized "receiving meetings" which sought God's blessing through such physical "signs" of his power and indwelling presence.

There were other characteristic manifestations to be observed among the physical signs of the Blessing. While some members of a congregation fell to the floor under the alleged "power" of God, others staggered around in what was described, by those involved, as a "spiritual drunkenness" – laughing or displaying slurred speech and uncontrolled spasms of the limbs. Alternatively, individuals would sit sobbing or gently weeping. Some moved their bodies rapidly and rhythmically, even erotically, others made judo-like chopping actions with their forearms or shook as if experiencing an epileptic seizure. Two of the more curious physical expressions that I personally witnessed almost defied description. One amounted to a kind of frantic running-on-the-spot, with a rapid shaking of the head, accompanied by arms outstretched and held high. The other constituted a rapidly repeated "bowing" jerk. Later came the more extreme manifestations witnessed in some charismatic fellowships with members of the congregation roaring like lions, clucking like chickens, speeding around their church imitating motor cars, or women groaning and claiming to be birthing in God's Kingdom to come.

The manifestations associated with the Toronto Blessing, given its nature, are open to wide interpretation. The view of some opponents in the churches (mostly but not exclusively non-charismatics) regarding the phenomena was often expressed with a scathing detachment. In Britain, for example, in January 1995, the Blessing was described in the preface of the *Church of England Yearbook* as "an expression of mass hysteria." In sociological terms, by contrast, the Blessing was accounted for by way of such variables as shifting attitudes toward bodily disinhibition, changing communication patterns, and new gender perceptions of God;[4] the influence of popular psychology;[5] the attempt to revive the Pentecostal movement;[6] or as an expression of pent up psychological hope for revival.[7] While all these renditions have provided insights into the Blessing, such interpretations have, to one extent or another, tended to ride rough-shod over the explanations given by those caught up in the events as they unfolded.

GLOBALIZATION OR GLOCALIZATION?

A good number of the scholarly accounts mentioned above rightly stress the global dimensions of the Toronto Blessing in its rapid dissemination. In a very short space of time the associated phenomena appeared in churches in such diverse places as Europe, South Africa, Australia, and South-East Asia. Perhaps the most impressive account to date of the globalizing aspects of the Blessing is that provided by Philip Richter who partly explains its spread through the age-old activity of the pilgrimage to sites believed to have special religious significance and where the sacrifices incurred are rewarded by divine blessing of one form or another. Put succinctly, in the context of the Blessing, charismatic Christians travelled to the Toronto Airport Vineyard Church and expected to experience the phenomena as a "reward" for their sacrifice in respect to the cost and time incurred.[8] However, there remains considerable room to investigate the further dynamics of globalization and usefully explore extant theoretical frameworks, especially in relation to contemporary religious movements.

Globalization and its consequences for religion have proved to be a popular theme for sociologists specializing in the area. Perhaps the most significant contribution has been offered by Roland Robertson[9] who is at pains to point out that while religion may, at first glance, appear to be peripheral to globalizing tendencies, it is, in fact, at the heart of it. What he terms "national societies" are related to different cultures and traditions as the economic and power structures of these societies become increasingly interdependent at a global level. This remains true of numerous expressions of religiosity as well as other social activity.

If religion is central to the globalizing processes, there undoubtedly exists considerable disagreement as to what are the most prominent dynamics involved. There are perhaps two polarized views. The first tends to be derived from notions of Western economic hegemony largely derived from the work of Wallerstein.[10] In simple terms, the nations of the world are subject to the power and influence of the Western industrialized nations; economically, politically, and culturally. It follows that the disproportionate global impact of Western forms of religion can best be understood in these terms. This point of view is powerfully espoused in Brouwer et al's *Exporting the American Gospel* which considers the global impact of US-style fundamentalist Christianity.[11] Another popular dimension to the theme of Western cultural hegemony comprises accounts of the global processes of "McDonaldization"[12] which suggest that economic products, along with accompanying cultural attributes, are suitably packaged and disseminated across the world. The potential and actual processes involved in McDonaldization of some forms of religion have rarely been explored although I have made some attempt to analyse the possibilities with reference to recent evangelizing initiatives emerging in Britain.[13] Attributing the rise and spread of the Toronto Blessing to the dominant mode of Western esoteric and therapeutic-type charismatic/evangelical experience and praxis remains, therefore, of considerable attraction. The Blessing seemingly "began" in a North American church and was subsequently packaged for global diffusion as a distinct cultural manifestation.

There are a number of problems with this "hegemonic" approach which can be briefly mentioned here. First, there is the danger of seeing the consequences of globalization for religion as something that marks a radically new departure.[14] Evidence suggests otherwise. Hence, Bryan Wilson has detailed the rapid global spread of such sects as the Church of Latter-Day Saints, Jehovah's Witnesses, and Pentecostalism, at the end of the nineteenth and beginning of the twentieth centuries from the US to Europe and beyond.[15] Second, the exported aspects of religiosity, as with other culture attributes, are not merely "one way." Hence, Campbell has explored the potent forces of Easternization, especially by way of religion, from the East to North America and Europe which seem to counterbalance Western cultural hegemonic processes.[16]

Third, it cannot be assumed that such processes emerging in the West are ascribed the same meaning as originally attributed to them, since people in different places look at the world through their own cultural lenses. In short, there are dynamics related to Featherstone's[17] notion of "glocalization" – a concept that marks the opposite pole from that of the hegemonic model. It follows that as a result of multi-dimensional aspects of globalization, religion becomes a "cultural site," since any part of the world can be influenced by the ebbs and flows of numerous expressions of religiosity which subsequently generate infinite variations and localized expressions of belief and practice.[18] While, for example, the impact of Easternization is modified by Western cultural themes,[19] North American evangelizing ministries, especially those espousing the prosperity gospel, have had an impact in different ways and to different degrees across the world.[20]

THE LIMITS OF GLOBALIZATION: THE CASE OF THE TORONTO BLESSING

How might we proceed to throw light on the global dissemination of the Toronto Blessing? Can we plausibly make sense of it in terms of extant sociological frameworks? To begin with I think that there is a danger of being wholly subsumed by theoretical paradigms in coming to terms with the Blessing and hence limiting our understanding of some of its most important dimensions. This is particularly so given its esoteric nature. Expressions of the Blessing were not merely restricted to its curious physical manifestations since there were more "hidden" dimensions, profoundly subjective experiences – references to prophecies, visions, and "pictures" which seemed to increase throughout its duration. Two examples from my survey in Britain may suffice. At a leading charismatic Anglican church, at the height of the Blessing's impact, several individuals reported having experienced a vision of large angelic figures bathed in orange light. At a Baptist church a young woman recounted to her congregation her experience of "seeing the Lord" appear at a mid-week prayer group who then proceeded to playfully throw "rainbows" at her.

The nature of such experiences is debatably outside the remit of sociology. Yet, other claimed esoteric experiences are more accountable to the realm of urban myths, even globalized urban myths, with rumour providing a powerful mechanism. One such rumour during the time of the Blessing related to further widespread tales of angelic visitations. In one narration an angel, in the guise of a hitch-hiker, accepted a lift in a car belonging to two Christians and then suddenly disappeared, but not before proclaiming that "revival is coming." There were at least, to my knowledge, nine variations of this story which were related in very different parts of the world.

Despite reservations in employing globalization theories in comprehending the wide impact of the Toronto Blessing some of the above frameworks do provide insights into its dissemination. One traces its spread from the Toronto Airport Vineyard Church by various mechanisms which suggests hegemonic aspects, while its localized impact across the world must also be taken into account. Nevertheless, it is important to reiterate the point already made that it is wrong to assume that the Blessing somehow "started" in Toronto and was merely "exported" in the fashion of a McDonaldized "product." Such assumptions tend to endorse, although for obviously different reasons, the narrative surrounding its origins in Canada shaped by many in the charismatic movement (especially from the Toronto Vineyard Church) caught up with events and which produced an uncritical and simplified account of complex developments.

In proceeding to explore the significance of the Airport Vineyard Church, and the way in which the Blessing was understood and appraised, I would suggest that we can draw parallels with the initial emergence of the Pentecostal movement, especially in the realm of Pentecostal-charismatic mythology which I have detailed elsewhere.[21] The alleged origins of the Pentecostal movement have been incorporated into the charismatic narrative in such a way as to display strong parallels with the manner in which the Blessing is appraised in terms of chronological developments. In 1900, the holiness evangelist Charles Parham started the Bethal Bible College in Topeka, Kansas. Parham maintained that there was a level of spiritual power which most Christians had not yet experienced which could be gained through holiness and repentance.[22] With Parham's inspiration the revival which began in Topeka spread to Houston and then to Los Angeles, and was especially evident at the famous Azusa Street mission.[23]

Numerous evangelical ministries visited Azusa for renewal, found their faith reinvigorated and subsequently helped to spread Pentecostalism internationally along with its ecstatic phenomena exemplified by speaking in tongues. However, the selective emphasis on this particular episode tended to hide the fact that the momentum for this version of ecstatic Christianity could also be found elsewhere and that earlier revival meetings had, as it were, prepared the way for full-blown revivalism. Moreover, the Azusa Street mission is often credited with giving Pentecostalism its distinguishing feature of speaking in tongues. Again, this is not strictly true since there had been several isolated cases of glossolalia leading up to the Azusa Street revival.[24] Not dissimilar observations can be made of the emergence of the second wave of Pentecostalism in the 1960s, which has subsequently come to be designated as the "charismatic movement."[25]

THE "ROOTS" OF THE BLESSING

So what are the roots of the Toronto Blessing? The answer to this question clearly hints at globalized events – developments which highlight processes at work long before they were suitably "packaged" and disseminated from the Airport Vineyard Church. Certainly, most of the characteristic features of the Toronto Blessing had been reported in a number of charismatic churches and meetings even before they were witnessed in Toronto and thereafter referred to as the Toronto Blessing. Their intensity, frequency, and spread are documented in copious amounts of popular charismatic and other evangelical literature. Nonetheless, it is very difficult to date the precise beginnings or the true tapestry of much wider events and thus divorce the reality from the myths that arose around one particular church in Toronto.

According to the leading charismatics involved in the Blessing whom I have interviewed and who sometimes contradict renditions in the charismatic literature, the manifestations had been occurring on a global level for some time and were evident across Europe (particularly Scandinavia), Argentina, the us, and elsewhere in Canada. It was speculated by some that in New Zealand manifestations associated with the Blessing had been periodically and spontaneously breaking out for perhaps four years previously but that the reports were suppressed by church leaders. This remains unsubstantiated. Even earlier is the record of a weekly prayer meeting held at Digby Stuart College in London in the late 1980s where allegedly "people were bouncing, convulsing, trembling, laughing, crying and falling over."[26]

Rõmer has impressively detailed the developments leading up to the Blessing's apparent sudden arrival.[27] In Rõmer's reading the beginning of events can be traced back to when the church's principal pastor, John Arnott, visited Argentina in late 1993 where he attended a conference for North American ministers. Certainly, it is clear that Arnott laid claim to having been particularly impressed by the Argentine pastor Hector Jiminez who headed a healing ministry and maintained that at his Assemblies of God Church, King of Kings Church, a revival had seen the congregation grow to 4,000 members.[28] Already witnessed at this church were members in the congregation who had "fallen under the power" (of the Holy Spirit) with uninhibited laughter being a trademark of the meetings. Around the same time Arnott also visited Florida where he was "prayed over" by Benny Hinn. The latter is perhaps the world's best known Pentecostal healing evangelist. Hinn had developed a strategy of "blowing" the Holy Spirit over people on stage, who would then fall to the floor, apparently healed or otherwise blessed.

At the end of 1993 a Vineyard pastor, Randy Clark from St Louis, also laid claim to revival at his church which was accompanied by the same curious phenomena. Clark was invited to Toronto in January 1994. Both Clark and Arnott scheduled a series of meetings to further stimulate revival. At this point another root to the Blessing became evident. Previously, Clark had witnessed the ministry of Rodney Howard-Brown during the latter's crusade meetings in St Louis. This was part of his tour of the US during 1993 where he brought large crowds "under the power." Howard-Brown also practised the habit of "blowing" the Holy Spirit over audiences and commanding them to laugh. According to Richter, it was Howard-Brown who provided the channel for the outbreak of the Blessing in January 1994.[29] The Airport Vineyard Church, however, became the localized catalyst for further developments. For one thing, it could claim a revival of its own with the congregation having risen from 300 to over 1,000 since 1990. This had, in turn, fulfilled a prophecy evidently announced through a member of the pastoral team, Marc Dupont. Prophecies then abounded in some number including that which foretold that world revival would stem from the localized revival in Toronto.

That the phenomena witnessed at the Airport Vineyard church immediately impacted other Vineyard churches in the locality, and then throughout North America, should be no surprise and not only because the church is centred in an unused warehouse situated in an industrial estate in close proximity to the city's airport. The Vineyard churches, under the auspices of the late healing evangelist John Wimber, were already renowned for their emphasis on "signs and wonders" as an essential ingredient of power evangelism. The Association of Vineyard Churches was established in 1986 and had grown rapidly to become a fully fledged international movement. From its heart in California, it boasted a membership of around 50,000 in some 500 churches globally and claimed networks open to mainline churches in North America, Europe, and elsewhere.[30] For a decade before the emergence of the Blessing a powerful array of signs and wonders had already done the round of charismatic churches on a global scale (with Wimber having first encountered such phenomena at the beginning of his ministry in the late 1970s).[31] This point is stressed by Richter who writes that "'the 'Wimber Wobbles' predated the 'Toronto Trots' by ten years."[32] Accompanying the phenomena was the talk of revival. The globally disseminated "Equipping the Saints" conferences and the like, organized by Vineyard, more than hinted that "equipping" God's people meant preparing for revival. This was given further emphasis through Vineyard's connection with Paul Cain and the other so-called Kansas City Prophets for whom the coming revival was associated with the eschatology of the Last Days.

My view is that such notions of preparing the Church had deep roots in the post-millenarian position of many contemporary charismatics. This eschatology allowed the possibility of "forcing the end" and the triumph of a world view in which the time of the Second Coming depended on revival and the actions of the "saved."[33] From its beginnings neo-Pentecostalism had established a link between the emergence of the movement itself and eschatological longings. Enhancing such longings was the acceptance of the spiritual gifts and esoteric phenomena which had the effect of making heaven appear closer by demonstrating the reality of the supernatural, instilling a sense of the imminence of God, and rekindling the desire for the full realization of the final Kingdom.

"PACKAGING" THE TORONTO BLESSING

The impression given by leaders of the larger charismatic churches across the world that looked favourably on the Blessing was that it began spontaneously in their churches and was interpreted as a global outpouring of the Holy Spirit. This then became more formulized through the "receiving meetings." In these meetings the phenomena typically commenced with the laying on of hands by church leaders or visiting "anointed" individuals from the Vineyard organization or other churches. There was a prevailing consensus at the time, however, that the Blessing could be observed most powerfully at the Toronto Airport Vineyard Church where the manifestations seemed to be more extreme and intense.

Given the apparent spontaneity of the Blessing there were those leading charismatics who were content to speak of a "time of blessing" when God periodically drew close to his Church. For others the theme was that of revival. Hence, "receiving meetings" were frequently replaced by "preparation for revival meetings." The Toronto Vineyard

Church had its own interpretation of events although this was by no means universally accepted. The central theme was that God was preparing his Church for the greatest revival ever which could lead to the Second Coming of Christ; that God was cleansing his Church for this purpose and, in the words of one leading charismatic involved, "God is coming to His people before He comes for His people."[34] The Toronto Vineyard Church also began to formulate what the Blessing meant in theological terms, clearly expressed in John Arnott's statement: "This is a time of restoration in the body of Christ similar to the time of John the Baptist's ministry prior to the coming of the Messiah." This put the Toronto Vineyard Church not only at the core of events but the centre of eschatological designs.

Within a very short space of time the Toronto Vineyard Church came to be associated with the most powerful manifestations of the Holy Spirit. While the charismatic literature and the pronouncements of church leaders of the time recognized that certain events (the impact of ministries of Howard-Brown, Benney Hinn, and others) had led to revival at Toronto, the Toronto Vineyard Church was designated as playing a special part in developments, hence the prefix "Toronto" to the characteristic esoteric manifestations.

The outpouring of the "power" of God at Toronto attracted pastors and lay people from North America, and later from other parts of the world, who travelled to Canada to witness and experience the manifestations which were believed to be of a greater intensity than elsewhere. By the end of the summer of 1994 over 10,000 people had visited Toronto. At this time there was the strong impression developing that Toronto was a kind of "fountain" of the Holy Spirit where visitors took the Blessing back to their own churches. Among the first visitors was a contingent from the large Anglican church in central London, Holy Trinity, Brompton (HTB), with whom Vineyard had long enjoyed strong connections.[35]

This representation was soon followed by others from mainline charismatic churches across the various denominations within Britain as well as those from the so-called "New Churches." All these churches represented interrelated evangelizing networks which "carried" the Blessing back to the local context in Britain where belief in a coming revival was also strong and where, in the case of HTB, it was prophesied that revival would extend nationally from the church. While some UK churches could claim to have already experienced the Blessing in part, it was the pilgrimage to Toronto that led to the intensification of the characteristic phenomena. For other churches, visiting Toronto meant experiencing the phenomena for the first time.

The flow and impact of the Blessing was then reinforced when Howard-Brown led a large church leaders' meeting in Birmingham which ended with the now familiar manifestations. Non-charismatic churches, however, would have nothing to do with the Blessing, and even more traditional Pentecostal churches, primarily represented by Elim and the Assemblies of God, were torn by what they regarded as excessive manifestations and even heresy on the one hand, and demands of their congregations on the other – producing a dilemma which also divided them over US-styled prosperity teachings. In this respect local church Pentecostal leaders became the "gate-keepers" in deciding whether or not their churches would embrace the "Blessing."[36]

There is more to consider concerning the dissemination of the Blessing from Toronto. Marketing had always proved to be an integral part of the Vineyard success story. There is evidence to suggest that in the US the majority of Vineyard's middle-class membership had conducted their share of "church shopping" and found the movement particularly attractive because it advocated a strong belief system which could be "acted out" through "experience."[37] Moreover, Vineyard has encouraged the individual believer to sustain a feeling of fulfillment and continued spiritual growth, frequently through popular books, many written by John Wimber himself, as well as specialized conferences. Much of this exemplified Smark's view that, in the hands of many evangelical churches, God was increasingly being mass marketed.[38] In true McDonalized fashion the Toronto Blessing was suitably "packaged" with best-selling books, audio and visual tapes, and other paraphernalia including T-shirts with such logos as "I'm a Jerk for Jesus" or "I have been Torontoed." There is little doubt that much was in response to the demands in the charismatic marketplace, since, as Richter notes, the membership of charismatic churches had begun to decline due to the inevitable process that Roy Wallis has designated as the "precariousness of charisma."[39] What was needed was more of the esoteric phenomena that had accompanied the charismatic movement in the first place.[40] Enter the Toronto Blessing.

THE GLOBAL SPREAD OF THE TORONTO BLESSING

While acknowledging that the Blessing required localized global receptivity, particularly against a background of an expected revival (this seemed to be especially important where church attendance had declined rapidly such as Australia, the UK, and Sweden), the standardized nature of much of the physical phenomena associated with it is noteworthy. This is all the more remarkable given their peculiar nature. How the Blessing was "acquired" is of major concern at this point. The Blessing was an esoteric experience but in many ways constituted a learned experience which depended on a number of observable dynamics.

In Britain, as elsewhere, the Blessing seemed to have occurred *impromptu*. This is difficult, however, to fully justify. Many of the churches first involved (and this was certainly the case with the UK) already enjoyed prior contacts with Vineyard, although not necessarily directly with the Toronto Airport Vineyard Church. A good deal in this respect mirrored the events during the early stage of charismatic renewal in the mid 1960s where a number of key individuals in the mainline churches had channels established with the classical Pentecostal churches and had witnessed firsthand the phenomena associated with them, most obviously glossolalia.

In Britain, as elsewhere, certain churches became "fountains" themselves or what Richter calls "epicentres"[41] for the Blessing – displaying the characteristic manifestations. These tended to be the larger charismatic churches which were visited by the leaders of smaller congregations who "took" the phenomena back to their churches. It is undoubtedly true to say that the arrival of the Blessing generally depended on the initiative of sympathetic leaders within any given church. Such local church leaders also became, in a sense, role models. This is important because, as Richter insists, normally a person would experience the Blessing only after accepting that the experience existed and what it meant or, at least, after weighing carefully the idea of its experience and after it had been reenforced and legitimated by the leadership.[42] This would seem to justify the insistence of Poloma and Pendleton that Pentecostal-type manifestations are frequently experienced by an individual only after they had been observed first-hand.[43]

Richter essentially interpreted "acquiring" the Blessing as a learning process. He points out how technical and practical tips were passed on as part of transference of personal guidance for the individual who was probably also attempting to receive the experience through sometimes reading Christian magazines and books or viewing video tapes. Even those sympathetic to the Blessing pointed out that many services and meetings in which it occurred were orchestrated in such a way that early on there were practical demonstrations of church members being prayed over and falling after they had publicly testified about the experience.[44] The ministry teams who guided the "Blessing" in their churches would normally have been through an "apprenticeship" period themselves[45] and trained according to certain accepted guidelines within a specific church as was evident in the Toronto Vineyard Church and Holy Trinity, Brompton, London.[46]

In my judgment it is impossible to know precisely how many churches were impacted by the Blessing, but certainly they numbered many tens of thousands world-wide. Most of the sizeable charismatic churches across the globe displayed the characteristic manifestation. The pattern of dissemination was predictable and constant. Church leaders had visited the Toronto Airport Vineyard Church or an "epicentre" of the Blessing in their own country or abroad. Alternatively, individuals or congregations had read accounts in the popular Christian media or seen videos produced in Toronto. At the same time representatives from the Toronto Airport Vineyard Church, other Vineyard churches, or internationally renowned churches visited other countries and spread the characteristic phenomena. It frequently followed, then, that the more remote a country and the more remote a locality, the longer the Blessing took to arrive. For instance, according to Pentecostal ministers in Australia, the Blessing seemed to be reaching churches in very remote areas long after it had disappeared elsewhere.

CONCLUSION

Over a decade has passed since the initial outbreak of the Blessing in Toronto. It is clear that the global impact of the Blessing means that it constitutes an ideal study in the context of extant theories of the globalization of religion whether subscribing to a hegemonic model or, alternatively, exploring the significance of "glocalization." Clearly, the dissemination of the phenomena manifest in the Blessing displays aspects of both although, if such an appraisal is at least partly derived from the account of the actors involved, it remains difficult to extract fact from myth and elaboration. There is a very real sense, however, in which the Blessing was *not* somehow "imposed" by a North American church that was at the time enjoying a growing reputation and had become the focus of interest for a number of charismatic ministries. Certainly, it would be wrong to conjecture that the Blessing was merely some vast charismatic/evangelical marketing exercise. Moreover, given the esoteric phenomena involved, it is hard to suggest that the Blessing was merely transplanted to localized global settings. On the other hand, the esoteric phenomena associated with the Blessing in the Toronto Vineyard Church were rarely subject to localized variations and, furthermore, if some were of local origin then they certainly did not find their way back to the church to add to its broad range of manifestations.

In many respects, the Blessing would seem to offer support for the rational-choice/"supply-side" theorizing that has proved to be so popular among North American sociologists for some two decades and been initially largely espoused by the theorizing of Rodney Stark and his associates[47] and once cogently described as *the* most significant emerging paradigm in the sociology of religion.[48] It is clear in Richter's application of the supply-side of the Toronto Blessing that charismatic churches were prepared to invest in more "charisma" in the form of the esoteric phenomena that accompanied it. In short, the Toronto Vineyard Church constituted the supply-side of a marketplace for the needs of a distinct set of religious consumers in the charismatic community. It was not, however, a hegemonic supply-side that cajoled and obligated that constituency to buy its wares in either a literal or metaphorical sense.

Such a rational choice/supply-side approach cannot be rejected wholesale. There is a very real sense in which the Blessing was a localized event (although earlier developments had clearly fed into it) that was thoroughly globalized through systematic marketing via Toronto. The packaging of the characteristic manifestations, the commercial business built up around it, and its subsequent spread are all relevant dimensions of the Blessing. At the same time localized features were significant. Some charismatically inclined Christians, particularly in North America and Europe, were more readily convinced than others of its virtues, especially where revival had long been expected and where the relevant "signs" were unquestionably embraced. Elsewhere, the Blessing penetrated areas untouched by the charismatic phenomena or brought to charismatic churches a dimension of Western therapeutic-type neo-Pentecostalism.

The Toronto Blessing, largely because of its multi-dimensional attributes, did not readily conform to a broad hegemonic model identified by its marketability and dominant set of theological interpretations of what it all amounted to. The diffuse and esoteric nature of the phenomenon was always open to interpretation in the local context and discussions as to what exactly the "revival" meant even if localized cultural "lenses" largely shared in common a charismatic worldview that set cognitive parameters to interpretations of what the Blessing was all about. Thus, despite its theological paucity, the Blessing retained a fairly "glocalized" understanding of its eschatological significance. This fairly standardized dimension of the Blessing should not distract from its remarkable nature and the way in which it signified the accumulation of four decades of charismatic-type phenomena. Equally remarkable was its brevity. The Toronto Blessing has disappeared as rapidly as yesterday's news, now rarely discussed in charismatic and Pentecostal quarters, perhaps rendering it less of a fad and more an end of the charismatic movement in its Western variant.

NOTES

1 Cox, *Fire from Heaven*; Martin, *Tongues of Fire*.
2 Hunt, "The 'Toronto Blessing': A Rumour of Angels?," 257–71; Poloma, *Main Street Mystics*; Römer, *The Toronto Blessing*.
3 Percy, *The Toronto Blessing*; Richter, "GOD is Not a Gentleman! The Sociology of the Toronto Blessing," 5–37; Richter, "The Toronto Blessing: Charismatic Evangelical Global Warming," 97–119.
4 Richter, "The Toronto Blessing."
5 Römer, *The Toronto Blessing*.
6 Poloma, *Main Street Mystics*.
7 Hunt, "The Toronto Blessing."
8 Richter, "The Toronto Blessing."
9 Robertson, "Community, Society, Globality, and Category of Religion."
10 Wallerstein, *The Capitalist World Economy*.
11 Brouwer, Gifford, and Rose, *Exporting the American Gospel*.
12 A term usually attributed to the work of Ritzer. See *The McDonaldization of Society*.
13 Hunt, *Anyone for Alpha?*; Hunt, *The Alpha Initiative*.
14 Davies, "The Creation, Mortality, the After-life and the Fission of Religious Tradition."
15 Wilson, *Religious Sects*.
16 Campbell, "The Easternization of the West."
17 Featherstone, "Global Culture," 1–14.
18 Albrow, *The Global Age*.
19 Khasala, "New Religious Movements Turn to Worldly Success," 233–47.

20 Hunt "'Winning Ways'": Globalisation and the Impact of the Health and
   Wealth Ministries"; Hunt, "The British Black Pentecostal 'Revival,'" 104–24;
   Hunt, "The 'Health and Wealth' Gospel in the UK," 89–104.
21 Hunt, "The Toronto Blessing."
22 Hocken, Steams of Renewal, 13.
23 Bartleman, Azusa Street.
24 Hollenweger, The Pentecostals.
25 Hunt et al., Charismatic Christianity, 1997.
26 Tablet, 20 August 1994, 1056.
27 Römer, The Toronto Blessing, 32–4.
28 Hunt, "The Toronto Blessing," 261.
29 Richter, The Toronto Blessing, 11.
30 Hunt, "The Success of Kensington Temple."
31 Hunt, "The Anglican Wimberites"; MacNutt, Overcome by the Spirit.
32 Richter, "The Toronto Blessing," 11.
33 Hunt, Christian Millenarianism.
34 Allen, "Catching the Fire," 18.
35 Hunt, "The Anglican Wimberites."
36 Hunt, "Doing the Stuff."
37 Perrin, "Signs and Wonders."
38 Smark, "Mass Marketing God," 19–20.
39 Wallis, The Elementary Forms of New Religious Life, 86–118.
40 Richter, "The Toronto Blessing," 22–4.
41 Ibid., 13.
42 Ibid., 15–16.
43 Poloma, and Pendleton, "Religious Experiences, Evangelism, and Institutional
   Growth within the Assemblies of God," 428.
44 Roberts, The Toronto Blessing, 78
45 Ibid., 69.
46 Richter, "The Toronto Blessing," 18.
47 See Stark, Finke, and Guest, "Mobilizing Local Religious Markets," 203–18;
   Stark and Iannaccone, "Rational Choice Propositions about Religious
   Movements"; Stark, and Iannaccone, "A Supply-Side Reinterpretation of the
   'Secularization' of Europe," 23–52.
48 Warner, "Work in Progress: Towards a New Paradigm for the Sociological
   Study of Religion in the United States," 1044–93.

12

Transforming Pentecostalism:
The Migration of Pentecostals to Canada

MICHAEL WILKINSON

INTRODUCTION

When a group of Tamil-speaking Christians arrived in Toronto in the early 1990s, they contacted the Pentecostal Assemblies of Canada (PAOC) and asked to affiliate with the denomination. Displaced by the civil war in Sri Lanka, these Pentecostal Christians left behind the few material belongings they had as well as family members, their church, and their pastor. Not easily discouraged, they quickly organized and began meeting as a small group sharing a facility with a large English-speaking congregation and several other ethnic congregations in Toronto.

As they established a new congregation in Canada, they found it was difficult without a pastor, and especially the one they left behind in Sri Lanka. Almost immediately, the parishioners solicited the help of the PAOC to bring their pastor to Canada. Letters were exchanged and an invitation was made to Rev. Thaya Rasiah to come and provide leadership for his former congregation. Initially, Rasiah felt he could not leave his homeland. As the war intensified, however, the church was burnt to the ground and most of the members moved to the capital city, Colombo. Finally, he came to Canada to pastor the Agincourt Pentecostal Tamil Church as a "religious worker" on a two-year missionary visa. Now, Rasiah's transplanted Sri Lankan congregation ministers from its new local base in Canada. Its ministry, however, is global in focus characterized by a variety of transnational social ties.

This example illustrates one facet of a larger process that this chapter seeks to address. While many aspects of religious life are global, contemporary migration is increasingly characterized by a proliferation of transnational relationships, practices, and organizations. These various networks facilitate religious life in many ways for new immigrants. They are also points of tension between ethnic congregations and the denominations they seek to join in Canada.

This chapter focuses on some of the social relationships and practices that characterize the current phase of globalization. Certainly, transnational networks are not specific to Pentecostals or to the present time. There is, however, evidence of a thickening of social ties since the early 1990s.[1] The various networks among Pentecostals include a range of global relationships and practices such as new denominational affiliations, pastoral searches, theological training, special events and conferences, prayer networks, Internet sites, international ministries, publications, music, and television, not to mention continued global migration itself. In addition, the various affiliations that I discuss here consist of both sending and receiving links. Furthermore, the flow along the links is multidirectional. Yet for the PAOC, the increase in global networks is problematic. Unable to keep up with the level of change, the PAOC finds itself in the midst of a transformation. Social change raises questions about identity and the nature of Pentecostalism in Canada and worldwide.

Social relationships and practices increasingly carry Pentecostalism as a global culture. These transnational Pentecostal networks point to the relationship that exists between Pentecostals and the specific links that interconnect them. In addition, networks are maintained through the reciprocation of a variety of flows, including relationships, practices, ideas, money, information, and material goods. I have identified three broad types of Pentecostal networks. They are congregational ministry flows, special event and conference links, and denominational affiliations.

Congregational ministry flows refer to a variety of exchanges between Pentecostal congregations and their members. They occur through such means as the Internet, telephone, letters, videotapes, cassette tapes, mail, travel, and migration. The types of ministry flows manifest themselves in pastoral searches, theological education, prayer, worship, the building of facilities, promotion, and support. In each congregation I researched, congregational ministry flows maintained ties between local congregations in different places.

The second type of Pentecostal network is the special event and conference link. There are two kinds of special event and conference links. First, there are the conferences for the pastors and members of ethnic congregations. Generally, Pentecostals travel to these large global conferences and participate with other Pentecostals from around the world. The conferences I heard about were either seminars for pastoral training or motivational worship conferences. The second kind of special event and conference link is more local in nature. That is, it occurs at the local level for the local congregation but it still has a global focus. The special event and conference serves to tie ethnic Pentecostals at the local level to the larger community of Pentecostals globally.

The third type of Pentecostal network is the denominational affiliation. As a variety of Pentecostalisms mutually inform one another, new affiliations are created between existing organizations. What is evident is the proliferation of affiliations and the kinds of relationships, both formal and informal, which exist in Pentecostalism globally. The tension experienced at the level of Pentecostal organizations demonstrates the extent of change and shows how the history, nature, and religious character of Pentecostalism almost encourage certain strategies and orientations. What follows is an examination of these global networks and how they are transforming Canadian Pentecostalism.

The findings are based on a study of global migration and ethnic congregations in the PAOC between 1995 and 1999. Observations, interviews, and survey data were gathered from Spanish-speaking, Tamil, Korean, Eritrean, and Ethiopian congregations in Toronto and Ottawa. Since the collection of the data, the analysis and interpretation of the findings continues in light of recent theoretical debates about globalization, religion, and migration.[2]

THEORETICAL DEBATES

While there is a growing literature on the role of religion and immigrant communities, there is an appeal for social scientific understanding of the process.[3] The movement of people, ideas, and practices across borders has led researchers to accept that theories of assimilation or plurality miss out on many important practices for migrants between "home" and "host" countries. Migration is not unidirectional. Migration is a multifaceted process with social, cultural, political, economic, and religious implications. There are a number of important research findings that illustrate this point.

One important study was the "New Ethnic and Immigrant Congregations Project" (NEICP) which resulted in the publication *Gatherings in Diaspora: Religious Communities and the New Immigration* by R. Stephen Warner and Judith G. Wittner. The book is a collection of case studies that explores how new immigrants (those that have arrived since the late 1960s) have interacted with American cultural institutions. The researchers argue that new religious communities are adopting the congregational model. The project is an important contribution to the understanding of these organizational adaptations. Unfortunately, it only briefly acknowledges that migration is characterized by transnational practices with implications for migrants. It fails to explore in detail what those social practices are or how the connections with "home" transform the American congregational model.

A second and important project is the "Religion, Ethnicity and New Immigrant Project" (RENIR) which explored the city of Houston as a multicultural and multi-religious setting. The findings for the project were published in *Religion and the New Immigrants: Continuities and Adaptations in Immigrant Congregations* with other important related publications.[4] The theoretical focus of this project was the maintenance of ethnic identity through religious practices, institutions, social events, and cultural activities as new immigrants were incorporated into American life. Occasionally some of the case studies examined transnational ties and influences but not in any consistent manner. Missing from the research is a systematic discussion of globalization and transnational practices.

Canadian research on religion and new immigrants is even more recent but with some very exciting potential for the future of research on religion and migration. For example, *Religion and Ethnicity in Canada* by Paul Bramadat and David Seljak is a thorough examination of the topic that requires an extended discussion. The editors of this volume have brought together a collection of essays that explore the complex interaction between religious and ethnic identity among six religions: Judaism, Hinduism, Sikhism, Buddhism, Islam, and Chinese religions. More specifically, the authors incorporate a transnational perspective that identifies how religion is transformed through the process of migration and religious networks.

Probably the most thorough research on transnational practices to date is the work of Peggy Levitt.[5] Levitt identifies how transnational religious practices between Boston and the Dominican Republic are reciprocally transformed through a variety of exchanges between these two points. Even more interesting is the contribution these exchanges make to the process of globalization. Levitt argues that migration and transnational practice "reconfigure macro-level religious space and its relationship to other worldwide regimes."[6] My view is that worldwide, religion is undergoing a transformation in relation to globalizing processes. Transnational links are an important component of this change but they must be understood in relation to the dilemmas of global systematization. I will return to this point later.

Network research is a tool for understanding patterns of relationships – social ties that represent the numerous flows of resources, friendships, and communication.[7] A network refers to the links between people and the groups or organizations that they associate with. In general, the relationship between individuals and networks can both constrain individuals and also provide certain resources.

A network analysis has a number of characteristics.[8] First, it allows for an analysis of trans-organizational and transnational relationships and practices. Global relationships and practices increasingly characterize our world. Second, a network analysis attempts to understand the relationship between individual actors within and between organizations. Third, a network analysis assumes that these relationships and practices affect the operation of organizations. This is certainly the case for the PAOC. Fourth, the organization is viewed as one of many in a network of networks. Finally, the focus of a network analysis is on the relational nature between networks. The link between networks is an important element that needs further elaboration.

The various links between networks have been described in different ways as ties,[9] social remittances,[10] flows,[11] and transnational flows.[12] Each idea conveys a sense of movement across boundaries. Network exchanges include relationships, practices, ideas, money, information, and material goods. As Rouse[13] states, "Through the continuous circulation of people, money, goods, and information, the various settlements have become so closely woven together that, in an important sense they have come to constitute a single community spread across a variety of sites." Thus a network of global relationships and practices points to how Pentecostal culture is structured and how it functions globally. Yet, it also has transforming qualities at the local level.

A network approach is also helpful for explaining individual behaviour at the macro level. More specifically, it is an important concept that allows one to see the two-directional relationship between the micro and macro, the individual and social action, and the local and the global.[14] In addition, a network approach helps to understand how people find support and maintain community, especially following a recent move, or in this case, migration.[15] It is concerned with the constraints of the system as a whole, the social ties across local cultural systems, the effect of networks on the social system, and the relational nature of the social structure.[16] A network approach also assumes that social systems can be examined according to the relationships between members of organizations and the specific links that characterize their interconnectedness.[17]

As migrants increasingly maintain important support links that span geographical boundaries they do so through the spread of new technologies.[18] For Pentecostals, the connections they maintain with other Pentecostals through things like prayer groups and international conferences allow them to participate with Pentecostals around the globe. The personal community aspects of these networks are loosely bound, sparsely knit networks with specialized ties. They are long distance ties that stretch beyond local areas or neighbourhoods which become the important focal point for Pentecostal migrants.[19] They also contribute to the global systematization of Pentecostalism through the espousal of a Pentecostal culture.[20]

The concept of social network best describes the underlying global structure of contacts in and between the many different Pentecostals in the world. By identifying some patterns of behaviour among Pentecostal networks, I can examine the consequences for local denominations like the PAOC. Pentecostal networks are part of a larger religious system that is interconnected to other spheres of a global society.[21] The study of ethnic Pentecostal congregations is meant to supplement understanding of a global religious system and the interconnections with a global society. This chapter is more than a case study of independent units of analysis. It is a theoretical exploration into the nature of a global religious system and the networks within a specific religious culture – the Pentecostals.

TRANSNATIONAL RELIGIOUS NETWORKS

Global Congregational Ministry Flows

One change centres on the problem of a lack of pastors for the ethnic congregations. The PAOC has attempted to deal with this issue in several ways. First, pastoral searches have extended beyond the borders of Canada. As one PAOC official explained, there are an insufficient number of qualified pastors for ethnic congregations. For example, when new Chinese immigrant congregations emerged in the 1990s, especially with Pentecostals from Hong Kong, the PAOC thought there would be no problem with a Mainland Chinese pastor overseeing the congregation. It became apparent that even though the pastor and the congregation were Chinese, culturally, they were far apart. With no Hong Kong Chinese pastor available in Canada, the search for a pastor was made in Hong Kong. The intention was to have this person come to Canada and pastor the congregation. The Tamil congregation is another example of a global pastoral search. The parishioners contacted their minister in Sri Lanka and invited him to come and pastor them in Canada. He now serves as the pastor of the Tamil congregation in Toronto. One Spanish-speaking pastor, originally from Cuba, was temporarily preaching in the United States when he was invited by the PAOC and a local Spanish congregation to come to Toronto. In each case the PAOC was involved in assisting the pastors to secure the proper immigration papers for ministry in Canada.

Related to a lack of pastors are the requests for theological education by ethnic congregations. In 1990, the Executive Director of Home Missions for the PAOC approved the establishment of a Spanish leadership centre. El Verbo, a Spanish Bible college for ethnic Pentecostals, came into existence with the leadership of Rev. Otoniel Perez. The college is under the supervision of the Academic Dean of Eastern Pentecostal Bible College, Peterborough, Ontario (now Master's College). Classes, however, are convened in Toronto. In 1994, El Verbo became an official extension school of EPBC. Graduates of El Verbo pastor new ethnic congregations in Canada. One graduate returned to Latin America to pastor a congregation. As well, El Verbo now provides courses on the Internet. In 1997, Perez travelled to Latin America to recruit students for the college. He told me he had five potential students and one registered student for the fall semester of 1998. These students will stay in their home countries and study at El Verbo as distance education students. Perez administers the college from the PAOC's international office in Mississauga, Ontario.

A group of Tamils also requested theological education from the PAOC. Tamil students studying at EPBC explained that it was difficult to study at the college because of language and cultural differences. Dr Lyman Kulathungam, a Sri Lankan Tamil who teaches at EPBC, teaches courses for the Tamils. Kulathungam explained to me that it is a challenge for a variety of reasons. For example, in one class he has a female student who wants to be a pastor. The men in the class are trying to discourage her. Kulathungam told me the class had a discussion about women in ministry. Eventually, it became clear that the Tamil Pentecostal men do not believe women should be pastors. This issue is problematic for the men because the PAOC ordains women and allows them to pastor PAOC congregations. Kulathungam explained to me that gender, language, and related theological issues represent varying shades of theology. Kulathungam also told me students are requesting classes in law and legal issues, and human rights, courses not traditionally offered as part of the Bible college curriculum. The PAOC and EPBC are endeavouring to accommodate the requests of the immigrant groups.

SPECIAL EVENT AND CONFERENCE LINKS

Second, Canadian Pentecostalism is transforming through special event and conference links between ethnic congregations in Canada and the many global Pentecostal events they participate in in Africa, Latin America, Asia, and Canada. Special event and conference links serve to construct and maintain cultural identity. Yet ethnic Pentecostals also struggle with maintaining an ethnic identity while living in Canada. Global networks suggest another option between assimilation and pluralism – the mixing and multiplying of identities.[22]

What may not be understood in the PAOC is the role social networks play among ethnic congregations in Canada. Specifically, special event and conference links serve to maintain ties between Pentecostals at a global level. There are several examples I will describe here. Each one illustrates how Pentecostalism as a global culture supports and expresses itself in Pentecostalism locally. The first two examples focus on the global nature of the conference. The final two examples focus on the local nature of the event. Both serve to foster ethnic identity in the congregation.

First, the pastor of the Korean congregation is involved in an annual conference that takes place in Korea. The conference is for pastors of all Korean Pentecostal congregations around the world. Yonggi Cho of the Full Gospel Church organizes the conference. The Korean pastor told me that once he arrives in Korea, Yonggi Cho's ministry provides for all the participants. The conference connects him with other Korean pastors around the world and ideas for ministry are exchanged. As well, the participants are spiritually motivated through times of prayer, worship, and preaching. The congregation in Canada then benefits from the conference.

Members of the Spanish congregation in Toronto also participate in global conferences. The pastor told me that the young people travelled to Mexico for a worship conference that was attended by Spanish-speaking Pentecostals from Canada, the United States, and Latin America. He explained that it is important for Spanish Pentecostals to worship with other Spanish Pentecostals. He said that ministry in Canada can be very discouraging. In contrast, the church is alive in Latin America and as he told me, it is good for him to celebrate the victories of other Spanish Pentecostals.

The Eritrean and Ethiopian Pentecostals also hold conferences for local congregations in North America. In 1995, a special conference was held in Toronto with nine different congregational leaders from Canada and the United States, for prayer, leadership training, and outreach planning. One of the elders told me that it is a very important event for the participants as they share together both the joys and the difficulties of living in new countries.

Another event that serves to link ethnic Pentecostals and maintain their ethnicity is the annual "Parade of Nations." Each year, the Spanish congregations of the PAOC celebrate their congregation's anniversary. The problem is that as many as thirty-five different countries can be represented in one congregation at the anniversary celebration. Each cultural group is very loyal to their country and at every anniversary celebration they will sing the national anthem of each country represented in the congregation. During the meeting someone will walk in with, for example, a Nicaraguan flag, and everyone who is from Nicaragua will stand and sing the national anthem. This will continue until every country represented in the congregation has had their flag paraded in and the national anthem sung. It often turns out to be an all-day event.

I had the opportunity to experience an anniversary celebration in Toronto in 1997. The "Parade of Nations" occurred on a Sunday, the final day of the three-day missions convention and anniversary celebration. The congregation was extremely excited about the weekend as they anticipated the "Parade of Nations" and the ministry of their guest speaker, an evangelist originally from Latin America and now in the United States where he coordinates ministry among Spanish people in the Assemblies of God. His radio broadcasts are heard throughout Latin America from his base in Florida. Musical guests for the weekend were from Mexico and added to the cultural and global quality of the celebration.

The climax of the weekend was the three-hour Sunday meeting of the "Parade of Nations" when flags from twenty-two countries were waved and members from their respective countries rose to their feet to sing their national anthem. I was told that people come for the anniversary celebration each year that have no association with the congregation just to sing their national anthem. During the ceremony many cried, clapped, shouted, sang, and saluted. It was a very emotional experience linking religion and national pride. The pastor, originally from Cuba, shouted "Viva la Cuba," waved to the flag, and cried as he sang his national anthem. At the conclusion of the ceremony, children came marching into the auditorium waving banners reading "Jesus is Lord" and singing "The Lord Reigns." The pastor explained that it is an important time when they can thank God for the country they were born in, the new country they live in, and the world that needs revival.

Ethnic congregations represent members from disparate cultures with different histories and ethnicities. The social and historical construction of these ethnic congregations, along with their employment of global resources for the expression of Pentecostalism, demonstrates how Pentecostalism functions under the constraints of globalization. The congregations use ethnicity differently, sometimes with sharp boundaries, sometimes not, sometimes with internal divisions encouraged, sometimes not. This is precisely the "optional" nature of what is usually considered to be a "natural," ascribed category.[23] That is, after all, one of the ways that globalization works: the local is global, the necessary is optional.

NEW DENOMINATIONAL AFFILIATIONS

There are a variety of views in the congregations about the needs of ethnic congregations, the programs and objectives of the PAOC, and finances. The ethnic congregations believe they should support the endeavours of the denomination. At the same time, there is the perception that ethnic congregations do not support the programs and objectives of the PAOC. For the ethnic congregations, though, it is not a matter of choosing one organization over another. Generally, ethnic congregations maintain multiple affiliations and practices. The issue becomes clearer when examined in the context of global networks and, specifically, new denominational affiliations. Furthermore, it is at the level of organization that the greatest diversity of opinion is expressed among the congregations. There are several reasons why. First, Pentecostals from other regions of the world organize their congregations differently from the PAOC. As well, Pentecostals have always been suspicious of a rational bureaucracy that stifles the moving of the Spirit.[24] Third, and more importantly, the interaction between the different models has led to some disagreement over how congregations organize. Yet PAOC officials claim they are learning to respond appropriately, and if necessary, differently to each congregation. There is evidence of new strategies for congregational organization in the PAOC. Important aspects are the global networks among ethnic congregations.

In my discussions with the leaders of the PAOC, it is clear that the organizational implications of global migration for the PAOC centre on how the congregations organize and second, how they share facilities with a variety of language and culture groups. In an interview with one PAOC official we discussed some misunderstandings between the PAOC and the ethnic congregations. Specifically, we discussed the interaction between the PAOC and two Ethiopian congregations over church organization. The varied responses illustrate the difficulty the PAOC had in dealing with cultural variations of Pentecostalism, yet also its flexibility to change.

It was explained to me that the PAOC "lost" an Ethiopian congregation in Ottawa because of a rigid expectation regarding church organization. The PAOC learned to be more flexible and to even allow for an informal constitutional change giving the Ethiopians in Toronto the ability to organize around a group of Elders as opposed to a pastor. This change, however, came too late as the congregation of Ethiopian Pentecostals in Ottawa no longer seeks affiliation with the PAOC.

According to a PAOC official, Finnish Pentecostal missionaries, who apparently had a different form of church government, evangelized the Ethiopian Pentecostals who came to Canada. The Finnish missionaries used a structure in Ethiopia whereby they established congregations led by a group of lay leaders or elders with a pastor, if any at all, taking an equal role. The Ethiopian congregations, therefore, based their own congregations on a similar form of organization or church government, transplanting it in Canada. In the PAOC, where churches are organized hierarchically with a pastor giving leadership as opposed to a group of elders, the confrontation was inevitable.

In the Ottawa case, a young Ethiopian man came to Canada via Greece where he had co-pastored a congregation and demonstrated pastoral abilities. At the time, the pastor of the Ottawa congregation, which gave space to the Ethiopians to meet, wanted to recognize this person as the pastor. The English congregation felt it had good intentions, only wanting to recognize someone as the pastor of the congregation. The differences in organization, though, created a crisis. The leadership at the English-speaking congregation told the Ethiopians that they would recognize the young man as the pastor and that the congregation should endorse this decision or perhaps consider worshipping somewhere else, not thinking they would leave. Over 60 per cent of the Ethiopian congregation left and began meeting in another facility in Ottawa. Distraught over the crisis, the Ethiopian congregation invited an evangelist from Ethiopia to come and minister to the congregations in Ottawa. After several meetings the split Ethiopian congregations reconciled but no longer sought affiliation with the PAOC. The young man whom they asked to be recognized as the pastor of the Ethiopian congregation no longer worships with the Ethiopian community.

The differences in church government between the Ethiopian Pentecostals and the PAOC almost resulted in a split in an Ethiopian congregation in Toronto. I asked if there was any way of compromising with the Ethiopians regarding church leadership and organization. One official said they could have dealt with the Ottawa situation better "if we had not been so rigid." In the Toronto Ethiopian congregation, the PAOC allowed an informal constitutional change in order for the church to be governed by a group of elders and thus provide room in the PAOC for the Ethiopian Pentecostals. The differences in organization and the ensuing conflict illustrate issues of authority and the struggle over who defines how the congregations will organize in the PAOC.

While the Ethiopian congregation in Ottawa decided not to join the PAOC, the Eritrean congregation is in the process of organizing. While they have not officially joined the PAOC, one elder explained to me that when the time is right they will talk about whether or not to join. For now they worship in a PAOC church facility and are clearly Pentecostal. Some of their members were part of the Ethiopian congregation in Ottawa that experienced the split and they are not anxious to join the PAOC. They do, however, desire to have an affiliation with other Pentecostals. Currently, the Eritrean congregation shares an affiliation with other Eritrean congregations in Toronto and Washington, DC.

One effort is to have a yearly seminar or conference for the leadership of the ethnic congregations that are led by ethnic leaders and other national PAOC leaders to deal with specific issues in the ethnic churches. A PAOC official stated: "the PAOC is a fellowship of churches and it has to be flexible with all of the diversity. We are still learning. We lost a

Korean church. They wanted to have affiliation with us but also have an affiliation with their church in Korea with Paul Yonggi Cho. We felt it wasn't going to work out organizationally. So they never affiliated. But we are learning to be flexible. We are learning not to hamper but facilitate the work of God for these people who are believers." In 1997 the PAOC changed. Korean congregations can now have dual affiliation. They can maintain their ties with the home country and with the host country. Korean pastors in Canada hold dual affiliation for various reasons. For the Koreans, the name "Pentecostal" is suspect in Korea, but "Full Gospel" is not. Holding affiliation with the Full Gospel organization in North America and globally allows them to use their name and maintain a sense of their Korean Pentecostalism. As the Korean pastor explained to me, the change in name will appeal to new immigrants and may result in growth for his congregation.

Another example of dual affiliation is found in the Ghanaian congregations in Canada. A PAOC official in the Western Ontario District explained that the PAOC has a partnership with the Assemblies of God of Ghana for the purpose of arranging funeral rites. I was told that Ghanaians in Canada want to be buried in Ghana after they die. The church in Ghana, however, will not bury them unless they demonstrate they were members of a congregation affiliated with the PAOC. The PAOC is more than willing to work with the Assemblies of God of Ghana to meet this request. Thus, members of Ghanaian congregations have dual affiliation. This occurs precisely because the global culture allows it and the two denominations agree to do it.

GLOBAL RELIGION AND THE TRANSFORMATION OF PENTECOSTALISM

Danièle Hervieu-Léger[25] argues that religion in the contemporary era is going through a process of reconfiguration. Her work, while focusing on charismatic Catholics in France, has application for global Pentecostalism. The five key tendencies are as follows. First, there is an increasing emphasis on individual and personal experience as authoritative versus the religious organization. While one may argue that personal experience has always been a hallmark of Pentecostalism, it is not the same today. In the past, denominations and other persons in places of authority defined the role of personal experience. Hervieu-Léger's point is that institutions play a lesser role. Identity is increasingly constructed from the vantage point of the individual. Personal experience and spiritual pilgrimage are the measuring rods of authentic faith.

Second, the social construction of identity is facilitated through global networks. The diffusion across national boundaries of Pentecostal/charismatic communities characterizes the mobility of experience itself. No longer does religion require institutions for it to spread. A third trend is the deregulation of religious belief whereby individuals pragmatically select what works best for them – this in contrast, again, to the authority of institutions to decide what is an authentic or theologically correct expression. This, however, may lead to another tendency – an increase in clashes among Pentecostals with differing values and experiences. Again, this may account for the debate about origins, the role of non-Western Pentecostals, or the theological debates about the vast experiences reported at the Toronto Blessing. Finally, while there continue to be local debates about who is a Pentecostal, increasingly, there is an awareness and identification with the global movement. Pentecostalism, however, continues to change as it negotiates the dilemmas of systematization.

CONCLUSION

The transformation of the PAOC is largely related to the globalization of religion and specifically global migration and the various social relationships and practices maintained by ethnic congregations. Global networks such as congregational ministry flows, special event and conferences links, and new denominational affiliations indicate how the PAOC and the ethnic congregations are adjusting to the global systematization of religion. As new global networks are established and immigrants continue to establish and maintain ties with "home" countries, the PAOC is challenged to rethink questions of identity, authority, and authenticity. Still, the consequences of these global networks for the "home" countries are still to be determined. For example, how are Pentecostals in Africa, Asia, or Latin America adapting to global networks with Pentecostals in Canada? What contributions do immigrants in Canada make to Pentecostalism in their "home" country? How do these global networks contribute to the globalization of Pentecostal identity? Global analyses of Pentecostalism, however, can be enhanced with a better understanding of global networks and the globalization of Pentecostalism.

NOTES

1 See Robertson, *Globalization*, 59.

2 See the appendix in Wilkinson, *The Spirit Said Go* for the details about methodology. Generally, the case study included multiple methods such as participant observation, over twenty interviews with denominational leaders and immigrant pastors, and congregational surveys with new immigrant congregations from Latin America, North Africa, Sri Lanka, and Korea.

3 Kivisto, "Religion and the New Immigrants," 92–108; Ebaugh, "Religion and the New Immigrants," 225–39; Levitt, "Redefining the Boundaries of Belonging," 1–18.

4 See Yang, *Chinese Christians in America: Conversion, Assimilation, and Adhesive Identities*; Yang and Ebaugh, "Religion and Ethnicity," 89–107; Yang and Ebaugh, "Transformations in New Immigrant Religions and Their Global Implications," 269–88.

5 Levitt, "Local-Level Global Religion," 74–89.

6 Ibid., 76.

7 Wellman and Berkowitz, *Social Structures*.

8 Wellman, "Structural Analysis," 19–61.

9 Ibid.

10 Levitt, "Local-Level Global Religion."

11 Berkowitz, "Afterword: Toward a Formal Structural Sociology," 477–97.

12 Basch et al., *Nations Unbound*.

13 Rouse, "Mexican Migration and the Social Space of Postmodernism," 15.

14 Mitchell, "Social Networks," 279–99; Robertson, *Globalization*.

15 Fisher et al., *Networks and Places*.

16 Wellman, "Structural Analysis."

17 Wellman and Berkowitz, *Social Structures*.

18 See Albrow, *The Global Age*; Castells, *The Rise of the Network Society*; Cairncross, *The Death of Distance*.

19 Wellman, *Networks in the Global Village*.

20 Albrow, *The Global Age*, 141–2; Lyon, *Jesus in Disneyland*, 97–119.

21 See Beyer, *Religion and Globalization*; "Religion, Residual Problems, and Functional Differentiation: An Ambiguous Relationship," 219–35; "The Religious System of Global Society," 1–29; "The Modern Emergence of Religions and a Global Social System for Religion," 151–72.

22 Cornell and Hartmann, *Ethnicity and Race*.

23 Fenton, *Ethnicity*.

24 Poloma, *The Assemblies of God at the Crossroads*.

25 Hervieu-Léger, "Faces of Catholic Transnationalism," 104–18.8.

13

Movements, Markets, and Social Contexts: Canadian Pentecostalism in Global Perspective

PETER BEYER

INTRODUCTION

Among the many transitions and transformations relevant to twentieth-century Pentecostalism, one that has perhaps received less attention is the shifting attitudes of outside observers toward the movement. Until relatively recently, those attitudes have more often been negative than positive. Those not involved in the phenomenon, when they paid any attention at all, tended to dismiss Pentecostalism as at best a religion of the marginalized and the unsophisticated, as something closer to a Melanesian Cargo Cult than "serious" religion. Indeed, as an example, it was not that long ago that the 1960s film, "Holy Ghost People,"[1] about Pentecostals in American Appalachia – itself the marginalized zone of "moonshine" and "Hill Billies" – was regular fare in North American introductory social anthropology courses, a social scientific discipline whose domain has historically been "primitive," small-scale, non-literate, and "pre-modern" cultures as opposed to the supposedly modern and cosmopolitan societies to which sociology devoted its attention. Moreover, the latter discipline has been, at least until quite recently, dominated by a perspective which considered religion as somehow at odds with modernity; a modern society was ipso facto a secularizing society because it was an increasingly rationalized society and religion was fundamentally "irrational." In that context, the subdiscipline of the sociology of religion was itself "isolated" within the larger discipline, reflective of the marginal status of its subject matter.[2] A profound shift has occurred over the last three to four decades, a transformation

among the outside observers of Pentecostalism that is perhaps best sym-
bolized in the contrasting nature of Harvard theologian Harvey Cox's
most well known publications. His famous book of the 1960s, *The Secular City*,[3] analyzed the decline of religion in the public life of modern
urban society. In the 1990s, by contrast, he was best known for *Fire
from Heaven*,[4] a work which not only announced the renewed importance of religion, but saw this resurgence as best exemplified in the rapidly growing and global Christian phenomenon of Pentecostalism.
From a strange curiosity, Pentecostalism had been transformed into a
paradigmatic movement exemplary of the world in which we live.

CONTEXTUAL FACTORS

The fact of this turnaround is interesting enough in itself, but so is the
changing context in which it has occurred. Certainly the rapid growth
of the movement since the 1960s is one aspect. Whether in sub-Saharan
Africa, Latin America, Korea, North America, or various other regions,
the sheer number of Pentecostal practitioners has increased to the point
where it is far more difficult to ignore. The rise of neo-Pentecostalism or
charismatic Christianity outside the classical Protestant Pentecostal
fold has undoubtedly also played a role, as has the connected fact that
Pentecostals and charismatics alike are less socio-demographically
marginalized – at least in some regions – than they have been in the
past. Accordingly, it seems that the turnaround in outside attention
began in the early to mid–1960s and burgeoned in the decades thereafter.[5] Nonetheless, Pentecostal growth was certainly not limited to these
decades, the indications being that the movement grew steadily
throughout the twentieth century from its modern origins in the 1900s.[6]
It is in that light that contextual factors may have played a significant
role, not just in the shift in attention outsiders paid to the movement,
but also in the growth and character of the movement itself.

   The acknowledged high points in the history of the Pentecostal movement, to a large degree reflected in the various contributions to this
book, are the beginning phase of the early 1900s up to the post World
War I period, the rise of mainline charismatic renewal in the 1960s, and
then the perhaps more ambiguous neo-Pentecostal renewal associated
with the Vineyard Church and the "Toronto Blessing" of the 1990s.
The in-between periods may by contrast be described as ones of consolidation, so long as it is kept in mind that these are not also periods of
stagnation against which the high points are the periods of growth.

Without suggesting that these seminal developments were caused by contextual factors, it is nonetheless striking that they correspond to identifiable and much discussed transitions on the wider global scale. Whether we are looking at the beginning of the twentieth century, the post-1960s period, or the post-Cold War period, Pentecostalism's highlights are in each case far from isolated as hinge developments, whether in the religious or broadly secular spheres.

The period from the late nineteenth to the early twentieth century was one which saw, among other developments, accelerated industrialization and urbanization in European and North American countries, important innovations in communications from steamships and telegraph to the beginnings of telephone and radio, unprecedented movements of migrant populations to various countries of the Americas, intensified European nationalisms and interstate imperial rivalries with continued expansion of European influence around the world – especially in sub-Saharan Africa – and culmination in the First World War, the intensified rise of socialist movements eventuating in the Bolshevik revolution, stirring nationalist movements in India, the ascension of Japan to an imperial power, and the overthrow of the two-millennia-old imperial order in China. On the religious side, restricting ourselves to Christianity, it was correspondingly the era of the rise of Fundamentalism in the United States, a high point of European missionary activity in virtually all parts of the world, and in that context the beginning of the twentieth-century mainline Christian ecumenical movement. Pentecostalism's modern birth occurred directly in that context, not as a direct manifestation of these other developments, but, as it were, riding on and contributing to the currents that they created, not the least of which was the accelerated means of communication and flow of people. The oft remarked, rapid transnational expansion of the movement in its first decades would have been far more difficult without them. Moreover, that spread showed graphically how global religious developments were in no sense only the province of the more powerful Christian denominations and organizations. Beneath the radar of dominant observation, a great deal else was flowing along the intensified paths of communication, including Pentecostalism. On the whole, however, few observers noticed.

Turning to the post-Second World War period up to the fall of the Soviet empire in 1989, we find an analogously distinctive set of world developments paralleling equally distinctive developments in global Pentecostalism. The forty- year Cold War period saw both the qualitative and quantitative intensification of worldwide communications with, for instance, the creation of an ever thickening network of regularly scheduled air travel, the emergence of television and then satellite television, and sharply increased efficiency in already existing technologies like telephone and radio. Politically, the era not only pitted the two ideological superpowers against each other in a competitive battle to enlarge their respective spheres of influence and thus weave more and more of the world more tightly into a single political web, but it also witnessed an explosion in the number of newly independent states, especially in sub-Saharan Africa and the previously colonial regions of Asia. Economically, the first three post-war decades were ones of economic expansion in virtually all parts of the world, including the rise of the so-called East Asian "tiger" economies like South Korea, and a marked growth in international trade and transnational corporations. This was followed by two decades of equally dramatic economic difficulty, again affecting most regions. Cultural developments were no less dramatic. They included, in the later 1960s and early 1970s, the simultaneous emergence of a number of social movements; including the Western counter-cultural, second-wave feminist, gay liberation, and in the United States civil rights and Black power movements; the first concerted wave of environmentalism; and in regions like North America and Australasia movements of Aboriginal resurgence. Corresponding to these, most First World countries liberalized their immigration policies, leading to a significant and sustained intensification of transnational migration from virtually all corners of the world. Charismatic renewal and neo-Pentecostalism arose in this context as well, as one manifestation of more complex religious developments in the latter half of this period. If we take the mid–1960s as our starting point, the simultaneity of events is remarkable. Again restricting ourselves for the moment to Christianity, these include the rise of liberation theology and liberation theological movements, first primarily in Latin America, but then more broadly in Southern Africa, East Asia, the Philippines, and to some extent in North America and Western Europe. In the post-Vatican II decades from 1965 until 1979 and the reign of Pope John Paul II, the Roman Catholic Church more generally went through a period of profound questioning, turmoil, and renewal of which, of course, Catholic charismatics were a notable part. An important outcome during this time was a significant de-centring of this church from a primarily Western and Western European to a more globally focused institution. The postwar era also saw the founding of the mainline

Protestant-dominated World Council of Churches in 1948. After the mid-1960s, it too experienced internationalization in a way quite parallel to what was happening among Roman Catholics. In both cases, the demographic centre of gravity (if not the finances) of these Christian organizations shifted from the Western to the non-Western world as the era proceeded. It is in the context of these sorts of transformation that, during the same decades, the "explosion" of Pentecostalism in Latin America, but also its rapid rise to prominence in sub-Saharan Africa, South Korea, and elsewhere has to be understood.[7] For it is also at that time that the shift in attention of outside observation began to happen.

A further category of religious event during the last decade of the forty-year postwar period has probably also contributed significantly to the greater attention that Pentecostalism has received from outside observers. These are the series of highly visible and often highly effective religio-political movements that arose after the late 1970s. Beginning in 1979 with the New Christian Right in the United States and the revolutions in Iran and Nicaragua, followed over the next decade by comparable movements in various Muslim majority countries (e.g., Afghanistan, Palestine, Lebanon, Pakistan, Malaysia, Algeria, Sudan), in South Asia (Sikhs in Punjab, Hindus in the rest of India, Buddhists and Hindus in Sri Lanka), and in other countries such as Israel, religion once again rose to prominence as a powerful public and political force in a way that the world had not seen (or noticed) for quite some time. While these sorts of movements are very different from Pentecostalism and most of the other religious developments mentioned above, they made religion in general more visible even to those inclined to ignore it; they demonstrated that religion could still be important in the contemporary world and thus had the effect of making various non-political religious developments, like the rapid expansion of Pentecostalism, more apparent. And in fact, it was during the 1980s that social scientists began seriously to question the self-evidence of the idea that modern contemporary society was inherently secularizing.

While perhaps still too recent to be assessed properly, the post-Soviet era has already yielded significant developments in much the same areas as those just adumbrated for the two previous eras. The loss of the disciplining power of the old superpower rivalry has resulted not in the final victory of the remaining giant, but rather in geo-political uncertainty and certainly neither the "end of history" as Francis Fukuyama suggested nor a "clash" of multiple "civilizations" along the lines of Samuel Huntington's famous thesis.[8] To be sure, capitalism no longer seems to have a clear economic rival and sharply different worldviews exist side by side and often do clash in today's globalized society. Yet this has thus far not amounted to the straightforward and nefarious homogeneity feared by many anti-globalization activists nor the structural division of the world into rival, geographically centred units. In the domain of technology, the web of worldwide communication has thickened appreciably as a result of the accelerated and continuous development of the Internet, the truly global spread of the cell phone, and the further intensification of the already existing techniques. On the religious side, the trends of the earlier period are also continuing and in some cases multiplying. One thinks in particular of extremist Islamist militancy, but the religio-political conflicts of the eighties continue in most places, with the possible exception of Northern Ireland and Punjab. In addition, religion has taken on greater and sometimes highly conflicted importance in the different parts of the former Soviet-dominated Eastern Block, whether one is thinking of the importance of Islam and sometimes Islamism in countries/regions like Chechnya and the Central Asian republics, the wars in the former Yugoslavia in which the various sides have identified themselves explicitly in religious terms, or the greater prominence and even assertiveness of the Eastern Orthodox churches in countries such as Russia or Ukraine. In this context, the worldwide Pentecostal movement has shown more continuity than discontinuity, and yet there are some, admittedly very inconclusive, indicators that uncertainty may be interrupting the continuous curve of development that it had experienced for almost a century. Straws in the wind in this regard are the ambiguity and the comparative brevity of the nonetheless very visible revival associated with the so-called Toronto Blessing, and evidence that Pentecostal growth has slowed, halted, or perhaps even reversed in very different areas such as Korea and Canada.[9] I return to this point below.

The suggestion, therefore, is that Pentecostalism has reflected and exemplified larger and indeed global social and religious trends since the beginning of the twentieth century and probably continues to do so. That contextualization also helps explain the relatively recent shift in outside attention. Yet this is at best only half the story. For no movement, religious or otherwise, is just a global phenomenon. Its concrete reality is always also local, and at this level, generalities rapidly give way to variable specifics. This has been especially the case with Pentecostalism. One might say that its globalization has mostly expressed itself through an intense localization, but a localization that has included wider and often global connections and awareness. This clearly *glocal* character of the Pentecostal movement is arguably also one of the reasons that it now, in contrast to the past, receives such sustained outside attention.

LOCALIZING A MOVEMENT

The focus of previous chapters on different aspects of Canadian Pentecostalism shows very well that, while there is almost always an awareness of the global spread of the movement virtually at all times, the dominant range of geographical attention is usually no broader than Canada and the United States. Whether, for instance, one is looking at theological developments such as the role of apocalypticism or oneness theology, or institutional matters like the founding of Bible colleges and the place of women in Pentecostal ministry, the important factors to take into consideration occur within that limited region. That, of course, does not detract from Canadian Pentecostalism's universalism, the idea that its message and mission, as a manifestation of a global movement, is valid for everyone everywhere. It merely means that, in order to understand the details of Pentecostalism in Canada, its particularity as it were, one need not be overly concerned with what is happening in other parts of the Pentecostal world. Conversely, one must understand precisely those more local trends and institutional developments, their peculiar history and particular Canadian and North American social and cultural context. Naturally, exactly the same conclusion applies to the study of Pentecostalism in all the other regions and localities of the world, whether they are in Korea, Sweden, Brazil, Sri Lanka, Eritrea, Polynesia, or any number of other places.

The question of globalism/localism in Canadian and worldwide Pentecostalism is more than one of simple geography, a matter of different folk doing the same thing differently in different places. It is also a question of authority, authenticity, institutionalization, and indeed growth or decline. Modern Pentecostalism since its inception and consolidation as a Christian religious movement in the early twentieth century has conceived, styled, and partially structured itself as a spontaneous, decentralized, and non-hierarchical movement "of the Spirit." Translated somewhat, this means that it has tried to lay not only theological but also institutional or organizational stress on non-human agency, an emphasis that has manifested itself through the consistent and even characteristic valorization of individual religio-ecstatic experience (glossolalia, healing, prophesying, etc.) and, strictly related to this, what one might call a fluid congregational voluntarism as concerns collective form. No centralized agency was primarily responsible for founding the movement or spreading it around the globe, even though the Azusa Street mission in Los Angeles receives a kind of symbolic place of honour in this regard. Organized missions seeking converts in foreign lands have not been the most prominent method of propagation. Rather more typical have been, as in the Canadian case, the Hebdens, the McAlisters, and the Argues (see, for instance, Di Giacomo, chapter 1 in this volume), to name only a few, people who, as it were, "went and got" the message and the mission elsewhere and then of their own initiative "brought it home." Thus, while charismatic leadership is not at all absent from this story – indeed charisma, however understood, is clearly at the core of what the movement has been all about – arguably charismatic figures like Parham, Seymour, Gee, Bennett, or du Plessis, while important, have not played the critical role of charismatic founders as, for instance, did Mary Baker Eddy for Christian Science, Charles T. Russell for the Jehovah's Witnesses, or William and Catherine Booth for the Salvation Army, the latter two also direct manifestations of nineteenth-century Holiness impulses in Europe and North America. Charismatic Pentecostal figures there have been, but almost too many to count. Nonetheless, as with these other Christian organizations, this characteristic has raised the constant question of how to manage that charisma, and in social terms how to institutionalize this charismatic authority. It points to what Thomas O'Dea called the dilemmas of institutionalization, in particular the one he called "organizational elaboration vs. movement effectiveness."[10]

INSTITUTIONALIZING CHARISMA

Twentieth-century Pentecostalism has not lacked the organizations that have, historically and today, been so typical of Christian religion. Not only have there been a great many local organized congregations with their typical distinction between members and non-members, along with the rules that structure these, larger denominational organizations have been a constant feature from very near the beginning. In the North American context, the American Assemblies of God and the Canadian Pentecostal Assemblies of Canada are among the more notable that have played a significant role in not just the maintenance but also the propagation of Pentecostalism in North America and on other continents (and one notes in this regard how frequently the PAOC is the specific focus in the analyses of the preceding chapters). Yet such overarching organizations have always maintained a decentralized quality that puts the most emphasis on the independence of the local congregation and more than allows for the constant formation of independent Pentecostal groups alongside and even breaking away from the established and organizationally incorporated churches without thereby ceasing to be part of the overall movement. Even at the local congregational level, clear standards of membership are very often of far less importance than they are in most mainline Christian bodies, and anything like a geographically based parish system such as that which is at the heart of Roman Catholic organization hardly exists at all. Such organizational flexibility has been one of the ways that the Pentecostal movement in Canada, in North America, and indeed worldwide has lent itself necessary and regular social form – if one wishes, "community" – without discouraging or putting too much control on the possibilities of "spontaneous" expansion into new territories or among new groups and often surprising renewal in the places where it has been long established. One could say that, by and large, the worldwide Pentecostal movement has responded to O'Dea's dilemmas rather successfully to date.[11]

There is, however, another side to this question, one that may not be peculiar to Pentecostalism as such, but refers rather to features of the broader local (national) and global social context in which both social movements and organizations are today located. Social movements, like the charismatic authority that often accompanies them, have an evanescent and even temporary quality about them. They depend on continued mobilization, of people and resources, failing which they will tend either to fade or translate their impulse and rationale into another social form with greater long-term stability, notably in the present case, the regular (as opposed to social movement) organization. Movements, like Weber's charisma, tend toward routinization if they do not continue to mobilize. Yet that is not the end of the matter, a simple alternative. Looked at from a slightly different angle, social movements and organizations, as the styling of O'Dea's dilemma indicates, have parallel although somewhat opposite strengths and challenges. If the organization is relatively stable and depends only on the ability to maintain access to its characteristic social resources (e.g., narrative discourse, members, buildings, finances), it also carries the risk which is the other side of stability, namely loss of dynamism and comparative sluggishness in transforming itself in response to different contexts and new situations. Social movements present a mirror image: they are highly responsive and have a corresponding fluidity, but thereby little stability; they cannot rest. In Canadian religious history, perhaps the paradigmatic case is the history of the Methodist movement and the Methodist churches from the late eighteenth to the beginning of the twentieth century. In the early period, Methodist circuit riders took advantage of their mobility to, as it were, "ride rings around" the more staid and organized representatives of the Church of England. The Methodist movement thereby becomes the dominant religious presence on the expanding Upper Canadian frontier and thereafter an increasingly important part of the nineteenth-century Canadian religious landscape. By the end of the nineteenth century, however, a largely unified Methodist church had transformed itself into a dominant Christian organization alongside the older Anglican and Presbyterian "establishments," but thereby leaving room for more flexible and dynamic movements such as the Salvation Army or the Missionary Alliance to respond to new "urban frontiers" and challenges.[12] Canadian Pentecostalism was another wing of that mobilization. A comparison of the twentieth-century fate of these three manifestations of the larger Holiness movement will move the argument forward.

Restricting ourselves for the moment to the Canadian context, the relative growth of the three is already instructive. All three grew slowly until the end of the First World War; during the interwar decades Pentecostalism expanded well beyond the other two and has maintained that relative size advantage ever since. One could suggest that this may be a reflection of its lesser commitment to organized form and its greater maintenance of an emphasis on mobilization, but this would be speculative. In the post–Second World War context, all three gained significantly in absolute numbers and in terms of overall percentage of the Canadian population, at least up until the 1980s. At that point the Salvation Army began to decline on both measures, a fate that the other two were able to avoid for another decade. As of 2001, all three were in demographic decline in Canada.[13] At the very least, these figures indicate that all three have lost momentum, whether in terms of organizational or social movement strength. One must be careful, however, including careful to put these developments in their more global context. Christian affiliation overall has ceased to grow and is even in slight decline in Canada; if it were not for the continued influx of immigrants, up to 40 per cent of whom are still arriving as Christians, that decline would be far more noticeable.[14] What this outcome indicates is that balancing form between the flexibility of the social movement and the stability of the organization is only part of the "dilemma" that Pentecostalism has been facing. The national and global contexts are also germane to the story, as they have been from the beginning of the modern movement.

As noted, part of the context of the growth of the Pentecostal movement in Canada in the early part of the twentieth century was the rise of an "urban frontier" to replace the rural one in which the Methodists did so well a century earlier. Pentecostals were able to take advantage of and respond to that development and the vast social changes that went along with it to become an important feature of Canadian religion, especially in the second half of the century. That parallels what has been happening in other parts of the world more recently. Whether in sub-Saharan Africa, Korea, Latin America, or even in Polynesia, the sometimes explosive growth of Pentecostalism has in good measure been a reflection of its ability to provide meaningful and empowering personal narratives along with a sense of community and cosmic place to people in significant states of transition, very often from rural destitution to less dire urban poverty, but also as national states and the global economy incorporate an ever higher proportion of the world's population. Transnational migration is, of course, also part of that picture.[15] This is not to suggest that the appeal of Pentecostal Christianity is in any sense limited to such people in radical transition, but periods of "explosive" growth may well have been contingent upon such contextual factors. The implication is that, like any instance of religious revival, Pentecostalism's fate in particular localities or regions depends not just on how well the movement manages institutional dilemmas or even on the kinds of larger global trends discussed above, but also on the shifting character of what one might call "local markets." More specifically, given that Pentecostalism is never just global but always necessarily local, and that "present trends" in any particular locality never continue indefinitely, there will come a time when the movement will have arrived at or near the asymptotic apogee of its growth potential, irrespective of how dedicated and evangelistic its proponents are or of how effectively they mobilize resources. Alternatively, the people who were once in radical transition will eventually have accomplished their transformation, and Pentecostalism may well have played a critical role in that achievement. Some of them will continue to mobilize with energy and zeal; most will not. Locally, therefore, Pentecostal growth will eventually have run its course. Yet this is precisely where the global context enters once again. If, for instance, the Pentecostal movement in a country like Korea reaches this asymptotic and regularized state, the alternative to local growth is to put one's evangelistic motivation and resources into other parts of the world that still seem to hold great potential, perhaps sub-Saharan Africa. The same question and prognosis would apply to Canadian Pentecostalism. The question of whether the global possibilities have similar "limits to growth" can be left open. Since, as discussed above, the globalization of society has not and is unlikely to eventuate either in the "end of history" or a *cloisonné* clash of civilizations, some part of the world can always be expected to be in serious transition and thereby provide fruitful ground for religious renewal. The ex-Soviet Union, for example, may yet provide such ground, as may the People's Republic of China over the next decades, together regions with about 1.5 billion people. In the meantime, in globalized circumstances, the regions such as Canada, where Pentecostalism already has a long localized history, can participate in this potential dynamism of the movement elsewhere, but perhaps in the realization that its own numbers may decline or the next "Toronto Blessing" may be as ambiguous as the last.

NOTES

1 Boyd and Adair, *Holy Ghost People.*
2 Beckford, *Religion and Advanced Industrial Society.*
3 Cox, *The Secular City.*
4 Cox, *Fire from Heaven.*
5 An electronic search of the catalogues of Harvard University and University of Toronto libraries yielded exceedingly few publications of any kind on Pentecostalism as a movement before the 1960s that were not those of insiders or detractors.
6 Canadian census statistics, as an example, show this steady growth from the 1911 to the 1991 census – in terms of percentage of the population a dramatic increase from 1921 to 1931 and then a steady increase for the remaining decades. See Statistics Canada, *Canada Year Book 1978–79*, 155, 62; Statistics Canada, *Religions in Canada*, 102.
7 See, from among many, Coleman, *The Globalisation of Charismatic Christianity*; Corten and Marshall-Fratani, *Between Babel and Pentecost*;

Dempster, Klaus, and Petersen, *The Globalization of Pentecostalism*; Martin, *Pentecostalism*; Martin, *Tongues of Fire*; Poewe, *Charismatic Christianity as a Global Culture*; Stoll, *Is Latin America Turning Protestant?*

8 Fukuyama, *The End of History and the Last Man*; Huntington, *The Clash of Civilizations and the Remaking of World Order.*

9 For Korea, see Kim, "Modernization and the Explosive Growth and Decline of Korean Protestant Religiosity." Between 1991 and 2001, according to the Canadian censuses, the number of self-identified Pentecostals actually declined by 15 per cent. See Statistics Canada, *1971, 1981, 1991 & 2001 Census Custom Tabulations. DO0324*, vol. CD-ROM (Ottawa: Statistics Canada, Advisory Services Division, 2003).

10 See O'Dea, *The Sociology of Religion.*

11 This is, for instance, the major structuring theme of Poloma's analysis of the American Assemblies of God in the 1980s. See *The Assemblies of God at the Crossroads.*

12 The classic analysis is still Clark, *Church and Sect in Canada*. See also Semple, *The Lord's Dominion.*

13 The analysis is based on Census Canada data. The sources are Statistics Canada, *Canada Yearbook 1948* (Ottawa: Statistics Canada, 1949); Statistics Canada, *1971, 1981, 1991 & 2001 Census Custom Tabulations. DO0324*; Statistics Canada, *Canada Year Book 1978–79*; Statistics Canada, *Religions in Canada: The Nation.*

14 See Wilkinson's chapter in this volume and, more broadly, his book *The Spirit Said Go*. While the evidence is somewhat inconclusive, the Christian subdivisions that are growing, above all the domain of independent (and largely conservative) Protestant churches, are also the ones that are benefiting most from current immigration, and those attracting the fewest immigrants, liberal Protestant denominations, are in the sharpest decline. The evidence is drawn from Statistics Canada, *1971, 1981, 1991 & 2001 Census Custom Tabulations. DO0324.*

15 See, as examples, Fer, *Pentecôtisme en Polynésie française: L'Évangile relationnel*; Martin, *Pentecostalism*; Meyer, "Commodities and the Power of Prayer".

Bibliography

Albrecht, Daniel E. *Rites in the Spirit: A Ritual Approach to Pentecostal/Charismatic Spirituality*. Sheffield: Sheffield Academic Press, 1999.

Albrow, Martin. *The Global Age*. Stanford: Stanford University Press, 1996.

Alexander, Charles. *Anglican Renewal Ministries: The First Four Years – A Report to the Archbishops and Bishops of the Canadian Church*. Nepean, ON: privately published, 1987.

Allen, Richard. *The Social Passion: Religion and Social Reform in Canada 1914–28*. Toronto: University of Toronto Press, 1971.

– "Catching the Fire." *Renewal* (December 1994): 18.

Althouse, Peter F. "The Influence of Dr. J.E. Purdie's Reformed Anglican Theology on the Formation and Development of the Pentecostal Assemblies of Canada." *Pneuma* 19, 1 (1997): 3–28.

– *Spirit of the Last Days: Pentecostal Eschatology in Conversation with Jürgen Moltmann*. London: T&T Clark International, 2003.

– "The Ideology of Power in Early American Pentecostalism." *Journal of Pentecostal Theology* 13, 1 (2004): 99–118

Anderson, Alan. *An Introduction to Pentecostalism: Global Charismatic Christianity*. Cambridge: Cambridge University Press, 2004.

Anderson, Robert Mapes. *Vision of the Disinherited*. New York: Oxford, 1979. *Anglican Renewal Ministries: The First Four Years – A Report to the Archbishops and Bishops of the Canadian Church*, Nepean, ON: privately published, 1987.

Atter, Gordon F. "The Pentecostal Movement: Who We Are and What We Believe." By the author, 1937; Rev. ed., 1957.

– *The Third Force*. 2nd ed. Peterborough, ON: College Press, 1965.

Baer, Jr., Richard A. "Quaker Silence, Catholic Liturgy, and Pentecostal
    Glossalalia – Some Functional Similarities." In Spittler, *Perspectives on the
    New Pentecostalism*.
Bakhtin, Mikhail. *Speech Genres and Other Late Essays*. Translated by Vern
    W. McGee, edited by Caryl Emerson and Michael Holquist. Austin:
    University of Texas Press, 1986.
Barfoot, Charles H. and Gerald T. Sheppard. "Prophetic vs. Priestly Religion:
    The Changing Role of Women Clergy in Classical Pentecostal Churches."
    Review of Religious Research 22, 1 (1980): 2–17.
Barrett, David. "Statistics, Global." In Burgess et al., *Dictionary of
    Pentecostal and Charismatic Movements*.
Bartleman, Frank. *Azusa Street*. Plainfield: Logos International, [1925] 1980.
– "How Pentecost Came to Los Angeles." In *Witness to Pentecost: The life of
    Frank Bartleman*, edited by Donald Dayton. New York: Garland
    Press,1985.
Basch, Linda, Nina Glick Schiller, and Cristina Szanton Blanc. *Nations
    Unbound: Transnational Projects, Postcolonial Predicaments and
    Deterritorialized Nation-States*. Switzerland: Gordon and Breach
    Publishers, 1994.
Beckford, James A. *Religion and Advanced Industrial Society*. London:
    Unwin Hyman, 1989.
Bennett, D. *Nine O'clock in the Morning*. Plainfield: Logos International,
    1970.
Bennett, D. and R. Bennett. *The Holy Spirit and You*. Plainfield: Logos
    International, 1971.
Berger, Peter L. *The Sacred Canopy*. New York: Anchor Books, 1967.
Berkhof, Hendrikus. *The Doctrine of the Holy Spirit*. Richmond: John Knox
    Press, 1964.
Berkowitz, S.D. "Afterword: Toward a Formal Structural Sociology." In
    Wellman and Berkowitz, *Social Structures: A Network Approach*.
Bernard, David K. *A History of Christian Doctrine*. Hazelwood, MO: Word
    Aflame Press, 1999.
Beverley, James A. *Holy Laughter and the Toronto Blessing*. Grand Rapids:
    Zondervan, 1995.
Beyer, Peter. "Roman Catholicism in Contemporary Quebec: The Ghosts of
    Religion Past?" In *The Sociology of Religion: A Canadian Focus*, edited by
    W.E. Hewitt. Toronto: Butterworths, 1993.
– *Religion and Globalization*. London: Sage, 1994.
– "Religion, Residual Problems, and Functional Differentiation: An
    Ambiguous Relationship." *Soziale Systeme* 3 (1997): 219–35.

- "Religious Vitality in Canada." *Journal for the Scientific Study of Religion* 36 (1997): 272–88.
- "The Religious System of Global Society: A Sociological Look at Contemporary Religion and Religions." *Numen* 45 (1998): 1–29.
- "The Modern Emergence of Religions and a Global Social System for Religion." *International Sociology* 13, :2 (1998): 151–72.
- "Social Forms of Religion and Religions in Contemporary Global Society." In *Handbook of the Sociology of Religion*, edited by M. Dillon. Cambridge: Cambridge University Press, 2003.
- *Religions in Global Society*. New York: Routledge, 2006.
Bibby, Reginald W. *Anglitrends: A Profile and Prognosis – A Study Carried Out for the Anglican Diocese of Toronto*. Lethbridge: The University of Lethbridge, 1986.
- *Fragmented Gods*. Toronto: Irwin, 1987.
- *Unknown Gods*. Toronto: Stoddart, 1993.
- *Restless Gods*. Toronto: Stoddart, 2002.
Birch, Kenneth B. and Eusebio Perez. "Ethnic and Anglo Churches in Partnership." In *Missions Within Reach: Intercultural Ministries in Canada*, edited by E. Wan. Hong Kong: China Alliance Press, 1995.
Blumhofer, Edith L. *The Assemblies of God: A Chapter in the Story of American Pentecostalism, Volume 1 – to 1941*. Springfield, MO: Gospel Publishing House, 1989.
- *The Assemblies of God: A Chapter in the Story of American Pentecostalism, Volume 2 – Since 1941*. Springfield, MO: Gospel Publishing House, 1989.
- *Restoring the Faith. The Assemblies of God, Pentecostalism and American Culture*. Champaign: University of Illinois Press, 1993.
- "All Shook Up." *Books & Culture* (January/February, 2002).
Blumhofer, Edith L. and Randall Balmer, eds. *Modern Christian Revivals*. Chicago: University of Illinois Press, 1993.
Blumhofer, Edith, R. Spittler, and G. Wacker, eds. *Pentecostal Currents in American Protestantism*. Chicago: University of Illinois Press, 1999.
Boyd, Blair and Peter Adair. *Holy Ghost People*. Del Mar, CA: Contemporary Films/McGraw-Hill Films, 1968.
Britton, Bill. *Sons of God – Awake*. Springfield, MO: The Voice of the Overcomer, 1967.
Brouwer, S., P. Gifford, and S. Rose. *Exporting the American Gospel*. New York: Routledge, 1996.
Brown, Harold O.J. *Heresies: The Image of Christ in the Mirror of Heresy and Orthodoxy*. Grand Rapids: Baker Book House, 1984.

Brumback, Carl. *"What Meaneth This?" A Pentecostal Answer to a Pentecostal Question*. Springfield, MO: Gospel Publishing House, 1947.

Bruner, Frederick Dale. *A Theology of the Holy Spirit: The Pentecostal Experience and the New Testament Witness*. Grand Rapids: Eerdmans, 1970.

Buntain, Mark. *Why He Is a Pentecostal Preacher*. Toronto: Full Gospel Publishing House, 1944.

Burgess, Stanley and Gary M. McGee, eds. *Dictionary of Pentecostal and Charismatic Movements*. Grand Rapids: Zondervan, 1988.

Burgess, Stanley M. and Eduard van der Maas, eds. *New International Dictionary of Pentecostal and Charismatic Movements*. Grand Rapids: Zondervan, 2002.

Burkinshaw, Robert K. "Pentecostalism and Fundamentalism in British Columbia." *Fides et Historia* 24 (1992): 68–80.

– *Pilgrims in Lotus Land: Conservative Protestantism in British Columbia, 1917–1981*. Montreal & Kingston: McGill-Queen's University Press, 1995.

Byrne, J. *Threshold of God's Promise – An Introduction to the Catholic Pentecostal Movement*. Notre Dame: Ave Maria Press, 1970.

Cairncross, Frances. *The Death of Distance*. Cambridge: Harvard University, 1997.

Campbell, C. "The Easternization of the West." In *New Religious Movements: Challenge and Response*, edited by B. Wilson and J. Cresswell. New York: Sage, 1999.

Canada, Statistics. *Canada Yearbook 1948*. Ottawa: Statistics Canada, 1949.

Castells, Manuel. *The Rise of the Network Society*. Oxford: Blackwell Publishers, 1996.

Caulier, Brigitte, ed. *Religion, sécularisation, modernité. Les expériences francophones en Amérique du Nord*. Quebec: PUL, 1996.

Cerillo, Augustus and Grant Wacker. "Bibliography and Historiography of Pentecostalism in the United States." In Burgess and van der Maas, *New International Dictionary of Pentecostal and Charismatic Movements*.

Chaves, Mark. *Ordaining Women: Culture and Conflict in Religious Organizations*. Harvard: Harvard University Press, 1999.

Christensen, Larry. "Pentecostalism's Forgotten Forerunner." In *Aspects of Pentecostal-Charismatic Origins*, edited by V. Synan. Plainfield: Logos International, 1975.

Choquette, Robert. *Canada's Religions*. Ottawa: University of Ottawa Press, 2004.

Clark, S. *Unordained Elders and Renewal Communities*. New York: Paulist Press, 1976.

– *Man and Woman in Christ*. Ann Arbor: Servant Books, 1980.

Clark, S.D. *Church and Sect in Canada*. Toronto: University of Toronto Press, 1948.

Clarke, Brian. "English-Speaking Canada from 1854." In *A Concise History of Christianity in Canada*, edited by Terrence Murphy and Roberto Perin. Oxford: Oxford University Press, 1996.

Cnaan, Ram A. *The Invisible Caring Hand: American Congregations and Provision of Welfare*. New York: New York University Press, 2002.

Coates, Ruth. *Christianity in Bakhtin: God and the Exiled Author*. Cambridge: Cambridge University Press, 1998.

Coleman, Simon. *The Globalisation of Charismatic Christianity: Spreading the Gospel of Prosperity*. Cambridge: Cambridge University Press, 2000.

Comeau, Robert, ed. *Jean Lesage et l'éveil d'une nation: les débuts de la Révolution Tranquille*. Sillery: Presses de l'Université du Québec, 1989.

Cornell, Stephen and Douglas Hartmann. *Ethnicity and Race: Making Identities in a Changing World*. Thousand Oaks, CA: Pine Forge, 1998.

Corten, André and Ruth Marshall-Fratani, eds. *Between Babel and Pentecost: Transnational Pentecostalism in Africa and Latin America*. Bloomington and Indianapolis: Indiana University Press, 2001.

Corum, Fred T. and Rachel A. Harper Sizelove, eds. *Like as of Fire*. Washington: Middle Atlantic Press, 1985.

Côté, Pauline. *Les transactions politiques des croyants. Charismatiques et Témoins de Jéhovah dans le Québec des années 1970 et 1980*. Ottawa: Les presses de l'Université d'Ottawa, 1993.

Cox, Harvey. *The Secular City*. New York: MacMillan, 1966.

– *Fire from Heaven*. New York: Addison Wesley, 1995.

Craig, James D. "R.E. McAlister, Canadian Pentecostal Pioneer." *Eastern Journal of Practical Theology* 3 (1988).

– "'Out and Out for the Lord': James Eustace Purdie, An Early Anglican Pentecostal." MA thesis, University of St. Michael's College, 1995.

Creech, Joseph W. Jr. "Visions of Glory: The Place of Azusa Street in Pentecostal History." *Church History* 65, 3 (1996): 405–24.

Davies, C. "The Creation, Mortality, the After-Life and the Fission of Religious Tradition: Modernity not Postmodernity." *Journal of Contemporary Religion* 14, 3 (1991): 339–60.

Dayton, Donald W. *Witness to Pentecost: The life of Frank Bartleman*. New York: Garland Press, 1985.

– *Theological Roots of Pentecostalism*. Grand Rapids: Francis Asbury, 1987.

– ed. *Three Early Protestant Tracts*. New York and London: Garland, 1985.

Dayton, Donald W. and Robert K. Johnston, eds. *The Variety of American Evangelicalism*, Knoxville: University of Tennessee Press, 1991.

De Arteaga, William. *Quenching the Spirit: Examining Centuries of Opposition to the Moving of the Holy Spirit*. Lake Mary, FL: Creation House, 1992.

Del Colle, Ralph. "Theological Dialogue on the 'Full Gospel': Trinitarian Contributions from Pope John Paul II and Thomas A. Smail." *Pneuma* 20, 2 (1998): 141–60.

– "Pentecostal/Catholic Dialogue: Theological Suggestions for Consideration." *Pneuma* 25, 1 (2003): 93–6.

Dempster, Murray W. "Christian Social Concern in Pentecostal Perspective: Reformulating Pentecostal Eschatology." *Journal of Pentecostal Theology* 2 (1993): 51–64.

Dempster, Murray W., Byron D. Klaus and Douglas Petersen, eds. *The Globalization of Pentecostalism: A Religion Made to Travel*. Oxford: Regnum Books, 1999.

Di Giacomo, Michael. "Les pentecôtistes québécois, 1966–1995: histoire d'un réveil." PhD diss., Université Laval, 1999.

– "La Vieille Capitale : son importance pour le pentecôtisme au Canada français dans les années 1970." *Études d'histoire religieuse 70* (2004).

Doberstein, Horst, ed. *Grace & Glory: The Story of the German Branch of the Pentecostal Assemblies of Canada*. St Catherines, ON: German Branch of the Pentecostal Assemblies of Canada, 1990.

Dombrowski, Kirk. "Against Culture: Contemporary Pentecostalism in Native American Villages along Alaska's Southeast Coast." PhD diss., City University of New York, 1998.

Drewitz, Arthur. *A History of the German Branch of the Pentecostal Assemblies of Canada*. Kitchener, ON: German Branch of the Pentecostal Assemblies of Canada, 1986.

Dumont, Fernand. *Genèse de la société québécoise*. Montreal: Éditions du Boréal, 1996.

Du Plessis, David. *The Spirit Bade Me Go*. Plainfield: Logos International, 1970.

– *A Man Called Mr. Pentecost*. Plainfield : Logos International, 1977.

Durkheim, Emile. *The Elementary Forms of the Religious Life*. New York: Free Press, 1965 [1915].

Ebaugh, Helen Rose. "Religion and the New Immigrants." In *Handbook of the Sociology of Religion*, edited by Michele Dillon. Cambridge: Cambridge University Press, 2003.

Ellington, Scott. "The Costly Loss of Testimony." *Journal of Pentecostal Theology* 16 (2000): 8–59.

Ellul, J. *The Presence of the Kingdom.* New York: Seabury Press, 1967.

– *The Technological Society.* New York: Vintage Books, 1967.

Emberley, Peter C. *Divine Hunger.* Toronto: Harper Collins, 2002.

Espinosa, Gastón. "El Azteca : Francisco Olazabal and Linto Pentecostal Charisma, Power, and Faith Healing in the Borderlands." *Journal of the American Academy of Religion* 167, 3 (September 1999): 197–616.

"Est-ce le climat religieux du Québec est vraiment si unique?" Montreal: Christian Direction, n.d..

Evans, H.M. "Tertullian: 'Pentecostal of Carthage.'" *Pnuema* 9 (1975): 17–21.

Ewart, Frank J., with W.E. Kidson. *The Phenomenon of Pentecost (a history of "The Latter Rain").* Houston: Herald Publishing House, 1947.

Falardeau, Jean-Charles, ed. *Essais sur le Québec contemporain.* Quebec: Presses de l'Université Laval, 1953.

Faupel, D. William. "The Function of 'Models' in the Interpretation of Pentecostal Thought." *Pneuma* 2 (1980) : 51–71. "Whither Pentecostalism?" *Pneuma* 15 (1993): 9–28.

– *The Everlasting Gospel: The Significance of Eschatology in the Development of Pentecostal Thought.* Sheffield: Sheffield Academic Press, 1996.

Featherstone, M. "Global Culture: An Introduction" *Theory, Culture, & Society* 7 (1990): 1–14.

Fenton, Steven. *Ethnicity.* London: Polity, 2004.

Fer, Yannick. *Pentecôtisme en Polynésie française: L'Évangile relationnel.* Geneva: Labor et Fides, 2005.

Filson, Floyd. "Journey Motif in Luke-Acts." In *Apostolic History and the Gospel,* edited by W. Gasque and R. Martin. Exeter: Paternoster, 1970.

Finke, R. and P. Wittberg. "Organizational Revival from Within: Explaining Revivalism and Reform in the Roman Catholic Church." *Journal for the Scientific Study of Religion* 39 (2000): 154–70.

Fisher, Claude S. et al. *Networks and Places: Social Relations in the Urban Setting.* New York: The Free Press, 1977.

Froese, Walter. *Sounding Forth the Gospel on the Prairies: A History of the Church of God Reformation Movement in Western Canada.* Camrose, AB: Gospel Contact Press, 1982.

Fudge, Thomas A. *Christianity without the Cross: A History of Salvation in Oneness Pentecostalism.* Parkland, FL: Universal Publishers, 2003.

Fukuyama, Francis. *The End of History and the Last Man.* New York: Avon Books, 1993.

Gerlach, Luther and Virginia Hine. *People, Power and Change: Movements of Social Transformation*. New York: Bobbs-Merrill, 1970.

Gifford, Paul. *African Christianity: Its Public Role*. Bloomington and Indianapolis: Indiana University Press, 1998.

Gill, Deborah and Barbara Cavaness. *God's Women: Then and Now*. Springfield: Grace and Truth, 2004.

Goff, James R. *Fields White unto Harvest: Charles F. Parham and the Missionary Origins of Pentecostalism*. Fayetteville: University of Arkansas, 1988.

Goss, Howard A. and Ethel E. Goss. *The Winds of God: The Story of the Early Pentecostal Days (1901–1914) in the Life of Howard A. Goss*. New York: Comet Press Books, 1958.

Grant, John W. *Moon of Wintertime: Missionaries and the Indians of Canada in Encounter since 1534*. Toronto: University of Toronto Press, 1984.

Guenther, Bruce L. "Training for Service: The Bible School Movement in Western Canada, 1909–1960." PhD diss., McGill University, 2001.

Hawkes, Paul. "Pentecostalism in Canada: A History with Implications for the Future." DMin thesis, San Francisco Theological Seminary, 1982.

– *Songs of the Reaper: The Story of the Pentecostal Assemblies of Canada in Saskatchewan*. Altona, SK: PAOC Saskatchewan District, 1985.

Held, David and Anthony McGrew, eds. *The Global Transformations Reader: An Introduction to the Globalization Debate*. Cambridge: Polity, 2000.

Hervieu-Léger, Danièle. "Faces of Catholic Transnationalism: In and Beyond France." In *Transnational Religion and Fading States*, edited by Susanne Hoeber Rudolph and James Piscatori. Boulder, CO: Westview Press, 1997.

Hildebrandt, E. "A History of the Winnipeg Bible Institute and College of Theology from 1925–1960. " MTh thesis, Dallas Theological Seminary, 1965

Hill, M. *The Religious Order*. London: Heinemann Educational Books, 1973.

Hindmarsh, Bruce. "The Winnipeg Fundamentalist Network, 1910–1940: The Roots of Transdenominational Evangelicalism in Manitoba and Saskatchewan." In *Aspects of the Canadian Evangelical Experience*, edited by George A. Rawlyk. Montreal & Kingston: McGill-Queen's University Press, 1997.

Hird, Ed. "Anglican Pioneer in Renewal." *Anglicans for Renewal Canada*. Summer 1992.

Hocken, P.D. *Steams of Renewal: Origins and Development of the Charismatic Movement in Britain*. Exeter: Paternoster Press, 1986.

_ "Alpha Course." In Burgess and van der Maas, *New International Dictionary of Pentecostal and Charismatic Movements*.

– "Charismatic Movement." In Burgess and van der Maas, *New International Dictionary of Pentecostal and Charismatic Movements*.

Hollenweger, Walter J. *The Pentecostals*. London: SCM, 1972.

– "Methodism's Past in Pentecostalism's Present: A Case Study of a Cultural Clash in Chile." *Methodist History* 20, 4 (1982): 169–82.

– *Pentecostal Origins and Development Worldwide*. Peabody: Hendrickson, 1997.

– "Rethinking Spirit-Baptism: The Natural and the Supernatural." In *Pentecostals after a Century: Global Perspectives on a Movement in Transition*, edited by Allan Anderson and Walter Hollenweger. Sheffield: Sheffield University Press, 1999.

Holm, Randall. "Organizational Blues: The Struggle of One Pentecostal Denomination with the Bugbear of Institutionalism." Paper presented at the Society for Pentecostal Studies Annual Meeting, Wheaton, Illinois, 1994.

– "A Paradigmatic Analysis of Authority within Pentecostalism." PhD diss. Laval University, 1995.

Holmes, Paula Elizabeth. "Charismatic Fundamentalism and Orality." MA thesis, University of Calgary, 1995.

Hunt, Stephen. "The 'Toronto Blessing': A Rumour of Angels?" *Journal of Contemporary Religion* 10, 3 (1995): 257–71.

– "The Anglican Wimberites." *Pnuema* 17, 1 (1995): 105–15.

– "The Success of Kensington Temple, Britain's Largest Church. Market Forces and Theological Dilemmas." Paper presented at the Society for Pentecostal Studies Annual Meeting, San Francisco, 1997.

– "'Doing the Stuff.' The Vineyard Connection." In *Charismatic Christianity: Sociological Perspectives*, edited by S. Hunt, M. Hamilton, and T. Walter. Basingstoke: MacMillan, 1997.

– *Anyone for Alpha? Inside a Leading Evangelising Initiative*. London: Darton, Longman and Todd, 2000.

– "'Winning Ways.' Globalisation and the Impact of the Health and Wealth Ministries." *Journal of Contemporary Religion* (2000).

– *Christian Millenarianism*. London: Hurst Publishing, 2000.

– "The British Black Pentecostal 'Revival.' Identity and Belief in the 'New' Nigerian Churches." *Ethnic and Racial Studies* 24, 1 (2001): 104–24.

– "The 'Health and Wealth' Gospel in the UK: Variations on a Theme." *Culture and Religion* 3, 1 (2001): 89–104.

– *The Alpha Initiative: Evangelism in the Post-Christian Era*. London: Ashgate, 2004.

Hunt, S., M. Hamilton, and T. Walter, "Tongues, Toronto and the Millennium." In Hunt, Hamilton, and Walter, *Charismatic Christianity: Sociological Perspectives.*

Hunt, S., M. Hamilton, and T. Walter, eds. *Charismatic Christianity: Sociological Perspectives.* Basingstoke: MacMillan, 1997.

Huntington, Samuel P. *The Clash of Civilizations and the Remaking of World Order.* New Delhi: Viking Penguin, 1996.

Hurtado, Larry W. *Lord Jesus Christ: Devotion to Jesus in Earliest Christianity.* Grand Rapids: Eerdmans, 2003.

Irish, C.M. and C.B. Fulton, Jr. "Acts 29 Ministries." In Burgess and van der Maas, *The New International Dictionary of Pentecostal and Charismatic Movements.*

Jacobsen, Douglas. "Knowing the Doctrines of Pentecostals: The Scholastic Theology of the Assemblies of God, 1930–55." In Blumhofer, Spittler, and Wacker, *Pentecostal Currents in American Protestantism.*

Jaenen, Cornelius J. "The Pentecostal Movement." MA thesis, University of Manitoba, 1950.

Janes, Burton K. *The Lady Who Stayed: The Biography of Alice Belle Garrigus, Newfoundland's First Pentecostal Pioneer.* St. John's: Good Tidings Press, 1983.

– *History of the Pentecostal Assemblies of Newfoundland.* St. John's: Pentecostal Assemblies of Newfoundland, 1996.

Jenkins, Philip. *The Next Christendom: The Coming of Global Christianity.* Oxford: Oxford University, 2002.

Johnson, Luke Timothy and William Kurz. *The Future of Catholic Biblical Scholarship: A Constructive Conversation.* Grand Rapids: Eerdmans, 2002.

Jubilation: Five Decades in the Life of Western Pentecostal Bible College. Abbotsford, BC: WPBC, 1991.

Kept By His Grace, Ebenezer 75: Trossachs Camp Meeting Association. Pangman: Trossachs Camp History Book Association, 1988.

Khasala, G. "New Religious Movements Turn to Worldly Success." *Journal for the Scientific Study of Religion* 25, 2 (1994): 233–47.

Kim, Byung-Suh. "Modernization and the Explosive Growth and Decline of Korean Protestant Religiosity." In *Christianity in Korea*, edited by Robert E. Buswell, Jr. and Timothy S. Lee. Honolulu: University of Hawai'i, 2007.

Kivisto, Peter. "Religion and the New Immigrants." In *A Future for Religion? New Paradigms for Social Analysis*, edited by William H. Swatos, Jr. London: Sage, 1993.

Klan, Donald T. "Pentecostal Assemblies of Canada Church Growth in British Columbia from Origins until 1955." MCS thesis, Regent College, Vancouver, 1979.

Kulbeck, Gloria. *What God Hath Wrought: A History of the Pentecostal Assemblies of Canada.* Toronto: The Pentecostal Assemblies of Canada, 1958.

Kurz, William. "Narrative Models for Imitation in Luke-Acts." In *Greeks, Romans and Christians: Essays in Honor of Abraham J. Malherbe,* edited by David L. Balch, Everett Ferguson, and Wayne A. Meeks. Minneapolis: Fortress, 1990.

– "Open-ended Nature of Luke and Acts as Inviting Canonical Actualization." *Neotestamentica* 31 (1997): 289–308.

Kydd, Ronald A.N. "The Pentecostal Assemblies of Canada and Society." Paper read at the Canadian Society of Church History, Queen's University, June 1973.

– *I'm Still There! A Reaffirmation of Tongues as the Initial Evidence of the Baptism in the Holy Spirit.* Toronto: PAOC, 1977.

– "H.C. Sweet: Canadian Churchman." *Journal of the Canadian Church Historical Society* 20, 1–2 (1978): 19–30.

– "Pentecostals, Charismatics and the Canadian Denominations." *Église et Théologie* 13 (1982): 211–31.

– "The Contribution of Denominationally Trained Clergymen to the Emerging Pentecostal Movement in Canada." *Pneuma* 5, 1 (1983): 17–33.

– *Charismatic Gifts in the Early Church.* Peabody: Hendrickson, 1984.

– "Pentecostal Assemblies of Canada," in Burgess and McGee, *Dictionary of Pentecostal and Charismatic Movement.*

– "The Impact of the Charismatic Renewal on Classical Pentecostalism in Canada." *Pneuma* 18 (1996): 122–5.

– "Canadian Pentecostalism and the Evangelical Impulse." In Rawlyk, *Aspects of the Canadian Evangelical Experience.*

– *Healing through the Centuries: Models of Understanding.* Peabody: Hendrickson, 1998.

– "A Retrospectus/Prospectus on Physical Phenomena Centred on the 'Toronto Blessing.'" *Journal of Pentecostal Theology* 12 (1998).

– "Canada." In Burgess and Van der Maas, *The New International Dictionary of Pentecostal and Charismatic Movements.*

– "Pentecostal Assemblies of Canada." In Burgess and van der Maas, *The New International Dictionary of Pentecostal and Charismatic Movements.*

Land, Steven. *Pentecostal Spirituality: A Passion for the Kingdom.* Sheffield: Sheffield Academic Press, 1997.

Larden, Robert A. *Our Apostolic Heritage*. Calgary: Apostolic Church of Pentecost, 1971.

Lawless, Elaine. *Handmaidens of the Lord: Pentecostal Women Preachers and Traditional Religion*. Philadelphia: University of Pennsylvania Press, 1988.

Lederle, Henry. *Treasures Old and New: Interpretations of 'Spirit Baptism' in the Charismatic Renewal Movement*. Peabody: Hendrickson, 1988.

Lesage, Marc and Francine Tardif, eds. *Trente ans de Révolution tranquille: entre le je et le nous: intinéraires et mouvements*, papers of colloquium "Elle aura bientôt trente ans, la Révolution tranquille." Montreal : Éditions Bellarmin, 1989.

Levitt, Peggy. "Local-Level Global Religion: US-Dominican Migration." *Journal for the Scientific Study of Religion* 37, 1 (1998):74–89.

– "Redefining the Boundaries of Belonging: The Institutional Character of Transnational Religious Life." *Sociology of Religion* 65, 1 (2004): 1–18.

Linteau, Paul-André, René Durocher, Jean-Claude Robert, François Ricard. *Histoire du Québec contemporain: Le Québec depuis 1930*, vol. 2. Montréal : Boréal, 1989.

Lougheed, Richard, Wesley Peach, and Glenn Smith. *Histoire du protestantisme au Québec depuis 1960*. Québec: La Clairière, 1999.

Lynn, Carman W., ed. *Truth Aflame: Across the Nation and around the World, A History of Eastern Pentecostal Bible College, 1939–89*. Peterborough, ON: Eastern Pentecostal Bible College, 1989.

Lyon, David. *Jesus in Disneyland: Religion in Postmodern Times*. Cambridge: Polity Press, 1999.

Lyon, David and Marguerite Van Die, eds. *Rethinking Church, State, and Modernity: Canada between Europe and America*. Toronto: University of Toronto Press, 2000.

Macchia, Frank D. *Baptized in the Spirit: A Global Pentecostal Theology*. Grand Rapids: Zondervan, 2006.

MacNutt, F. *Overcome by the Spirit*. Guildford: Eagle, 1994.

MacRobert, Ian. *The Black Roots and White Racism of Early Pentecostalism in the USA*. New York: St Martin's Press, 1988.

Marshall, I. Howard. *Luke: Historian and Theologian*. Grand Rapids: Zondervan, 1970.

Martin, David. *Tongues of Fire: The Explosion of Protestantism in Latin America*. Oxford: Blackwell, 1990.

– *Pentecostalism: The World Their Parish*. Oxford: Blackwell, 2001.

Martin, R. "Covenant Communities." In *As the Spirit Leads Us*, edited by K. Ranaghan and D. Ranaghan. New York: Paulist Press, 1971.

– "About This Issue." *New Covenant* 2: index page, 1973.

Mattill, A.J. "The Jesus-Paul Parallels and the Purpose of Luke-Acts: H.H. Evans Reconsidered." *Novum Testamentum* 17 (1975): 15–46.

McConaghy, Stanley. "Down Memory's Lane." *UPC Home Mission News*. Doaktown, NB. September 1963.

McDonnell, K. "The Baptism of the Holy Spirit as an Ecumenical Problem." Notre Dame: The Charismatic Renewal Services and cited in Larry Christensen, "Pentecostalism's Forgotten Forerunner." In *Aspects of Pentecostal-Charismatic Origins*, edited by V. Synan. Plainfield: Logos, 1972.

– "Catholic Charismatics." *Commonweal* 96 (1972).

McGee, Gary B., "Initial Evidence." In Burgess and van der Maas, *New International Dictionary of Pentecostal and Charismatic Movements*.

– "Missions, Overseas," In Burgess and van der Maas, *New International Dictionary of Pentecostal and Charismatic Movements*.

– "Shortcut to Language Preparation? Radical Evangelicals, Missions, and the Gift of Tongues." *International Bulletin of Missionary Research* 25, 3 (2001).

McGinn, Bernard, John J. Collins, and Stephen J. Stein, eds. *The Encyclopedia of Apocalypticism*, 3 vols. New York: Continuum, 2000.

McPherson, Aimee Semple. "Lost and Restored: Dispensation of the Holy Spirit from Christ's Ascension to His Return." Reprinted in *World Map Digest* 23 (July / August 1983).

– *This Is That*. Los Angeles: Bridal Call Publishing House, 1919.

McQueen, Larry R. *Joel and the Spirit: The Cry of a Prophetic Hermeneutic*. Sheffield: Sheffield University, 1995.

Menzies, William W. *Anointed to Serve: The Story of the Assemblies of God*. Springfield, MO: Gospel Publishing House, 1971.

– "The Non-Wesleyan Origins of the Pentecostal Movement." In Synan, *Aspects of Pentecostal-Charismatic Origins*.

Meyer, Birgit. "Commodities and the Power of Prayer: Pentecostalist Attitudes towards Consumption in Contemporary Ghana." In *Globalization and Identity: Dialectics of Flow and Closure*, edited by Birgit Meyer and Peter Geschiere. Oxford: Blackwell, 1999.

Miller, Thomas William. "The Pentecostal Assemblies of Canada: Origins and Antecedents." *The Pentecostal Testimony* (July 1983): 15–16.

– "The Canadian 'Azusa': The Hebden Mission in Toronto." *Pneuma* 8, 1 (1986): 5–29.

– "The Significance of A.H. Argue for Pentecostal Historiography." *Pneuma* 8 (1986): 120–58.

- *Canadian Pentecostals. A History of the Pentecostal Assemblies of Canada*, edited by William A. Griffin. Mississauga, ON: Full Gospel Publishing House, 1994.

Mitchell, J. Clyde. "Social Networks." *Annual Review of Anthropology* 3 (1974): 279–99.

Mittelstadt, Martin William. *Spirit and Suffering in Luke-Acts: Implications for a Pentecostal Pneumatology*. London: T & T Clark, 2004.

Moltmann, Jürgen. *The Spirit of Life: A Universal Affirmation*. Minneapolis: Fortress, 2001.

Moltmann, Jürgen and Karl-Josef Kuschel, eds. *Pentecostal Movements as an Ecumenical Challenge*. Maryknoll: Orbis, 1996.

Morehouse, Joyce Macbeth. *Pioneers of Pentecost*. Doaktown, NB: by the author, 2000.

Murphy, Terrence and Roberto Perin, eds. *A Concise History of Christianity in Canada* Oxford: Oxford University Press, 1996.

Myland, D. Wesley. "The Latter Rain Covenant and Pentecostal Power." In *Three Early Pentecostal Tracts*, edited by D. Dayton. New York: Garland, 1985.

Nesbitt, Paula D. *Feminization of the Clergy in America*. New York: Oxford, 1997.

New Covenant. Ann Arbour: Servant Publications, 1972.

Neylan, Susan. *The Heavens Are Changing: Nineteenth-Century Protestant Missions and Tsimshian Christianity*. Montreal & Kingston: McGill-Queen's University Press, 2003.

Niebuhr, H. Richard. *The Social Sources of Denominationalism*. New York: Meridian, 1957.

Nienkirchen, Charles. *A.B. Simpson and the Pentecostal Movement: A Study in Continuity, Crisis, and Change*. Peabody: Hendrickson Publishers, 1992.

Noll, Mark A. *The Scandal of the Evangelical Mind*. Grand Rapids: Eerdmans, 1995.

Nygaard, John. *Beyond the Hammer and the Sword*. Kelowna, BC: Regatta Press, nd (but c 1985).

O'Connor, E. *The Pentecostal Movement in the Catholic Church*. Notre Dame: Ave Maria Press, 1971.

- "The Hidden Roots of the Charismatic Renewal in the Catholic Church." In Synan, *Aspects of Pentecostal-Charismatic Origins*.

O'Dea, T. *The Sociology of Religion*. Engelwood Cliffs: Prentice Hall, 1966.

Orsini, J. "When I Let God Come Near." *Logos* 40, 3 (1972):18–20.

Osmer, Richard R., *A Teachable Spirit: Recovering the Teaching Office in the Church*. Louisville: Westminster/John Knox Press, 1990.

Parham, Charles F. *The Everlasting Gospel*. Baxter Springs, KA: privately printed, 1942.

Parham, Sarah E. *The Life of Charles F. Parham: Founder of the Apostolic Faith Movement*. Joplin, MO: Hunter Printing, 1930.

Pawson, David. *The Fourth Wave*. London: Hodder and Stoughton, 1992.

Pentecostal Testimony. CDS I-XII. Mississauga, ON: The Pentecostal Assemblies of Canada, 2003.

Percy, M. *The Toronto Blessing*, Oxford: Latimer Press, 1997.

Perrin, R. "Signs and Wonders. The Growth of the Vineyard Fellowship." PhD diss., Washington State University, 1989.

Peters, Erna Alma. *The Contribution to Education by the Pentecostal Assemblies of Canada*. Homewood, MB: By the author, 1971.

Petroski, G. "Professed Religious Ideals and Realities: A Case-Study of Dissonance in a Religious Grouping." MA thesis, University of Saskatchewan, 1979.

Poewe, Karla, ed. *Charismatic Christianity as a Global Culture*. Columbia: University of South Carolina Press, 1994.

Poloma, Margaret. *The Assemblies of God at the Crossroads: Charisma and Institutional Dilemmas*. Knoxville: University of Tennessee Press, 1989.

– "The Spirit and the Bride: The 'Toronto Blessing' and Church Structure." *Evangelical Studies Bulletin* 13, 4 (1996): 1–5.

– "By their fruits ... A Sociological Assessment of the 'Toronto Blessing.'" In *The Toronto Report*. Bradford-on-Avon: Terra Nova Publications, Ltd, 1996.

– "The 'Toronto Blessing': Charisma, Institutionalization, and Revival." *Journal for the Scientific Study of Religion* 36, 2 (1997): 257–71.

– "Inspecting the Fruit of the Toronto Blessing: A Sociological Perspective." *Pneuma* 20 (1998): 43–70.

– "The Spirit Movement in North America at the Millenium: From Azusa Street to Toronto, Pensacola and Beyond." *Journal of Pentecostal Theology* 12 (1998): 83–107.

– "The 'Toronto Blessing' in Postmodern Society: Manifestations, Metaphor and Myth." In Dempster et al., *The Globalization of Pentecostalism: A Religion Made to Travel*.

– *Main Street Mystics. The Toronto Blessing and Reviving Pentecostalism*. Walnut Creek, CA: Altamira Press, 2003.

Poloma, M. and B. Pendleton. "Religious Experiences, Evangelism, and Institutional Growth within the Assemblies of God." *Journal for the Scientific Study of Religion* 28, 4 (1989): 415–31.

Poloma, M. and Lynette Hoelter. "The 'Toronto Blessing': A Holistic Model of Healing." *Journal for the Scientific Study of Religion* 37, 2 (1998): 257–71.

Praeder, Susan. "Jesus-Paul, Peter-Paul and Jesus-Peter Parallelisms in Luke-Acts: A History of Reader Response." *Society of Biblical Literature Seminar Papers*, 1984.

Prosser, Peter E. "A Historical and Theological Evaluation of the Charismatic Renewal." MA thesis, University of Montreal, 1978.

Purdie, J. Eustace. "The Principles of Our Balanced Course." *Western Bible College Yearbook*, 1938–39.

– "The Vision Glorious." *The Gleaner*, 11 April 1950.

– *Concerning the Faith*. Toronto: Full Gospel Publishing House, 1951.

– "What God Hath Wrought: Historical Sketch of the College, 1925–1950." *The Gleaner* 11, 1 (April 1950).

Ranaghan, K. and D. Ranaghan. *Catholic Pentecostals*. Paramus, NJ: Paulist Press, 1969.

Ranaghan, K. and D. Ranaghan, eds. *As the Spirit Leads Us*. New York: Paulist Press, 1971.

Rawlyk, George A. *Is Jesus Your Personal Saviour? In Search of Canadian Evangelicalism in the 1990s* (Montreal & Kingston: McGill-Queen's University Press, 1996).

Rawlyk, George A., ed. *Aspects of the Canadian Evangelical Experience*. Montreal: McGill-Queen's University Press, 1997.

Reed, Bruce. *Dynamics of Religion: Process and Movement in Christian Churches*. London: Darton, Longman and Todd, 1978.

Reed, D.A., "From Movement to Institution: A Case Study of Charismatic Renewal in the Anglican Church of Canada." Paper read at the 21st annual meeting of the Society for Pentecostal Studies, Lakeland, FL, 1991.

– "Oneness Pentecostalism." In Burgess and Van der Maas, *The New International Dictionary of Pentecostal and Charismatic Movements*.

– "Pentecostal Assemblies of the World." In Burgess and Van der Maas, *The New International Dictionary of Pentecostal and Charismatic Movements*.

Reimer, Sam. *Evangelicals and the Continental Divide: The Conservative Protestant Subculture in Canada and the United States*. Montreal & Kingston: McGill-Queen's University Press, 2003.

Reimers, Al. *God's Country: Charismatic Renewal*. Burlington, ON: Welch, 1979. *Rejoice: A History of the Pentecostal Assemblies of Alberta and the Northwest Territories*. Edmonton: The Pentecostal Assemblies of Canada, c. 1984.

Reynolds, Ralph Vincent and Joyce Macbeth Morehouse. *From the Rising of the Sun. A History of the Apostolic Truth across Canada and the Reflections of a Pioneer Preacher.* Conexions Publishing, 1998.

Richter, P. "'God Is Not a Gentleman! The Sociology of the Toronto Blessing." In *The Toronto Blessing– Or Is It?*, edited by P. Richter and S. Porter. London: Darton, Longman and Todd, 1995.

– "The Toronto Blessing: Charismatic Evangelical Global Warming." In Hunt et al., *Charismatic Christianity: Sociological Perspectives.*

Riss, Richard. *The Latter Rain Movement of 1948 and the Mid-Twentieth Century Evangelical Awakening.* Etobicok, ON: Kingdom Flagships Foundation, 1987.

– *A Survey of 20th-Century Revivals in North America.* Peabody: Hendrickson, 1988.

Ritzer, G. *The McDonaldization of Society.* Newbury Park, CA: Pine Forge, 1996.

Robeck, Cecil M. Jr. "The International Significance of Azusa Street." *Pneuma* 8, 1 (1986): 1–4.

– "Pentecostals and Ecumenism in a Pluralistic World." In Dempster et al., *The Globalization of Pentecostalism: A Religion Made to Travel.*

– "McDonnell, Killian." In Burgess and Van der Maas, *New International Dictionary of Pentecostal and Charismatic Movements.*

– *The Azusa Street Mission & Revival: The Birth of the Global Pentecostal Movement.* Nashville: Thomas Nelson, 2006.

Roberts, D. *The Toronto Blessing.* Eastbourne: Kingsway, 1994.

Robertson, Roland. *Globalization.* London: Sage, 1992.

– "Community, Society, Globality, and Category of Religion." In *Secularization, Rationalism, and Sectarianism*, edited by E. Barker, J. Beckford and K. Dobbelaere. Oxford: Clarendon, 1993.

Robinson, Anthony B. *Transforming Congregational Culture.* Grand Rapids: Eerdmans, 2003.

Robinson, Martin and Dwight Smith. *Invading Secular Space.* Grand Rapids: Kregel Publications, 2004.

Robinson, Thomas A. "The Conservative Nature of Dissent in Early Pentecostalism: A Study of Charles F. Parham, the Founder of the Pentecostal Movement." In *Orthodoxy and Heresy in Religious Movements: Discipline and Dissent*, edited by Malcolm R. Greenshields and Thomas A. Robinson. Lewiston: Mellen, 1992.

Roebuck, David G. "'Go and Tell My Brothers'? The Waning of Women's Voices in American Pentecostalism." Paper presented to the Society for Pentecostal Studies Annual Meeting, 1990.

Rogers, Nelson. "And Your Daughters Shall Prophesy: The Impact of
    Dominant Ideology of Canadian Society on the Role of Women in the
    PAOC." MSW thesis, Carleton University, 1992.
Römer, J. *The Toronto Blessing*. Helsinki: Åbo Akademi University Press,
    2002.
Ross, Brian R. "The Emergence of Theological Education within the
    Pentecostal Assemblies of Canada." MTh thesis, University of Toronto,
    1971.
– "James Eustace Purdie: The Story of Pentecostal Theological Education."
    Journal of the Canadian Church Historical Society 17, 4 (1975): 94–103.
Rouse, Roger. "Mexican Migration and the Social Space of Postmodernism."
    Diaspora 1 (1991): 8–24.
Ruby, Robert H. and John A. Brown. *John Slocum and the Indian Shaker
    Church*. Norman: University of Oklahoma Press, 1996.
Rudd, Douglas. *When the Spirit Came Upon Them: Highlights from the
    Early Years of the Pentecostal Movement in Canada*. Burlington, ON:
    Antioch Books, 2002.
Schinkel, C. Mark. "James Eustace Purdie and Biblical/Theological Education
    in the Pentecostal Assemblies of Canada: The Formative Years."
    Unpublished paper, 1986.
– "The Pentecostal Assemblies of Canada: The Influence of Fundamentalism
    on Articles Appearing in the *Pentecostal Testimony*." MRel thesis, Wycliffe
    College, 1990.
Scholte, Jan Aart. *Globalization: A Critical Introduction*. Rev. Ed. London:
    Palgrave McMillan, 2005.
Semple, Neil. *The Lord's Dominion: A History of Canadian Methodism*.
    Montreal: McGill-Queen's University Press, 1996.
Sheppard, Gerald T. "Pentecostals and the Hermeneutics of
    Dispensationalism: The Anatomy of an Uneasy Relationship." *Pneuma* 6, 2
    (1984): 5–33.
– "Pentecostals, Globalization, and Postmodern Hermeneutics: Implications
    for the Politics of Scriptural Interpretation." In Dempster et al., *The
    Globalization of Pentecostalism: A Religion Made to Travel*.
Slauenwhite, David. *Fresh Breezes: An Historical Perspective on the
    Pentecostal Assemblies of Canada*. Mississauga, ON: PAOC Dept. of
    Spiritual Life, 1996.
Small, Franklin. *Living Waters* 1, 2 (June, 1918).
– "Historical and Valedictory Account of the Origins of Water Baptism in
    Jesus' Name Only, and the Doctrine of the Fulness of God in Christ, in
    Pentecostal Circles in Canada." *Living Waters* 1:, 4 (April 1941): 1–6.

– "Our Trip to Eastern Canada." *The Apostolic Church Advocate* 1, 8 (November–December 1926), 6–7.
– "Our Trip through the Maritime Provinces." *Living Waters* 1, 1 (January 1930), 14–17.
– "Perplexed Christians." *Living Waters* 4, 3 (November 1923), 1–2.
Smark, P. "Mass Marketing God." *Atlas* 25 (1978): 19–20.
Smith, Christian. *Moral, Believing Animals: Human Personhood and Culture.* Oxford: Oxford, 2003.
Spiritual Health of the Episcopal Church. Survey conducted by The 1990 Gallup Organization, Inc., for The Episcopal Church Center. Washington, DC: Episcopal Parish Services, 1990.
Spittler, Russell P., ed. *Perspectives on the New Pentecostalism,* Grand Rapids: Baker Book House, 1976.
– "Spirituality, Pentecostal and Charismatic." In Burgess and van der Maas, *The New International Dictionary of Pentecostal and Charismatic Movements.*
– "Glossolalia." In Burgess and van der Maas, *The New International Dictionary of Pentecostal and Charismatic Movements.*
Stark, R. and R. Finke. *Acts of Faith: Explaining the Human Side of Religion.* Berkeley and Los Angeles: University of California Press, 2000.
Stark, R., R. Finke, and A. Guest. "Mobilizing Local Religious Markets: Religious Pluralism in the Empire State, 1855–1865." *Sociological Review* 6, 2 (1996): 203–18.
Stark, R. and L. Iannaccone. "Rational Choice Propositions About Religious Movements." In *Handbook on Cults and Sects,* edited by D. Bromley and J. Hadden. Greenwich, CT: JAI Press, 1993.
– "A Supply-Side Reinterpretation of the 'Secularization' of Europe." *Journal for the Scientific Study of Religion* 33, 1 (1994): 23–52.
Statistics Canada. *1971, 1981, 1991 & 2001 Census Custom Tabulations.* DO0324. Ottawa: Statistics Canada, Advisory Services Division, 2003.
Statistics Canada. *Canada Year Book 1978–79.* Ottawa: Statistics Canada, 1980.
Statistics Canada. *Religions in Canada: The Nation.* Ottawa: Industry, Science and Technology Canada, 1993.
Stephenson, John. "The Centrality of a Common Interpretation of History to the Self-Definition of the Early Pentecostals." MTh thesis, Wycliffe College, 1990.
Stiller, Brian C. "The Evolution of Pentecostalism: From Sectarianism to Denominationalism with Special Reference to the Danforth Gospel Temple, 1922–1968." MRel thesis, Wycliffe College, 1975.

Stoll, David. *Is Latin America Turning Protestant? The Politics of Evangelical Growth.* Berkeley: University of California Press, 1990.

Stronstad, Roger J. "Dr. J.E. Purdie and Western Bible College." Unpublished paper, 1974.

– *The Charismatic Theology of St. Luke.* Peabody: Hendrickson, 1984.

– *The Prophethood of All Believers: A Study in Luke's Charismatic Theology.* Sheffield: Sheffield Academic Press, 1999.

Suurmond, Jean-Jacques. *Word and Spirit at Play: Towards a Charismatic Theology.* Grand Rapids: Eerdmans, 1994.

Swenson, D. "The Charismatic Movement within Denominational Christianity." MA thesis, University of Calgary, 1972.

– *Society, Spirituality and the Sacred: A Social Scientific Introduction to Religion.* Peterborough, ON: Broadview, 1999.

Swenson, D. and J. Thompson. "Locus Theologicus and Constructing a Sacred Past: Charismatic Renewal among Catholics as a Movement of Renewal." Paper presented at the Annual Canadian Sociology and Anthropology Association, Winnipeg, Manitoba, 1986.

Synan, Vinson. *The Holiness-Pentecostal Movement in the United States.* Grand Rapids: Eerdmans, 1971.

– "Pentecostalism: Varieties and Contributions." *Pneuma* 8, 2 (1986): 31–49.

– *The Spirit Said Grow.* Monrovia, CA: MARC, 1992.

– *The Century of the Spirit.* Nashville: Thomas Nelson, 2001.

– "Classical Pentecostalism." In Burgess and van der Maas, *New International Dictionary of Pentecostal and Charismatic Movements.*

Synan, Vinson, ed. *Aspects of Pentecostal-Charismatic Origins.* Plainfield: Logos International, 1975.

Tennant, Agnieszka. "Tallying Compassion." *Christianity Today* (February, 2003).

Thigpen, T.P. "Catholic Charismatic Renewal." In Burgess and van der Maas, *New International Dictionary of Pentecostal and Charismatic Movements.*

Thomson, Dale C. *Jean Lesage and the Quiet Revolution.* Toronto: Macmillan, 1984.

Torrey, R.A. *Is the Present "Tongues" Movement of God?* Los Angeles: BIOLA Book Room, n.d. [c. 1913].

Tyson, James L. *The Early Pentecostal Revival: History of Twentieth-Century Pentecostals and the Pentecostal Assemblies of the World, 1901–30.* Hazelwood, MO: Word Aflame, 1992.

Valverde, Mariana. *The Age of Light, Soap, and Water: Moral Reform in English Canada, 1885–1925*. Toronto: McClelland & Stewart, 1991.

Verge, Carl. "Pentecostal Clergy and Higher Education." *Eastern Journal of Practical Theology* 2 (1988): 41–7.

Volf, Miroslav. "On Loving with Hope: Eschatology and Social Responsibility." *Transformation* 7 (1990).

Wach, J. *Sociology of Religion*. Chicago: University of Chicago, 1967 [1944].

Wacker, Grant. "Are the Golden Oldies Still Worth Playing? Reflections on History Writing among Early Pentecostals." *Pneuma* 8, 2 (1986): 81–100.

– "Travail of a Broken Family." *Journal of Ecclesiastical History* 47, 3 (1996): 505–28.

– "Early Pentecostals and the Almost Chosen People." *Pneuma* 19, 2 (1997): 141–66.

– *Heaven Below*. Cambridge: Harvard University, 2001.

Wagner, C. Peter. *The Third Wave of the Holy Spirit – Encountering the Power of Signs and Wonders Today*. Ann Arbor: Servant Publications, 1988.

– "Wimber, John." In Burgess and van der Maas, *New International Dictionary of Pentecostal and Charismatic Movements*.

Walker, John, ed. *What Really Happened at "Azusa Street"?* Northridge, CA: Christian Publications, 1962.

Wallerstein, I. *The Capitalist World Economy*. Cambridge: Cambridge University Press, 1980.

Wallis, R. *The Elementary Forms of New Religious Life*. London: Routledge and Kegan Paul, 1984.

Walmsley, Christopher. "Changing the Future: A Social Development Plan for the Nuxalk Nation." In *Nuxalk First Nation Community Profile, Bella Coola, BC*. Compiled by Rhonda Carriere. Burnaby, BC: Simon Fraser University, 1999.

Warner, R. Stephen. "Work in Progress: Towards a New Paradigm for the Sociological Study of Religion in the United States." *American Journal of Sociology* 98, 5 (1993): 1044–93.

Waters, Malcolm. *Globalization*. 2nd ed. New York: Routledge, 2001.

Wellman, Barry. "Structural Analysis: From Method and Metaphor to Theory and Substance." In Wellman and Berkowitz, *Social Structures: A Network Approach*.

Wellman, Barry, ed. *Networks in the Global Village*. Boulder: Westview, 1999.

Wellman, Barry and S.D. Berkowitz, eds. *Social Structures: A Network Approach*. Cambridge: Cambridge University Press, 1988.

Wenk, Matthias. *Community Forming Power: The Socio-Ethical Role of the Spirit in Luke-Acts*. Sheffield: Sheffield University, 2000.

Westley, F. *The Complex Forms of the Religious Life: A Durkheimian View of New Religious Movements*. Chico, CA: Scholars Press, 1983.

Whiteheand, Margaret. *Now You Are My Brother: Missionaries in British Columbia*. Sound Heritage Series, Provincial Archives of British Columbia, No. 34, 1981.

Whitt, Irving Alfred. "Developing a Pentecostal Missiology in the Canadian Context (1867–1944): The Pentecostal Assemblies of Canada," DMiss thesis, Fuller Theological Seminary, 1994.

Wilkins, Charles. *Walk to New York: A Journey out of the Wilds of Canada*. Toronto: Viking Canada, 2004.

Wilkinson, Michael. "The Globalization of Pentecostalism: Asian Pentecostals in Canada." *Asian Journal of Pentecostal Studies* 3, 2 (2000): 219–26.

– *The Spirit Said Go: Pentecostal Immigrants in Canada*. New York: Peter Lang Publishing, 2006.

– "Religion and Global Flows." In *Religion, Globalization, and Culture*, edited by Peter Beyer and Lori Beaman. Leiden: Brill, 2007.

Williams, J. Rodman. "Baptism in the Holy Spirit." In Burgess and van der Maas, *New International Dictionary of Pentecostal and Charismatic Movements*.

Williams, R. *The Era of the Spirit*. Plainfield: Logos International, 1971.

Wilson, B. *Religious Sects*. London: Heineman, 1970.

Yamane, D. "Charismatic Movement." In *Encyclopedia of Religion and Society*, edited by William Swatos, Jr. Walnut Creek, CA: Altamira Press, 1998.

Yang, Fenggang. *Chinese Christians in Amercia: Conversion, Assimilation, and Adhesive Identities*. University Park: Penn State University Press, 1999.

Yang, Fenggang and Helen Rose Ebaugh. "Religion and Ethnicity: The Impact of Majority/Minority Status in the Home and Host Countries." *Journal for the Scientific Study of Religion* 40 (2001): 89–107.

– "Transformations in New Immigrant Religions and Their Global Implications." *American Sociological Review* 66 (2001): 269–88.

Yong, Amos. *Discerning the Spirit(s): A Pentecostal/Charismatic Contribution to Christian Theology of Religions*. Sheffield: Sheffield Academic Press, 2000.

Zaleski, Alexander (1971). "Report of the American Bishops." *New Covenant* 1, 3 (1971).

Zimmerman, Thomas. "The Reason for the Rise of the Pentecostal Movement." In Synan, *Aspects of Pentecostal-Charismatic Origins.*

Index